I0130914

Peacebuilding and National Ownership in Timor-Leste

Originally published in 2013, *Peacebuilding and National Ownership in Timor-Leste* is an insightful, analytical presentation of developments that took place in Timor-Leste from July 2002 to September 2006. It reflects an intimate knowledge of events during this period, and provides a detailed focus on the Timorese people and their leaders who struggled to lay a foundation for a free, peaceful and democratic nation. The book's central theme is that of the commitment of national leaders to national interest, rather than the establishment of perfect institutional mechanisms that determines the success of a post-conflict country in achieving its stability.

Peacebuilding and National Ownership in Timor-Leste

Sukehiro Hasagawa

Routledge
Taylor & Francis Group

First published in 2013
by Routledge

This edition first published in 2018 by Routledge
2 Park Square, Milton Park, Abingdon, Oxon, OX14 4RN
and by Routledge
711 Third Avenue, New York, NY 10017

Routledge is an imprint of the Taylor & Francis Group, an informa business

© 2013 United Nations University

Publisher's Note
The publisher has gone to great lengths to ensure the quality of this reprint but points out that some imperfections in the original copies may be apparent.

Disclaimer
The publisher has made every effort to trace copyright holders and welcomes correspondence from those they have been unable to contact.

A Library of Congress record exists under LCCN: 2013024655

ISBN 13: 978-1-138-48147-3 (hbk)
ISBN 13: 978-1-351-06015-8 (ebk)
ISBN 13: 978-1-138-48156-5 (pbk)

United Nations University Press is the publishing arm of the United Nations University. UNU Press publishes scholarly and policy-oriented books and periodicals on the issues facing the United Nations and its peoples and member states, with particular emphasis upon international, regional and transboundary policies.

The United Nations University was established as a subsidiary organ of the United Nations by General Assembly Resolution 2951 (XXVII) of 11 December 1972. The United Nations University undertakes a wide range of activities focused on knowledge generation (basic and applied research, and foresight and policy studies), education and capacity development (developing human and organizational capabilities), and knowledge transfer and sharing (communications, dissemination and outreach). The University operates through its institutes and programmes located throughout the world, and its planning and coordinating centre in Tokyo.

Primordial leadership

Peacebuilding and National Ownership in Timor-Leste

Sukehiro Hasegawa

United Nations University Press

TOKYO · NEW YORK · PARIS

The views expressed in this publication are those of the authors and do not necessarily reflect the views of the United Nations University.

United Nations University Press
United Nations University, 53-70, Jingumae 5-chome,
Shibuya-ku, Tokyo 150-8925, Japan
Tel: +81-3-5467-1212   Fax: +81-3-3406-7345
E-mail: sales@unu.edu   General enquiries: press@unu.edu
http://www.unu.edu

United Nations University Office at the United Nations, New York
2 United Nations Plaza, Room DC2-2062, New York, NY 10017, USA
Tel: +1-212-963-6387   Fax: +1-212-371-9454
E-mail: unuony@unu.edu

United Nations University Press is the publishing division of the United Nations University.

Printed in the United States of America for the Americas and Asia
Printed in the United Kingdom for Europe, Africa and the Middle East

ISBN 978-92-808-1224-4
e-ISBN 978-92-808-7193-7

Library of Congress Cataloging-in-Publication Data: 2013024655

Endorsements

"This book is an insightful analytical presentation of developments that took place in Timor-Leste during the period of four years and three months Professor Sukehiro Hasegawa served first as Deputy Special Representative and then as Special Representative of the UN Secretary-General (SRSG) and head of UN peace missions, UNMISET, UNOTIL and UNMIT from July 2002 to September 2006. It reflects not only his intimate knowledge of events that happened during this period but also his genuine care about Timorese people and their leaders who struggled to lay a foundation for a free, peaceful and democratic nation.

As Professor Hasegawa points out, the United Nations and other external supporters played a critically important role in Timor-Leste in facilitating the process of building the national capacity for self-governance based on the principles of democracy. But, it was the national leaders' commitment to national interest that made it possible successful peace and state building.

I am grateful to the United Nations for having provided its assistance since 1999 through peacekeeping and peace building missions together with UN agencies. Along with other SRSGs and senior staff of UN missions and agencies assigned to Timor-Leste, Professor Hasegawa played a most valuable role in extending his advisory services and support to the Timorese leaders and people. As I said in my speech welcoming back Professor Hasegawa to Timor-Leste in September 2009, he is a good friend of Timor-Leste who has been with us through both difficult times and periods of progress set on the path to development.

I recommend highly this book to those who are interested in knowing how the Timorese people carried out peace and nation building efforts with the assistance of the international community."

Kay Rala Xanana Gusmão, President (2002–2006) and Prime Minister (2007–2012), The Democratic Republic of Timor-Leste

"It is with much appreciation that I find in this book what I did together with Hasegawa as head of UN peacekeeping missions and UN agencies. He sat right next to me at a countless number of meetings that I chaired as the Foreign Minister and the Prime Minister. When security crisis took place, as SRSG and Deputy SRSG, Hasegawa was always in touch with me and other Timorese leaders in search of immediate secession of hostility and sustainable solutions to security problems.

The central theme of his book is the commitment of national leaders to national interest rather than the establishment of perfect institutional mechanisms that determines the success of a post-conflict country in achieving its stability and the sustainability of democratic governance. Hasegawa re-enacts in detail how the Timorese leaders endeavoured to find their roles in their own areas of strength and struggled to serve the national interest of Timor-Leste sometimes at the expense of their personal gains.

Anyone who is interested in knowing how the leaders and people of this nascent country of Timor-Leste gained their self-confidence in building peace and stability should read this book."

José Ramos-Horta, Nobel Peace Laureate, Foreign Minister (2002–2006), Prime Minister (2006–2007) and President (2007–2012), The Democratic Republic of Timor-Leste

"In order to achieve peace building in a post-conflict country like Timor-Leste, I consider as Professor Hasegawa points out, that it is the relationship of trust and confidence that UN mission leaders need to build with national leadership in order to bring about a change in the mind-set and mentality of both national leaders and people of a host country. For this to happen, UN and other international officers should not just find the shortcomings of any post-conflict society and merely insist on imposing a legal and institutional model of governance. The mission leaders need to develop a more productive approach that are culturally oriented to the society in which they work. The international community needs to find and support national leaders in post-conflict countries until the rule of law can be fully accepted and internalized by the people and society as a whole.

I highly recommend this book to those who are interested in knowing how the Timorese leaders and people have transcended old mentality and acquired new mind-set needed for making democracy work in the country."

Fernando La Sama de Araújo, President, National Parliament (2007–2012) and Deputy Prime Minister (since 2012), The Democratic Republic of Timor-Leste

"This is a book you should read if you want to understand how Timorese struggled to establish our own judicial system after we regained our political independence. Professor Hasegawa helped us a lot. As he rightly highlights the complexity of factors such as judicial traditions and languages, we had to address conflicting demands in order to build a viable justice system in Timor-Leste. He also points out rightly the need to reconcile competing desires by international partners in installing their own judicial system and the need to establish a simple and coherent judicial national system."

Claudio Ximenes, President, Court of Appeal, The Democratic Republic of Timor-Leste

"I was honored, together with my wife Babli, to have the opportunity to serve the people of Timor-Leste as the first Special Representative of the UN Secretary-General to independent Timor-Leste. We were present at the dawn of their first day as a new nation after long years of trial and tribulation for them. Such a moment comes but once in the history of a people and is worthy of being recorded in every way possible for posterity. Sukehiro Hasegawa, who was my Deputy and subsequently took over as the Special Representative himself, is therefore well suited to do so. All those with an interest in nation building in Timor-Leste are in debt to Suki for his having turned his hand to this valuable task with the dedication which we know from his service to the three UN peace missions.

Uniquely for the United Nations our team was made responsible for successive peace missions in Timor-Leste. The responsibility entrusted to us to serve the Timorese people was onerous, pioneering and uplifting at the same time. In our minds we will always be part of their journey as a nation. I congratulate Suki for capturing the onset of the journey.

What made it possible for us to be at the start with confidence and hope was the partnership with the leaders of Timor-Leste. The Timorese people are immensely fortunate in the leaders that guided their first steps as a nation. History will applaud the guidance they have given. We will always wear the distinction with pride that we were there in solidarity at the beginning."

Kamalesh Sharma, Commonwealth Secretary-General, SRSG UNMISET 2002–2004

"You hold in your hands a book that is remarkable, both in the story that it tells and in the analysis that it provides. Professor Sukehiro Hasegawa gives us a comprehensive look at the development of Timor-Leste during the period immediately following the restoration of independence in 2002 up to and including the crisis in 2006. In doing so, he highlights the achievements of the Timorese people and their leaders, which were often accomplished against considerable odds. He also describes the work of the UN and the international community, including lessons learned with respect to the challenges of peacekeeping and peace building in a post-conflict society. His reflections on transitional justice are of particular interest, as is his discussion of the serious crimes process, on which he sheds some new light.

Professor Hasegawa has twice served the people of Timor-Leste: first, as Deputy Special Representative and then Special Representative of the UN Secretary-General, and second, as the author of this book. With the publication of this volume, no future commentator will be able to discuss the recent history of Timor-Leste without referring to Professor Hasegawa's narration of events there and his analysis of their significance both to that country and the international community."

Phillip Rapoza, Chief Justice, The Appeals Court, Commonwealth of Massachusetts, Former International Judge and Coordinator Special Panels for Serious Crimes (2003–2005)

"Dr. Hasegawa has written an encyclopaedic history of the first crucial years after the restoration of East Timor's independence. He has all the advantages of having been a close observer, and often a participant, in the important events about which he writes, and yet he reports fairly and calmly about these events. The book reflects the commitment to principle and the scrupulous regard for the interests and feelings of others that Dr. Hasegawa managed to combine during his service as chief of the United Nations mission in Timor. We were all lucky to have him then, and now we are fortunate to have the benefit of his observations and reflections."

Grover Joseph Rees, United States Ambassador to Timor-Leste (2002–2006)

Contents

Acknowledgements

After 37 years of service to the United Nations and returning home from my last peacebuilding mission in Timor-Leste, I was asked by Hosei University to submit the curriculum I would be teaching. In preparation, I assembled as much relevant literature as I could find on global governance, international organizations and peacebuilding operations, with a particular focus on theories and doctrines.

Yet, once I started teaching, I soon discovered that the students were interested to know what actually happens on the ground. The more I talked about my experiences, the more I realized that I should share the lessons learned more widely during my period in Timor-Leste from 2002 to 2006, as Special Representative of the UN Secretary-General.

The focus of this book is the Timorese leaders and people; their warmness towards me was as deep as their commitment to peace and national interest. I am grateful for their openness and forthrightness in expressing their views and sentiments during our encounters. Special thanks to Xanana Gusmão and José Ramos-Horta, former presidents of Timor-Leste, and Fernando La Sama, former president of the National Parliament, for meeting with me in Japan and Timor-Leste even after my retirement. President Taur Matan Ruak also spoke to me at length when he was still commander of F-FDTL. FRETILIN leaders; Mari Alkatiri, the former prime minister; and Francisco Lú-Olo Guterres, the former president of the National Parliament, talked to me whenever I asked for meetings during my visits to Timor-Leste after my retirement. Ministers José Luís Guterres, Mario Carrascalão and Estanislau da Silva, along with Justice Claudio Ximenes, shared their understandings and views of the events that I recollected and are described in this book. Ágio Pereira and Emilia Pires spoke with me for endless hours during and after my UN mission assignment in Timor-Leste.

At UN Headquarters, Secretary-General Kofi Annan and Under-Secretary-General Jean Marie Guéhenno guided me with indication of the overall policy approach, and Assistant Secretary-General Hédi Annabi provided me with timely advice while he was in charge of peace-keeping operations at DPKO New York and before his tragic death in Haiti. I am most grateful to them for their guidance and advice. I also appreciated valuable support extended to me by Lisa Buttenheim, Director of the Asia and Middle East Division, and operational assistance provided by Ingrid Hayden, the late Andrew Greene, Nina Lahoud, Lin Bai and Daria Ferrari.

Atul Khare, Ameerah Haq and Finn Reske-Nielsen, who succeeded me as Special Representatives of the Secretary-General, welcomed me back whenever I visited Timor-Leste. My deputy General Anis Bajwa, and Chief of Staff Michiko Kuroda, helped me in recollecting the events in April and May 2006. My assistants Lisa Reefke and Nelia da Costa were most forthcoming whenever I needed their help.

Special thanks go to Vesselin Popovski of United Nations University who encouraged me to write this book, and the staff of UNU Press in making its publication possible. In assembling my records, I benefitted a great deal from Hillel Loew's tireless work in locating relevant papers, reports, documents and records of communication.

I am grateful to my wife Anita, and our three children, Erika, Corinne and Stefan, who endured my extended absences during my numerous UN assignments, including this one in Timor-Leste. Erika helped me tremendously in preparing and editing the final draft of my manuscript for this book.

Thank you, dear reader, for your interest in my book and my peace-keeping and peacebuilding missions. I hope you will benefit from this story about the Timorese people's quest for sustainable peace and development.

Sukehiro Hasegawa
Tokyo, October 2012

Abbreviations and Acronyms

AAC	Associação dos Antigos Combatentes das FALINTIL (Association of Former Combatants)
ABC	Australian Broadcasting Corporation
ACABQ	Advisory Committee on Administrative and Budgetary Questions
ACP	Summit of Asian, Caribbean and Pacific Countries
ACVTL	Associação Comunidade Vitimas de Timor-Leste (Community Association of Victims of Timor-Leste)
ADB	Asian Development Bank
ASDT	Associação Social Democráta Timorense (Social Democratic Association of Timor- Leste)
ASEAN	Association of Southeast Asian Nations
ASSEPOL	Association of Former Political Prisoners
BDT	Border Demarcation Team
BPA	Banking and Payments Authority
BPU	Border Patrol Unit
CAT	Convention against Torture and Other Cruel, Inhuman or Degrading Treatment or Punishment
CAVR	Comissão de Acolhimento, Verdade e Reconciliação (Commission for Reception, Truth and Reconciliation in East Timor)
CCF	FRETILIN Central Committee
CEDAW	Convention on the Elimination of All Forms of Discrimination against Women
CEDAW-OP	Optional Protocol to the Convention on the Elimination of All Forms of Discrimination against Women
CNE	Comissão Nacional de Eleições (National Electoral Commission)

CNRM	Conselho Nacional de Resistência Maubere (National Council of Maubere Resistance)
CNRT	Conselho Nacional de Reconstrução de Timor (National Congress for Timorese Reconstruction)
COE	Commission of Experts
COI	Commission of Inquiry
Colimau	Comando de Libertação do Povo Maubere
CPD-RDTL	Conselho Popular pela Defesa da República Democrática de Timor-Leste (Popular Committee for Defence of the Democratic Republic of Timor-Leste)
CPLP	Comunidade dos Países de Língua Portuguesa (Community of Portuguese Speaking Countries)
CRC	Convention on the Rights of the Child
CRC-OP-AC	Optional Protocol to the Convention on the Rights of the Child on the involvement of children in armed conflict
CRC-OP-SC	Optional Protocol to the Convention on the Rights of the Child on the sale of children, child prostitution and child pornography
CSG	Civilian Support Group
CTF	Commission of Truth and Friendship (between Timor-Leste and Indonesia)
DOA	Director of Administration
DPA	Department of Political Affairs of the United Nations
DPI	Department of Public Information
DPKO	Department of Peacekeeping Operations of the United Nations
DSRSG	Deputy Special Representative of the Secretary-General
EAD	Electoral Assistance Division of the Department of Political Affairs
ETPS	East Timor Police Service
FALINTIL	Forças Armadas de Libertação Nacional de Timor-Leste (Armed Forces for the National Liberation of East Timor)
FAO	Food and Agriculture Organization
F-FDTL	FALINTIL - Forças Armadas de Defesa de Timor-Leste
FPI	Baucau Frente Política Interna
FRAP	Reintegration Assistance Programme
FRETILIN	Frente Revolucionária do Timor-Leste Independente (Revolutionary Front for an Independent East Timor)
G-RDTL	Government of the Democratic Republic of Timor-Leste
HC	Humanitarian Co-ordinator
HRU	Human Rights Unit
HRW	Human Rights Watch
IBRD	International Bank for Reconstruction and Development – World Bank
ICAO	International Civil Aviation Organization
ICCPR-OP2-DP	Second Optional Protocol to the International Covenant on Civil and Political Rights (aimed at the abolition of the death penalty)

ICCR	International Covenant on Civil and Political Rights
ICERD	International Convention on the Elimination of All Forms of Racial Discrimination
ICESCR	International Covenant on Economic, Social and Cultural Rights
ICG	International Crisis Group
ICIET	International Commission of Inquiry on East Timor
ICRC	International Committee of the Red Cross
ICTR	International Criminal Tribunal for Rwanda
ICTY	International Criminal Tribunal for former Yugoslavia
IDP	internally displaced person
ILO	International Labour Organization
IMF	International Monetary Fund
INTERFET	International Force for East Timor
IOM	International Organization for Migration
IRI	International Republican Institute
IRU	International Response Unit
ISF	International Security Forces
JBC	Joint Border Committee
JEG	Japan Engineering Group of the Japan Self-Defence Force
JP	Junction Point
JSMP	Judicial System Monitoring Programme
KKN	Korupusi, Kolusi, Nepotisme (Corruption, Collusion and Nepotism)
MLG	Military Liaison Group
MLO	Military Liaison Officer
MOP	Movement of Personnel
MP	Military Police
MPR	Majelis Permusyawaratan Rakyat (People's Consultative Assembly)
MTA	Military Training Adviser
MTAG	Military Training Advisors Group
MWC	International Convention on the Protection of the Rights of All Migrant Workers and Members of their Families
NGO	Non-Governmental Organization
NOC	National Operations Centre
OHCHR	Office of the United Nations High Commissioner for Human Rights
OLA	Office of Legal Affairs
PBSO	Peacebuilding Support Office
PD	Partido Democrático (Democratic Party)
PDC	Partido Democrata Cristã (Christian Democratic Party)
PKF	Peacekeeping Force
PNTL	Polícia Nacional de Timor-Leste (National Police of Timor-Leste)
POLRI	Indonesian National Police
PSD	Partido Social Democrático (Social Democratic Party)

PST	Timor Socialist Party
RC	Resident Co-ordinator of the United Nations System's Operational Activities for Development
RDS	Rapid Deployment Services
RDTL	República Democrática de Timor Leste (Democratic Republic of Timor-Leste)
RENETIL	Resistência Nacional dos Estudantes de Timor-Leste Resistencia Nacional dos Estudantes de Timor-Leste
RESPECT	Recovery, Employment and Stability Programme for Ex-combatants and Communities in Timor-Leste
RIU	Rapid Intervention Unit
S/CRS	US Department of State Office of the Coordinator for Reconstruction and Stabilization
SAF	Singapore Armed Forces
SCIT	Serious Crimes Investigation Team
SCIU	Serious Crimes Investigation Unit
SCP	Serious Crimes Programme
SCU	Serious Crimes Unit
SPTL	Timor-Leste Prison System
SPU	Special Police Unit
SRSG	Special Representative of the Secretary-General of the United Nations
SSMTA	Senior Sector Military Training Adviser
SSPTA	Senior Sector Police Training Advisor
STAE	Technical Secretariat for Electoral Administration
SUP	Special Unit Patrol
TCL	Tactical Coordination Line
TLDPM	Timor-Leste Development Partners Meeting
TMR	Taur Matan Ruak
TNI	Tentara Nasional Indonesia – Indonesian National Armed Forces
TOR	Terms of Reference
TWG	Transition Working Group
UDC	União Democrática Cristã (Christian Democratic Union)
UDT	União Democrática Timorense (Timorese Democratic Union)
UIR	Unidade Intervenção Rápida (Rapid Response Unit)
UNAMET	United Nations Assistance Mission in East Timor
UNDAF	United Nations Development Assistance Framework
UNDERTIM	Unidade Nacional Democratica da Resistancia Timorense (National Democratic Unity of Timorese Resistance
UNDP	United Nations Development Programme
UNESCO	United Nations Educational, Scientific and Cultural Organization
UNFPA	United Nations Fund for Population Activities
UNHCR	United Nations High Commissioner for Refugees
UNICEF	United Nations Children's Fund
UNIOSIL	United Nations Integrated Office in Sierra Leone

UNMIN	United Nations Mission to Nepal
UNMISET	United Nations Mission of Support in East Timor
UNMIT	United Nations Integrated Mission in Timor-Leste
UNMOG	UN Military Observers Group
UNOPS	United Nations Office for Project Service
UNOSOM	United Nations Operations in Somalia
UNOTIL	United Nations Office in Timor-Leste
UNPOL	United Nations Police
UNTAC	United Nations Transitional Authority for Cambodia
UNTAET	United Nations Transitional Administration in East Timor
UNTL	Universidade Nacional Timor Lorosa'e (National University of East Timor)
UNU	United Nations University
UNV	United Nations Volunteer
UPF	Unidade Patrulhamento Fronteira (Timor-Leste Border Patrol Unit)
URP	Unidade de Reserva da Polícia (Police Reserve Unit)
USAID	US Agency for International Development
USG	Under-Secretary-General
WFP	World Food Programme
WHO	World Health Organization

Map of Timor-Leste

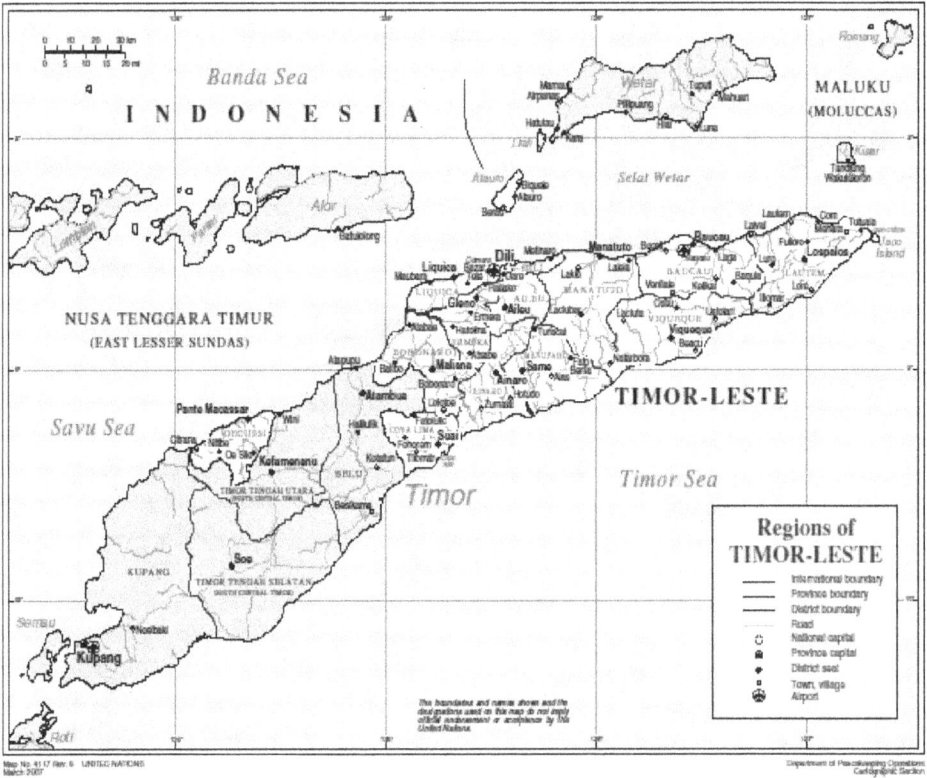

Map of Timor-Leste. Source: UN Department of Peacekeeping Operations, Cartographic Section, 2012 (http://www.un.org/Depts/Cartographic/map/profile/timoreg. pdf, accessed 15 January 2013).

Introduction

This book provides a detailed account of my interactions with the Timorese national leaders during my assignment in Timor-Leste from July 2002 to September 2006. In this period, the UN Security Council maintained, in succession, three peacekeeping and peacebuilding missions: the United Nations Mission of Support in East Timor (UNMISET), the United Nations Office in Timor-Leste (UNOTIL) and the United Nations Integrated Mission in Timor-Leste (UNMIT).

Upon my arrival in Dili, I first acted as deputy head of UNMISET, the UN peacekeeping mission that succeeded the United Nations Transitional Administration in East Timor (UNTAET) in May 2002. Two years later, upon the departure of Ambassador Kamalesh Sharma, I was appointed Special Representative of the Secretary-General (SRSG) and Head of UNMISET. Finally, I continued as the SRSG and Head of UNOTIL until August 2006. Upon the closure of UNOTIL, I remained in Timor-Leste as SRSG and continued to manage UNMIT for a brief period until 30 September 2006. Throughout this period of four-plus years, I also acted concurrently as Resident Coordinator of the United Nations operational system's activities for development and as the Resident Representative of the United Nations Development Programme (UNDP), and sometime as the Humanitarian Coordinator when the situation required a humanitarian response from the United Nations.

Chapter I describes the start of my UN peacekeeping assignment in Timor-Leste in July 2002 and assesses the significance of a referendum called "popular consultation" conducted by the United Nations on 30

August 1999. The work undertaken by UNTAET to prepare for Timorese self-governance is reviewed.

Chapter II explains how Timorese leadership established the national judiciary system, including prison facilities. It identifies the difficulties encountered by the National Parliament in carrying out its legislative work, and the challenges the national judiciary faced in building its professional competence are described. Discussed also are the negotiations with Australia on oil and natural gas resources in the Timor Gap, and with Indonesia on land border demarcation and management.

Chapter III reveals the tension among Timorese leadership regarding the manner and direction of national governance and development. It shows the gradual centralization of governing power by the Prime Minister, whose authoritarian management style disenchanted many, including some soldiers of the Forças Armadas de Libertação Nacional de Timor-Leste (FALINTIL, Armed Forces for the National Liberation of East Timor) – Forças Armadas de Defesa de Timor-Leste (F-FDTL). The implications of anti-police and anti-government demonstrations, including the Dili riots in December 2002, are reviewed. The need for a Security Council mandate for UN involvement in security sector reform is explained, as is the government's decision to make religious teaching at public schools optional, causing confrontation between church and state.

Chapter IV analyses how the struggle for supreme power intensified between the two main leaders, triggering armed confrontations between their followers in April and May 2006. This chapter identifies the three most serious events leading up to the armed clashes and discusses how the crisis inadvertently caused an ethnic division between lorosae and lolomonu groups. The reactions of the Security Council and the Core Group to the crisis are explained in detail.

Chapter V provides an explanation of how the Timorese dealt with several post-conflict transitional justice issues. Diverse notions and concepts that were identified during the process of achieving truth, justice, reconciliation and peace are presented and analysed. The Comissão de Acolhimento, Verdade e Reconciliação (CAVR, Commission for Reception, Truth and Reconciliation) was successful in unearthing human rights violations committed by both the Indonesians and the Timorese. The Serious Crimes Programme (SCP) achieved tangible results in investigating, prosecuting and bringing to trial those who perpetrated crimes against humanity. It did, however, face a major geopolitical obstacle that prevented any prosecutions and trials of Indonesian security personnel and the Timorese who fled to Indonesia.

Chapter VI describes how the roles of UN peace missions changed between 1999 and 2006. It gives an account of comprehensive consultations that were carried out in eight Transition Working Groups (TWGs), in preparation for a rapid and smooth transition from peacekeeping to a peacebuilding phase, and finally, to a sustainable development framework. The policy committee chaired by Secretary-General Kofi Annan, and meetings with the members of the Security Council and the Core Group, indicated divergent views. The security crisis of May 2006 is considered; this led to a reversal of the Security Council decision, and the re-establishment of a peacekeeping mission in August 2006.

Chapter VII explains how SRSGs, and other mission leaders, acted to integrate mission components and build cohesive teams in pursuit of strategic goals. It also addresses the issue of UN staff security, particularly in conflict-prone countries.

Chapter VIII identifies the principal factors that contributed to the successful outcome of Timor-Leste's pursuit of stability, peace and development. These include Indonesia's acceptance of Timor-Leste's independence as a sovereign nation state, and the solidarity of the members of the Security Council and the Core Group in support of the continued engagement of the United Nations and the international community. This final chapter concludes with the identification of five key attributes that I call "primordial leadership", essential for sustainable peacebuilding of a post-conflict country. They are (i) indigenous and original, (ii) authentic and legitimate, (iii) local and universal, (iv) primal and emotional, and (v) transformative and sustainable. In the aftermath of the security crisis in 2006, the primordial leaders of Timor-Leste were determined to bring about the necessary change in the mindset and mentality of the Timorese people and transform the indigenous political culture into one of democratic governance and sustainable development.

I

The beginning of a peacebuilding mission in Timor-Leste

The world is celebrating with us, but the world is also watching us,
to assess our will and our ability to govern ourselves.

Kay Rala Xanana Gusmão[1]

The incidents in Dili last week were a wake-up call to us,
the East Timorese leadership, as well as to the international community,
that we must not take for granted the apparent tranquillity in the country and
that urgent preventive measures must be taken in a resolute manner
to prevent a relapse into the past of violence and instability.

José Ramos-Horta[2]

I declare I am ready to resign my position as prime minister of the government
. . . so as to avoid the resignation of His Excellency the President of the
Republic Xanana Gusmão

Mari Bin Amude Alkatiri[3]

Arrival in Dili and the start of my UN mission assignment in Timor-Leste

On 15 July 2002, I travelled to Dili, Timor-Leste, on a Merpati flight from Denpasar, Bali. It took nearly two hours. The atmosphere in the aircraft was calm as we landed. The runway was just long enough to accommodate

Primordial leadership: Peacebuilding and national ownership in Timor-Leste, Hasegawa,
United Nations University Press, 2013, ISBN 978-92-808-1224-4

our medium-sized Boeing 737 aircraft. The airport and its adjacent areas appeared empty except for two UN transport aircraft in a parking area. The sky was blue and the air was dry.

As I walked down the ramp onto the tarmac, a tall Indian gentleman greeted me with a serene smile. It was the beginning of a cordial professional relationship with Ambassador Kamalesh Sharma, Special Representative of the Secretary-General (SRSG), who was accompanied by his assistant, Atul Khare.

My assignment in Timor-Leste was an opportunity to interact with Timorese leadership in peace- and nation-building for more than four years. Timor-Leste had gained international recognition of its independence, which had been declared on 20 May 2002. The newly founded country then embarked upon strenuous efforts to build both peace, and a new nation, with international assistance.

The road from the airport to the central part of Dili was livelier than I remembered it. My first visit in 2000 was as a Japanese government aid advisor on an assessment mission. At the time, there was hardly anyone on Comoro Road, and not a single hotel with a vacant room. Like most international personnel arriving in the wake of East Timor's independence, I found a place to stay in one of two floating hotel ships anchored off Dili's rocky coast.

During my brief visit, I met with the SRSG at the time, Sérgio Vieira de Mello. The rain was pouring outside and it was difficult to hear one another, yet Sérgio's enthusiasm reverberated through the noise. I felt certain at the time that he would achieve his goals of establishing security and stability for the people, that he would lay a solid foundation down for stable governance. Sérgio was a charismatic leader who possessed an extraordinary ability to inspire people.[4]

I also met additional senior mission officials, such as David Harland. We had collaborated earlier in Afghanistan and Somalia. David served with the United Nations Transitional Administration in East Timor (UNTAET) from November 1999 to June 2000, as Acting Deputy Special Representative of the Secretary-General (DSRSG) for Governance and Public Administration. He advocated an integrated approach in conducting mission operations.[5] All the UN mission staff looked busy and enthusiastic. The atmosphere in Dili was surprisingly congenial compared with my previous experiences in Kabul and Mogadishu.

Upon my arrival in Dili two and a half years later, I moved into a proper hotel known as the Crystal Hotel. Several other UN officers were also staying there. I had one simple room on the second floor, with a shower and a private toilet. There was even a Portuguese restaurant downstairs. Having lived in Kabul, Phnom Penh, Mogadishu and Kigali, where proper accommodation facilities were scarce, I was quite content with the Crystal Hotel. I enjoyed staying there for two weeks until my official residence became available.

The house had been the official residence of United Nations Development Programme (UNDP) Resident Representative Finn Reske-Nielsen until his departure in mid-2002. It had a comfortable living room, a small dining room with a table for six people and two small bedrooms, one of which I converted into a study.

Across the street from the residence was a building complex kept for the Embassy of Indonesia. Along with many other buildings in the Faro area, the Indonesian Government and security personnel had occupied the complex. There were stories that many houses in the area had been used for the interrogation and torture of Timorese independence activists. It was suspected that many of them had died in these houses.

Once I checked into the hotel, my first order of business was to have a long meeting with my boss, SRSG Sharma. My goal was to find out exactly what his expectations of me were. I had a standard UN post description; I was well aware of the importance of maintaining the official duties and functions. One lesson, learned after many years working in the UN system, was that my usefulness to the mission depended upon how much confidence the Head of Mission had in me.

I had no doubt that the primary task of any deputy should be to help the Chief carry out his work, to achieve the mission goals as mandated by the Security Council. Therefore, I indicated to Sharma that I was ready to take up any of the functions he wanted to entrust or delegate to me. The core of his response was that, while he expected me to assist him in managing the mission's work, I should be active in directing capacity-building, humanitarian assistance and socio-economic programmes.

In his absence from the mission area, I would assume all responsibilities entrusted to him. He also expressed his expectation that I would advise him on the implications of any events or actions being taken by UN Headquarters. After this meeting, we worked well together as a team. Sharma was primarily concerned with political and security developments, and my own strengths and interests lay in building the capacity of national institutions for democratic governance.

I had spent nearly 30 years with the UNDP. My experience involved development assistance for nation-building in several countries including Nepal, Indonesia, Samoa and Rwanda. I had acted as the Resident Coordinator and UNDP Resident Representative in Samoa and Rwanda. Sharma felt strongly that my focus should be to coordinate and integrate the development assistance programmes of various agencies and other aid institutions.

Writing the job description and meeting the SRSG Executive Team

As required by the Department of Peacekeeping Operations (DPKO) Headquarters in New York, I then drafted my own job description. I listed the functions that I would carry out in my dual roles as Deputy Head of the United Nations Mission of Support in East Timor (UNMISET) and UN Resident Coordinator/UNDP Resident Representative.

As Deputy Head of UNMISET, I would be responsible for co-ordinating the implementation of governance and institutional capacity-development programmes of the mission implementation plan, with specific responsibilities for:

- Overseeing the investigation and fair trial of serious crime cases.
- Strengthening the core functions of the East Timorese public administration.
- Strengthening of the East Timorese judiciary.
- Supporting the development of the East Timor Police Service (ETPS).[6]
- Providing strategic direction for the mission's executive policing functions.
- Presenting the budget of the mission to the Advisory Committee on Administrative and Budgetary Questions (ACABQ).

As UN Resident Coordinator and UNDP Resident Representative, I was to:

- Coordinate humanitarian, rehabilitation and development activities undertaken by the UN agencies and international finance institutions such as the World Bank, International Monetary Fund (IMF) and the Asian Development Bank, with a view to ensuring an integrated and coherent approach towards sustainable development in the country.
- Facilitate inter-agency support for implementation of the National Development Plan through the development of projects of recovery, employment and income generation.
- Perform the duties of the designated official for security in respect of UN agencies, programmes and funds, including chairing monthly security meetings.

Upon assumption of my new functions, I decided to spend a considerable amount of my time formulating a strategic development plan for the justice sector. I sought to engage international donor agencies to request funding for 200 "development advisor" posts. I also embarked upon the task of coordinating the UNMISET programmes with the wider UN system of agencies, funds and programmes. Included in my plan were bilateral players and civil society organizations, in both national and international NGOs.

SRSG Sharma was already busy consolidating the relationship between the UN mission and the nascent national government. For example, he held weekly meetings with Prime Minister Alkatiri and Foreign Minister Ramos-Horta, and periodic meetings with President Gusmão. He interacted regularly with civil society organizations, including NGOs. He visited several districts in rural areas in order to open direct communication channels with local leaders. The Prime Minister had appointed district administrators, whom Sharma met. However, he made a point of interacting with community leaders as well.

Another major undertaking SRSG Sharma was engaged in was to help establish a cordial working relationship between Timor-Leste and Indonesia, in line with Security Council Resolution S/RES/1410 (2002), paragraph 12. He visited Jakarta from 23 to 25 July 2002 and held meetings with senior officials, including President Megawati Sukarnoputri; Coordinating Minister for Political and Security Affairs, General Susilo Bambang Yudhoyono; Coordinating Minister for People's Welfare Kalla; and Foreign Minister Wirajuda.

Atul Khare played an increasingly important role in policy coordination and decision-making within the executive office of the SRSG.[7] He was highly intelligent and had a great memory. I was impressed with his ability to analyse a myriad of incoming faxes, correspondence materials, voluminous reports and documentation. Atul was the first to provide Sharma with the latest information on any issues that needed his immediate attention. He had a rare combination of qualities: those of a consummate political negotiator and good personnel manager, while managing international civil servants and security personnel.

Sue Ingram, who advised the SRSG on the implications of any developments, was another member of the senior staff in the executive office. Sue had extensive historical knowledge of the UN's previous work in the country. She also coordinated preparation of the budget and staffing proposals, supervised the recruitment process and reported on the implementation of the UN mission mandate.

As a newcomer, I provided the SRSG with relatively dispassionate and global perspectives on various issues. Issues in this newly founded country had a tendency to become rather complex and intractable, given their implications for the UN system as a whole. I took it as my duty to discuss with the SRSG about how the entire mission staff could work together, particularly at the executive level. I had heard that during the UNTAET period, the Chief of Staff at the time, Nagalingam Parameswaran from Malaysia, felt left out of the inner working circle of senior management.[8] He had resigned from the position, as he claimed that the mission was run in an exclusive manner. SRSG Sharma and I were determined to prevent that sort of situation from reoccurring.

The main information sharing and coordination assembly was the senior staff meeting held twice a week at 9:15 a.m. Several departments attended the meeting, including the SRSG, DSRSG, Chief of Staff, Special Assistant to the SRSG, the Force Commander, the UN Police Commissioner, Director of Administration, Chiefs of the Political and Legal offices, Head of the Human Rights Division, Chief of Public Information and Chief of the Security Unit. In addition to the role of DSRSG, I participated in the meeting as the coordinator of all UN agencies, funds and programmes. The meeting usually started with a short introductory remark by SRSG Sharma. He spoke briefly on broad policy issues as well as on any specific developments that had taken place during the preceding days. The participants were then in turn given an opportunity to present their views on any of the issues touched upon by the SRSG, or any matters of concern to them.

During the first two years of UNMISET from June 2002 to May 2004, security and stability were the primary issues that occupied most of the morning meetings. The Force Commander Winai Phattiyakul from Thailand, and his deputy, Justin Kelly from Australia, always spoke about security developments in a matter-of-fact manner. Their presentation and analysis of issues were factual and precise. As a Thai, General Winai spoke gently and in a most reassuring manner. He was experienced in dealing with the insurgency, as he had served as Chief of Office for the Thai–Myanmar border security coordination. He always displayed sincere concern for his staff. This was contrary to my expectation of a general in military uniform as being a disciplined and stern person.

Major General Huck Gim Tan of Singapore, who was equally factual, but also highly analytical, succeeded General Winai. He excelled in presenting his views on security matters in a very systematic manner. The third and last Force Commander was General Khairuddin Mat Yusof of Malaysia. Similar to General Winai, General Khairuddin showed much humane interest and concern for his troops. Having served as the assistant military adviser at the Department of Peacekeeping Operations, New York, from 1991 to 1993, he was familiar with the procedures of UN peacekeeping operations. Among the three force commanders, he remained in Timor-Leste for the longest period of nearly two years from August 2003 to May 2005. I learned that these military chiefs emphasized the maintenance of a relationship of trust and confidence with their troops and associates.

Peter Miller of Canada was the UN Police Commissioner upon my arrival in Dili. He was very much engaged in laying the groundwork for a gradual transfer of national policing responsibility to the Timorese police forces. They were called PNTL, an acronym in Portuguese for Policia Nacional de Timor-Leste. There were more than 1,000 UN Police (UNPOL) personnel when I arrived in Timor-Leste. During the course of the following 20 months, they completed their assignments and left the country. Sandra Peisley of Australia replaced Peter Miller in June 2003. She was the first UN female Police Commissioner, and had a wide variety of experience in police training, management and investigation. She exercised discipline among her police officers.

All in all, the spirit of cooperation encouraged by the mission leaders and the congenial relationships among the senior staff of UNMISET resulted in good teamwork. The UN Headquarters staff repeatedly stated that UNMISET was one of the most cohesive teams they had seen.

Administering the Special Fund

My first assignment, as DSRSG and UNDP Resident Representative, was management of the Special Fund, which compensated former Indonesian public servants and pensioners for their loss of employment following Timor-Leste's separation from Indonesia. This Fund had been established by the Transitional Administrator, Sérgio Vieira de Mello, upon an agreement reached between the United Nations and the Indonesian Government on 23 November 2001.

The UNDP managed the Special Fund in partnership with UNMISET, the United Nations High Commissioner for Refugees (UNHCR) and bilateral donor countries that had contributed to the Fund. Australia, Portugal and the European Commission had contributed most significantly to the Fund, along with Indonesia. The idea was to entice former Timorese civil servants and pensioners who had fled to West Timor to return to Timor-Leste.

The Fund was initially budgeted at US$25 million for payments ranging from US$500 to US$1,500 to each former Indonesian civil servant. However, only US$5.5 million had been raised. There was no prospect of obtaining additional contributions to the Fund. It became apparent that with the resources available, we could only make payments ranging from US$50 for an Indonesian employee with one to five years of service, to US$350 for a longer-term pensioner. The payments had been calculated based on the years of service. The total number of beneficiaries was estimated at 29,200. Some 22,000 had registered, while 2,500 had not, even though they were thought to be living in Timor-Leste. Furthermore, we estimated that about 4,700 were still in the Indonesian province of West Timor.

As with any operation carried out by the United Nations, we had to establish and follow a principle of payment that was fair and accountable. This required us to devise a formula of payment based on the length of service with the Indonesian Government. Financial resources were insufficient for the pension payments. Therefore, the Special Fund payments were not presented as any entitlement vis-à-vis the Indonesian Government. It was clearly communicated that these payments were different from the Indonesian pension, housing scheme and severance payments. They were part of a different agreement signed earlier, on 10 July 2001, by UNTAET and the Indonesian Government. According to the agreement with UNTAET, Indonesia decided to pay back pension contributions and other related benefits owed to its former employees in Timor-Leste, calculated up until 20 May 2002.

In the end, lump-sum payments ranging from US$70 to US$460 were made, depending on the beneficiaries' years of service. The UNDP, with the assistance of UNPOL and the United Nations Peacekeeping Force (PKF), made cash payments to 22,596 former civil servants in the two years 2002–2003. Many former Indonesian civil servants viewed this as inadequate, and I was pressed to keep the promise made a few years earlier.

Several mass demonstrations took place, and their main organizer – the Associação Comunidade Vitimas de Timor-Leste (Community Association of Victims of Timor-Leste) (ACVTL) – made a variety of complaints, statements and accusations. Occasionally, the group questioned the UN's failure to fulfil its responsibility to former Indonesian civil servants. I met with the leaders of ACVTL several times. Additionally, on 29 May 2003, I met with 19 ACVTL representatives, including the leaders of 13 districts.

The ACVTL leaders demanded an immediate response to their "claim" made a week earlier. They asked me to require the governments of Indonesia and Timor-Leste to make proper pension payments. I explained that the United Nations and UNDP were international organizations. They did not have the authority to force the governments of these two countries to make payments to them. This came as a surprise, as apparently they thought the United Nations was powerful enough to command Member States.

The Tripartite Agreement of 5 May 1999 pertained only to the holding of a referendum on Timor-Leste's future under the control of the Republic of Indonesia. It did not mention the rights of the Indonesian government employees. I stressed that the United Nations was not in a position to force the Indonesian government to meet with the ACVTL. When I asked a Timorese colleague at UNMISET, I was told that these were activists who did not have the broad support of the people.

After numerous meetings, I decided to decline any further requests for meetings with the ACVTL activists, lest they could hold the United Nations responsible for pension entitlements. Based on their understanding of the agreement reached between UNTAET, Indonesia and other countries, the ACVTL activists believed they could legitimately claim additional payments from the international community on top of the Indonesian pension payments.

I found myself torn on legal and moral grounds. I had no means of mobilizing funds to honour the original promise made before my time. Therefore, we made a decision to distribute only what we received from donor countries, even though the total amount made available was far smaller than expected. Yet, it appeared that this proved to be both a realistic and acceptable decision. There were no significant or major protests once we started making payments in Dili on Monday, 4 November 2002.

People formed long lines in the hot sun and remained in place until late at night. There was a danger of disturbances as so many people stood in the dark. At my request, the Japan Engineering Group of the Japan Self-Defence Force (JEG) brought mobile lighting vehicles that kept the street lit and orderly. The UNDP staff headed by Anthony Wood worked long and hard to complete the payments, remaining resilient throughout the ordeal. Their work contributed to restoring some sense of trust and confidence among people towards the United Nations. I was pleased to learn from the UNDP staff that 99 per cent of the recipients had shown their appreciation and did not question the appropriateness of payments. It was also reassuring that the ACVTL activists did not organize any further demonstrations during the two-month period when we made the payments from the Special Fund.

Notes

1. Xanana Gusmão, *Timor Lives!: Speeches of Freedom and Independence* (Woollahra, Australia: Longueville Media, 2005), p. 8.
2. Statement made by Foreign Minister Ramos-Horta to the United Nations Security Council on 5 May 2006. See the record of the Security Council 5432 meeting, S/PV.5432.
3. Statement made by Prime Minister Alkatiri at a press conference held on 26 June 2006 and reported by Agence France-Presse. Alkatiri was Prime Minister of the Democratic Republic of Timor-Leste from 20 May 2002 to 26 June 2006.
4. For a detailed account of Sérgio Vieira de Mello, see Samantha Power, *Chasing the Flame: Sérgio Vieira de Mello and the Fight to Save the World* (London: Penguin Books, 2008).
5. David Harland emphasized that the basic directions that SRSG Sérgio de Mello set were in the right directions, although there were some weaknesses in planning, budgeting, consultations and service delivery. See his paper entitled "UN peacekeeping operations in post-conflict Timor-Leste: Accomplishments and lessons learned", presented to a conference I organized in Dili in April 2005 to review what had been accomplished and what challenges remained.
6. Management of the executive Parameswaran functions were, however, retained by the UN Police Commissioner who reported directly to the SRSG.

7. Secretary-General Kofi Annan appointed him as my deputy in 2004, and later as his Special Representative for Timor-Leste in December 2006. In 2010, he was appointed Assistant Secretary-General for UN peacekeeping operations at UN Headquarters in New York. In June 2011, as Head of the Change Management Team, he spearheaded efforts to implement a reform agenda aimed at streamlining and improving the efficiency of the world body.

8. Reflecting on society's tendency to characterize any international institution, I discovered that Parameswaran was quoted as saying that UNTAET had become "a 'white' mission, an Eastern mission with a Western face" (*South China Morning Post*, Thursday 10 January 2002). A similar accusation was made in the local press that UNMISET was too Asian, as both the SRSG and DSRSG were of Asian descent.

II

First acts of national governance (2002–2004)

Launching of the first constitutional government

The restoration of Timor-Leste's political independence on 20 May 2002 marked the beginning of a genuine national self-rule. It built the foundations for an independent nation, based on the principles of democracy, where the people hold sovereign power to determine their own destiny. The Timorese people had acquired freedom to govern themselves. The leaders appeared most willing to promote a broad-based, participatory democracy and to heed their citizens' concerns. Yet, there was an expectation that the people would not only be freed from any further oppression, but also from poverty. The Timorese leaders would later find out that this was a tall order.

Pleased with the appearance of democratic spirit in Timor-Leste, international donors started to provide funding for programmes designed to strengthen the institutional capacities for governance. In particular, they supported the government, the judiciary, the parliament and the office of the President. The government took up office under the leadership of Prime Minister Alkatiri in May 2002. The national institutions took on responsibility for the conduct of its affairs with substantive assistance from the United Nations Mission of Support in East Timor (UNMISET), other UN agencies, the World Bank, the IMF and other multilateral aid agencies.

The Timorese responded to the offer of external support with respect towards the international community. For example, they demonstrated

Primordial leadership: Peacebuilding and national ownership in Timor-Leste, Hasegawa, United Nations University Press, 2013, ISBN 978-92-808-1224-4

their commitment to the principles of democratic governance by incorporating internationally accepted norms of human and civil rights. Furthermore, they heeded the advice of international experts and began to make some tangible progress in building the institutions of governance.

However, the Timorese leaders soon discovered differences among their values, interests and aspirations. The reconciliation of these differences would prove more difficult than fighting together against foreign occupation. They started to discover that their old mindset had been nurtured during a long period of foreign colonialism and occupation. This old mentality had become detrimental to accepting democratic governance.

Among the state institutions, the government was the most active and assertive. The ministers displayed their dedication to work even in a resource-starved environment. Yet, they suffered from a lack of technical and administrative capacity in their departments and ministries. This impeded implementation of their policies and programmes. Decision-making and management capacity remained weak, particularly at middle and senior management levels. Furthermore, the operational capacity at lower levels was very limited. The capacity limitations also made it difficult for the ministers to empower officials to make decisions at appropriately lower levels. Additionally, in many cases, their tendency to comply fully with the wishes of the Prime Minister resulted in delayed decision-making and implementation of programmes.

Alkatiri appoints diverse ministers for his government

To start governing a fragile country, still dominated by international institutions, Mari Alkatiri formed a tightly controlled cabinet in May 2002. It consisted of loyalists and technocrats. Alkatiri also paid due attention to the need for gender balance.

The appointment of José Ramos-Horta was one expected by both the Timorese society and the international community. He had been very active in pursuing diplomatic recognition at the United Nations and elsewhere, during the struggle for independence. When a Nobel Peace Prize was bestowed on him in 1996, Ramos-Horta had gained international recognition.

He was a cosmopolitan statesman who thought in terms of universal values and principles. These were rare qualities to find on a remote island in the Indonesian archipelago. Ramos-Horta was fully acquainted with the norms and standards developed at the United Nations. He was also up to speed with other forms of emerging global governance. He was cognisant of the principal needs for the Timorese people: the right of self-determination, protection from political persecution and other human rights that all people are entitled to.

His commitment to this international principle was demonstrated in an international incident in 2002 when a boat carrying Sri Lankan asylum seekers appeared near the shore of Timor-Leste in 2002 en route to Australia. While Prime Minister Alkatiri and Interior Minister Lobato were unsure how to deal with the situation, Ramos-Horta made it clear that Timor-Leste should take them onshore and house them in temporary accommodation. Since then, he repeatedly showed his determination to stand up for human rights and other universal values.

Ramos-Horta was senior to the other ministers in ranking. His official title was: "Senior Minister and Minister of Foreign Affairs and Cooperation". Yet he was not as close to the Prime Minister as were Maria Boivida and Ana Pessoa. These two ladies were part of the core of the Alkatiri cabinet: Maria Boivida as the Minister of Finance and Planning, and Ana Pessoa as the Minister of Justice. Boivida was loyal to Alkatiri; she followed his instructions diligently. Ana Pessoa was also loyal, but she was strong-willed and independent-minded. Many diplomats found her sometimes rigid and uncompromising. However, we all respected her for her straightforwardness. Nobody questioned her integrity.

Among the cabinet members, there were ministers with excellent technical competence. Estanislau da Silva, the Minister of Agriculture, Forestry and Fisheries, had studied engineering in Portugal. Additionally, Da Silva had spent more than ten years in Australia during his exile from 1975 to 1999. His interest in natural sciences and agriculture was evident in 2005, during a visit to an experimental rice farm in a rural district of Manatutu. In May 2007, he became the interim Prime Minister for three months when José Ramos-Horta was elected President.

Rui Araujo was another high-performing professional as the Minister of Health. He was respected in the international community. We met in Geneva in 2004 during a joint meeting of the executive boards of the United Nations Development Programme (UNDP), the United Nations Children's Fund (UNICEF) and the United Nations Fund for Population Activities (UNFPA). I asked him to join me in presenting on Timor-Leste's engagement in national development. He later became Deputy Prime Minister of the interim government in 2006.

The Minister of Defence, Rodrigues, spoke English fluently but insisted on speaking Portuguese. He liked being considered a professor and enjoyed conceptualizing subject matters in an abstract form. The senior members of the Alkatiri Government were intelligent and educated. Most of the members had been abroad before the restoration of independence, so they were comfortable collaborating with one another. They formed a group around Mari Alkatiri, the Prime Minister, who was their dominant leader.

Mari Alkatiri was a man of intellect and reason with a strong will. He believed in tight governmental control in all segments of the society and economy. He was aware of the need for foreign investment, but was also careful about its adverse impact. He felt that national independence and interest should be protected at all costs. For this reason, he was not in favour of borrowing funds from the World Bank. I respected his strong spirit of independence, which made him reluctant to borrow from foreign sources. However, I also understood that there was a place for pragmatism. Therefore, I advised him that strict discipline was admirable, but it was also necessary to activate the economy. People needed gainful employment. I emphasized that job creation had to be the government's key goal. He should achieve tangible economic recovery and growth, lest people would start to turn on him.

Ramos-Horta, by contrast, was more open to adopting a liberal economic policy, such as borrowing funds from the World Bank in order to stimulate the economy. He was a Keynesian at heart: ready to borrow money; ready to undertake massive public works, such that the government could create jobs for the people who needed income. Mari Alkatiri, on the other hand, was fearful. If too much money were injected into the economy too hastily, from his perspective, it would be a waste.

To secure adequate financial resources, the Alkatiri Government endeavoured to establish a regulatory and technical framework with Australia, to develop oil and natural gas resources in the Timor Gap area. On 20 May 2002, the government signed the Timor Sea Treaty with Australia, which would provide Timor-Leste with 90 per cent of the revenues from the Bayu-Undan field. A "Memorandum of Understanding" was also signed on the same day, which provided a 31 December 2002 deadline of an International Unitization Agreement. This agreement promised the efficient taxation, regulation and administration of the gas and oil field. In addition, Timor-Leste initiated technical discussions with Australia regarding the exploitation of the reserves in the Joint Petroleum Development Area.

The understanding was that this venture would not prejudice its position on the maritime boundary negotiations. This was specifically created to overcome the differences between the two governments on the ownership of oil and natural gas resources located in the Timor Sea. While Australia considered the location to be within the extended area of the continental shelf adjacent to Australia, Timor-Leste insisted that it was within the area of its exclusive economic zone.

International recognition and assistance for financial management

The President and the government acted together swiftly to establish the country's status in the international community, in order to secure assistance for financial management. During the first few months after the launch of the first constitutional government, the President concentrated his attention on foreign affairs, with trips as an Observer to the 3rd African, Caribbean and Pacific (ACP) Summit in Fiji in July 2002, and the 4th CPLP (Comunidade dos Países de Língua Portuguesa, Community of Portuguese-Speaking Countries) Heads of State and Government Summit in Brazil.

On 27 September 2002, Timor-Leste was admitted as the 191st member of the United Nations. The ceremony, which President Gusmão attended along with Prime Minister Alkatiri and Minister for Foreign Affairs José Ramos-Horta, marked the formal realization of their aspiration for independence as a sovereign nation.

In the same year, Timor-Leste became a member of the World Bank, the Asian Development Bank and CPLP. The country established diplomatic relations with nearly all Member States of the Association of Southeast Asian Nations (ASEAN). Timor-Leste started to participate in ASEAN meetings as an invited Observer.

As the first act of national governance, the government wanted to strengthen the core administrative structures critical to Timor-Leste's viability and political stability. The development of the East Timor Police Service (ETPS) received first priority because of the importance of law enforcement and maintenance of security.[1]

The government further recognized the need to provide people with basic social services, such as schools and health centres. For this purpose, it started the annual budgeting process in order to secure a minimum amount of resources. However, the government had neither the experience nor expertise to undertake proper budgeting of financial resources. Given the need for funds and technical expertise, it decided to accept the assistance of Bretton Woods Institutions when the preparation of the 2003–2004 national budgets took place.

UNMISET and UNDP recognized Bretton Woods Institutions' specialized expertise. At the same time we were sensitive to what we regarded as the short-sightedness of the IMF and World Bank staff. They seemed to take our cooperation for granted and dictate their terms to us. On 12 August 2003, UNMISET received a four-man delegation from the IMF's monetary and financial systems department, led by Mr Cheek Sung Lee. He discussed the status of advisory services provided by five joint IMF and UN experts to the Banking and Payment Authority of Timor-Leste. The delegation included Mr Luis Quintaneiro, Banking and Payments Authority (BPA) General Manager; Mr C. Ake Lonnberg, IMF Senior Economist; and Mr Cadim A. Al-Eyd, IMF Senior Resident Representative based in Timor-Leste. Contrary to my earlier expectation, Mr Cheek Sung Lee was polite and appreciative of the support extended by the United Nations to the cost-sharing agreement in support of the Government of Timor-Leste. Instead of making demands, he gently expressed his hopes that the cost-sharing arrangement would continue until the end of the UNMISET mandate.

Also, he said that a similar arrangement could be made to fill the BPA's critical need to continue functioning as a central bank of the country and to manage the monetary policies and operational responsibilities. I acknowledged that with the assistance of the IMF and the United Nations, the monetary policies and operations of the new country had started without any major problems. However, concerning the cost-sharing funds, I had to inform him that there was no firm assurance for any resources beyond May 2004.

The Security Council wanted to reduce the funding of capacity-building tasks. Furthermore, it sought to transfer this to agencies with voluntary funding as much as possible. The end of the UNMISET mandate period was considered the suitable time for transition to a sustainable framework. Noting this point, I told the IMF delegation about the need to explore alternative means of securing funds, should any of the international advisory posts be absolutely required.

I pointed out to the IMF delegations the need to adopt a new approach for institutional capacity-building. The current arrangement was designed to simply fill the gap for technical expertise by foreign experts. The IMF delegation leader listened and said that he agreed to shift the approach towards building national capacity. He indicated that the two posts of the Deputy General Manager for Payments and the Director of Administration could be taken over by Timorese. He felt, however, that the positions of General Manager and Chief Accountant still needed to be filled by international experts appointed by the IMF. Furthermore, to counteract my suggestion, he said that the funds needed to be secured to meet the short-term assignments to undertake training and coaching activities. Concerning the appointment of any advisors, Mr Lee gave an assurance that candidates would be presented to UNMISET for concurrence before IMF recruited them.

In conclusion, I suggested that IMF finalize the cost-sharing arrangements for the remaining UNMISET mandate period with the Director of Administration and the Civilian Support Group. They should take into account the need to obtain the approval of UNMISET for recruitment of any individual experts and to increase the activities for national institution capacity-building.

National parliament finds its task highly technical and problematic

The parliament passed its first piece of legislation, the Publication of Acts Bill, on 28 June 2002. Subsequently, it enacted additional legislation including the Judicial Magistrates Statutes, the Citizenship Bill, the Passport

Law and the Law on the Maritime Borders of the Democratic Republic of Timor-Leste. Yet, the National Parliament moved rather slowly, as it faced the difficulty of dealing with highly technical pieces of legislation. Neither the committees nor the plenary made any aggressive move to take the opportunity to call on outside technical experts. Although there was an admittedly small pool of individuals in Timor-Leste who were knowledgeable of the bills currently under consideration, only government ministers and their international advisors addressed the plenary.

An example of the lack of technical expertise was seen in the amount of time it took for consideration of a bill on maritime boundaries. The review stretched over two weeks of at times intense debate. At one point, a proposal was drafted to eliminate a provision that defined Timor-Leste's continental shelf. The clause was a standard component of most countries' legal framework for maritime boundaries. Despite this fact, and considering that its elimination would be seriously problematic, many members took it to be indicative of extra-territorial claims by the Timorese Government. The plenary spent well over an hour negotiating the proposal, and it was defeated in a closed vote.

The lack of technical expertise was also hampering the work of the Standing Committee on Constitutional Rights, Freedom and Guarantees. The Committee considered the bills on judicial magistrate, amnesty and pardon. The Committee Chair, Vicente Guterres of União Democrática Cristã/Partido Democrata Cristã (UDC/PDC), expressed the view that the committee members were not able to properly evaluate the bills and offer amendments, due to their inexperience in dealing with such issues. They had no library or access to documents or comparative legislation. This was a continuing constraint, especially as many of the bills were to lay the foundation for critical areas such as commercial law, the judiciary and nationality.

This detrimental situation was compounded by the poor quality of some of the bills submitted by the Council of Ministers to parliament. An example of such poor quality was the Bill on Judicial Magistrates. Independent legal experts, including the UN Special Rapporteur on the Independence of Judges and Lawyers, Dato Param Comaraswamy, and the local NGOs, particularly the Judicial System Monitoring Programme (JSMP) expressed serious concerns regarding this bill. These concerns included the emphasis on disciplinary control of judges, assumption of a fully formed judiciary with limited provisions to address the nascence of the judicial system, and its inconsistency with principles of judicial independence.

The lack of interaction between parliament and the government was demonstrated in the fact that the Standing Committee Chair Guterres was completely unaware of the Rapporteur's visit. He knew nothing of the Rapporteur's concerns regarding the bill even a week after he had left. This was despite the fact that the Rapporteur met with various ministers, including both Vice-Ministers for Justice. The Rapporteur was due to deliver an advisory letter to the National Parliament on the Bill in August. This Standing Committee of the Parliament, in a first act of post-independence, invited the head of the UNMISET Human Rights Unit, to address its public hearing on the bill.

The 'Bill on Amnesty and Pardons'[2] provided yet another example of a problematic bill. Although there was much public discussion, there was little progress in parliamentary decision-making on the bill. On 29 June Bishop Belo issued a pastoral letter on amnesty. He stressed the absolute need for justice for serious crimes, in conjunction with forgiveness by those wronged. Additionally, in order for the reconciliation process to succeed, he found it necessary for perpetrators of serious crimes to admit their guilt. He spoke of justice as being one of those basic needs to be fulfilled; that justice was the main goal in the Timorese struggle for freedom. Belo said there was no justification for an automatic amnesty for those who committed the most serious crimes. He stressed that the inadequacy of the justice system could not be used as a reason for forgoing litigation. This would only lead to a weakening of the rule of law and the continuing violation of human rights.

On 16 July 2002 Human Rights Watch (HRW) issued a public letter addressed to President Gusmão that detailed three concerns about the bill: (1) vague definitions of those eligible for amnesty; (2) unequal treatment of resistance and pro-autonomy individuals; and (3) lack of details regarding the process for selecting who would be eligible for amnesty. The NGO JSMP also criticized the bill, agreeing with some of the HRW observations, while questioning the constitutionality of some of the provisions. The NGO also addressed the difficulties involved in implementation due to the bill's imprecise language.

In responding to these criticisms, Alkatiri defended the bill as a platform around which to promote national debate on the issue. He also defended the different treatment of pro-independence and pro-autonomy groups. Finally, he criticized the NGOs, saying that they brought up issues in order to justify their own existence. They did not understand the reality of the country. These remarks were consistent with Alkatiri's reluctance to accept advisory input from civil society groups, especially when they issued very public statements. It was clear that the Prime Minister was more receptive to a low-key personal approach.

On 17 July 2002 the Commission for Reception, Truth and Reconciliation (CAVR) and the NGO Forum held a one-day seminar entitled "Amnesty or Reconciliation". Speakers included the UN Human Rights Unit; Chief of Staff for the President Pereira; and Bishop Belo. Speakers did not address specific provisions of the bill on amnesty or offer concrete alternatives. It was understood that while the President initially supported the bill as a means to reduce the number of prisoners in pretrial detention, and those serving sentences for ordinary crimes, he had lost interest in the draft law.

After the Secretary-General informed the Security Council, the leaders of Timor-Leste endeavoured to promote a broad-based democracy. They made efforts to respond to concerns expressed by their citizens.[3] Diverse interest groups including lawyers, taxi drivers, students and pensioners started to show their discontent with certain aspects of government policy or specific executive decisions.

The government and the President sought dialogues to promote a better understanding of the limited financial and human resources capacity they had to address those demands. Among the groups, former combatants and veterans expressed increasing dissatisfaction with the government over a perceived lack of recognition for their role in the struggle for independence. Some threatened to create civil unrest. President Gusmão had long been concerned with this issue. He established two commissions, to determine the roles played by various groups and individuals in the resistance movement, and to identify appropriate means of recognition.

Opening of the National Parliament 2004–2005

On 22 September 2004, I attended a ceremony to mark the opening of the 2004–2005 session of the National Parliament. The programme consisted of statements by representatives of the party benches, the President of the Court of Appeal, the Prime Minister, the President and the Speaker of Parliament. The bench representatives spoke on a wide range of challenges confronting Timor-Leste including Polícia Nacional de Timor-Leste (PNTL, the National Police of Timor-Leste), the justice sector and veterans. The President of the Court of Appeal concentrated on capacity issues affecting the judicial system, mentioning the assistance that UNMISET had provided. The Prime Minister called on the country's leaders to contribute to the development of a democratic state. The Speaker devoted most of his speech to a review of the previous year's legislative output and institutional development activities. Most of the parliament members who were invited by the Speaker made generally positive remarks. They concentrated their comments on the progress to date, while recognizing the institutional and legislative challenges ahead. The Associação Social Democráta Timorense (ASDT, Social Democratic Association of Timor- Leste) stressed a need for urgent resolution of the veterans' issue. PDC urged the government to address the internal disunity of PNTL, such as groups of nationalists and pro-integrationists. Other parties including the Liberal Party pointed out inadequate functioning of the National Parliament, particularly overseeing the government's work.

The President characteristically took the occasion to offer *inter alia* a wide-ranging speech that ranged from attacks on the conduct of the Interior Minister Chief-of-Staff to matters of international diplomacy. He elaborated on his views with four broad themes: justice/international tribunal; Timor Sea negotiations; veterans; and future needs for the State Institution building. The two most interesting issues he dealt with were justice and veterans.

On the issue of justice, Gusmão offered a surprising critique that seemed to equate making domestic efforts towards reconciliation with granting forgiveness for crimes that Indonesians had committed in Timor-Leste. He claimed at one point that this was based on pragmatism. However, he went on to critically compare Timor-Leste with Indonesia. He stated that Indonesia was certainly changing towards political reform, while Timor-Leste was still very feebly initiating the construction of a democratic state. He further stated that Indonesia had given Timor-Leste a lesson in individual freedoms and pluralistic democracy.

Gusmão's doubts regarding an international tribunal were well known. However, his willingness to chastise the people of Timor-Leste, while praising the Indonesians, was a striking example of the extent to which he was willing to go to placate Timor-Leste's neighbour in order to persuade the people that there should be no further justice processes for serious crimes committed during Indonesian occupation. Local media chose to highlight this aspect of the speech in their reporting.

Regarding veterans, the President criticized Interior Minister Lobato for his involvement in engineering a pro-government demonstration on 3 December 2002. This event effectively sabotaged an important meeting between the Prime Minister and Cornélio Gama ("Commander L7"), organized during the National Dialogue on Veterans. This was the second time that the President had so publicly condemned the minister, giving the clear signal that he disapproved of Lobato's manipulation of the veterans' issue. This received much coverage from the local media. Lobato offered his own defence to the effect that all citizens had the right to demonstrate.

In a meeting with me, the President explained his critical remarks of Lobato by stressing the importance he placed on ensuring that repressive government and internal dissents did not result in civil conflicts. Also, he insisted that the wealth from the Timor Sea not be disposed of without full knowledge of the people. The President's concern was well justified, while it was not certain that his concern could be redressed sufficiently by the existing governance structure and players at the time.

Open governance initiatives

Shortly after they took office, both President Gusmão and Prime Minister Alkatiri initiated the programmes of "Open Presidency" and "Open Governance". Both campaigns had the same explicit purpose of communicating with the general public at large with regard to what they were doing, and what people wanted from the leaders. They shared the same objective of gaining and sustaining the popular support essential in democracy. I was invited to many of the public gatherings hosted by both the President and the Prime Minister in 2003 and 2004. These events were well organized. Large crowds of people numbering from several hundred to a few thousand attended. Taking advantage of his Presidency, Gusmão from time to time held "National Dialogues" aimed at airing out some issues of contention that had wider national implications. Meanwhile Alkatiri, as the Prime Minister, took his cabinet members along to the districts.

Prime Minister Alkatiri takes his ministers to districts

In one of his weekly meetings with Prime Minister Alkatiri, SRSG Sharma spoke about the idea for the government to hold open governance meetings. Alkatiri took his advice, and exceeded our expectations. He decided to hold an open council of ministers meeting in each of 13 districts and sub-districts. Typically, these lasted three to four days. They were then followed by a final consultation, a "town meeting", at the district capital. The first town meeting of the council of ministers was held in Viqueque on 24 February 2003. The Prime Minister opened the meeting by stressing the importance of the open council of ministers to which he invited UNMISET and the parliament.[4] He thereby showed his adeptness in influencing peoples' minds concerning the relationship between the government and the people.

Prime Minister Alkatiri started his remarks by informing the participants that the open council meeting was a means for the government to communicate with the citizens throughout the country as a practice of transparency. He explained that independence was not the end of the struggle, but just the beginning of a new struggle for betterment of their livelihood. He urged the people not to expect the government to achieve miracles. Instead everyone had to understand new roles and responsibilities. Political independence had provided the people of Timor-Leste with democracy to exercise their rights and responsibilities. The government was most willing to understand the needs of its people, while the citizens had the obligation to support the government. Everyone should be careful not to let any individuals or groups exploit the situation and make use of the circumstances to destabilize the country.

The opening remarks were then followed by a question-and-answer session between government officials and citizens of the Viqueque district. The first round was given to the village chiefs (Chefes do Suco) and the remaining time was given to several villagers. The villagers were vocal and raised some controversial issues. The first speaker pointed out inconsistency in the recruitment of police agents and civil servants. He said the practice of KKN[5] allowed nepotism and the unfair recruitment process to persist. Another speaker noted that public education was non-functional due to a lack of qualified teachers and educational facilities such as laboratories, houses for teachers and school spaces for students. He also pointed out the lack of health facilities and services, particularly staff such as nurses. Additionally, the issue of the lack of transport facilities to carry the deceased back to villages was raised. Furthermore, the lack of road access to remote villages and hamlets (aldeias) was brought up. Several questions and issues were raised about the uncertainty in the local government structure, especially at the village level. Of concern was the uncertain status of village chiefs, which resulted in inadequate public services being provided by the local government. Village concerns included:

- Lack of irrigation infrastructure and agricultural tools, particularly tractors for agricultural production of seeds.
- Lack of health facilities and nurses in several villages, including the need for transport to carry the deceased back to villages.
- Land tenure, especially on the status of lands around main roads.
- Recognition of former clandestine members.
- Sanitation issues, especially the possibility of establishing a Community Service day.
- Security in the villages; absence of police force.
- Government involvement to ensure the rights of Timor-Leste citizens to pension and special funds.
- Continuing use of explosives in fishing and hunting practices, although banned.
- The status and activities of the "Borge da Costa" foundation.
- Possible rehabilitation of buildings to support women's activities in the districts.
- Transparency over the collection and use of income tax.

The Prime Minister was quite receptive to these issues, but also firm in his response. He stated clearly that the villagers should not expect the government to solve all of their problems. There were no budget resources to meet all of these needs. He went on to explain that in order to secure the necessary financial resources, the government would regulate the extraction of natural resources at the district level, and keep part of the revenue generated from that extraction for the district concerned. The resources then could be used for improvements in sanitation and other basic social infrastructure facilities. He did not specify clearly what kind of resources, be they oil or mineral. Nor did he reveal their existence – on land or offshore of the Timorese territory.

With regard to the governance structure at the village level, Alkatiri assured the villagers that they would elect their own village chiefs. He went on to explain that the government was working on the draft legislation regarding the local governance structure, and to clarify the role and status of the village chiefs, whether the positions should be made as political or professional appointments.

He then addressed the sensitive issue of land tenure. Without giving a conclusive answer, Alkatiri explained that the law on land was yet to be approved and any dispute on land tenure would be settled only after the passage of the law by parliament. Meanwhile, he advised the people that the first thing to be resolved was the problem of assets, and that the district would have registration authority.

The civil servants would be selected based on standard criteria regardless of their place of origin. Alkatiri was saying in essence that anyone with the right qualification could occupy such a post in any part of Timor-Leste, regardless of one's place of birth. In other words, he advocated a unitary state approach. When people asked for jobs, Alkatiri told them clearly it was impossible, as the government had already filled 12,000 government positions, and had no more capacity to employ additional people. He told them that the private sector had to be developed to create jobs. In order for this to happen there had to be stability in the country to attract foreign investors.

Furthermore, Alkatiri explained to the people that the government was already spending a great deal of its budgetary resources to pay for teachers who numbered about 6,000 or half of all civil servants. If some villages did not have enough teachers, it was a problem of distribution of teaching staff. The Ministry of Education had to review the distribution

Alkatiri addressed former "clandestine" workers who did not engage in actual combat, but who wanted recognition and assistance from the government nonetheless. He told them that he had first to address the problems faced by members of the former Forças Armadas de Libertação Nacional de Timor-Leste (FALINTIL, Armed Forces for the National

Liberation of East Timor), who had fought in combat, before he could find ways to help the former clandestine workers. However, he assured them that they would not be forgotten.

As I accompanied Alkatiri to several of the open governance meetings in many parts of the country, I felt that he played the role of a professor or a preacher. He explained to the people the complexity of governing the fragile country. He was skilful in resorting to dialectic arguments in making his points and was extremely careful in his speeches not to raise people's expectations. He appealed to them to be more self-reliant, and not to count on the government. In responding to calls for more assistance to people living in villages, Alkatiri acknowledged the difficult conditions they lived in, but contended that the government could do little given the scarcity of available resources.

At these open governance meetings, the Prime Minister and various ministers took turns in speaking and responding with facts and figures to questions raised by local people. In most cases, the issues raised included security matters, public works, schools and health facilities. They were factual and analytical.

In Viqueque, the Minister of Internal Administration, Lobato, was the first to speak after Alkatiri. He explained how government security should be maintained at the district level. He admitted there was some concern about collusion and nepotism in the recruitment of civil servant and police officers. He said that the people had to provide specific information and evidence, if available, so that the government could charge any persons involved in wrongdoing. He then said that people needed to put those complaints in writing and send them to the government. This was a logical explanation but not conducive of resolving the problem.

There was a sense of irony that Lobato was making people responsible for producing evidence, instead of taking the initiative in investigating accusations of wrongdoing. Lobato was defensive with regard to the capacity of the police forces to be deployed in villages, as the police personnel available were very limited. He then told the villages that the government was considering the establishment of community self-defence groups to inform the police of any security-related developments. What he did not explain was that this could become part of an elaborate intelligence-gathering network about any anti-government movements.

Lobato told the people that the government was discussing with UNMISET the possibility of obtaining additional equipment for the police force, such that they could counter any major civil disturbances. What he had in mind was equipping police units so that they could deal with the sort of riots and demonstrations that had taken place in Dili two months earlier in December 2002. He also hinted that the Timor-Leste Defence Force had been deployed in several districts to assist the police in maintaining security. This raised a great deal of concern as Lobato was clearly preparing the use of all security forces to counter any anti-government movements.

Ovideo Amaral, the Minister of Transportation, Telecommunications and Public Works, said that the priority was to create a network of main roads that would connect the districts. As this was to cover about 6,500 km of main roads and included 11 bridges, the government had to spend all available budget resources to maintain and expand the main transportation network. It meant that it had no funds to fix secondary village roads. With regard to power and energy supply, the government needed to secure the 24-hour energy supply in Dili. In other districts it would be a 12–18-hour supply.

Amaral further explained that the government was considering the possibility of turning the government's electricity department into an independent entity to enable people to access cheap energy. He further stated that a new fee for energy users had been established: 16 cents/unit for household users and 20 cents/unit for industry. Noting that many users had not paid for their use of electricity, Amaral told them about the installation of a recovery programme for past non-payments. He also mentioned the introduction of a new collection system.

The Minister of Education, Culture, Youth and Sports, Maia, fielded questions regarding the recruitment of teachers at the village level. He explained that there was not just a lack of teachers, but also that they preferred to stay in Dili and other cities. He said that within the total available quota, an additional 200–300 new teachers were to be hired within the year. However, these new teachers had to sign an agreement of willingness to be deployed anywhere in the country, otherwise it would be impossible to cover the isolated villages. The government was making basic and primary schools a priority, so new high schools might not be contemplated in the near future. The quality of teachers was also a concern, and citizens were requested to participate in monitoring their work. He asked for the support of villages to secure housing for teachers, as the government could not cover this due to limited financial resources.

The Vice-Minister of Health clarified the government policy on the establishment of health centres, which had the ratio of 1 to as many as 2,000 local residents. He further said that the accessibility was another major problem. Around 730 new nurses would be recruited to cover nationwide needs. However, the villages that did not qualify to have a health centre had to be covered by mobile clinics. The ministry also had around 16,000 mosquito nets available for residents that lived in malaria-prone areas, and the first 1,000 would be distributed to the Uatu-Carabau sub-district. A group of nearly 50 Timorese students who were studying in the Faculty of Medicine could be integrated to the existing team of 11 ministry doctors after their graduation.

The response from the Vice-Minister of Agriculture was that to date, the irrigation facilities built by the government amounted to around 300 units. The community had to take responsibility for their use and maintenance. The use of explosives in fishing was prohibited and hunting of certain species was not allowed. The community was requested to support the Ministry in monitoring due to the limited number of officers in the Agricultural Department.

In July 2003, Alkatiri held another open governance meeting, this time, in Lautem District. As an established procedure by now, he started it with series of visits to all sub-districts. The meetings took the same format as in other districts, with similar needs raised by local people, such as repairs and improvements of roads, new schools, health facilities and assistance for the agricultural sector.

A notable concern specific to the Lautem District was the prospect for tourism development in the area. In response to local aspirations and concerns, Alkatiri and other government members continued to underline their primary message of community involvement and responsibility in the development process. They stated that the government would do its best to create the conditions necessary for development in areas with access to markets, through improved infrastructure. It would address human resource development through educational and health facilities. However, it was the responsibility of individual communities to actively take advantage of these conditions. This was an important point, and probably one of the most difficult challenges faced by the government, especially in rural areas that had been accustomed to paternalistic support, provided by the occupying Indonesian authorities in the past.

In his open governance meeting in Oecussi, Alkatiri, as before, first spent four days visiting various part of the district and held meetings in a number of villages. Almost all of the Ministers attended the session in Bako village and addressed some 800–1000 local villagers, village chiefs and district administration officials. As in other open governance meetings, the proceedings were open and frank, with the Ministers responding to people's concerns in a direct manner. This time, two sensitive issues of corruption in the government and local elections were raised. Typically, most were familiar social issues such as school rebuilding and health facilities. This time, however, people also asked about the role of police in reducing violence against women, and about the recruitment criteria for police officers.

The Prime Minister, in response to the delivery of reports by village chiefs, tried to dampen increasing expectations of what the government could achieve, shifting some responsibility from the government to the people. To a long list of requests for services, he responded by telling local leaders that they needed to report what they had achieved and not just make requests. He also told them not to talk too much about KKN (corruption, collusion and nepotism) in the government-recruiting procedures, implying it had much to do with jealousy and the desire of some people to work harder than others. He bluntly told people that the time had come to show to the international community that the people of Timor-Leste were capable. Furthermore, the days when they could ask for everything from others such as Lisbon and Jakarta were over.

The Minister of the Interior promised to investigate any reported nepotism in police recruitment procedures. However, he cautioned against referring to the former police officers in the Indonesian National Police (POLRI) as "collaborators". Instead, he put their presence in the police force in the context of reconciliation and accommodation. In an attempt to demonstrate transparent recruitment procedures, Lobato gave the current example of the Rapid Deployment Service, indicating his intention to recruit 550 of the 1,000 people who had already passed the entry exam. They were all former clandestine workers, 80 of whom had applied from Oecussi. Around 30 of the applicants would be chosen. Interestingly he praised the performance of the Oecussi police and remarked that undisciplined police in Dili could well learn from them.

One of the measures Alkatiri took, as a result of his enhanced awareness of the events taking place in rural communities, was to expand and strengthen his capacity for administration at the sub-district level. The 65 Sub-District Coordinators were recruited at the L3 level. Under the new structure, this post would be upgraded to an L5, supported by two L3 officers – a Community Development Officer and a Local Government Officer, to be filled automatically by the incumbent Sub-District Coordinator. This move was motivated by the Prime Minister's desire to increase not only administrative efficiency, but also political control. The new posts were advertised in the districts, but were mostly filled by party loyalists from the Frente Revolucionária do Timor-Leste Independente (FRETILIN, the Revolutionary Front for an Independent East Timor).

Presidential initiative for National Dialogue

On 25 January 2003, the National Dialogue was held in the former Conselho Nacional de Reconstrução de Timor (CNRT, National Congress for Timorese Reconstruction) compound in Dili. The programme largely followed the original agenda, with only minor changes due to frequent interruptions from electrical power outages. President Gusmão moderated the first session in the morning, and the Vicar General, Father José Antonio, moderated the second session. Approximately 300 people attended the event. Key members of the government participated, including Prime Minister Alkatiri, Justice Minister Pessoa, and Secretary of State for Defence Rodrigues. At times, Alkatiri called on National Police Commissioner Paulo Martins and Brigadier General Taur Matan Ruak to respond to questions on security issues. President Guterres ("Lú-Olo") came and spoke, frequently in the name of his party, FRETILIN, as well as for the parliament.

Among the invited participants were 50 members of Conselho Popular pela Defesa da República Democrática de Timor-Leste (CPD-RDTL, Popular Committee for Defence of the Democratic Republic of Timor-Leste), including Egas da Costa, Ai-Tahan Matak and Cristiano da Costa, who were key members of the executive body; and a student leader named Ivo.[6] Contrary to some people's fear and expectations, the CPD-RDTL members were mostly well mannered, with only a couple of emotional presentations towards the end of the day. There was also significant representation from the FRETLIN party, minority political parties, the media, the diplomatic and donor community, a few former FALINTIL members of the Assoçiação dos Antigos Combatentes,[7] civil society, the civil service and district administration.

During the first session, CPD-RDTL and UNMISET read their prepared statements. Although CPD-RDTL's prepared statement used its usual forceful rhetoric, the CPD-RDTL members were more conciliatory in their spoken interventions, explaining that they sought clarification on consultation mechanisms. They agreed with the mandate, but said that there were problems with its "implementation", and exhibited confusion on various UN resolutions. President Gusmão directed most questions from CPD-RDTL and the audience to members of the government. CPD-RDTL also exhibited considerable concern regarding the role of UNMISET in impinging on the sovereignty of Timor-Leste and controlling the national budget. This was clearly rebutted by Prime Minister Alkatiri and SRSG Sharma, who told the participants that UNMISET operated only with the consent of the government, which exercised sovereign power of the new State. Taur Matan Ruak and Paulo Martins also clearly rebutted claims that the support for security by the United Nations Police (UNPOL) and the United Nations Peacekeeping Force (PKF) in some way endangered Timor-Leste's national sovereignty. In summary, President Gusmão offered an appreciative assessment of the UN role in Timor-Leste, and tactfully nullified the CPD-RDTL assertions.

During the second session, which was rather protracted, CPD-RDTL advanced its proposal for a "constitutional readjustment". It brought in associated issues such as the restoration of FALINTIL as the national defence force, the legitimacy of currently registered political parties and the use of national symbols. National Parliament President Lú-Olo explained how the Constitution had been drawn up through the electoral and consultative processes. Prime Minister Alkatiri also noted that he had been one of the writers of the 1975 Constitution, and had used it as a reference for the current Constitution.

Lú-Olo and Alkatiri also made attempts to project the FRETILIN party as the authors and guardians of independence. Again, in his summary, Gusmão subtly undermined some of CPD-RDTL's arguments, himself defending FALINTIL–Forças Armadas de Defesa de Timor-Leste (F-FDTL, FALINTIL–Armed Forces for the National Liberation of East Timor) from CPD-RDTL charges of Indonesian-style dual functions ("dwifungsi"). He pointed out some of the contradictions in their arguments, and praised Alkatiri and Lú-Olo for their willingness to participate in the Dialogue. It is noteworthy that in 2003, the President was still very much in charge with the full support and admiration of the people. He was relaxed and able to couch his comments in an open manner, and with humour that did not appear to offend CPD-RDTL. As CPD-RDTL received much attention, Cristiano da Costa called for future dialogues. However, Alkatiri and Lú-Olo made it clear that they had no desire to participate with CPD-RDTL in any similar events in the future. It was clear that they participated in the meeting only as the President had convened it.

The Dialogue took place in a cordial atmosphere, with the organizers respecting the interventions and management of the moderators. It could be debated whether or not the event was really a dialogue. The Prime Minister and other government officials received the various participants' presentations of their views, yet they did not engage in serious discussions with their interlocutors. It could be that, given the intractability of the CPD-RDTL demands, there was no opportunity for a possible compromise or for finding common ground.

One of the goals of the Dialogue, as stated by the organizing committee in private conversations, was to deprive CPD-RDTL of public support by showing the public the unreasonableness of their demands. In Dili, with a relatively more sophisticated audience, it may have had this effect. However, in many villages where CPD-RDTL operated, conversations about UN resolutions and the difference between a constitutional readjustment and an amendment must have appeared esoteric.

CPD-RDTL support in villages relied not so much on the reasonableness of its arguments, as on the dissatisfaction of societal elements and the emotional resonance of their rhetoric. Also, despite the fact that it was widely broadcast on television and radio, there was still not much penetration of the mass media to the interior parts of the country. However, as almost all CPD-RDTL interventions came from people in the eastern part of the country, this reinforced the perception that it was made up primarily of "troublemakers" from Baucau and Viqueque Districts. This would certainly do nothing to help them attract additional support in the central and western parts of Timor-Leste.

The day after the National Dialogue, Cristiano da Costa said that CPD-RDTL would wait for the report of the organizing committee before deciding on any further action. During the Dialogue itself, CPD-RDTL said that it would inform the "masses" of the outcome of the event, and let them decide on any need for follow-up actions. CPD-RDTL appeared to be under the impression that it would be the driving force behind future dialogues that the President had promised on such issues as security, unemployment and the economy.

However, members of the organizing committee indicated that these Dialogues were independent of CPD-RDTL. Despite the possible weaknesses of the CPD-RDTL presentation, the party had managed to manoeuvre itself into a highly publicized event. The party sat at a table across from the President of Parliament and the Prime Minister, and this could be considered a success, demonstrating a level of influence that the oppositional political parties had been unable to muster. It should be noted that the Dialogue also served to raise the status and authority of President Gusmão, continuing a trend of assertion of a leadership role on questions of national interest and in crisis situations. It could well be a reason why the Prime Minister and the President of the Parliament, both of whom were leaders of FRETILIN, were adamant about not participating in a similar meeting again.

President Gusmão then convened another public consultation meeting on 3 May 2003 in Gleno, located about an hour's drive from the capital city of Dili. It was a culmination of a series of dialogues held with local populations and leaders from different social groups, including youth and ex-combatant organizations. Among the participants were Victor Dos Santos, the District Administrator of Ermera, and former FALINTIL Commander Dudu. The meeting took place under a roofed market building complex with more than 200 participants spilling out of the place. It was dominated by ex-combatants, who poured out their grievances and needs, their aspirations for recognition and for material assistance. They said that the government should neither forget nor ignore the contributions they had made in the fight for independence. The government should provide them with employment and other means to sustain and improve their living conditions. More specifically, they noted that most of ex-combatants who had applied for employment with PNTL had not been chosen. They demanded that the government should correct the unfair recruitment practices for national police officers.

Gusmão responded to the emotional appeals of ex-combatants with a strong personal statement, showing how much he appreciated their predicament. Referring to himself as one of them, Gusmão reminded them that he had stayed in the jungle and fought the Indonesian soldiers even after the deaths in December 1978 of the then Commander in Chief of FALINTIL and President of FRETILIN, Nicolau Lobato, and of most independence fighters. With the loss of a majority of the central committee members of FRETILIN, he had to organize its first National Conference. He had to serve as the elected leader of the Resistance and commander-in-chief of the FALINTIL.[8] Gusmão also reminded them that a year after the Santa Cruz massacre he was captured on 20 November 1992, after 17 years of guerrilla warfare.

Having convinced the ex-combatants that he was one of them, he assured them that their contributions to independence would never be forgotten by the new State of Timor-Leste. Gusmão told them how deeply he understood their daily hardships, as much as those faced by other members of the community. He explained that Timor-Leste as a nascent country had severe limitations in meeting people's needs. The government was doing its best. It would do more in cooperation with international development partners to provide the citizens with jobs, housing, education and health facilities.

As an example, the President referred at length to the Recovery, Employment and Stability Programme for Ex-combatants and Communities in Timor-Leste (RESPECT) project, which had been designed to assist and empower vulnerable members of communities including ex-combatants, widows and youths. He expressed his hope that with additional support from the international community, RESPECT could provide ex-combatants and other vulnerable people with more employment opportunities. The meeting developed into a direct dialogue, as Gusmão wanted to respond to the grievances of the ex-combatant group, and was skilful in turning these into a common cause for unity. He had demonstrated this before during the struggle against the Indonesians, when he took the initiative and developed a clandestine network for national unity, ultimately forming the Conselho Nacional de Resistência Maubere (CNRM, National Council of Maubere Resistance) in 1988.

In concluding the Gleno meeting, Gusmão told the crowd about the need to trust one other and in the government with the same resilience they had displayed during 24 years of independence struggle. Gusmão showed his remarkable talent to become emotionally involved with the ex-combatants' concerns, and to establish synergy with them on the need to endure the new challenge.

On 4 August 2003, as part of his open presidency programme, Gusmão visited the Baucau District, the third district to receive such a visit. This was the same week that the government visited Oecussi District for its similarly named Open Governance initiative. This was the second occasion that the President's visit to the countryside had coincided with the government's visit to another part of the country. Given the late planning by his office, the timing could have been purposeful. The competing initiatives could have been an indicator of Gusmão's efforts to extend his influence by engaging with the government. He interpreted the President's constitutionally defined role as a symbol and guarantor of national independence and unity of the State. He himself thereby indicated that the smooth functioning of democratic institutions included acting as a sort of mediator between the public and government. This was just one of several examples of the President establishing parallel processes to those of the government. Further examples include his national dialogue on local power, conducted at the same time that the government was developing an option paper for local government, and his formation of the Veterans Commissions when the government already had an Office of Veterans Affairs. Given the President's stature, the Prime Minister and others had been careful not to offer any public criticisms of presidential initiatives.

In September 2003, Gusmão started to hold reconciliation meetings with discontented groups and individuals within Timor-Leste. The sub-districts he chose to visit can be characterized as areas where there had been past violence (Ermera district) or where groups such as CPD-RDTL and Colimau 2000 were known to operate. On 15–16 September Gusmão, accompanied by Xavier do Amaral, President of ASDT, visited the isolated community of Orsenaco near Turiscai in Manufahi district. It was the headquarters of self-styled community leader Marcos da Costa, who claimed that he developed the facility as a rest home for former combatants.

Some 1,500 villagers from surrounding areas looked on as the President landed on a newly constructed helicopter pad and received military-style salute from about 100 ex-combatants. The population gave the impression of being tightly controlled by Costa and his aides, many of whom acted in a military manner, carrying hand-held radios and saluting. In the afternoon, after much ceremony and the raising of the ASDT, FRETILIN and national flags, Marcos da Costa presented the grievances of the population. The President addressed the population at large, but did not hold any dialogue with individual members of the community.

There were some 20 F-FDTL members on site for security purposes, in addition to PNTL. Lt Col. Falur, former FALINTIL commander of the region and commander of the first F-FDTL battalion, was asked by the President to address the gathering. He spoke critically and emotionally against groups such as CPD-RDTL and others that remained outside existing official structures. President Gusmão replied calmly and briefly, referring to the achievements of the community. He emphasized the need for unity among the population, asking the community not to engage in violent activities. He invited them to become members of existing parties and structures such as ASDT and not to organize themselves in unofficial groups. Xavier do Amaral likewise invited the people to become members of ASDT "as an act of free choice" and stressed the need to unite as well as to fight against problems such as famine and disease in order for the people to be truly independent. Marcos da Costa was deferential towards Gusmão. He responded calmly to the hard-hitting remarks of Falur, while denying links with Colimau 2000 or militia groups. He also denied allegations that he was harbouring fugitives and engaging in criminal activities, and urged politicians to address the needs of those who had fought for independence.

Implications of the contrasting personalities and approaches

It was fascinating to observe how the President and the Prime Minister each spoke to the Timorese people and responded to their concerns. I found similarities and differences in how they addressed political, security and socio-economic issues. They both showed a remarkable competency in talking to ordinary people and addressing their concerns. Neither man blamed the Portuguese or Indonesian colonialists for the lack of development and current difficult living conditions. Instead, both leaders emphasized the need for discipline and self-reliance. This approach was an encouraging sign of what I refer to primordial leadership. It was in complete contrast to some African leaders, who simply blamed past wrongdoings by the colonialists for their present predicament.

The Prime Minister visited several sub-districts for three to four days, which ended with an open meeting of the Council of Ministers in the district capital. Meanwhile, the President chose to concentrate his shorter visits on a few sub-districts, avoiding the district capital. His popularity was obvious in the enthusiastic receptions he received. On at least one occasion he was lifted above the crowd and paraded around in triumph.

The Prime Minister had a much tougher time. He was forced to address difficult questions about service delivery and government programmes, explain national budget restraints and lower the public's expectations of what the State could provide. Although Prime Minister Alkatiri had become increasingly at ease in these settings, he clearly did not yet have the populist touch of President Gusmão.

Gusmão was always passionate in displaying his empathy towards the crowds. He responded with emotional speeches to those who asked questions. Sometimes he even wept and conjured images of the struggle for independence. In addressing concerns, he took an individual rather than an institutional approach. He promised that he would personally do what he could to resolve specific problems. At the same time he pointed out that overall socio-economic programmes were the responsibility of the government. In other words, Gusmão often spoke in a manner that seemed to echo the government's desire to set realistic expectations, and increase community involvement in development efforts. This seemingly supportive stance was sometimes followed by comments that could be considered as being simultaneously critical, portraying the government as being incompetent, corrupt and unresponsive.

In one instance, in the Baucau District, Gusmão told a crowd of people that the international donor community preferred to give money to NGOs, because it was afraid that the government was corrupt and would misuse the funds. At the same time, Gusmão said that the people should support the government in carrying out its responsibility and should maintain unity and a sense of realism about the overall situation. He visited potential trouble spots in an attempt to develop a channel of communication with individuals and groups. His aim was to encourage people to join the newly founded democratic structures of governance. I recall his urging L-7, one of the ex-combatant leaders, to form a political party and run for a seat in parliament.

Gusmão and Alkatiri's differences in style and the content of their individual communications reflected their characters and personalities. These played a major role in shaping the relationship between the two top national leaders. Gusmão was suave, humorous, witty, charming and easy to approach. He was venturesome and could be reckless in pursuit of his goals once he his mind was set. Occasionally, he showed another side of his character that was explorative and adventuresome. The meetings organized by Gusmão could be seen as campaign stops to boost his popularity.

In contrast to Gusmão, Alkatiri might best be characterized as a "cool architect" of ideas, systems and organizations. He was a solitary intellectual, who loved working quietly, reading, analysing and pontificating alone. As an intuitive scholar, Alkatiri preferred planning the future of governance logically, to better explain it to people with little knowledge and understanding. He believed in authority based on strength in reason and rationality. Public opinion, for him, was a liberal indicator of popular sentiment, not conducive to safeguarding national interest in the long run.

Alkatiri was the incumbent who had to defend his accomplishments during the most formative years. Meanwhile, Gusmão was in the advantageous position of overseeing the government on behalf of the people. One could see that the covert strategy behind the open presidency and open governance meetings was for both to demonstrate that they were the true leader of the new-born country of Timor-Leste. It was a harbinger of emerging divisions between the Alkatiri-led government and the Gusmão Presidency that would gradually increase the tension in the country. Contrary to their wishes, they were both placed in competition for the guardianship of national interests. People increasingly expected the emergence of a single leader, regardless of the constitutional design for the distribution of power to govern the country.

Security and justice issues become divisive

During the initial period of national governance, several security- and justice-related incidents began to divide the state institutions. The taxation bill placed the President against the government and parliament. Incidents of violence at the district level by security- and political-issue groups such as the Associação dos Antigos Combatentes das FALINTIL (AAC, Association of Former Combatants), Colimau 2000 and CPD-RDTL compelled the President to act.

During the months of May and June, a branch of the former clandestine movement most recently associated with CNRT went on the offensive in Baucau against another group, the CPD-RDTL. A series of incidents also took place during these months between CPD-RDTL and a group called the Youth Front Against Violence, which identified with the CNRT wing of the resistance and its offshoots.

Concentrated mainly in the villages of Wailili (a Baucau sub-district) and Kampung Baru (Vemasse sub-district), these incidents were characterized by underground ("caixa") and former FALINTIL commanders capturing CPD-RDTL members who allegedly carried illegal weapons.

The two groups associated with these events varied in their backgrounds, activities and stated goals. The AAC was a group claiming to represent the interests of former FALINTIL and resistance members, whose needs were not being met by the State. The activities of some components of the Associaçao had long hovered on the verge of legality.

Colimau 2000 was the successor to a clandestine organization, Comando de Libertação do Povo Maubere (Colimau), which was established in Bobonaro in the mid-1990s. The original Colimau was formally disbanded on 1 January 2000. Colimau 2000 was founded a few months later, under different leadership. Powerlessness is a theme that seemed to unite many of the leaders of Colimau 2000. Although other conflicts over land, reconciliation (a particularly fraught issue in this former heartland of João Tavares' Halilintir militia group) and relations with other former clandestine groups also played a part. In some cases, the aim was to unite displaced CNRT officials with ex-FALINTIL commanders who were rejected for entry into the FALINTIL-F-FDTL.

During the month of July, district security groups caused two incidents of violence. The AAC (but also going by the name FALINTIL Baixo de Apoio) staged a violent demonstration on 9 July at UNPOL Headquarters in Suai, Covalima District. They protested the arrest of one of their members the day before. Fourteen people were arrested during and after the attack, including the two leaders José dos Santos Lemos (Commander Labarik Maia) and Bruno Do Rosario Da Costa Magalhães.

Colimau 2000 had also engaged in violence in Bobonaro District that resulted in life-threatening injuries to one individual. The violence was spurred when local residents detained and turned in three members of Colimau 2000. On 23 July, in retaliation, 100 members of Colimau 2000 attacked the Maliana market. When UNPOL and PNTL officers moved in to control the situation, the Colimau 2000 members fled into the bush. By 29 July, 28 members of the semi-religious group were detained, including their self-styled "Bishop" Gabriel Fernandes.

Colimau 2000's fringe status was more pronounced than that of AAC. It was anti-government, favouring a national unity government with representatives from many political parties. As a mark of its opposition to the government, its members allegedly destroyed irrigation works inaugurated by the Minister of Agriculture. It was also a religious cult with its own rituals and hierarchy that were a fusion of traditional and Catholic beliefs. In some places, its members had prevented people from attending Mass.

In Baucau, the Youth Front Against Violence had existed since August 2001 as a counter to CPD-RDTL. Its President, Manuel Pinto, was formerly chief of security in the Baucau Frente Política Interna (FPI) associated with CNRT. He was also the Baucau District Representative in the National Council during the United Nations Transitional Administration in East Timor (UNTAET). Additionally, he held titles of Partido Democrático (PD, Democratic party) District Co-ordinator and Baucau District Head of Civil Security.

Other leaders were members of the underground FALINTIL. They all had close ties to the FALINTIL commander David Alex, who was killed by the Indonesians in 1997. It appeared that the conflicts in Baucau were the result of antagonisms within the clandestine movement. These were triggered by the formation of the broad-based pro-Independence organizations, the CNRM and its successor, the CNRT.

Alex was a key ally of Gusmão and his national unity policy. Many of the CPD-RDTL members, although formerly clandestine, opposed the formation of CNRM and CNRT. Their ranks had been strengthened by the entry of individuals who were denied entry into FALINTIL-F-FDTL.

Sergeant Alin Laik was another concern. He was based with the FALINTIL-F-FDTL First Battalion in Lautem. As a former FALINTIL member close to Commander Alex, he had acted as his liaison to underground groups. Laik claimed that the FALINTIL-F-FDTL commander, Brigadier General Taur Matan Ruak, had sent him to Baucau to collect munitions from former clandestine members. He also claimed he was there to request the members of the Youth Front to cease their activities.

In a related development, Eurico Guterres, who was deputy commander to Tavares in 1999, was reported to have made anti-Tavares statements in Kupang. Apparently, he condemned Tavares for his reconciliation meetings with the government, and called on his supposed followers to reject Tavares' call to return to East Timor. This was the first time Guterres had been spotted in West Timor since Major General da Costa had been commander of Udayana IX. Guterres' sudden appearance in Kupang could be attributed to da Costa's reassignment to the Tentara Nasional Indonesia (TNI, Indonesian National Armed Forces) Staff College in Bandung. In Indonesia, this move was considered to be a demotion for a former provincial commander. It was clear that the reconciliation meetings would continue to keep the momentum of returns going. The meetings between ex-militia and the Government of East Timor sent the right signals to the people remaining in the camps, who were largely made up of former militia members, their families and relatives.

President Gusmão became actively involved in reconciliation activities. He appointed a Reconciliation Advisor, Feliciano Da Costa, to set up a working group that was composed of former CNRT members including David Ximenes, Guilhermina Saldanha and Paulo Assis. Most of these appointees were already in the reconciliation group coordinated by the Political Affairs Unit under UNTAET.

It was unclear how this would function *vis-à-vis* government-led reconciliation activities. For example, the Prosecutor General led the Tavares reconciliation meetings. Other reconciliation meetings, organized by the President's office and funded by Uppsala University, had also taken place in Darwin and Denpasar. Key to these meetings was the decision to reestablish a working group closely linked to the President, comprising many former CNRT members. This move could create friction with the Prime Minister's Office.

In August 2002 the President sent a letter to the Ad Hoc Tribunal in Jakarta asking the court to show leniency in the case of the former Governor of East Timor Abilio Soares. His sentence was due to be handed down on 14 August. Gusmão had long felt that the civilian East Timorese should not become scapegoats for the Indonesian military, which had orchestrated and carried out the violence. FRETILIN President Francisco "Lú Olo" Guterres publicly expressed concern that the President was writing to the court of another country with such a request, fearing that it would set a poor institutional precedent.

CAVR came in for some criticism from donors, particularly the British Government, during July. During the regularly scheduled monthly donors meeting held with Timor-Leste's Government, the Ministry of Finance represented by Vice-Minister Bassarewan was unable to provide adequate answers to inquiries dealing with the work of the Commission. Ms Bassarewan sent a letter to SRSG Sharma on 31 July raising concerns about the need for clarification of accountability and management of the Commission. Her concerns were based on the issues raised by the British Ambassador in Dili.

On 28 June 2003 the National Parliament passed its first piece of legislation, the Publication of Acts Bill, which subsequently legislated on a number of important issues. These included the Judicial Magistrates Statutes, the Citizenship Bill, the Passport Law and the Law on the Maritime Borders. Another thorny issue for the parliament was the Bill on Land and Property.

As for the protection of human rights in Timor-Leste, an embryonic institutionalization was undertaken through the establishment of the office of the "Provedor" for Human Rights and Justice. There was a great deal of expectation raised by the forthcoming emergence of the Provedor. Once enabling legislation was adopted, this Office combined the role of an Ombudsperson and a Human Rights Commission.

Progress was made in institution building, improving economic and social conditions, but changes for ordinary citizens remained stagnant. Dissatisfied with the lack of tangible benefits and progress, diverse interest groups staged demonstrations. Demonstrators included students, lawyers, taxi drivers, students, pensioners and others. At first, the government handled these demonstrations in an orderly and restrained manner and did not readily give in to the demands of the petitioners and demonstrators, seeking their understanding through dialogue.

During the early period, two issue groups were the most active. The first was concerned for pensioners of Indonesian civil services. The Prime Minister had refused to respond to any demands made by the pensioners of the former Indonesian civil service, as he considered them to be matters for which Indonesia was responsible. In his opinion, his government had no responsibility for this grievance. At the request of Portugal and other donors, UNMISET agreed to mediate the dispute and channel funds contributed by the donors.[9]

The second group consisted of former combatants and veterans, who felt increasingly dissatisfied with the government over a perceived lack of recognition for their role in the struggle for independence. Some indicated their readiness to create civil unrest. President Gusmão, who had long been concerned about this issue, established two Commissions to determine the role individuals had played in the resistance. His aim was to identify appropriate means of recognition, for which donor support would be sought. Despite encouraging first acts of governance by Timorese state institutions, the government was overwhelmed with high expectations from the population. These included hopes for an immediate economic recovery, and the reinsertion of former combatants within this new system.

Apart from the security issues, a difference of views emerged on the subject of taxation. The President vetoed the taxation bill passed by parliament in July. In a speech on 19 July, the day of the veto, he claimed that the increases in tax as proposed would have contradicted the government's stated plans to promote investment. He also said that the tax increases were being used by the government to cover expenditures unrelated to poverty reduction and economic development.

Gusmão then proposed to eliminate expenditures and lower civil servants' salaries. Given that FRETILIN and its allies in parliament had sufficient votes to override the veto, they argued that Gusmão rejected the taxation increases simply to gain public sympathy. The President's move was interpreted by some diplomatic sources as an overall dissatisfaction with the Prime Minister's manner of acting without full consultation. This interpretation became more credible when the President repeatedly called on the government to give an opportunity to civil society groups to offer input into the development of legislation.

Establishing the rule of law

The United Nations recognized that the East Timorese had suffered severe forms of human rights violations during the period of Indonesian occupation from 1975 to 1999, and also immediately before and after the Popular Consultations that took place on 30 August 1999. The Security Council in Resolution 1272 called for investigations into "reports indicating that systematic, widespread and flagrant violations of international humanitarian and human rights law have been committed in East Timor, stressing that persons committing such violations bear individual responsibility."[10] The United Nations then launched a Serious Crimes Process by establishing a special prosecution unit, or a serious crimes unit; it also created hybrid panels of international and national judges, who were entrusted with judicial power. They were tasked with trying cases of serious crimes, including crimes against humanity, war crimes and individual offences of murder, torture and rape. The Security Council's decision appropriately addressed the need to provide a credible process of accountability for crimes committed within the specific period of ten months from 1 January to 25 October 1999. It was, no doubt, a major step towards bringing those responsible for serious crimes to justice. However, it had the effect of diverting the attention and energy of UN mission staff away from the need to build a competent and professional national judiciary.

In this section, I review the efforts made Timorese nationals in building the national judiciary. Later on, in Chapter V, I will also explain how the Serious Crimes Process was carried out.

Challenges in establishing a competent and professional national judiciary

Many Timorese had expected that the departure of Indonesian soldiers would result in a free and safe country, in which they would be treated fairly and justly. For this reason, a credible justice system had to be introduced and developed without delay. Yet, as stated before, the international community was more interested in achieving transitional justice than establishing a viable national judiciary. When I arrived in Dili in July 2002, a major portion of UN civilian staff resources was allocated to the Serious Crimes Process, while little attention was paid to building the national judiciary.

The UN Transitional Administrator did appoint the judges, prosecutors and public defenders in early 2000. However, few of them had any previous legal experience and many had just recently finished law courses in Indonesia. Thus, inexperienced East Timorese were pushed into administering a system that had not been properly developed. Courts had no buildings, no legal regime and no legal support staff. There were practically no trained interpreters in a system where Portuguese was re-introduced as a legal language, while the majority of people spoke the Indonesian dialect.

Additionally, there were disagreements between the national and international officials concerning the judiciary. The Timorese judiciary had long called for a system by which their professional achievements could be measured. A professional standards and ethics code for judges and prosecutors had been proposed by UNTAET in September 2001. The Ministry of Justice, however, found this code unacceptable on the grounds that it lacked sufficient detail with regard to investigations and sanctions on judges, and proposed its own alternative code to the international advisors. This lacked fundamental principles such as the independence of the judiciary, and failed to adequately define transgressions such as "insubordination". Consequently, at the time of independence, a legal code for judges and prosecutors was not in existence.

Furthermore, on 20 May 2002, the day after the restoration of independence, the contracts of a number of national judges and prosecutors appointed by UNTAET expired in accordance with their own wishes. Their performances over the previous two years had to be reviewed by the new government before they received fresh appointments and contracts. Unfortunately, in the absence of a professional code, these reviews could never take place in a fair manner.

Additionally, the Constitution foresaw the establishment of the Supreme Council for the Judiciary, responsible, *inter alia*, for the appointment of judges. Legislation establishing the Supreme Council for the Judiciary was still pending, and the members of an eventual Council had not yet been named. The government felt that the Constitution provided ample authority to the judges to continue to hear cases. Despite these circumstances the judges felt otherwise.

Those judges who did have valid contracts extending beyond 20 May 2002 either stopped working, in solidarity with their colleagues, or were unable to continue to hear cases that had begun before a panel of three judges. The court system effectively ground to a halt when the first constitutional government came into being. This led to the illegal detention of many whose warrants of arrest and detention had expired.

To address this crisis situation, the Timorese judges asked for UN intervention. UNMISET staff persuaded the government to receive a UN Special Rapporteur on the independence of judges and lawyers to advise them. Dato' Param Comaraswamy visited Timor-Leste from 11 to 14 July 2002. He was able to provide constructive advice and assistance to redress the situation. After the visit, those members of the judiciary who had considered themselves unable to function in the absence of due process of appointment, agreed to start working again. The incident was just a tip of the iceberg. The challenges before the judicial system were numerous and enormous. They ranged from lack of adequate human resources to the complex legal issues listed below:

- Lack of experienced personnel (judges, prosecutors, defenders).
- Inadequate facilities and resources.
- Lack of resources for the Public Defender's office, leading to a disparity in comparison with the Prosecutor's office.
- Insistence on use of Portuguese language, a language which most of the judges, prosecutors, victims and defendants were generally not familiar with.
- Civil law versus common law issues.
- Lack of due process and well-paced resolution of cases.
- Inadequate and inappropriate training and absence of mentors.
- Difficulties in the functioning of the Court management systems, including the Court Registry and the absence of a coherent case management system.
- Non-functional Court of Appeal.

- Law on nationality of judges (only East Timorese).
- Non-integration with parallel systems (police).
- Non-appointment of Attorney General.

The Ministry of Justice had made an attempt to address the serious lack of jurist training. However, the demands of training impeded the full-time workload already imposed upon the judges. Also challenging was the fact that the young jurist trainees, who had grown up speaking Indonesian, had difficulty understanding what was being presented to them, as the training was conducted in Portuguese.

The SRSG sensitized the two key leaders of Timor-Leste, President Gusmão and Prime Minister Alkatiri, about the need to effectively and urgently address these issues. It soon became apparent that the issues had to be managed as a two-pronged exercise. On one side, immediate and short-term measures were needed to ensure a functioning judiciary, which enjoyed public confidence. On the other side, medium- to long-term action plans needed to be put in place to assist national efforts towards policies with a longer gestation.

In developing the judiciary in a country like Timor-Leste, the traditional justice system needed to be fully recognized as a useful means of resolving disputes. The basic principles of the traditional justice system revolved around mediation, arbitration and reconciliation. It therefore required a mature and impartial adjudicator, a role that was performed by the village chiefs. Most had actually attempted to perform this duty, despite a lack of formal legal training and disruptions in the social fabric. When such judicial structures operated alongside the emerging formal courts, it was important to ensure that these systems avoided any tendency to compromise human rights standards. For example, in gender-related crimes, such as sexual abuse and domestic violence, women's rights might not be fully respected.

Inadequate prison facilities

The second aspect of the judiciary that required much attention from the Timorese government, as well as the supporting UN missions, was the handling of detainees and the need for the renovation of detention facilities. During the period of UNTAET administration, the three correctional facilities located in Dili, Baucau and Ermera districts had been re-established under international management. International staff was then gradually withdrawn, and since independence, the prison service had been administered almost entirely by Timorese national staff.

When I visited the prisons, 36 UNPOL and PNTL officers remained deployed there due to the absence of trained prison wardens to ensure prison security. The total prison population on 1 August 2002 numbered only 330, a relatively small number even for a population of slightly fewer than 1,000,000. The delay with which papers were prepared, and trials held, led to a situation where a majority of inmates were in pre-trial detention status. Furthermore, another 25 per cent of inmates were being detained on expired detention warrants. During the first two years of UNMISET, SRSG Sharma mentioned this fact quite often in his conversations with government officials and international visitors. Delays in the appointment of a Director of Prisons, and managers for each of the prisons in Baucau and Gleno, continued to hamper the development of the system. The absence of an oversight mechanism to monitor standards, and to investigate complaints, further complicated the situation. This led to prison riots.

On 9 June 2002, a riot by inmates in Becerra required police intervention, during which a few inmates suffered minor injuries. Then, on 16 August, there was a breakout at the Becora Prison. It was a major blow to the government and the UN mission. Almost all of the inmates were able easily to slip out of the prison, although later, to our surprise, most of the escapees returned. The incident generated wide debate among the government and the diplomatic community. Senior officials of the government started speaking about the need to move the Becora Prison out of the suburbs of Dili, and wanted to construct a new facility away from the capital city. They started negotiating further possible assistance from Malaysia and New Zealand, even though they said they were appreciative of the training done by UNMISET specialists. At this juncture, SRSG Sharma entrusted me with the task of addressing, in a coordinated manner, all the problems encountered with the administration of prisons.

The more familiar I became with the prison situation, the more I was convinced that a systematic review was needed to assess the situation, and that an appropriate way to improve their management was necessary. I assembled a group of experts to do the assessment. The Joint UNMISET-UNDP-Donors Prison Needs Joint Mission came to Timor-Leste in October 2002. The purpose was not only assessing problems in the management of prisons and detention facilities, but also advising the United Nations, the government and particularly the Ministry of Justice. What was needed was a proposal for a medium- to long-term strategy for the structures and modality of operations.

At first, the Prison Joint Mission carried out interviews at the four prison sites: Becora, Baucau, Gleno and Suai. It also visited one possible new prison site in Metinaro. The mission team also met with the most relevant players in the sector including civil society, the church, social workers and parliamentarians. At the conclusion of the visit, the Joint Mission leader, Mr Eric Scheye, suggested a two-track immediate and strategic approach to address the Timor-Leste correctional services.

The first immediate approach was to make specific, concrete improvements within the correctional services in Timor-Leste. The Joint Mission identified nine short-term projects with an estimated cost of approximately US$250,000. These were designed to address the need to improve the following aspects of prison management:

Code of conduct for prison staff.
Inmate employment workshop.
Inmate discipline.
Inmate redress.
Transportation for social workers.
Juvenile facilities.
Transportation for the Timor-Leste Prison System (SPTL).
Penal institution oversight team.
Laminated human rights cards for prison officers.

The second strategic long-term approach was identified as building a national consensus on the purpose and type of national correctional system. To address this issue the team recommended the establishment of a National Corrections Commission in which the church, Ministry of Justice and civil society would become main members. This recommendation was regarded as an expression of a lack of confidence in the government, which considered neither the church nor civil society an appropriate partner in prison management.

In order to reduce the number of unlawfully detained inmates, the Joint Mission pointed out the immediate need to improve the entire justice system. This was significant. As noted earlier, unlawful detainees numbered nearly one-third of the prison population. More specifically, the Joint Mission identified specific needs to address several shortcomings. The most noteworthy were:

• The absence of a coherent and publicly accepted correctional philosophy.
• A weak management in structure, oversight capabilities and execution.
• Underdeveloped organizational structure.
• The projected decrease in the prison system budget over the next four years.
• Various operational weaknesses such as poor practices in perimeter security, withdrawal of staff from certain areas of the prison and a lack of interpersonal relationships necessary for dynamic security.

To the surprise of many, the Joint Mission recommended the continued operation of the Becora Prison in its current location. This recommendation became controversial since the government had proposed to move the Becora Prison to an area far away from the capital city of Dili. Another noteworthy Mission observation was the lack of major human rights violations in Timorese prisons since the country's independence.

The Timorese Government warmly welcomed the findings of this Joint Mission. Minister of Justice Pessoa was moderately appreciative of

UNMISET and UNDP for having invited the needs joint mission. However, she remained careful in her remarks. She simply stated that she would examine the proposals and then consider what action should be taken. Regarding the long-term strategy, she thought that the National Dialogue led by President Gusmão was the best forum to discuss issues such as the prisons system in Timor-Leste. She asked the international community to support this already established initiative. Minister Pessoa also pointed out that the church had already extended special assistance to the prisons, but that this was suspended after the 16 August breakout from Becora Prison.

On the issue of construction of a new prison, Ms Pessoa reasoned that even though the Ministry of Justice was aware that the Becora Prison matched international standards in terms of physical arrangements for security, there was still a need for training and inmate social reintegration. This could not be carried out because of lack of human resources staff and space. She referred to the significant issues of the sanitary situation, and the mixing of different categories of inmates in the same facilities. She indeed noted the lack of separation between women and juveniles from the rest of the inmate population. In conclusion, Minister Pessoa was keen to emphasize the fact that the August breakout in Becora had been organized from outside the prison, so pointing out a security problem of a different nature.

Following the government's response to the Joint Mission findings, Beate Bull, a Norwegian junior professional officer of UNDP, asked whether the team could further elaborate on its stance of not constructing new prisons or detention facilities. Mr Eric Scheye took into account the Ministry of Justice's stated need for detention and prison facilities for the Suai District Court to process trials. He suggested, however, that as long as the court would not be open for business, there would be no need to build extra detention or prison facilities.

At the end of the debriefing meeting, I highlighted three points that I felt should still be addressed. First, there was a need for a clear policy from the Ministry of Justice on the management of the correctional services. Ana Pessoa had agreed to do this through the National Dialogue. Second, I suggested that the donor community should provide funding to implement the physical improvement of the prisons as recommended by the Assessment Team. Third, I advised the government acknowledge the Joint Mission's recommendation to keep the Becora Prison in its current location. This put an end to the debate on the need to move the prison out of the vicinity of Dili.

On Friday 2 April 2004, I visited Baucau where I met with the Vice-Minister of State Administration Conceiçao, Acting District Administrator Ximenes, and UNMISET District Administration Advisor Udumyan.

We discussed the need to maintain security in the area of Baucau in the post-May 2004 period. Conceiçao then raised two main issues. First, he pointed out the importance of ensuring equipment donated by UNMISET to the Government of Timor-Leste be handed over before buildings were vacated. This precaution was to avoid theft during a period without security presence. An advanced inventory list was requested. Secondly, Conceiçao raised concerns about the departure of the PKF, including UN Military Observers, from the Baucau area after May 2004. Only a few UNPOL technical advisors were expected to remain. Daily patrols of UN Military Observers were reported to have had a positive impact for the communities in the area. Their presence was appreciated, and concerns were voiced that their discontinuation could provide an opportunity for something to happen. Ximenes reported rumours that once the PKF left, something would happen, due to previous bad experiences. The overall awareness of the PNTL's role and functions in the communities had improved during the last two years. Public support was a positive contribution to the ability of the PNTL to handle potential security situations.

It was stated that the ability of 60 officers of the Rapid Intervention Unit posted in Baucau to respond rapidly would be limited due to logistic issues, such as the poor condition of vehicles and lack of fuel. A point was made that UNPOL technical advisors and PNTL should continue to be located as physically close as possible in order to be readily available for hands-on support. UNPOL advisors and PNTL were located in the same compound, but in different buildings.

Moreover, Acting District Administrator Ximenes highlighted the fact that Baucau had been without power for three months. My visit to the power station later that day was sobering. It was devoid of staff and 100 per cent non-operational. I was informed that the power station was awaiting a delicate process to be completed in order for repairs to be started, and it was expected that this would take at least another month.

Exercising national sovereignty in international relations and negotiations

Joining the United Nations and securing international visibility as an independent country

President Gusmão, Prime Minister Alkatiri and Foreign Minister Ramos-Horta attended the ceremony signifying the admission of Timor-Leste to the United Nations on 27 September 2002 as the 191st member. This marked the formal culmination of its people's aspiration for independence as a sovereign nation. It was also an occasion of great pride for the international community, particularly the United Nations, for having assisted in the birth of a nation.

Apart from addressing internal affairs of domestic governance and nation-building, the Timorese leaders showed their inclination to travel abroad and attend international conferences. President Gusmão visited Australia, Fiji, Indonesia, Japan and the Republic of Korea within one year of my arrival in Dili. The visits to Australia and Indonesia added further momentum to Timor-Leste's relations with two of its important neighbouring countries. He also made a state visit to Brazil in conjunction with his participation in the Summit of the Community of Portuguese Speaking Countries. Timor-Leste became the first Asian member. He also travelled to Nadi, Fiji, to participate as an Observer in the Summit of the ACP countries.

Prime Minister Alkatiri also made overseas trips to several countries, including Australia, Malaysia, Philippines, the United Kingdom and the United States. In Washington DC, Alkatiri signed agreements for Timor-Leste to become a member of the IMF and the World Bank..

In these overseas trips, the Timorese leaders sought to assert Timor-Leste's identity as a newly independent country. Also, they wanted it to be known as a Least Developed Country, a Southeast Asian country and a Portuguese-speaking nation. The diversity of its affiliations in fact reflected a difficulty in establishing its own distinctiveness, and its identity as an Asian country was not emphasized at first. This perhaps reflected that some sentiment existed among those who were partly Portuguese and tended to consider that they were not Asians. Nevertheless, José Ramos-Horta was quite clear in his view that Timor-Leste should be an integral part of Asia and the Pacific, and particularly ASEAN. He cultivated close links with the ASEAN countries and established diplomatic relations with all ASEAN member states except for Myanmar.

Ramos-Horta received a Nobel Peace Prize in 1996 along with Aung San Suu Kyi. He felt strongly about the illegitimacy of the military junta governing Myanmar. In 2004, Ramos-Horta visited Myanmar and hoped to meet with Aung San Suu Kyi, but was unable to obtain the permission of the government to meet his fellow Nobel Peace Prize recipient.

The Timorese leaders worked hard to maintain cordial relations with other states in the region, and particularly with Indonesia. The participation of President Megawati of Indonesia in the independence celebrations was a major achievement for President Gusmão, who later made a State Visit to Jakarta on 2 July 2002. He succeeded in obtaining the Indonesian President's agreement to create a Joint Ministerial Commission for Bilateral Cooperation to address issues of mutual concern. No doubt this was key to establishing a cordial relationship between the two countries. In a further significant step forward, the Joint Ministerial Commission decided on 8 October 2002 to maintain the Joint Border Committee (JBC) that had first been established under UNTAET. The Committee was tasked to finalize an agreement by 30 June 2003, on a line that constituted the border between the two countries. The agreement was to be in accordance with historic agreements and legal instruments.

The decision by the Joint Commission to sign the "Arrangement on Traditional Border Crossings and Regulated Markets" at the earliest opportunity marked further progress in the bilateral relationship. Also positive, for humanitarian and political reasons, was the Commission's adoption of a provisional agreement to allow persons residing in Oecussi to cross into neighbouring areas of West Timor without passports and visas. Its preliminary implementation was indeed crucial to allow the general population, who could not afford the visa fees, to travel once more by land to other parts of Timor-Leste via Indonesia.

After securing UN membership and having conciliated its relationship with Indonesia, the Timorese leaders worked vigorously to establish the country's membership with other international organizations. Timor-Leste became a member of the World Bank, the Asian Development Bank, and CPLP. It established diplomatic relations with nearly all ASEAN Member States. Timor-Leste also started participating in ASEAN meetings as an invited Observer, and the country's leaders participated in the Summit of African, Caribbean and Pacific countries.

At the invitation of President Gusmão, the former Foreign Minister of Indonesia, Alatas, visited Dili for two days in September 2003 to give a keynote address at a conference on international relations.[11] The President acted as the conference moderator. In addition to Alatas, Foreign Minister Ramos-Horta and the Ambassador of Australia made speeches, and SRSG Sharma also addressed the Conference on the "importance of the UN for Timor-Leste".

The visit of Alatas and his wife to Timor-Leste clearly reflected a strengthening of the ties between the two countries. At a formal reception at the Palace of Ashes during the evening of 8 September, the interaction between President Gusmão and Ali Alatas was warm. Alatas' obvious gratitude, as well as the positive tone of the conference, indicated a change in attitudes on both sides. At the very least there was a clear determination to move forward in their bilateral relationship.

Gusmão used his extraordinary ability to both charm and cajole old adversaries through choppy waters. This resulted in a relaxed approach being taken to serious subjects by all at the conference. Alatas added to the friendly approach by noting in his opening remarks that out of the hundreds of similar events he had been to over the years, this was the first time he had attended a conference "personally moderated by a President".

Alatas, in his current position as an advisor to President Megawati, touched on a few important themes and issues in the bilateral relationship. He stressed that the personal ties between Timor-Leste and Indonesia were close for historical, cultural and ethnic reasons. He emphasized, though, the need not to dwell on the past. He spoke of the common destiny which linked the two developing, non-aligned nations, and the significant progress made over the past two years. Alatas noted that Indonesia would open its embassy in Timor-Leste as soon as possible.

Alatas said that both sides had agreed to continue with the Joint Border Committee, due to the complexity of the border issues. He described the finalization of the border demarcation to ensure border safety, noting that "good borders make good neighbours" as a most pressing concern. Responding to a question, he added that Indonesia had great interest in ensuring that it had no trouble with its neighbours. However, he underlined that border delineation required goodwill on both sides, because borders were not just about the lines, which do not mean much to local people. A wide range of topics was covered in the approximately two-hour question-and-answer time allotment, including Timor-Leste's membership in regional groupings, the impact of terrorism, foreign investment, cultural identity, intimidation of East Timorese students in central Java, military bases in Timor-Leste and the situation in Aceh.

On Aceh, Alatas stressed that the situation was very painful for Indonesia. He dismissed those who said the Aceh problem was the same as East Timor. Interestingly, he said that East Timor had always been an international problem whereas Aceh was not. Alatas was confident that Indonesia's friendly policy towards Timor-Leste after the 2004 elections would remain unchanged. The highest body in the land, the Majelis Permusyawaratan Rakyat (MPR, People's Consultative Assembly), had established Indonesia's ties with Timor-Leste in 1999.

The mere fact that this meeting could take place in Dili was a significant testimony to Alatas' statements. In his remarks, Ramos-Horta admitted that both sides were still wounded by what they had done to one another, and at the same time he praised Indonesia for its statesmanship and goodwill towards Timor-Leste. At the public reception Gusmão jokingly described Ramos-Horta as the "arch-enemy" of Ali Alatas in the past. Horta expressed his respect and admiration for Alatas as one of the most highly recognized foreign ministers, who happened to work for the wrong boss. Taking the opportunity to talk with him during the event, SRSG Sharma quietly suggested that Ali Alatas might provide the necessary political impetus to the finalization of agreement on the land border and for resettlement of East Timorese refugees away from West Timor. At Sharma's suggestion, President Gusmão also made similar démarches. We hoped that the intervention of Alatas on these issues would provide additional momentum to the process.

On 23 October 2003 the Prime Minister of Malaysia, Mahathir Mohamed, paid his first visit to Timor-Leste. In a busy and productive period, he signed an agreement on bilateral cooperation, contributed 32 trucks to the F-FDTL, addressed the National Parliament and conducted a dialogue with the business community. He also held a private meeting with me. Mahathir Mohamed visited Timor-Leste with a delegation of some 80 members, including the Ministers of Foreign Affairs, Employment, Defence and International Trade. Members of the media and his security team were also present. Highlights of the visit were:

- Address to the National Parliament: The Malaysian Prime Minister's statement to the National Parliament focused on comparison among different forms of government in the parliamentarian and presidential systems. He also spoke on the authority of elected governments in contrast with the non-elected entities, such as NGOs, the media and the judiciary. He pointed out that although democracy in developed countries had "an idealistic beginning", it evolved to become an unjust and intolerant system. "Democracy can now be imposed by violence," he said. Stressing that free trade was not fair trade, he pointed out the unjust competition between the developed and developing countries, but concluded, however, that democracy remained the best available system of governance.
- Management of natural resources: In his address, the Malaysian Prime Minister was categorical in warning against "the oil majors" who had exploited the poor countries.
- Business dialogue: During a meeting between the Malaysian and East Timorese business communities, the Malaysian Prime Minister highlighted Timor-Leste's progress in reconstruction and nation-building, particularly in the areas of planning, institution capacity-building and in identifying development priority areas. Included in his positive review were: law and order, justice, strengthening of local administration, employment creation and poverty reduction. He expressed his commitment to continuing bilateral support in human resources development and education. Encouraging to Malaysian private investment in Timor-Leste, he pointed out that Malaysia ranked as the second largest foreign investor in 2002.
- Bilateral issues: Malaysia and Timor-Leste signed an agreement on economic, scientific, technical and cultural cooperation. A joint commission was established in order to facilitate the implementation of the agreement and the protection of intellectual property. In addition, Malaysia contributed 32 trucks and equipment to the F-FDTL.
- Government of Timor-Leste: Highlighting the close ties between the two countries, Prime Minister Alkatiri pointed out that Malaysia was one of the key partners in the region. He indicated that the contribution of Malaysia to the F-FDTL came at a crucial time in view of the

withdrawal of the international peacekeeping force and the need to prepare the F-FDTL to take over the defence responsibilities fully within a year. He indicated, however, that the key responsibilities of the F-FDTL were to abide by the Constitution and the laws, while respecting human rights and maintaining peace.

- UNMISET: Upon Prime Minister Mahathir's invitation, I held a private meeting with him for nearly half an hour from 6:30 to 7:00 p.m. Besides briefing the Malaysian Prime Minister on the Mission's main activities, I stressed the need for assistance in providing necessary equipment for the Rapid Deployment Service (RDS) training to start as soon as possible. On the topic of aviation support for UNMISET, I asked for possible Malaysian support for helicopters. I confirmed with the Malaysian Prime Minister that the helicopters would be used to transport PKF members.

This first State Visit by the head of a foreign country since the independence of Timor-Leste marked a positive development in the nation-building process. Additionally, it reflected Timor-Leste's strength in developing neighbourly relations with countries in the region, particularly ASEAN members. The speech to the National Parliament was "vintage Mahathir". The Malaysian Prime Minister avoided controversial remarks about the Middle East. He focused on his customary themes of the limitations of Western-style liberal democratic systems and the exploitation of poor countries. There was little specific reference to Timor-Leste in the speech. Nevertheless, a number of the themes undoubtedly resonated with the East Timorese leadership. The Malaysian Prime Minister highlighted the potentially threatening roles of the judiciary, which should not "usurp the law-making role" of the parliament. He also addressed the roles of NGOs and remarked that they "should not unduly harass the Government".

The speech received a standing ovation from the members of the parliament. There had been speculation that the visit was aimed at countering Australian interests in the region. This led Foreign Minister Ramos-Horta to voice assurances that "Australia need not be worried" about the visit. At the same time, Foreign Minister Ramos-Horta had added that the Malaysian state oil firm Petronas had been invited to explore for oil in Timor-Leste, as had the state oil firm of China. The Timorese leaders instinctively knew there was a need to balance the influence exerted by various powers.

The most telling point made by Mahathir in his speech to National Parliament was that unless petroleum-rich countries got smart in negotiating concessions, they would be "cheated", as the rich countries gained the advantage by exploiting, refining and retailing the oil resources. At his press conference, the Malaysian Prime Minister said that Malaysia had no intention of taking East Timor's oil, but rather to give advice on how to deal with multinational companies. He remarked on the implications of becoming a democratic country, observing that there was no assurance the country would become peaceful by saying "It is important to remember that nuclear bombs have only been dropped by a democratic country."[12]

The Malaysian Prime Minister's speech in the Timor-Leste–Malaysia Business Dialogue was typical of his pragmatic economic approach, noting the importance of attracting foreign investment. He emphasized that for economic development, it was important to put in place the necessary policies, incentive schemes and infrastructure facilities to provide a pro-business environment beneficial to the private sector. He had taken note, with keen interest, of UNMISET's concerns with the RDS and request for aviation support. As a result of effective security planning and close cooperation with the national police, military components and the Mission police, the visit took place in a peaceful and orderly fashion with no incidents.

The Timorese leaders had succeeded in building a cordial relationship with Indonesia and other countries of the region such as Australia and Malaysia. Timor-Leste also established its visibility as a new member of the international community; the country had been integrated, as an independent sovereign state, into the Asian region and the Portuguese-speaking world.

Addressing human rights concerns

The international press frequently reports major human rights violations in the developing world, particularly in crisis-prone countries. Such major human rights violation, however, did not take place in post-independence Timor-Leste. National leaders, particularly José Ramos-Horta, were conscious of Timor-Leste's image, particularly in view of the global concern for human rights violations committed in many parts of the world. Both the government and UNMISET insisted upon a prominent place in their programmes for the protection and promotion of human rights.

Before the country's independence, an Advisor on Human Rights to the Prime Minister was appointed with the support of UNTAET. The Prime Minister invited this official to convene a Working Group to facilitate the establishment of the Provedor for Human Rights and Justice, an institution provided for in the Constitution. It also combined Ombudsman and Human Rights Commission functions. UNMISET staff participated as members of the Working Group and helped organize a workshop on 14–15 June 2002. This was supported by the Office of the United

Nations High Commissioner for Human Rights (OHCHR) and attended by experts from Portugal, Sweden, India and Australia. The necessary legislation was adopted soon after the workshop. This led the way for the creation of the Office of the Provedor in 2003.

Furthermore, setting up institutionalized human rights protection organs enabled the government to ratify core international human rights treaties. This was a significant step towards acquiring respectability on the international scene. The nascent State of Timor-Leste thus submitted its instrument of accession to these treaties when it became a Member State of the United Nations on 27 September 2002.

Another example of addressing of human rights concerns as a priority was the series of successful seminars on the Convention on the Rights of the Child. UNICEF organized these in conjunction with the government and UNMISET on 19 July 2002. The one on the Convention on Elimination of Discrimination Against Women took place on 7 August, with UNMISET support. Prime Minister Alkatiri participated in both events, demonstrating his personal interest in the promotion and protection of human rights.

UNMISET also supported human rights training programmes in Timor-Leste. In April 2002, the HRU (Human Rights Unit), UNICEF and UNPOL conducted a "Training of Trainers in Human Rights and Child Rights" for ETPS officers. The ETPS trainers continued this training, by constituting a working group to support training of ETPS officers in each district. The working group involved the HRU, UNPOL, ETPS, UNICEF and the NGO Yayasan Hak. The district training programme was designed to cover every district during 2002, using UNICEF and HRU training manuals as a reference guide.

Added momentum came with the visit of the High Commissioner for Human Rights, Mary Robinson, from 23 to 25 August 2002. This was her final visit before she completed her term in office on 11 September 2002. She met the Timorese leadership and addressed parliament on the ratification of international human rights treaties. I accompanied her to Suai to meet with the victims of the 1999 church massacre there. She also participated in a ceremony organized by the CAVR. During her visit, the High Commissioner pledged to provide cooperation with Timor-Leste to enhance the national capacity for human rights protection. Mary Robinson's visit demonstrated the importance of international leadership, particularly in conflict-prone countries, to advance the cause of human rights.

On 31 August 2003, the issue of trafficking of women and prostitution in Timor-Leste was addressed, following the report of Under-Secretary-General Nair on the subject.[13] Upon UNMISET's request, the Ministry of Foreign Affairs and Cooperation had been co-chairing meetings of the transition working group (TWG), which I had initiated in April. Relevant

Timorese authorities including members of the PNTL participated in the group discussion, to formulate appropriate strategies to prevent, detect and prosecute trafficking of persons. The objective was to protect the victims in accordance with international standards. UNMISET had secured the Government of Timor-Leste's active participation in TWG in order to foster a sense of government ownership. It was also hoped to encourage increased participation in the TWG meetings that had begun in June 2003.

The TWG delegated UNMISET HRU, the International Organization for Migration (IOM), UNICEF and UNPOL National Investigations to consider a proposal on a draft strategy to investigate cases of suspected trafficking. The draft included coordination for various types of services in order to facilitate investigation and victim protection. Following an agreement upon the general principles of the document, it was hoped that the TWG would be able to flesh out further details. Attention was directed to crucial and practical steps to assist investigation. Included were proposals for the funding and establishment of overnight accommodation, interview rooms at the national airport and a safe house for victims of trafficking and sexual exploitation.

Meanwhile, the HRU assisted UNPOL in dealing with the alleged victims of trafficking. In close cooperation with UNPOL and IOM, HRU supported a victim of alleged trafficking, arranged secure accommodation, and provided counselling support and food for a four-week period while she was waiting to be repatriated to her home country. The HRU was ready to assist UNPOL and IOM in similar cases should the need arise.

The HRU also assisted UNPOL in cases when women were arrested for alleged involvement in prostitution. Specifically, they interviewed the women to determine that their rights were being respected and their safety ensured. We were concerned that some women arrested for prostitution may have been trafficked. Owing to lack of adherence to judicial procedure, such problems were causing difficulties in determining the actual level of trafficking in Timor-Leste.

More cases of collaboration among the members of TGW were expected. UNPOL and PNTL identified five business premises allegedly involved in prostitution and possibly trafficking women, and planned proactive investigations into these premises. In order to prohibit UNPOL officers from entering any premises where prostitution or non-medical massage was offered for service, a "Commissioner's Directive" was issued to all UNPOL officers. The new Directive mentioned specific premises that should not be visited by UNPOL officers and UNMISET staff. I am confident that these measures reduced to a negligible number any UN-related personnel visiting such establishments.

On 17 October 2005, a Policy Review and Coordination Meeting on Democratic Governance and Human Rights was held. The objective of the meeting was to provide an overview of the specific mandate of the United Nations Office in Timor-Leste (UNOTIL) HRU, and to outline the key activities. The aim was to place these activities within the larger context of leaving behind a strengthened post-UNOTIL environment, one where human rights principles and state institutions complemented the building of democratic governance. The Chief Justice and Head of the Court of Appeals, the Civilian Support Group (CSG), UNDP and bilaterally funded advisors in the field of human rights attended the meeting. Further attendees included representatives from the diplomatic corps and development partners, civil society, UNOTIL officials, UNDP representatives and UNICEF.

The following major points were highlights of the discussion:

- Human rights were one of the main components of the principles governing democratic governance along with the rule of law, transparency and accountability, for which the state institutions were responsible.
- It was recognized that state institution-building was a long-term process, requiring time for good governance to flourish, and human rights-monitoring mechanisms to establish firm roots. It was the role of the international community to assist in this process.
- UNOTIL should leave a legacy of respect for human rights values and principles.
- Post-UNOTIL deployment of human rights officers to various state institutions as well as to the districts should be ensured in order to continue capacity-building and monitoring activities.
- The importance of sensitization of the population at the grassroots level to human rights values and principles was emphasized. To this end the role of civil society, including the media, should be strengthened.
- The government had to introduce laws and regulations that would enable proper procedures for investigation, prosecution and trials. This was particularly important in view of the return of former militia.

The suggested course of action was for stakeholders to consider continued support of capacity-building and the monitoring roles of national human rights officers, and to strengthen further the role of civil society awareness and media participation.

On 6 November 2002 the Council of Ministers of the Government of Timor-Leste discussed a package of human rights treaties, and subsequently agreed to forward the package to the National Parliament. The Council recommended that the National Parliament consider the treaties before 15 November, when it would rise for a two-month recess. The objective was for the State to accede to the treaties on or before International Human Rights Day, 10 December.

The following treaties were included in the package:
- International Covenant on Civil and Political Rights (ICCPR)
- International Covenant on Economic, Social and Cultural Rights (ICESCR)
- International Convention on the Elimination of All Forms of Racial Discrimination (ICERD)
- Convention against Torture and Other Cruel, Inhuman or Degrading Treatment or Punishment (CAT)
- Convention on the Elimination of All Forms of Discrimination against Women (CEDAW)
- Convention on the Rights of the Child (CRC)
- International Convention on the Protection of the Rights of All Migrant Workers and Members of their Families (MWC)
- Second Optional Protocol to the International Covenant on Civil and Political Rights (aimed at the abolition of the death penalty) (ICCPR-OP2-DP)
- Optional Protocol to the Convention on the Elimination of All Forms of Discrimination against Women (CEDAW-OP)
- Optional Protocol to the Convention on the Rights of the Child on the involvement of children in armed conflict (CRC-OP-AC)
- Optional Protocol to the Convention on the Rights of the Child on the sale of children, child prostitution and child pornography (CRC-OP-SC)

Overall, the Council's decision was welcomed as a substantial step forward for human rights protection in Timor-Leste, and was indicative of the country's commitment to the international human rights system. Significant among the treaties recommended for signature was the Migrant Workers Convention. There had been 19 signatories on this convention, and Timor-Leste's signature represented the 20th one needed to bring the convention into force. The only protocol which the Council did not approve was the Optional Protocol to the International Covenant on Civil and Political Rights, which would have provided individuals with the right to petition the Human Rights Committee of the OHCHR.

Signing the human rights treaties: Marking International Day in Support of the Victims of Torture

Timor-Leste acceded to the human rights treaties on 10 December 2002. Foreign Affairs Minister Ramos-Horta requested that the act of the President signing the documents be recorded on video to be shown to the United Nations in New York.

On 26 June 2003, activities were undertaken to mark the International Day in Support of Victims of Torture. The Association of Former Political

Prisoners (ASSEPOL) organized a number of events in Dili to mark the occasion. Events were supported and attended by members of the government, the National Parliament and UNMISET. Members of the diplomatic corps, civil society and the church also attended.

In the morning Jacob Fernandes, the Vice-President of the National Parliament, and I attended the event held at the seaport. In my speech I conveyed the Secretary-General's firm commitment to bring about a world free of torture. I also commended the government and parliament for having ratified the Convention against Torture and Other Cruel, Inhuman and Degrading Punishment.

As part of the ceremony, the participants strewed wreaths and flower petals into the water of the harbour. It was speculated that, during the occupation years, the bodies of many torture victims had been thrown into the water. The site was particularly significant to the Chinese community in Timor-Leste, and part of the ceremony involved the burning of incense and religious chanting by Chinese participants. The ceremony was followed by a seminar, at which Minister Pessoa spoke. She stressed the importance of learning from the lessons of the past, and how establishing institutions to prevent torture would ensure that such a situation would never be allowed to happen again in Timor-Leste.

One such step was the ratification in December 2002 of the UN Convention Against Torture and Other Cruel, Inhuman or Degrading Treatment of Punishment. In addition, the government strived to ensure that all agency and institution staff members were trained to observe international human rights standards, including the Convention. She added that these government efforts must be supported by teachings on how to live in peace and love.

Two East Timorese survivors of torture then spoke of the importance of recognizing victims of torture, emphasizing that this would prevent a culture of torture from being passed on to future generations. In later sessions, presentations were given by the General Prosecutor, representatives of F-FDTL and the PNTL. Also presenting were the National Parliament, church and human rights groups, including UNMISET's HRU.

Later in the afternoon, a tree-planting ceremony was held at the premises of the CAVR. The location was formerly a prison in which political prisoners had been held, many of them suffering at the hands of torturers. I participated in the ceremony and planted a memorial tree. Finally, a solemn mass was held to honour the victims of torture. In addition to the events outlined above, UNMISET's Public Information Office distributed a message from the Secretary-General in four languages internally and to the local media. Throughout the day, the local TV broadcast a 14-second message prepared by UNMISET. It showed a very quick sequence of torture scenes that took place in East Timor. A displayed message read: "Torture Never More/International Day in Support of Victims of Torture". The day's events served as a poignant reminder of the suffering endured for so long by this proud nation. At the same time, it sought to look to the future and brought into focus the positive steps that would ensure such events would never happen again.

Managing the border areas with Indonesia

UNMISET recognized the importance of normalization of the land border for the external security of Timor-Leste and for the timely withdrawal of PKF. Therefore, UNMISET formulated an action plan to deal with all border-related issues in a comprehensive manner. SRSG Sharma had emphasized the need to maintain the momentum achieved in the JBC between Indonesia and East Timor on Timorese leadership, including the President, the Prime Minister, the Minister of Foreign Affairs and Cooperation.

He also made similar démarches to Indonesian leadership, including President Sukarnoputri, Coordinating Minister for Political and Security Affairs Lieutenant General Yudhoyono, and Foreign Minister Wirajuda. All the leaders in both Timor-Leste and Indonesia indicated a willingness to proceed with border delineation and normalization, with the emphasis that the issues deserved.

Illegal markets operating on dry riverbeds at the time of independence had proved to be a magnet for smugglers and other criminal activities. The markets provided ex-militia with an opportunity to exert influence and levy illegal taxation. The markets generally shifted to the Indonesian side of the Tactical Coordination Line (TCL) following an incident on 18 June 2002. This allowed the Indonesian police to have better control over the maintenance of law and order at the markets. However, it did not significantly reduce the opportunities for crime and petty extortion. Indonesian authorities indicated that should Timor-Leste wish to organize regular markets on its side of the TCL, the proposal would be examined positively and constructively.

The Indonesian authorities also indicated to SRSG Sharma a willingness to consider issues related to the maintenance of a soft border, for example, special visa regimes or identity cards for residents of border areas. They would support a regular bus service connecting the Oecussi enclave via Atambua to Batugade in Timor-Leste. They indicated a desire to work with East Timor to curb smuggling of sandalwood and cattle from Timor-Leste. Subsidized goods, such as fuel and rice, were also being smuggled from Indonesia.

Refugee repatriation was proceeding apace. In July 2002, the highest number of returnees (5,304) was recorded. It was then estimated that around 37,000 refugees still remained on the Indonesian side of the is-land, West Timor. When the Government of Indonesia and UNHCR ended their programme on 31 December 2002, only about 15,000 were estimated to remain in Indonesia awaiting resettlement.

On 9 September 2003, the PNTL nominated 138 officers to be trained as RDS members. According to Police Commissioner Peisley, the total deployment of RDS members could reach 180 by the end of the UNMISET mandate. The initial deployment was 60 RDS members to Oecussi by the end of January 2004, with 60 RDS members being de-ployed to both Covalima and Bobonaro by May 2004.

The curriculum design was completed by the end of September as orig-inally planned, and the training of 60 RDS candidates began in October 2003. The intended start date of August had been delayed, primarily due to the lack of training facilities and complications in procurement of suit-able weapons. The government recognized the former as a top priority. I had instructed Police Commissioner Peisley to address urgently the need to start training without any further delays. I also reminded him of the requirement to institute discipline and human rights safeguards.

The issue arose of how the border would be managed if the RDS was not ready. I was of the view that the Border Patrol Unit (BPU), with its improved capability and increased strength, remained the police unit re-sponsible for the management of the border. The Mission's police con-tinued to cooperate closely with the military component. Their presence in the border areas increased the BPU's preparedness and capabilities. Australian PKF troops remained available for backup support should it become necessary in the border areas.

The primary role of the RDS was to perform special police functions, such as addressing internal security threats by armed and criminal groups. After the PKF withdrew its permanent presence in Oecussi, Cove Lima and Bononaro, the UN military observers (UNMOs) remained in Oe-cussi and the western districts. Many local and international observers were concerned that the presence of RDS and UNMOs would not be adequate in the event of any major armed attacks. In view of the post-UNMISET period, it seemed essential to contemplate deployment of a substantial number of international police, which would serve as an armed, multidimensional backup force. Of course, these issues needed to be debated by the Security Council in due course.

On 31 May 2005 I met with President Gusmão, and briefed him on the investigation by the Military Liaison Group (MLG) of a shooting inci-dent on 21 April, which had taken place on the border area near Junction Point Memo (JP-MEMO). The MLG's investigation had concluded that a BPU agent had fired a shot that hit a TNI soldier. I told him that I had advised the Prime Minister that the agent should be transferred away from the BPU. My reasoning was that his continued presence there could cause tension in the dealings of the BPU with the TNI. The Prime Minister had concurred, and Gusmão agreed that he would also take up the matter with the Prime Minister.

Gunfire reported on the Tactical Coordination Line

On 21 April 2005, an exchange of gunfire took place between TNI and BPU at the Tactical Coordination Line near Maliana. Being aware of the importance of gaining first-hand knowledge of the area, I immediately decided to visit the scene of the incident. The investigators from the PNTL National Investigation Unit, along with UNPOL technical advisors, came with me to the site. They started to gather some preliminary evidence, including photographs, bullet cartridges and evidence of blood from the Timor-Leste side. The information given to me on site by the BPU was sketchy, seeming to indicate that the TNI were in pursuit of smugglers, while the BPU was in a position to observe the incident. At the scene, UNPOL found were what were believed to be traces of blood, and also bullets and cartridges from both BPU and TNI. The evidence hinted that the incident might have taken place at least in part on the Timor-Leste side, although it could not be determined definitively.

The TNI battalion commander agreed to join in the discussion, and crossed onto the Timor-Leste side of the border. The TNI commander did not agree with the claim that any TNI personnel had crossed into Timor-Leste and indicated that his patrol might have been deliberately fired upon. He believed the bullet came from a high-velocity weapon (that is, a rifle), and repeated that the first shot came from the Timor-Leste side. He wanted to know the name of the BPU officer who had shot the TNI soldier, a lieutenant-colonel, in the leg; meanwhile, the BPU commander insisted that the shooting had taken place on the Timor-Leste side of the river.

The two sides clearly had different versions of what had actually happened. According to the BPU, the TNI chased a group of Timorese engaged in smuggling kerosene from the Indonesian side to Timor-Leste. The TNI then reportedly fired shots at the smugglers, with at least one TNI officer crossing the river into the Timor-Leste side. The BPU patrol returned fire with three warning shots, one in the direction of the TNI, which apparently hit the TNI soldier's left thigh. One of the BPU agents had in fact admitted to the Military Liaison Officer (MLO) that he fired a bullet in the direction of the TNI soldiers. The TNI soldiers' account of the incident was different. According to them, some unknown person had shot at them, hitting one in the leg, while they were chasing the smugglers on the Indonesian side of the river. The TNI then returned fire and continued firing for some time.

The Indonesians then asked the United Nations to carry out a full investigation into the incident. This is the first time that the Indonesians showed trust in the United Nations, and the incident highlighted the key role that should be played by the MLG in developing an effective communication system for border management. I expressed the importance of maintaining communication and dialogue, that sharing of information was key in order to piece together the events that had taken place. Furthermore, I urged both sides to look into the changes they could make to improve communication and working arrangements in order to avoid such occurrences. Both sides agreed, particularly indicating the need to formalize some way to communicate with each other. I also suggested that both sides investigate the incident from their side and then try and share the information in order to reach some agreement. It was confirmed that a further meeting would take place on 23 April at the border site of Motaain, in the presence of the Chief Military Liaison Officer, the Border Security Task Force (Indonesia) commander, the BPU commander and UNPOL technical advisors, so that BPU could progress the investigation.

Meanwhile, to add to the Timorese fear of a possible Indonesian threat of retaliation, Minister of Interior Lobato telephoned me later to say he had received an alarming report from BPU. Local inhabitants had noticed the movement of "two tanks" along the border. According to local observation, it could have been two armoured patrol cars that had been moved by TNI towards the TCL in the JP-MEMO area. I immediately asked UNPOL and MLOs to ascertain the validity of the report. Subsequently, MLOs were told by the BPU that armoured patrol cars were seen between Nanura and JP-MEMO. MLOs contacted the TNI Company commanders at Junction Point C and Junction Point A later in the evening and asked for confirmation. The Indonesian Border Security Task Force commander in Atambua was also contacted by MLOs. The Indonesians denied any such activity had taken place. The commander in Atambua further added that TNI did not have tanks or armoured patrol cars in the area. He agreed to discuss the issue at the meeting between the two sides on 23 April. The MLOs who visited JP-MEMO later in the evening also did not observe any unusual activity in the area.

On 31 May 2005 I met with President Gusmão, and briefed him on the investigation carried out by the MLG of the 21 April shooting incident in the border area near JP-MEMO. The MLG's investigation had concluded that a BPU agent had first fired a shot that hit the TNI soldier. I told him that I had advised the Prime Minister that the agent should be transferred away from the BPU as his continued presence there could cause tension between the BPU with the TNI. Gusmão agreed that he would also take up the matter with the Prime Minister.

Whether TNI soldiers crossed the TCL or not, the exchange of fire between the two border agencies and the firing of bullets directly at a TNI soldier was a matter of serious concern. This incident could have been a first step towards heightening the tension between the two border agencies. The BPU reports of tank movements across the border were an indication of how vulnerable they felt, and they had immediately reverted to the MLOs to verify such information. If not handled with care, such incidents could ultimately affect not only the working relationship between BPU and TNI, but also the improving bilateral relationship between Timor-Leste and Indonesia. The MLO had been a calming influence and played a key role as mediator in this incident, urging both sides to cooperate in the investigation, and also to move across the TCL for this purpose if necessary. The important role of the MLO as impartial facilitator for dispute resolution, dialogue and investigation in such incidents had been highlighted once again.

This incident also demonstrated that similar occurrences could happen with frequency on a long and porous border. Unless a workable arrangement was made, or communication and rules of engagement set, incidents of this type could continue to trigger conflict between BPU and TNI. With this in mind, when I met with Foreign Minister Ramos-Horta immediately upon his return to Timor-Leste, I proposed the establishment of an investigation commission, and he agreed. He thought such a commission could be established by UNMISET, and should include representatives from both the Timor-Leste and Indonesian sides. The Indonesian Ambassador Ahmed Bey Sofwan, to whom I had also spoken, indicated his agreement to establishing a UN investigating commission, as the news of "Lt Col. Teddy shot by Timorese Police" was being aired on Indonesian television, arousing nationalistic reaction to the incident.

An incident disrupting the border marking

On 12 September 2005, there was an incident disrupting border marking. The Border Demarcation Team (BDT) subsequently ceased its work to allow time for resolving local disputes involving fires being lit, causing damage to East Timorese corn crops.[14] These incidents were initiated by local Indonesians from the villages of Imbate and Sungai in West Timor. The Unidade Patrulhamento Fronteira (UPF, Timor-Leste Border Patrol Unit) national commander, Antonio da Cruz, advised UNOTIL Military Training Advisors Group (MTAG) that meetings had been conducted with their TNI counterparts with respect to these incidents. The TNI had agreed to take action to prevent further occurrences. The UPF was also to increase its presence in the areas to prevent escalation. A more thorough information-seeking campaign on the Indonesian side was planned, prior to recommencing demarcation activities.

The Senior Sector Military Training Advisor (SSMTA) in Oecussi was to shift his efforts in order to support the UPF leadership handling this problem. UPF action to date had been measured and appropriate, and liaison with TNI appeared to be working effectively at that stage. Military Training Advisors (MTAs) in Oecussi would continue to provide more detailed information on the specific nature of the dispute, and report the ongoing actions being taken to reach a resolution.

The next day DSRSG Bajwa travelled to Oecussi, where he visited UNOTIL's presence at the border and sought more immediate information. He also toured six junction points along the border of Timor-Leste and Indonesia. Bajwa's detailed sector and post briefings brought a number of challenges to light in relation to UPF capacity to patrol the border. Deputy Bajwa reaffirmed to UPF commanders that the necessary means to carry out border security functions would be met with UNOTIL's support and assistance.

On 13 and 14 September, DSRSG Bajwa, accompanied by members of UNOTIL MTAG and Police Training Advisors, visited three border junction points in Oecussi district and three in Covalima and Bobonaro districts. The purpose was to obtain first-hand knowledge of the situation along the border of Timor-Leste and Indonesia. UPF commanders reported overall peaceful situations at each of the sectors visited. In Oecussi the Secretary of State for Oecussi, Albano Salem, joined Mr Bajwa for a morning briefing by the SSMTA, Senior Sector Police Training Advisor (SSPTA) and UPF district commander on the sector and its structure. Also covered were current training activities being carried out with UPF officers. Mr Bajwa toured Oecussi Junction Points (JPs) 1, 2 and 5, where he received post-specific briefings from UPF post commanders.

In JP-5 a disputed boundary lay at a waterbed abutting the village of Citron. According to the UPF post commander, Indonesia had thus far not objected to his crew patrolling the actual border road along the TCL. Border markers were to be placed between Citron and Passabe starting on 15 September. This was the site of two recent incidents involving the burning of East Timorese fields by West Timorese villagers.

In Covalima, prior to the tour of a southerly junction point, the SSMTA, SSPTA and UPF District Commander provided an overview of the sector and of training activities within it. The district's training programme focused upon computer and administration skills in addition to policing skills. It was anticipated that donated equipment would be received, which the UPF could use.

A final sector briefing was held in Bobonaro district, where the UPF district commander advised that smuggling and illegal immigration activity existed. DSRSG Bajwa visited JPs there. In this district, 26 of 56 boundary markers were already erected. Notwithstanding, it also contained a boundary still in dispute, consisting of a small island between two JPs. While noting a positive response to the training programmes implemented thus far, a number of challenges for the UPF were identified during the site visits.

These included:

• the flat UPF rank and salary structure;
• lack of fully operational communication equipment; and
• lack of transportation.

They also had extremely basic living conditions. Their food supply was limited since the government's recent replacement of its previous food rations contractor. There were also health concerns due to a lack of mosquito nets in the barracks. The DSRSG stressed that UNOTIL would follow up on possible solutions to these challenges, examining how to ensure that the UPF could be provided with the necessary means to carry out its job. This would include identifying the equipment donated by UNOTIL to the government, which could fill the needs of the UPF. He suggested that Secretary of State for Oecussi Salem should contact the government office where equipment was centrally donated, to find out whether some of this equipment could be made available to meet the needs of this district.

Cautious start of the Timor Gap negotiation with Australia

The issue of ownership of natural gas, oil and other resources in the seabed of the Timor Gap[15] became a major issue once Timor-Leste achieved the restoration of its independence, although naturally it was not dealt with as such in the beginning. The then Prime Minister Alkatiri played a major role in asserting Timorese ownership; I vividly remember the very difficult negotiations he had with Foreign Minister Downer of Australia.

Downer was over 2 metres tall, and imposing in character. Downer felt that Timor-Leste should be grateful for the support given by Australia and tried to intimidate Mari Alkatiri, who was relatively short. Mari, however, was tough and outfaced him. Downer's stance was that the area was part of the continental shelf of Australia; therefore, he reasoned, it belonged to Australia. Under strong pressure, Mari Alkatiri skilfully agreed to a tentative plan. He said he would sign an agreement. However, he had already planned to send it to parliament, as part of the democratic process, and so frustrated the Australian position.

The maritime boundary and the sharing of natural resources were two separate issues. Australia and Timor-Leste could not agree on the definition of definite lines for the maritime boundaries, but they did agree on how to share the oil and gas. The moment they agreed on the line, they could claim ownership. Timor-Leste wanted to take the matter to the International Court of Justice, but Australia declined. In the end Mari Alkatiri agreed to a 50–50 split on the Joint Petroleum Development Area, referred to as the Greater Sunrise field.

At first, the Timorese leaders took a cautious approach to the exploitation of natural resources in the maritime area between Timor-Leste and Australia. They engaged pragmatically with Australia for the exploitation of the Bayu Undan oil field by Philips Petroleum, and collaborated to determine the share of revenues to be derived from the Greater Sunrise field area. With the assistance of UN and World Bank advisors, the Timor-Leste Government initiated technical discussions with Australia, referred to as "unitization talks", related to the exploitation of these shared reserves. The talks started without any prejudice to their position on the maritime boundary negotiations. As the negotiations continued, Mari Alkatiri demonstrated strength. He did not give into the demands made by the Australian government to share the resources in a predetermined ratio favourable to Australia. Furthermore, he insisted on the construction of a gas pipeline from the Bayu Undan field to Timor-Leste rather than to Australia.

Mari Alkatiri skilfully used the requirement for parliamentary ratification of any treaty as a means to stall acceptance of Australian demands. He introduced the Timor Sea treaty to the National Parliament, and on 25 November 2002 they started deliberations in preparation for its ratification. Later, in the afternoon, a member of the Office for Timor Sea Joint Development Area made a full presentation of the treaty. The Parliament was to take a long time to debate the treaty while the Prime Minister renegotiated it.

Mari Alkatiri was criticized for having agreed to even a 50–50 split, for there was a strong feeling that the area belonged to Timor-Leste. Nevertheless, the split still reflected great progress compared with Australia's original plan, and Alkatiri should be given full recognition for having defended the national interest of Timor-Leste. Finally, Alkatiri worked hard on a plan to establish a pipeline which would link to a refinery in Timor-Leste instead of to the one in Darwin, Australia. The oil refinery company ConocoPhillips claimed it would be very expensive, but Mari Alkatiri insisted, as it would create several thousand jobs. The Portuguese paper company Petrotimor sued ConocoPhillips for US$2.7 million for bribing the Prime Minister and parliament. It filed a suit in the District Court of Washington DC, but the case was dismissed.

It was initially estimated that the Timor Sea would provide oil and gas income for 17 years, at prevailing oil prices. The total revenue was estimated at almost US$1.7 billion for the lifespan of the whole resource.

The sustainable rate of government expenditure would have been only about US$100 million a year. Mari Alkatiri was very careful in his decision-making process, and felt that the revenue could be wasted, as people were not prepared for such an income stream. As Prime Minister, he expressed that he could wait, but the people wanted the revenue to be spent. Xanana Gusmão and Ramos-Horta preferred to spend as much as possible on building bridges, roads and other public works in order to create employment.

Mari Alkatiri established a "Norway Plus" Trust Fund with a Board of Directors for the management of oil resources, in New York. Money could be withdrawn from this account only with parliamentary approval; the government could not do it individually. NGOs and others spoke up in the local press against the position taken by the Government of Australia. There was considerable press coverage, and stories appeared asking why Australia was bullying such a little country.

Timor-Leste first signed the Timor Sea Treaty with Australia, which was to provide Timor-Leste with 90 per cent of revenues from the Treaty area. Prime Minister Alkatiri also signed the memorandum of understanding on the same day. This reflected the intention of both governments to conclude negotiations for the International Unitization Agreement by 31 December 2002. The second agreement, or the memorandum, stipulated arrangements for taxation, regulation and administration of the gas and oil in the Greater Sunrise Field.

The fruitful negotiations for the Timorese Government on the Timor Gap resonated as a demonstration of its ability to be seen as a serious player on the international scene. The Timorese leaders' unexpectedly strong reaction against Australian interests showed they were not intimated, despite their relative weakness.

Gaining trust and confidence among neighbouring countries

The President, Prime Minister and Foreign Minister were all energetic in promoting the relationship between Timor-Leste and its core partner countries, Australia, Indonesia and Portugal. In addition, they made concerted efforts to strengthen the economic ties with the ASEAN countries of China and Japan. Apart from their efforts to strengthen bilateral ties, the Timorese leaders recognized the importance of promoting the United Nations' efforts to prevent civil wars and genocides. For example, the Government of Timor-Leste supported a series of events organized by the United Nations for the International Day of Reflection on the 1994 Genocide in Rwanda.

On 7 April 2004, UNMISET held a memorial ceremony early in the morning. Director of Administration (DOA) Philip Cooper, Chief of

Staff Atul Khare, Deputy Force Commander Paul Retter, Acting UNPOL Commissioner Carlos Anastacio, with staff members of UNMISET and UN agencies and I, all participated in the ceremony. It began with a reading of the Secretary-General's message. A Rawandan survivor, Miss Violette Kabatesi, spoke about the experience of having lost all her family members in the 1994 Genocide. In my speech, I recounted the fact that I had served for nearly two years in Rwanda immediately after the genocide. I then emphasized the need to hold responsible not only the perpetrators of the crimes against humanity and genocide, but also those responsible for planning and organizing these crimes.

The National Parliament observed one minute of silence at noon. Later in the afternoon, the government and UNMISET launched a joint exhibition at the Hotel Timor, in the presence of President Gusmão, President of the National Parliament Francisco (Lú-Olo) Guterres and Prime Minister Alkatiri. Approximately 200 people participated. Representatives from the government, parliament, the church, diplomatic missions and the judiciary, as well as the UN system and civil society, took part in the event.

Prime Minister Alkatiri and President Gusmão expressed support for the initiative of the Secretary-General, as well as sympathy and solidarity with the people of Rwanda. The Prime Minister was emphatic about the need for a change in the United Nations' decision-making process in order to prevent genocide in the future. He even noted that many people would have died if due UN process had not been followed in the case of Timor-Leste. The Prime Minister then commended Australia for its role in the International Force for East Timor (INTERFET). The President mentioned the importance of reconciliation and tolerance in preventing genocide, in particular at high levels of the political leadership. He made reference to the CAVR public hearings that were held in December 2003. On this occasion, the political leadership of two major parties involved in the civil war in Timor-Leste admitted responsibility for crimes committed. Furthermore, they asked forgiveness from the people.

The following year, we decided to involve civil society more in fostering the spirit of peace. On 23 September 2005, the Timorese Government, civil society, church leaders and UNOTIL jointly organized a series of events in commemoration of the International Day of Peace. Typical of all commemorative events, it commenced with a public ceremony in the morning opened by Prime Minister Alkatiri. Representatives attended the event from the government, diplomatic corps, civil society and the United Nations. The afternoon activities included a March for Peace followed by a Peace Concert. The actual International Day of Peace was followed by a series of post-Peace Day events throughout the month of

October. The national press reported that the International Day of Peace was not only celebrated in Dili, but also that church leaders and communities organized peace vigils all across the country. Peace tree-planting ceremonies and musical events took place.

The October events began with a one-day national seminar entitled "Consolidation of Peace: The Role of Civil Society". This event involved political party leaders, the church, the media and civil society in four consecutive debates broadcast live on national television and radio.

From 14 to 24 October, the government hosted a photo exhibition entitled "The Face of Human Rights" in the national cultural centre. A special programme, including the screening of documentaries and poetry readings, were part of the exhibition. Further events included the commemoration of a number of international days, such as World Food Day on 16 October and the International Day for the Eradication of Poverty on 17 October. These led up to UN Day on 24 October. UNOTIL staff from appropriate sections played a full part in the planning and preparations for all these events.

Among the countries that extended invitations to Timorese leaders was Japan, which showed much interest in Timor-Leste. Even though there were no strategic ties between the two countries, Japan invited key Timorese leaders to Tokyo for official consultations. Foreign Minister Ramos-Horta's meeting with his Japanese counterpart Machimura, on 6 September 2005, was a good example of Ramos-Horta's successful efforts to gain the confidence of a major country in the region. Knowing of Japan's desire to become a permanent member of the Security Council of the United Nations, Ramos-Horta told Machimura that Timor-Leste strongly supported the G-4 proposal, and Japan's permanent membership of the Security Council. Ramos-Horta then conveyed his support for Thai Deputy Prime Minister Sathienthai for the post of the Secretary-General after Kofi Annan's departure.

Noting the importance of maintaining the cordial relationship between Timor-Leste and Indonesia, Ramos-Horta asked for Japan's support of the Commission of Truth and Friendship. He also sought Japan's support for UNDP institution-building projects to strengthen the capacity of government ministries, the parliament and judiciary. He expressed to the Japanese Foreign Minister that, while the mandate of UNOTIL would come to an end in May 2006, advisory assistance would continue to be needed, especially in the area of governance. Additionally, Ramos-Horta sought Japan's support for south–south cooperation for advisory assistance. It was noted that qualified advisors would possibly be provided from different Asian counties, such as Indonesia and Thailand, who could be funded by Japan. Foreign Minister Machimura endorsed the idea of south–south cooperation. He also commended the Timorese authorities for having achieved stability and tangible progress in democratic nation-building. He indicated to Ramos-Horta that the Japanese government would like to invite Prime Minister Alkatiri to visit Japan before the end of March 2006.

On the following day, 7 September, Foreign Minister Ramos-Horta visited Tokyo University and received an Honorary Doctorate in International Regional Development Studies. In awarding the doctorate degree, Professor Tomonori Matsuo, President of Tokyo University and Director of the Centre for Sustainable Development Studies, highlighted the major contributions made by Ramos-Horta in Timor-Leste's struggle for independence through 1999, and in democratic governance since the country regained its independence in 2002. Ramos-Horta gave a keynote speech on the topic of "A New Paradigm in International Cooperation". I also spoke on the topic of how the people and leaders of Timor-Leste succeeded in laying the foundation for sustainable democratic governance.

By the end of 2005, the Timorese leaders and people had demonstrated to the outside world that they were fully committed to peace. They were ready to build their country based on international norms and standards of decency. Nevertheless, the leaders also began to face the challenge of balancing national unity with a desire for supreme power and authority.

Notes

1. UNMISET provided this assistance as part of its overall objective of ensuring long-term security and stability of Timor-Leste according to the mandate given to UNMISET by Security Council Resolution 1410.
2. Bill of Pardons.
3. Report of the Secretary-General on the United Nations Mission of Support in East Timor, S/2002/1223, dated 6 November 2002.
4. As SRSG Sharma was abroad on an official mission, I participated in the meeting on his behalf.
5. KKN was an acronym of "corruption, collusion and nepotism", widely practised in Indonesia. Timor-Leste consisted of 13 districts, which were divided into sub-districts, which in turn had sucos and then aldeiras as the smallest unit.
6. CPD-RDTL/FRETILIN was a former resistance organization that surfaced after independence although it had been removed from the Forças Armadas de Libertação Nacional de Timor-Leste (FALINTIL, Armed Forces for the National Liberation of East Timor).
7. The group included Cornélio Gama ("Commander L7"), a high-profile guerrilla leader who fought with FALINTIL for over 20 years during the Indonesian occupation. Cornélio Gama L7 was a fierce nationalist and established a political party, Unidade Nacional Democratica da Resistancia Timorense (UNDERTIM, National Democratic Unity of Timorese Resistance) in 2005 and called for adoption of Tetum as the official national language and a new Timorese currency in place of the US dollar.

8. Forças Armadas da Libertação Nacional de Timor-Leste (FALINTIL) in Portuguese means the Armed Forces for the National Liberation of Timor-Leste in English.
9. I reviewed the issue with Prime Minister Alkatiri. He felt that the donor countries were providing support to the former Indonesian civil servants, who had acted as agents of the occupying power. In his mind, they did not deserve any support from the Timorese who suffered from the Indonesian rule.
10. UN Security Council 1272 (1999), 25 October 1999.
11. The conference took place from 8 to 10 September.
12. See the statement made in the National Parliament of Timor-Leste on 23 October 2003.
13. Investigation into Trafficking of Women for the Purpose of Prostitution in Timor-Leste (dated 21 August 2003).
14. Also other crops in the Fatubasin and Bobometo areas.
15. The "Timor Gap" is often used to refer to an area of ocean between Timor, Indonesia and Australia. In fact, it refers to a gap in a seabed boundary which Australia and Indonesia negotiated in 1972 – the part of the line they could not define because Portugal, which governed East Timor, declined to participate in the negotiations. East Timor subsequently came under Indonesian control, and Australia and Indonesia negotiated the Timor Gap Treaty in 1989. East Timor became independent in 2002, but has yet to establish maritime boundaries with its neighbouring countries, Indonesia and Australia. "The Timor Gap, Wonosobo and the Fate of Portuguese Timor", *Journal of the Royal Australian Historical Society*, vol. 88, pt. 1, June 2002, pp. 75–103.

III

Growing tensions in Timorese society

Emerging rivalry between two leaders of contrasting personalities

In 2002, the Timorese government and other state institutions assumed sovereignty and started to function in an atmosphere of jubilation, with smiling faces to be seen everywhere. In the early days, the leaders showed a spirit of confidence and tolerance towards one other. Yet, as in many other post-conflict countries, disharmony soon began to appear, and this developed into a schism between the two organs of governance. The rift began with an emerging difference of views and approaches advocated by the executive government and the National Parliament, dominated by FRETILIN and the Office of the President, respectively.

As the Timorese leaders wished to emphasize, they had "restored" political independence on 20 May 2002, for FRETILIN had declared independence back on 28 November 1975 and named the country República Democrática de Timor Leste (RDTL, Democratic Republic of Timor-Leste), with members of FRETILIN holding 55 of 88 seats in the National Parliament. This gave them dominant control over the government and the National Parliament, under the leadership of Mari Alkatiri as Prime Minister and Francisco "Lú-Olo" Guterres as the President of the National Assembly. As mentioned already, Mari Alkatiri was an intellectual with a strong spirit of independence and possessing enormous pride and confidence. A tireless worker who was relentless in the pursuit of his goals and interests, he worked day and night towards the end of his term.

Primordial leadership: Peacebuilding and national ownership in Timor-Leste, Hasegawa,
United Nations University Press, 2013, ISBN 978-92-808-1224-4

His approach was to safeguard his authority and independence at any cost, and he did not mind being disliked or unloved; his frame of reference was himself. Above all, he was driven to acquire and consolidate his authority and power, and as long as he retained these, none of his cabinet ministers or subordinates showed any sign of disrespect towards him. He exercised strict discipline among his cabinet ministers and ensured that they followed his instructions studiously.

However, in 2002 it was clear that power was still held by Xanana Gusmão. He had both the respect and affection of almost the entire Timorese population, due to his enduring leadership through the long struggle for independence. It was he who continued fighting Indonesian troops in the 1980s with only a few hundred freedom fighters,[1] until he was captured and imprisoned in 1992. Gusmão was a man of exceptional "emotional intelligence".[2] He was a fighter who exuded personal warmth, dealing with people with trust and affection, loving them and enjoying being loved. This relationship was most important to him, for his frame of reference was Timorese society and people. In our conversations he often stressed that he had fought for the independence of the Timorese people for 24 years and that they deserved a better life. He felt he had achieved his goal with the departure of the Indonesian troops, and wanted to retire as a champion of the independence struggle. It appeared to me that he saw himself as the Nelson Mandela of Timor-Leste.[3] On 12 June 2002 he delivered his first presidential address on the State of the Nation, praising the people for their endurance, but then reportedly criticizing the performance of the government. Giving the government a six-month period to improve its performance, this symbolic exercise of his presidential power reflected his understanding of the President's role.

When I arrived in Dili to start my assignment on 15 July 2002, Alkatiri was in Oecussi. Several ministers and senior government officials, including the Ministers of Internal Administration and Finance, the Vice-Minister for Foreign Affairs and Cooperation, and the Secretary of State for the Council of Ministers, had accompanied him. The delegation visited Junction Point (JP) 2, Bobometo, where the commander of the Korean battalion briefed the Prime Minister. Other officers briefed the Prime Minister on the problems associated with the levying of taxes, the lack of communication equipment, transport difficulties and health concerns in the area.

After Bobometo, Alkatiri went to hold two meetings in Oecussi with the heads of the departments and representatives of civil society. He announced that the Council of Ministers would hold an open meeting in Oecussi in September. Soon, this "open governance" became a high-profile exercise for both the Prime Minister and his government ministers. The idea was for him to visit and meet local inhabitants to ascertain opinions at the district level, and was very much in line with the advice Special Representative of the Secretary-General (SRSG) Sharma had given that he should get out of the capital city of Dili more frequently, and meet the people in rural areas. He conveyed to me his intent to visit districts and rural areas more often, so he could engage in dialogue with local inhabitants and learn their needs and demands for assistance from the government.

At his invitation, I accompanied him and his ministers to several of the open governance visits he made to 13 districts in a period of two years. As a large number of local inhabitants showed up to meet him, Alkatiri became confident that "the open governance" exercise was successful in solidifying his control of districts. He was enthusiastic about the initiative, and even stayed as long as one week at a time in a district.

It is noteworthy that Alkatiri felt strongly about having ownership of the Constitution, which, he reminded me on several occasions, he had drafted himself. He insisted that he not only knew each and every sentence and phrase, but also that he understood its spirit. The message was clear: nobody else should question his authority over the meaning of any clause of the Constitution, and he had the right to judge the constitutionality of any action taken by the government. He indeed used the Constitution and its provisions to secure legal justification for his conduct of governmental affairs. Regardless of popularly accepted norms and beliefs, which were important in a primitive community like Timor-Leste, he was convinced of the correctness of his intuitive insight. He was also a fast learner of any measures that he needed to take to strengthen his authority.

Gusmão was convinced that he was the true guardian of democracy and the genuine interests of the people. Prior to his departure to attend a conference in Fiji,[4] he held a press conference at the airport, when he read a short statement announcing that he had promulgated the bill on the national budget for the fiscal year 2002–2003. He stressed that, although he had approved the budget, he had some reservations about it and stated that his approval was conditional on a budgetary review by parliament. He then said that this parliamentary review should be open to wide participation by civil society organizations, for it was crucially important to involve civil society in the development of national policy. Gusmão reminded the members of parliament, especially those from FRETILIN, that they were representatives of the whole population and should not just follow blindly those in power. He also called on opposition parties to become more responsible and effective, instead of wasting time with petty political arguments. He emphasized that the government must implement the budget wisely, because it was accountable to both the public and the donor community. The tone of Gusmão's speech reflected his belief that he was the true leader of the people, regardless of the legal and organizational constraints imposed on him by the Constitution and the government.[5]

Upon his return from Fiji, Gusmão exercised his constitutional power for the first time. On 19 July he vetoed the taxation bill, which was then sent back to parliament for reconsideration. Gusmão asserted that the bill was intended simply to raise revenue to cover public expenditure. Instead, he proposed a restructuring of income tax rates and lowering of public expenditure through greater efficiency and elimination of corruptive practices.

For many in UNMISET and the diplomatic community, Gusmão's statement sounded rather confrontational, although his criticism was justified. To me, having just arrived in Dili, the president's assertion of political power appeared to reflect the overwhelming trust and confidence of the people that he enjoyed as their independence hero. However, the short time frame he gave to the government to prove itself seemed to some an impossible demand. There were some concerns that the differences between the two top leaders might spark political confrontation. The majority of the Timorese leaders had shown remarkable restraint and a spirit of tolerance. However, those close to the President explained to me that he was trying to dampen expectations about his role as the President, rather than raise them. The reactions to the President's speech, from both the Prime Minister and the President of the National Parliament, were surprisingly conciliatory and accommodating. Therefore, initially it appeared to outside observers that the Timorese people and leaders readily accepted Gusmão's advice and instructions.

Another key leader who was to become President of Timor-Leste in 2007 was the Nobel Peace Prize laureate José Ramos-Horta. Ramos-Horta was also a man of very high emotional intelligence. He was very committed to the well-being of the country and the people of Timor-Leste. His approach was pragmatic, and he tried to find a practical solution to any given problem, being aware that sometimes a workable solution to any complicated problem required a compromise, along with a change in perception and approach. He had a rational mind, but was emotional at heart. His frame of reference was the international community and more specifically the United Nations, believing in the universal values and principles it established, and specifically those defined in the Universal Declaration of Human Rights. Ramos-Horta repeatedly demonstrated his concern for upholding these values.

A first sign of the discord that led to schism in the Timorese leadership began to emerge in late 2002. President Gusmão spoke at the government's ceremony commemorating independence day on 28 November 2002.[6] He was highly critical of FRETILIN as a whole, saying that he saw a "disease" spreading whereby the ruling party attempted to place cadres into government posts to satisfy its supporters. He then created an uproar by demanding the dismissal of Minister for Internal Administration Rogério Lobato on the grounds of incompetence and neglect. Alkatiri reacted to this demand by stating that he was the Prime Minister who had appointed his ministers, including Minister Rogério Lobato, and that only he had the right and authority to dismiss any of them. He then added that he did not plan to make any changes to his cabinet members. Alkatiri later explained to me that he would not dismiss Rogério Lobato for personal as well as constitutional reasons; Lobato was a brother of independence leader Nicholau Lobato, who was most highly respected by all Timorese people. Furthermore, Rogério was a close and long-time associate since the very first FRETILIN government was formed in 1975.[7] According to UNMISET political officers, the Prime Minister was reportedly dependent on Lobato's support within FRETILIN.

In early 2003, opposition parties began to make attempts to counter the growing dominance of FRETILIN. Member of Parliament Carrascalão claimed that FRETILIN had lured away the Partido Social Democrático (PSD, Social Democratic Party) Vice-President with a promise of a ministerial posting that never materialized. He denounced similar tactics of co-option that were allegedly being used against the Partido Democrático (PD, Democratic Party), the second-largest party in parliament. Carrascalão described efforts made by some of the minority parties, namely PSD, PD and União Democrática Timorense (UDT, Timorese Democratic Union) and some of the smaller parties, to form some sort of coalition or common platform in an effort to resist the dominance of FRETILIN in government and parliament.

A series of meetings had been held to discuss this over the past few months. However, given the internal difficulties of the individual parties, forming a cohesive coalition seemed difficult. Several Alkatiri loyalists within FRETILIN described these meetings as evidence that the opposition parties were guilty of creating instability by trying to undermine the government. PD leader Fernando La Sama de Araújo complained that his party's efforts to expand its presence into sub-districts had been met by accusations from the FRETILIN leadership that PD was "planning a coup" against the government. I felt that this was yet another indication that the role of legitimate opposition parties was not yet understood nor accepted.

In April 2003, some tension emerged within the government leadership. The senior minister and Minister of Foreign Affairs, José Ramos-Horta, addressing a group of Portuguese businessmen in Lisbon, publicly criticized his government's decision to charge fees for issuing visas to foreigners entering Timor-Leste. He maintained that the government's new visa policy was counterproductive to encouraging foreign investment, and that the new policy procedures were too cumbersome to be implemented smoothly.

Ramos-Horta made this assertion as the government sought to amend a United Nations Transitional Administration in East Timor (UNTAET) Regulation, whereby a 90-day visa was granted to all foreigners entering the country. In practice, however, a new policy had already been implemented, with foreigners entering Timor-Leste on the limited basis of a maximum of 30 days. This was then subject to time-consuming bureaucratic procedures for extensions. Ramos-Horta instead advocated a policy of total openness, with strict checks at border posts. His comments and suggestions brought a swift and angry reaction from Alkatiri, who declared that all ministers were expected to exercise absolute institutional discipline and that Ramos-Horta's statements were unacceptable. Ramos-Horta responded that he would not withdraw his remarks, going a step further by suggesting that he disagreed with Alkatiri on other matters as well, and stating that the government had many faults and weaknesses at several levels. Many of us in the diplomatic circle were surprised by the public exchange of the two contrasting views by the two leaders.

Gusmão also began to demand publicly that Alkatiri should exercise "good governance" practices. He made this call during the third week of his semi-official visit to Australia. While not attacking the government directly, in a speech to public administration officials in Melbourne, he focused on his now very familiar theme of "local power and good governance" which he wanted to elevate as part of his "open presidency". His stated that his intention was to make sure that the grass roots community and local organizations were listened to in his forthcoming second National Dialogue. This was apparently a clear challenge to the government, for Xanana Gusmão's message was that there was no other forum for constructive debate and dialogue other than the National Dialogue. This move did little to ease the sense of tension between him and the Prime Minister.

In May 2003, President Gusmão continued to press his demand that the government live up to the expectation of the people and perform better. The President's speech on 20 May was the featured event of the government's celebration of Independence Day, being reported and discussed widely in the districts. As with previous speeches, in some areas he was critical of the government and its institutions. For example, Gusmão said that the public had confidence in court officials, but that the latter needed to strip themselves of xenophobia and devote themselves more assiduously to their duties. He said the Prime Minister's open governance initiative deserved praise, but added that it reflected the absence of a system of governance that was more effective in fulfilling the needs of people. He stated that the public was meant to benefit from democratic governance instituted after independence. However, democracy was being used to constrain the people, in order to protect the personal gains of certain leaders. A large part of the speech was devoted to the need for effective local government. Gusmão presented it as a medicine for a wide range of problems, such as nepotism, urban migration and local socio-economic issues. Part of this was couched in the language of self-help, with calls for the population to become less dependent on the State. However, Gusmão's call was remind the government of the need to perform better, as a higher authority was there to assess its performance.

It is noteworthy that the President Gusmão's speech reflected his conviction that he was the ultimate guardian of the people's welfare and the highest authority to evaluate the performance of the government. This belief was shared as legitimate by many who had lived with him through the struggle against the occupation by Indonesia. Yet Gusmão did not realize that he should not take for granted that in a democratic system of governance, the power to rule the country and the authority to determine what is good for the people, were held by the dominant political party that ruled the government and the National Parliament. As was seen later, the Prime Minister would challenge the President in asserting the right to rule the country as he saw fit. The Prime Minister was more aware than the President that in democracy there is a constant struggle for power, conducted without the use of guns and other means of violence, which may result in rivalry and non-violent conflict.

In spite of growing signs of rivalry, President Gusmão and Prime Minister Alkatiri maintained a remarkable degree of congeniality and mutual accommodation. They talked and joked a great deal in public. Underneath the surface of tolerance and understanding, however, Gusmão began to harbour a sense of frustration with the manner in which some decisions were made by Alkatiri without prior consultation with him. Subtle schism also began to emerge between the President and the Forças Armadas de Libertação Nacional de Timor-Leste (FALINTIL, Armed Forces for the National Liberation of East Timor) – Forças Armadas de Defesa de Timor-Leste (F-FDTL) commander, Tau Matan Ruak (TMR).

On 18 August 2003, Xanana Gusmão informed SRSG Sharma that he was cancelling his plan to participate in the FALINTIL Day celebration in Waimori (the last camp of FRETILIN). The President first said that there were many independence-related and national celebrations in the annual calendar and that FALINTIL Day was just one of them. He then noted that he was required to proceed to Covalima District on 20 August to meet and have a constructive dialogue with people describing themselves as Conselho Popular pela Defesa da República Democrática de Timor-Leste (CPD-RDTL, Popular Committee for Defence of the Democratic Republic of Timor-Leste) and other activists, before the reconciliation meeting scheduled to take place in Salele on 22 August.

The President contended that the Waimori event was not important enough to require his personal participation, whereas his presence in Covalima and personal encounters with disgruntled members of society were essential to maintaining stability in the country. In Gusmão's mind, it would be of significance that he received some firearms that were being surrendered. Also important to him were assurances of future good behaviour, and these were key to preventing such people from disturbing the meeting in Salele. Gusmão then explained in detail the vital role he had played in reconciling the differences between the expectations of CPD-RDTL and other groups.

SRSG Sharma was a highly experienced diplomat with an ability to see what was in the mind of his interlocutor and the will to express his views firmly and clearly when necessary. He told the President about the importance of his presence at the Waimori event as Commander-in-Chief of F-FDTL. His absence would cause unavoidable speculation in public about the discord within the leadership. Referring to the recent unhelpful political debates carried out in the media, Sharma furthermore told Gusmão the undesirability of giving a wrong impression to the public, which suggested that leadership at the highest level was not working closely. Sharma emphasized that stability had to be maintained at any cost, with which the President agreed. Sharma then urged Xanana Gusmão to maintain his scheduled appearance at the celebration in Waimori, even if it was brief, and offered to take him on the helicopter to Waimori and then to Suai.

Being pressed to go to Waimori, the President told Sharma that he had been led to understand by F-FDTL Commander Brigadier General TMR that his presence was not entirely necessary for the FALINTIL Day celebration in Waimori. It was a subtle message sent by TMR that, if the President were not available, he himself would still proceed to Waimori with the Prime Minister and the President of the National Parliament. This was taken as a sign by the President that he was not really needed. It also indicated where TMR was heading. Furthermore, the President admitted that he had heard about the Waimori event for the first time from SRSG Sharma and not from Commander TMR.

The President was clearly irritated at what he perceived to be neglect of his authority, and dissociated himself from the plan to bring the remains of martyrs from Waimori and create a heroes' cemetery near the main F-FDTL camp in Metinaro, describing the idea as culturally inappropriate. He declared himself in favour of a national monument which could be created over time, on which the names of all martyrs could be inscribed, like the Vietnam Veterans Memorial in Washington.

The President eventually accepted SRSG Sharma's advice and the offer of UN air transport, sharing Sharma's view on the need to maintain the morale of former independence fighters and the F-FDTL. The President and the SRSG then travelled together to Waimori in the morning of 20 August and then later proceeded to Covalima after his appearance for a couple of hours at the FALINTIL celebration.

These developments created some unease. TMR, accompanied by the Prosecutor-General, had met Sharma and talked about the celebrations and cemetery idea. Sharma had taken it for granted that TMR was acting in close consultation with the President, for TMR was a loyal and respectful person and both Xanana Gusmão and he were the main pillars of FALINTIL. All of us in the UN mission were worried that if a rift developed between Xanana Gusmão and TMR, it would have serious implications for stability.

Consolidation and centralization of the power of governance

Shortly after the formation of the first constitutional government in May 2002, FRETILIN attempted to consolidate its power throughout all of Timor-Leste's institutions. This reflected its desire for consolidating power as far back as the pre-independence period of the UNTAET administration.

In forming the constituent assembly, UNTAET ensured there was proper geographical representation in the distribution of seats. Of the 88 seats in parliament, 13 were reserved for the representatives of 13 districts. The Timorese leaders were, however, unconvinced of the need for representation of regional and district interests. FRETILIN in particular wanted to establish a strong governance structure, and did not find any merit in establishing a special bench for district representatives. Therefore, the party insisted on limiting the district representation to 13 seats.

During the first months of parliamentary sessions, smaller opposition groups spoke out on the content of a number of bills. However, they were overruled by FRETILIN which had the majority. At best, there was insufficient time allowed for their consideration, because all draft laws were available only in Portuguese. This was a language that most people, particularly younger parliamentarians, generally did not understand. The parliamentary committees considered a number of complex bills such as nationality, amnesty, judicial magistrate statutes and maritime boundaries.

The second-largest party in the National Parliament was the PD. It issued a note rejecting Prime Minister Alkatiri's statement on 2 July 2002 that FRETILIN was the only party in a position to rule the country. The PD leader, Fernando La Sama de Araújo complained that the government behaved as if it cared little for the feelings of the people, and argued that the government was not paying sufficient attention for the welfare of common people. He criticized the government for increasing import taxes, which would raise the prices of commodities for ordinary people. He was also critical of the pensions for former Indonesian civil servants, the growing number of illegal foreign workers and the rising number of prostitutes of different nationalities in Dili.[8]

La Sama's criticism of FRETILIN's arrogant manner of governance did not bother Alkatiri, who was not mindful that his attitude was alienating an increasing number of former independence fighters who had not been included in the government. As his confidence increased, Alkatiri began to act without due concern for the criticisms of others. This led other government officials to pay limited attention to the grievances of people about their exclusion from government jobs and other unfair treatment. Furthermore, the Prime Minister and certain cabinet members viewed some demands as hostile acts, and dismissed them as unworthy of their attention. This continued until the government was forced to address issues, such when petitioners called for an end to discrimination in 2006.

At the same time as being an executive eager to increase the efficiency of the administration, Mari Alkatiri also had genuine interest in strengthening the institutional capacity of his government. When he spoke to me at the airport on the occasion of President Gusmão's departure on 6 November 2002, he indicated that he greatly appreciated the workshop held on the role and functions of international advisers. He thought it was helpful in bringing out the requirements for transfer of skills and capacity building. He was pleased to learn that Sweden was willing to provide the equivalent of $3.2 million for technical assistance, without any conditions attached. He was also pleased to hear that the Swedish Ambassador was emphatic about the negative impact of "cherry picking" that many donors indulged in. The government, Alkatiri said, wanted to identify priority needs that would be met with the use of generous funds. He was in a relaxed mood and confidant that others, including the President, accepted his strong leadership. The Prime Minister later told me "the relationship between the President and me was now quite good".[9]

Alkatiri conveyed to me his intention to visit districts and rural areas more frequently, mentioning that he planned to stay for a week at a time in a district. This was to allow him to talk with local inhabitants, and to learn their needs for government assistance. As I expressed my support of the idea, Alkatiri suggested that I accompany him to Atauro Island the following week, and I agreed.[10] He then referred to the demand made by the people of Dili for an electric power supply, and proudly shared the news that Norway had agreed to provide emergency assistance to restore additional power supply. This Norwegian supply came with a metering system that would help recover the cost of power production and distribution.

Apart from the extreme poverty that existed throughout Timor-Leste, key concerns for Timorese leadership were the veterans and other independence fighters. There were big differences in views on how to proceed with defining the veterans and compensating them. The President had started working on the issue by constituting commissions. Prime Minister Alkatiri recognized the need to move forward with defining veterans. He suggested that all Timorese principal players, including the President, the Prime Minister, the Foreign Minister, the Minister of Internal Administration and the Speaker of the Parliament, speak with one voice. This directive was so the international community would be provided with consistent views. Especially noteworthy was the demonstration of the magnitude of tasks that needed to be carried out in recognition of veterans. Alkatiri said the government should address the issues, and then carry out necessary activities with the international community's support.

In December 2003, the government concentrated in the preparation for the third Timor-Leste Development Partners Meeting (TLDPM), which was attended by about 30 bilateral and multilateral development supporters. In his opening statement, Alkatiri made it clear that he was in the driver's seat and in control of the country. As in previous meetings, he had the strong support of the World Bank, which amplified this sense of authority. In this meeting, the last before the completion of UNMISET's mandate, Alkatiri took the opportunity to distance himself from UNMISET, strongly asserting his independent authority *vis-à-vis* the United Nations. He told delegates that the Polícia Nacional de Timor-Leste (PNTL, National Police of Timor-Leste) was assuming increasing responsibilities, as the United Nations was reducing the strength of its peacekeeping forces and police personnel. By January 2004, he said, PNTL would take over command from the United Nations Police (UNPOL).

Alkatiri appeared more confident than ever of his power and authority. He did not hesitate to go beyond the prepared statement, and to chastise UNMISET on three occasions in his opening statement. First, he reminded the development partners that political stability had been achieved just 18 months after the inauguration of his government, or one year after the riots of December 2002. He became so emboldened that he blamed the delegates of the UN peacekeeping forces for the poor state of the roads throughout the country, particularly in the border districts. His government was launching a Special Preventive Development Programme that would focus on the need to strengthen security and development. With regard to the posts of 100 advisers funded by the regular UN budget and 200 development advisers supported by bilateral and multilateral donors, he criticized long delays in their recruitment and the inadequate capabilities of some of them in mentoring their counterpart nationals. He even laughed at the United Nations for having brought in vehicles which fell apart easily. The Prime Minister's accusations of the United Nations were accompanied by a carefully planned visit with international media in tow, to his house, which had burned down on 4 December 2002 during the riots. Alkatiri reminded everyone that it was a result of poor UN police performance and would never have happened under his control.[11]

Following the proclamation of the Law on the Restructuring of the Government on 29 June 2005, the Prime Minister was expected to announce the composition of the new government in late July, upon his return from an official visit to Portugal. On 27 July, Alkatiri announced the new cabinet ministerial appointment as well as changes in his own responsibility. He relinquished the Development and Environment portfolios, and took charge of the new Ministry for Natural Resources, Minerals and Energy Policy. In addition to five new ministers, he appointed five new Secretaries of State for the five regions to report directly to him. This signified his intention to strengthen his control over regional affairs. The Cabinet, including vice-ministers and secretaries of state, now had a total of 41 members.

The new ministers were Arsenio Bano for Labour and Community Reinsertion; Roque Rodrigues, who was previously a Secretary for Defence, and was now elevated to the full rank of minister; Vice-Minister Abel Ximenes was also promoted to the rank of minister to replace Prime Minister Alkatiri who had held the position of Minister for Development and Environment before; Odete Vitor was brought in as the new Minister of Public Works; and Antoninho Bianco, who became the new minister in the Presidency of the Council of Ministers. The new appointees in the Cabinet also included four Secretaries of State, who were to act as regional coordinators for four new regions, encompassing 12 of the 13 districts. The 13th district, Oecusse, had been granted special autonomy; it was to be overseen by a new Secretary of State, whose title was "Resident of Oecusse".

There were also three new Secretaries of State: for the Council of Ministers, for Coordination of the Environment, and for Youth and Sports. All new Secretaries of State reported directly to Prime Minister Alkatiri. His decision to keep the new Ministry of Natural Resources, Minerals and Energy Policy directly under him was no doubt intended to give him greater control of matters related to oil and energy resources. Also, he had more power over developments in the Districts through the new Secretaries of State for the regions.

It is worth noting that while most of the Cabinet members came from or had close ties to FRETILIN, two of the new members of the Cabinet selected by the Prime Minister, namely the Minister of Public Works and the Vice-Minister of Development, had strong ties to the opposition party, PD. Significantly, all of the newly appointed regional coordinators were FRETILIN members. Also significant was that the matters related to youth and sports were no longer under the portfolio of the Ministry of Education.

In a post-conflict country, there is a tendency to bring in as many followers as possible to government positions. This political move is made in order to provide them with employment and authority, and is perhaps necessary to keep opposition party leaders in a coalition government and to maintain peace and stability. In the case of the Alkatiri Government, it was necessitated by the Prime Minister's desire to reward the faithful with senior government positions, and to consolidate his control of governmental power.

On 28 July 2005, the national police reportedly carried out operations for several days against the political group CPD-RDTL. Premises had been searched without warrants, and there were allegations that the police had committed human rights violations against CPD-RDTL members. Based on the report that operations had been ordered by the Prime Minister, I immediately went to see him, and asked why he had authorized such an operation. He was clearly irritated by my questioning and insisted that police had only been told to stop acts of intimidation by CPD-RDTL, such as raising the FRETILIN flag.

Contrary to the Prime Minister's explanation, it was alarming to me that the government was ready to disregard the law, when they wished to take action against those with a different political view from that of the ruling party. A nationally coordinated police operation had also been conducted in Baucau and Los Palos Districts against members of CPD-RDTL.

From 22 to 26 July, the police searched 12 CPD-RDTL compounds in three sub-districts in Baucau. CPD-RDTL members in the compounds at the time of the operation were then unlawfully detained during the search operation. One CPD-RDTL meeting was broken up by the police, who, CPD-RDTL alleged, fired warning shots as people fled the meeting. Three CPD-RDTL members were then arrested by PNTL without any clear reason, although they were released later the same day. There were also allegations of human rights violations by PNTL against members of CPD-RDTL during the operation. CPD-RDTL claimed that several of their members had been subjected to ill-treatment during the PNTL operation, including being punched, kicked, grabbed around the neck and slapped.

During the search operation, the police confiscated documents and items owned by CPD-RDTL members, including membership documents, correspondence, machetes and knives. On other occasions, police reportedly stopped CPD-RDTL members in the street and searched them, confiscating items such as machetes and documents. PNTL claimed to have found items such as military uniforms, boots, blankets, berets, machetes, knives, flags, and bows and arrows. PNTL also informed UNPOL that they found one Kalashnikov AK rifle and 40 rounds of ammunition, which were last known to have been held in the former FALINTIL compound in Aileu. CPD-RDTL members were also told by the PNTL that they could not raise the RDTL flag in CPD-RDTL compounds.

Upon receipt of the report, I immediately took the issue up with the Prime Minister, who insisted that he had ordered the police to stop CPD-RDTL from harassing and even harming people. He referred to a violent incident involving CPD-RDTL members and villagers in the town of Com in Lautem District on 22 July, which reportedly left two villagers seriously injured and led to the arrest of at least six CPD-RDTL members.

The PNTL operations were conducted without the proper legal authority: to our knowledge, the searches were all conducted without warrants. It appeared that there had been no involvement by the Office of the Prosecutor-General or the Court. When I asked the Chief Justice of the Court of Appeal, Cláudio de Jesus Ximenes, he told me that he had heard about the incident only in general terms. Most of the goods confiscated during the search operations were not prohibited items. It was unclear as to what illegal activities CPD-RDTL members were accused of. Police reported that they had removed CPD-RDTL documents, including some files proposing shadow governments that had been found in some of the premises, but had not filed any charges.

In response to my probing, PNTL General Commander Paulo Martins insisted that no serious mistakes had been made. Nevertheless, he had reportedly issued a written order to PNTL to conduct search operations of CPD-RDTL branches in Baucau and Los Palos. He had also reportedly ordered a search of CPD-RDTL members in the compounds. Apart from the fact that the police were acting without a proper legal basis, the operations revealed the government's tendency to disregard legal requirements when taking action against those with a differing political view from that of the ruling party. I instructed UNPOL, as well as the United Nations Office in Timor-Leste (UNOTIL) Human Rights Unit (HRU) to monitor the situation. I also wrote a letter to Prime Minister Alkatiri to voice my concern about the police actions. These events paved the way for the imminent abuse of power and violent confrontation among the contenders for power.

The CPD-RDTL letter dated 29 July 2005 was addressed to the UN Secretary-General, the General Assembly, the Security Council and other international institutions. Its contents described CPD-RDTL's version of the police operations in Baucau. It demanded that the United Nations should act in order to end what CPD-RDTL described as "brutal and in-humane acts" carried out by the police. It remained unclear whether the police would continue their operations against CPD-RDTL locations.

On 4 August, police officers removed CPD-RDTL signposts from two CPD-RDTL branches in Suai District. This time, there were no reports of maltreatment by the PNTL. It seemed that my petition to the Prime Minister and the CPD-RDTL's letter to the UN Secretary-General had had some effect on the government controlling police actions.

Growing public confusion and disenchantment

In November 2003, a first national opinion poll was conducted by the International Republican Institute (IRI), a US-funded NGO. The opinion surveys were carried out with 1,500 randomly selected residents of Timor-Leste, who were interviewed by students from 14 September to 3 October 2003. IRI had trained these students, who had been recruited from the University of Dili. Multi-stage sampling was used to select *sucos* and *aldeias* from each of Timor-Leste's 13 districts to be included in the sample.

The outcome of these opinion surveys revealed the perception of common people of the conduct of national leaders. The results showed that the ordinary people perceived most of the leaders and state institutions positively, and the overall prospect for democracy was also positive. At the same time, they were dissatisfied with economic stagnation, and specifically the lack of employment opportunities. Common people also felt that corruption or KKN had worsened during the previous year.[12] While the President was seen by 28 per cent of the respondents as doing a "very good" and 62 per cent a "good" job, the Prime Minister was viewed by 4 per cent as "very good" and 49 per cent "good".

The poll results were released at a seminar held on 11 November. FRETILIN reportedly declined an invitation to participate in a panel discussion at the seminar. FRETILIN party President Lú Olo had made a critical and dismissive response the previous day. However, the government was well served by Foreign Minister Ramos-Horta's comments. Ramos-Horta rightly criticized the poll for failing to ask questions about the functioning of the government while focusing instead on the popularity of the President, the Prime Minister and other personalities.

There were many questions about the methodology used for gaining opinions, and IRI admitted that the language issue was not handled well. All questions were in the Indonesian language and some 100 students from the University of Dili who had carried out the survey were given a two-day training course on how to translate the concepts from Indonesian into the relevant language on the ground. This could have resulted in discrepancies. Despite its obvious methodological drawbacks, the poll produced some tangible and significant revelations about the public perception of national leaders and state institutions.

First, the opinion poll results revealed that most people still thought about the leaders in terms of their personalities, and contributions made during the resistance period, rather than their performance since independence. The bishops and President Gusmão, who had not been directly involved in governance, were still highly regarded and popular. Gusmão was regarded as the leader most able to resolve the problems ranging from security to health and education.

Second, these results reflected a lack of understanding by common people about the exact roles of state institutions. Although Alkatiri was better recognized, his favourable rating of 53 per cent was well below that of Ramos Horta, who received 83 per cent. Although Alkatiri's rating was not as low in comparison with the ratings received by national leaders in any of the developed countries, he took the result of the opinion polls rather personally and negatively. The IRI was accused of trying to inaccurately project the perception of the Timorese people and the international community of the political situation in Timor-Leste.

Third, in spite of the shortcomings of the opinion polls, they did reveal the general sentiment of the population about the popularity of political parties. According to the IRI surreys, PD and PSD would be expected to obtain about 23 per cent of the vote if national elections were held then. This compared with a total of 28 per cent received by three parties, the PSD and Associação Social Democráta Timorense (ASDT, Social Democratic Association of Timor- Leste) (15.7 per cent), and PD (11.3 per cent) in 2007. The total votes received by PSD and PD were estimated to be around 22–23 per cent. The ASDT could have received 4–5 per cent of the total votes.[13]

As a whole, the results of the opinion surveys indicated that the ordinary people overall had a basically positive perception of most of the leaders and state institutions. They also saw positive prospects for democracy to grow, and to solve the problems they were facing. At the same time, they were disenchanted with the economic stagnation, lack of employment and increasing corruption.

While the survey results were revealing, there was a need for caution in accepting their accuracy. For example, Ágio Pereira, the then Chief of Staff of the Office of the President, and other commentators pointed out it was rather implausible for PNTL to receive as much as 73 per cent, F-FDTL 86 per cent and the United Nations 87 per cent of public endorsement. Ágio Pereira further noted that IRI's claims that the population had a very positive attitude towards the future of democracy needed further analysis. He also mentioned that the Timorese people had very little understanding of their democratic institutions such as the National Parliament. The respondents gave the National Parliament a very high rating of 67 per cent for carrying out a "good" and a "very good" job.[14]

Ágio Pereira was a quiet person but, I found, had the rare ability to penetrate the surface of events and identify the forces that were at work beneath. He had a strong will to carry out difficult duties and responsibilities he believed in, sticking to his values with passionate conviction, although he seldom expressed them vocally. He judged events by his inner ideals and personal values, and while he was tolerant and flexible in everyday work, he would not change his position if one of his inner loyalties and values was threatened. He had little desire to dominate others, but his devotion to his duty, and responsibility to the people and the country, generated much trust and confidence among those who worked closely with him.

On 5 December 2003 the newspaper Suara Timor Lorosae published an op-ed piece entitled "KKN Is the Root of All Evils". It spoke in general terms about the possibility of corrupt behaviour of officials and businessmen in Timor-Leste, drawing on comparisons with other countries. However, the op-ed did make a severe criticism of a "Maputo Club" within the FRETILIN political party. This harsh accusation prompted the Prime Minister to threaten the editor with a lawsuit.[15]

For several months starting in March 2004, stories of corruption were popular items appearing frequently on front pages. The suit filed in the United States by Oceanic Exploration against ConocoPhillips dominated headlines for weeks. Although the suit did not specifically name any East Timorese politicians as defendants, it alleged that the Prime Minister and members of the National Parliament received bribes from Conoco-Phillips. FRETILIN immediately issued strong denials. It is noteworthy that several politicians openly showed strong support of Prime Minister Alkatiri. Foreign Minister Ramos-Horta called the allegations an insult against the dignity and integrity of the Prime Minister, whom he had known personally for over 30 years. No members of the National Parliament publicly admitted any involvement. Yet, most unexpectedly, President Xanana Gusmão spoke in public and admitted that he had been offered and accepted 12 vehicles for the Conselho Nacional de Reconstrução de Timor (CNRT, National Congress for Timorese Reconstruction), which was headed by him as its president. There was no way to verify if the CNRT or any other entity accepted anything else.

On a positive note for Prime Minister Alkatiri, Aderito de Jesus Soares, a former FRETILIN member of the Constituent Assembly and human rights lawyer, agreed to represent him and members of parliament in a defamation suit. The strong backing of Alkatiri by President Gusmão and Foreign Minister Ramos-Horta helped to ensure the international community's ongoing confidence in the Alkatiri Government. Furthermore, four years later La'o Hamutuk, a respected non-governmental research institute, stated on its website that little hard evidence had been found and "prosecutors in the United States, Australia and elsewhere did not find the (Oceanic's) allegations of bribery, racketeering and corruption credible enough to bring alleged perpetrators to trial".[16] Nonetheless, for some time in 2004, the negative public image created became a serious problem for Alkatiri. Ordinary Timorese often mistakenly thought that the government leaders were receiving an inordinate amount of money from business. Regardless of the facts, continuing coverage of this case fed public perception that government funds were being signed off by corrupt government officials.

Most unfortunately for the Prime Minister, the allegations of corruption began to create a vicious cycle of accusations and counter-accusations, poisoning the political atmosphere. The opposition parties tried to obtain as much coverage of their allegations as possible in the print media, calling for the Prime Minister to step down. This hardened Alkatiri's will to counteract the opposition party leaders with threats of lawsuits that would employ a defamation clause against those who were accusing him.[17] The PSD stated that two of its members had received such threats via their mobile phones, claiming that these threats were connected to their calls for the Prime Minister to step down.

As growing concerns emerged over the use of defamation, the Prime Minister became determined to enact a defamation law. Key civil society players had privately expressed their concerns on the likely criminalization of defamation in the Penal Code. In an informal consultation held with some journalists, they acknowledged that the threat of action for defamation might serve to increase the professionalism of inexperienced press staff. However, most journalists felt strongly that defamation should not be criminalized.

Editorial staff of three of the daily newspapers admitted that journalists operated in fear and often resorted to self-censorship to avoid possible conflict with powerful people, and were concerned that self-censorship would increase under the Code. Their main concern was that legal suits for defamation should only be used to protect the good name of a person, and not to maintain public order or to protect political interests. They felt that using a civil procedure in response to defamation would be proportional to the damage done.

Editors and lawyers were not convinced of the ability of the judiciary to adjudicate impartially and fairly on defamation cases. A pertinent point was that the views expressed by the Timorese journalists and lawyers were very much in line with the position taken by the UN Special Rapporteur on Freedom of Opinion and Expression. He had stated that "sanctions for defamation should not be so large as to exert a chilling effect on the freedom of opinion and expression and the right to seek and receive important information; penal sanctions, in particular imprisonment, should never be applied".[18] The Rapporteur had also called on states to repeal criminal defamation laws and instead to use the civil judicial process to respond to defamation cases.

These concerns appeared to become a reality with the news of a possible defamation action to be taken by Prime Minister Alkatiri. His action was against one of his main political rivals, Fernando La Sama de Araújo, the leader of the PD, the largest opposition party in parliament. Lasama was accused of defamation for comments he had reportedly made to the media about a court case filed in the United States. The case accused the Prime Minister of having taken a bribe from an oil company as part of the Timor Sea deal. It was feared that if Alkatiri, whose adviser had reportedly made an initial complaint to the Prosecutor General, went ahead with the case, it would undoubtedly become one of the biggest legal cases in Timor-Leste since 1999.

Riots erupting in Liquiça, Baucau and Dili

The first sign of a major crisis emerged within a few months after my arrival in Dili in July 2002. The level of disappointment and dissatisfaction against the government had risen in the populace, particularly among the former independence fighters and other marginalized groups. Reflecting the mood, President Gusmão made a provocative speech that sparked a heated discussion on the "Independence Day" ceremony on 27 November 2002.[19] The President denounced Interior Minister Lobato for his ineptitude and demanded his resignation. Those of us sitting in the seats assigned to the diplomatic corps were startled by the vigour with which the President spoke. He categorically spoke of the need for a change in the government, giving the impression that the President was asserting his authority over the management of the government. Until then, the image of a strong and decisive president had been held by most of the population. However, it was soon put in doubt when Prime Minister Alkatiri declared that he had the authority granted by the Constitution to appoint and dismiss his cabinet ministers. The Prime Minister then made clear that he was not dismissing Rogério Lobato. Some diplomats thought that it was the first sign of confrontation between the President and the Prime Minister that contributed to the emergence of anti-government feeling, resulting ultimately in the riots of 4 December 2002.

Prior to the Dili riots, a series of security incidents had begun to take place, first in Liquiça and then in Baucau, some 120 km east of Dili. On

15 November the Liquiça police station was attacked, an event which was brought under control by a Portuguese battalion.

A violent demonstration next occurred in Baucau on 25 November. Two separate groups comprising several hundred civilians gathered outside the police station in Baucau town. The first group reportedly protested over the handling by the Timorese police of an incident the previous week in Wailili. The morning incident gained momentum when its numbers were swelled by demonstrators meeting to protest the recruitment policy within PNTL.

During the clash, one civilian was shot in the head, and was airlifted to Dili for surgery in the UN Military Hospital. The 27-year old victim of the gunshot wound, Calisto Soares, died despite all attempts to save him. I visited the hospital and offered my condolences to the family. With the agreement of the deceased's family, I then asked for a UN pathologist to carry out an autopsy, so that a thorough investigation into his death could be concluded.

The police station and nine police vehicles, including four UN cars, were damaged. The demonstrations against the police appeared to have been organized by Cornelio Gama (known as L7) and his Sagrada Familia[20] group members. Support for the riot also came from CPD-RDTL supporters, who were known to be critical of the Mari Alkatiri Government.[21] As I met with Prime Minister Alkatiri and his right-arm, Justice Minister Pessoa, they told me that L7 was involved in organizing the violent demonstrations. He and his group had to be dealt with sternly, or confidence would be lost in the national police and the government.

The Prime Minister insisted that violent tactics, if not stopped at the outset, would be used to make further demands against the government. He asked for the deployment of the United Nations Peacekeeping Force (PKF) to restore order and security in Baucau. In the absence of the SRSG, I authorized the deployment of PKF forces: two platoons of 60 Portuguese were flown into Baucau by two helicopters from Liquica and Dili to assist in restoring order. Also, as a pre-cautionary measure, I authorized the evacuation of all 13 international staff to the Baucau airport.

In view of the significance of the disturbances, UNPOL immediately carried out its own investigations on how the events had developed during the course of the day. It also looked into the extent of the weaponry in use by authorized police personnel and unauthorized civilians. According to preliminary UN Police investigations, 16 UNPOL officers, 21 PNTL officers and 10 national Special Police Unit (SPU) officers were initially involved in the operation. A further 10 SPU arrived some 20 minutes later. This level of deployment had been planned in a staff meeting the previous day to prepare for the demonstration.

UNPOL also reported on the existence of several automatic weapons and pistols in the crowd, and the local press reported that PNTL Commissioner Paolo Martins indicated some protestors carried AR15 guns. At least one shot was understood to have come from a long-barrelled weapon. UNPOL officers reported hearing shots; they believed these to have been fired by demonstrators prior to police discharging their own firearms.

It was reported that a crowd of more than 300 attacked the police station, throwing stones, damaging all office windows and 10 vehicles, and attempted to enter the police headquarters building. The mob shouted angrily at the Timorese police and threatened to kill them. It became clear that the command and control of police officers broke down as the situation became serious.

The UN Police reported that they had not at any time directed PNTL or SPU officers to use firearms to disperse the crowd with warning shots. Nonetheless, more than 100 shots seemed to have been fired, while none of the UNPOL officers reportedly discharged a firearm at any stage.

The availability of peacekeeping forces helped to control the situation within two hours of the deployment of 24 troops on the ground. An additional 24 soldiers arrived by helicopter from Dili within the hour, and a further 40 arrived by road shortly after that. With regard to the policy on firearms: the weapons and ammunition had been issued to qualified officers at the start of their shift. These were then returned at the end of the shift. These procedures were considered to be reasonable and appropriate for the issuing, control and safe storage of weapons. However, in view of these recent experiences, UNPOL determined certain areas in which this policy needed to be altered or more rigidly enforced.

As the situation demanded, I held a meeting with Prime Minister Alkatiri. After our meeting, the Prime Minister dispatched Ilda Maria da Conceição, the Vice-Minister of Internal Administration, along with other members of the commission he had established, to investigate the violent clashes. The commission members consisted of L7, the Inspector General, the Police Commander in Baucau and the Security Adviser to the Prime Minister. The UN Police Commissioner was also invited to be a key member of the commission. It met with chiefs of communities and villages, who reportedly demanded the exclusion of police officers from the commission.

The disturbances in Baucau, particularly the death of a demonstrator, transformed the public perception of current political and security forces in Timor-Leste. Overnight, the police became suspect, and the demonstrators were seen as protestors against the abuse of public power. The Baucau incidents furthermore revealed the underlying current of sentiment growing against the national police forces, reflecting resentment of a recruitment process that did not accommodate a sufficiently large number of ex-FALINTIL and other ex-combatants who sought employment as members of PNTL. A negative attitude had also emerged with respect to police behaviour and their frequent firing of warning shots. It had also become apparent that various local holders of power, who were against the current government, had begun to exploit the anti-police sentiment.

Both the Liquica and Baucau incidents had involved national police and military personnel. This further revealed a complex web of political factors, for the situation affected the government's ability to administer its security forces properly, and to govern this fragile new country adequately. The professionalism of both United Nations and Timorese police forces was to be tested again within a week in the capital city of Dili.

On 3 December 2002, the police entered a school building in Dili, searching for a youth suspected of having committed a murder. This resulted in a violent response by students at the school, who threw stones at the police officers and damaged two police motorcycles. Police retaliated and fired warning shots in the air to disperse the crowd. They took the suspect to the police station to place him in custody, and the school students and teachers then marched to the government building. They complained that the police had entered school and arrested the youth without the permission of the headmaster. The police insisted that the student was arrested because of the seriousness of the crime he was reported to have committed. By the evening, with the situation becoming precarious, PNTL decided to place the anti-riot SPU, also known then as the Unidade Intervenção Rápida (UIR, Rapid Intervention Unit), on stand-by. While the SPU was on standby, UNPOL and PNTL verified information that a group of students would make a presentation to the government and parliament the following day.

On 4 December, as government officials started work in the morning, a number of students came to the Palácio do Governo and started throwing stones at the office windows, and many were broken. The government occupied the centre and west wing of this elegant white building complex, with the Prime Minister's office being located on the second floor. Prime Minister Alkatiri went to the adjacent UNMISET office in the west wing, shouting: "Bring PKF! PKF!" meaning that the UN peacekeeping troops should immediately be deployed to counter the demonstrators.

PNTL and SPU members, under the supervision of UNPOL, dispersed the crowd using tear gas and by firing warning gunshots. The students and other demonstrators moved to the Parliament Building located nearby, entering the compound and breaking into a number of offices. Demonstrators, including a few hundred students, also gathered in front of the UNPOL Police Headquarters building and started to throw stones. Unable to control the crowd, some police officers discharged firearms in response to the stones being thrown at them. When President Gusmão learned about the developments, he rushed to the police centre in an effort to calm the crowd. He subsequently spent two hours listening to the concerns of demonstrators, and engaged in conciliation talks with the demonstrators for another two hours.

As the day progressed, the police were unable to control the situation. The crowds dispersed and burned down a foreign-owned supermarket, as well as a hotel and other premises throughout Dili. The Prime Minister approached us and asked again for the immediate deployment of the peacekeeping forces. I recall him saying then: "They are going after my house." We immediately relayed the Prime Minister's message to UNPOL and urged them to proceed to his residence, but the students set fire to it before UNPOL arrived. The riot lasted until late in the afternoon as UNPOL and PNTL police officers were not able to contain the rioters; two people were shot dead and about 30 buildings were burned including the Prime Minister's residence. There were no PKF forces available other than Japanese defence forces stationed in Taci Tolu, just outside of Dili. However, as was well known, the Japanese forces were there only to carry out the maintenance of roads and bridges, and were not authorized to engage in any security operations. Only when the Portuguese troops arrived from Baucau in the evening, and drove around town, did the rioting crowds disperse. There was no need for the Portuguese to fire even a single shot; the crowds disappeared as soon as they saw the PKF troops.

The Prime Minister felt strongly that UNPOL had failed to do anything to prevent the burning of his residence, accusing the United Nations for not having stopped the mob from entering and burning his house. He put the blame squarely on the UNPOL and UNMISET, as the UN Police Commissioner still held the executive policing power. The Secretary-General reported on the riots immediately, and in March 2003 he raised the significance of the incidents in the Security Council as follows.

> The potential for grave civil disturbance became clear with the riots that erupted in Dili on 4 December 2002. While earlier disturbances in Baucau from 18 to 26 November 2002 had suggested that the Timor-Leste police could deal with challenges in urban areas, the riot in Dili was on a quite different scale. It developed from a protest at the Parliament Building, and was manipulated by elements that directed those involved to targets that were apparently selected to undermine the authority and legitimacy of the government. As was reported to the Security Council at the time, in the course of these riots, numerous buildings were destroyed by arson, including houses owned by the Prime Minister and members of his family, and foreign-owned businesses, and other buildings were looted. Seventeen Timorese sustained gunshot injuries, and two of them died. The mosque in Dili was damaged, and houses within its compound were burned. Efforts to restore order were slow to take effect, revealing a number of

weaknesses that are discussed below. The violence left two civilians dead, 25 civilians and several police injured, and significant damage to property including the Prime Minister's residence.[22]

The outburst on 4 December 2002 raised a serious question about the progress made in building viable security agencies, particularly PNTL. UNPOL instructed SPU and other Timorese police units not to carry weapons to the sites of demonstrations, but the commanders of SPU and Dili District's PNTL had ignored this instruction. The Timorese police fired warning shots at first, and eventually aimed at demonstrators as they were stoned and attacked. The unexpected police behaviour triggered an intense debate within UNMISET.

UNPOL identified several critical areas of police training that had gone wrong and advised how the command and control tactics, use of force practices and crowd control could be much improved. Following the riots, UNPOL also drafted a Police Handbook to formulate and rationalize expected police behaviour in crowd-control situations. They also strengthened police disciplinary training.

The spark that had set the riots alight could be seen as an early assertion of the prominence of human rights over security concerns in the conduct of public affairs. Beyond the gaps identified in doctrine and police behaviour, in my view, the December 2002 riots had less to with the technical capacity of the police itself. It had more to do with the mindset and mentality of people in a post-conflict country like Timor-Leste.

Both the international and Timorese communities reviewed the series of security incidents in November and December 2002, apportioning responsibility for the loss of life and destruction of buildings. The government was adamant in blaming UNPOL for the failure to maintain law and order, convinced that this was still the responsibility of the United Nations. UNPOL was blamed for ineptitude and there was even a hint that the maliciousness of the UNPOL Commissioner had allowed the whole situation to take place and develop.[23] To counter the criticism, SRSG Sharma asked Sandra Peisley, the new UN Police Commissioner, to make a fresh investigation into the performances of UNPOL and PNTL officers. Following a detailed investigation of incidents that took place on 4 December 2002, the UNPOL Commissioner submitted her report to the SRSG who in turn forwarded it to the Prime Minister.[24]

The report took a broad overview of the riots and included issues of response, previous investigations and post-incident lessons learned. The fresh investigation undertaken by UNPOL was not able to identify individuals, whether police officers or otherwise, who were directly responsible for the fatal shooting of two youths. On 4 December 2002, UNPOL and PNTL Headquarters staff attendance records revealed that 106

UNPOL and 140 PNTL officers were on duty for the shift commencing at 8:00 a.m. An additional 120 SPU members were also either on standby or on duty that day. The roles and functions carried out by these officers were many and varied. According to Peisley's report, the vitality and escalation of the incident made it difficult for police to respond with the resources available, as they were dispersed at a number of locations throughout Dili. These factors made it extremely difficult for UNPOL, PNTL and PKF to attend and control systematic outbreaks of violence in up to ten different locations, at times simultaneously.

Police Commissioner Peisley referred to contradictory statements made by Timorese police officers concerning their movements, and the absence of projectiles, which could have led to the identification of specific firearms. Nonetheless, the report noted that 22 SPU, 9 PNTL and 2 UNPOL officers did discharge firearms on 4 December 2002.[25]

The report ascertained technical inadequacy in communication facilities and equipment, and further reported inadequate command and control. It also pointed out the implications of the level of responsibility expected of the United Nations, particularly of UNPOL, as it continued to exercise executive policing authority. Apart from the technical difficulties encountered, it correctly noted that the riots took place at time when there were considerable political, social and economic issues manifesting in Timorese society. Commissioner Peisley was concerned that the events of 4 December 2002 had a significant impact on the appreciation of threat perception of Timor-Leste as a nation.[26]

As noted in the Peisley report, it should be pointed out that several months before the incident took place, UNPOL had identified inadequacies in Timor-Leste's law enforcement capability. UNPOL had recruited a training officer and a capacity-building expert to help strengthen police officers' ability to handle unexpected developments. The 'Needs Assessment Mission' that had been formed with the participation of representatives from PNTL, UNMISET, UNPOL and UNDP examined police operations in late November 2002. It is worth recapitulating the findings of this group with regard to the shortcomings that existed in not only police training, but also policing operations. They included a weakness in the chain of command and control in policing roles; a lack of structured communication among the rank and file; inadequate training in use of force and firearms; a lack of discipline; a lack of and poor police equipment; a lack of understanding/knowledge of human right principles (a problem specific to PNTL members); generally, a lack of understanding of procedural practice and of further specialist skills training.[27]

The report also indicated the lessons learnt from 4 December 2002. These pertained to such factors as poor discipline and lack of understanding of human rights, the use of force practices, crowd control and procedural practices. These lessons substantiated some of the shortcomings already identified in the Timor-Leste law enforcement capability, as well as many necessary changes that were then implemented. Measures cited by the report included:[28]

- A remedial restructuring of the SPU (RIU) – immediate and "near" future.
- Improved communication process between UNPOL and PNTL command procedures – i.e. proper record-keeping, regular updating of staff mobile phone numbers and improved portable radio communications.
- Minimum staffing at headquarters, regulated to ensure a minimum presence of at least 50 per cent at any given time.
- Improved equipment for handling demonstrations, allocated to appropriate stations; personnel preparation; and promulgation of a PNTL 'Code of Conduct'.
- Preparation and promulgation of a 'Use of Force Policy'.

A more significant lesson learned from the incidents of 4 December 2002, according to the Peisley report, was how to make use of "strategic information". It was stressed that policing should be proactive in nature, involving the gathering, evaluating, analysing and disseminating of relevant information. Policing practices of this nature were said to clearly hold the potential to allow intervention, and to stop such a violent occurrence before it commenced.

It became apparent that the UN Police had to develop this capacity eventually if it were to perform its duty efficiently and effectively in conflict-prone countries. At the least, an awareness of such matters should lead to better anticipation and proactive measures to be taken to defuse such occurrences prior to their commencement or escalation.

In Timor-Leste's case, efforts have since been made to integrate the information-gathering team as part of the National Operations Centre (NOC), located in UNPOL Headquarters. This formed a foundation and became the central point where all information was to be received, processed and disseminated. Every section of the PNTL was to be tasked with forwarding "information reports", as necessary, on all facets of law enforcement.[29] In my view, these were the most pertinent observations made in the UN Police Commissioner's report. I would add that it is highly desirable for UNPOL officers and all other international staff to comprehend the mindset and mentality of national and local people in order to predict and prevent any violent acts by them.

In its concluding summary, the report referred to the assessment of the riots in a larger framework made by President Gusmão, who thought that individuals and groups took advantage of the situation as it went beyond acceptable limits. He felt that the riots involved manipulation of a situation of social–economical dissatisfaction; therefore, it was necessary to analyse the actual situation as a whole and not strictly in political or security terms. President Gusmão was reported also to think that there was a need to ensure a better and effective coordination of information and action between state institutions, namely, the government and UNMISET.

Furthermore, the President stated that the Timorese leaders should not have continued to tie themselves exclusively to political problems and the concept of democratic governance. They should have paid more attention to socio-economic issues, namely those that could contribute to improving the standard of living of the population. The fact that it was possible to manipulate and utilize the confusion clearly demonstrated a vacuum of information and communication from state institutions to the grassroots and the population.[30]

In other words, the riots and other security incidents in Liquica, Baucau and Dili were a manifestation of the root causes of violence often witnessed in many post-conflict countries. The government needed to take measures to address not only the immediate security threats, but also the root causes of such violence. There were many unemployed youths and other marginalized groups which had become increasingly dissatisfied with the government, feeling that it had failed to deliver the promises of development after independence. For this reason the government needed to embark upon massive public works, but it had no resources within the national budget, which amounted to a mere $70 million in the fiscal year 2002–2003.

I thought that the international community should have helped the government through the creation of income generation and employment opportunities. Also, Timor-Leste needed more development assistance for the people, particularly for former independence fighters, who had not benefitted thus far from the restoration of independence. Some demobilized soldiers had previously received a few payments through the Reintegration Assistance Programme (FRAP) set up by the US Agency for International Development (USAID) and implemented by the International Organization for Migration (IOM). This programme, however, created only token employment opportunities. Recognizing the importance of employment creation, I secured $4.5 million from Japan for the Recovery, Employment and Stability Programme for Ex-combatants and Communities in Timor-Leste (RESPECT). This comprised support to agriculture and rural rehabilitation, infrastructure reconstruction and skill development.

From time to time, the question came up as to why the President publicly demanded the firing of the Interior Minister, only to discover that the Prime Minister had no intention of doing so. Later on, I learned that there had been a meeting among the three leaders, Xanana Gusmão, Mari Alkatiri and José Ramos-Horta, whereby they reached an agreement that Rogério Lobato should indeed go. Later, Prime Minister Alkatiri seemed to have changed his mind. This led Xanana Gusmão and Ramos-Horta to feel that Alkatiri was trying to monopolize power for his personal interests. They then saw the need to take specific measures to halt the increasing concentration of power in the hands of the Prime Minister. The advice SRSG Sharma gave was that any change must take place peacefully, without violating the Constitution.

The attitude and behaviour of the Timorese leaders needed to be understood not just in terms of the self-interests they pursued, but also the historical roles they had played. During the period of Indonesian occupation, Gusmão remained in Timor-Leste, while Alkatiri was in Mozambique, and Ramos-Horta in New York campaigning for independence. They also held enormous respect for Nicolau Lobato, who had been killed by Indonesian troops in 1978. Mari Alkatiri confided several times that this was one of the reasons why he felt an obligation not to abandon Rogério Lobato as a relative of the early independence leader.

The Timorese authorities also formed their own independent parliamentary commission to investigate the circumstances leading to the riots of 4 December. Justice Minister Pessoa and Defence Secretary Roque Rodrigues met me on 16 December 2002 and reported how the commission intended to carry out the investigation. In doing so, they told me that some commission members had been threatened. Although Minister Pessoa did not give me precise details of the threats, her expression of concern struck me, as she was known as a tough lady who rarely showed fear or any misgivings. I immediately reported Ana Pessoa's request for UNMISET protection for the Commission members to SRSG Sharma. SRSG Sharma then instructed the Police Commissioner to meet with Commission members. He was to gather credible evidence in order to properly evaluate the authenticity of the threats, and take any precautionary measures.

At the meeting initiated by Minister Ana Pessoa and Defence Secretary Roque Rodrigues, it was conveyed to me that the government was losing confidence in UNPOL Commissioner Peter Miller. They said UNPOL's performance reflected incompetence and was lacking in responsibility; they even implied an intention not to guard the Prime Minister's residence. They further stated that unless "an appropriate action" was taken, the government might be forced to publicly state a lack of confidence in the ability of UNMISET as a whole to guarantee the internal security of Timor-Leste.

I felt their accusation was unfair. I told them it had not been the intention of either UNPOL or UNMISET to disregard the security of the Prime Minister and his residence. I also pointed out that the SRSG himself had already decided to establish a security management committee, which aimed to improve the analysis of intelligence information and tighten the management control of UNPOL and PNTL. The committee would also be tasked to improve the professionalism of police officers. It was also tasked to enhance the Rapid Intervention Unit's capacity to deal with mass demonstrations and riots. At the same time, I referred to the political aspect of the security situation. I underscored the importance of establishing inclusive policies and procedures, which could accommodate those with different viewpoints. I also addressed the need to provide the people with economic and employment opportunities.

After my meeting with the two ministers, I informed SRSG Sharma of the serious concerns held by the government about the performance of UNPOL, and we jointly assessed the meaning of their message. This was that the government was losing confidence in UNPOL's ability to continue its mandated executive policing role. Should this be taken more seriously, as emphasized by the Minister for Justice, and by the Secretary of State in relation to defence? Would UNMISET be obliged to show that it could carry out the restructuring of UNPOL management immediately, and appoint a new commissioner? Yet, any such move might be interpreted as agreement that UNPOL was solely responsible for the failure to guard government premises, particularly the Prime Minister's residence. After a discussion within UNMISET, some political affairs officers argued that UNPOL should not take the blame alone, as the government had not responded to the root of the problem. Its failure to address the people's need to improve their livelihood was the cause of the anti-government demonstrations and violence.

Apart from the political diagnosis of the causes of the riots, it was apparent that UNPOL needed to establish a proper command-and-control structure. This was needed not only physically, but also strategically, so that it could operate swiftly in a unified manner. The unification of command and control of UN police officers, however, proved extremely difficult as they came from so many different Member States. This meant that all mission components needed to act in a more integrated manner. It also became apparent that we needed to gather and share intelligence information with national authorities. They, in fact, had a more intimate knowledge and understanding of current goings-on in their society.

Outburst of violent acts by F-FDTL personnel

As early as November 2002, a sign of antagonism surfaced between PNTL police officers and F-FDTL soldiers. A group of more than 20 F-FDTL soldiers, wearing civilian clothes, were brought into town and dropped off at the Dili stadium for weekend liberty. As several of them reached the intersection of Hello Mister road, they encountered two PNTL police officers performing traffic duties. Two F-FDTL soldiers then assaulted the PNTL officers. One of the latter, Rui Lobato, sustained a cut in the head requiring five stitches, while the other officer, Joaqin Lopes, had a cut below his left eye and received blows to the body. PNTL Special Unit Patrol (SUP) responded to the scene and arrested two F-FDTL members. Meanwhile, a crowd of about 40 witnesses moved to the compound housing of the F-FDTL and adjacent United Nations Military Observers Group (UNMOG) office premises. There they threw stones, breaking windows of the UNMOG Headquarters. Police patrols dispersed the crowd, and subsequently prevented another crowd from marching to the F-FDTL compound.

Both F-FDTL Commander General TMR and PNTL Commissioner Paulo Martins worked closely together in defusing the tension and preventing any further incident. While police dispersed the crowd, the F-FDTL commander redirected more soldiers away from the F-FDTL Headquarters. The PNTL Police Commissioner calmed down his staff and provided medical service for the two injured police officers, going to the Military Hospital with them and staying with them for nearly two hours until they were moved from an emergency operation room. TMR told UNMISET staff that the two soldiers would be punished severely once the outcome of the investigation was known. Paulo Martins held a meeting with his counterpart and the F-FDTL commander, who informed us that the two soldiers had in fact been put into Becora Prison. The Prime Minister then indicated his intention to set up a board of inquiry consisting of representatives of PNTL, F-FDTL and the government, probably the Office of the Prime Minister. Upon our suggestion, the Prime Minister agreed to consider the inclusion in the board of a representative of the civil society, although he did not promise it.

The incident should be seen from a historical perspective. The conscientious manner with which the Timorese leaders dealt with the incident reflected their serious concerns about possible re-emergence of a military culture. This was reminiscent of the period of Indonesian occupation when Tentara Nasional Indonesia (NTI, Indonesian National Armed Forces) members ruled the country as they wished. Shortly after the assault took place, the Prime Minister made a public declaration, saying that he would not hesitate to prevent F-FDTL from turning into a force like TNI.

When I later asked for his views on the possibility of criminal prosecution of the two soldiers, Alkatiri categorically told me that they would be prosecuted for a criminal offence once the outcome of the inquiry indicated such an act took place. The incident revealed the fact that F-FDTL members had not been trained adequately about civilian control; the role of the military in a democratic society had not been fully understood and accepted by military personnel.

I felt it would not be sufficient to leave the military training to a few troop-supplying countries that had concentrated on combat actions. It was essential for UNMISET to be involved in enhancing the nature of training carried out for F-FDTL members. Yet, given the absence of a proper mandate authorizing UNMISET to be engaged in security sector reform, we were limited in our actions. The most we could do then was to ask UNMISET's human rights division to formulate and implement a training programme designed to prepare F-FDTL members to behave properly in a democratic society.

However, the abusive behaviour of F-FDTL personnel continued, and even increased after the November 2002 event. On 24 January 2004, the first large-scale incident took place in Los Palos, when as many as 50 F-FDTL personnel went to the police station and a hospital to track down two brothers. They had been involved in a physical fight with some F-FDTL members. On being refused entry to the hospital the soldiers went on a rampage, firing multiple shots with M-16 military weapons, and threatening people around them. Fear spread rapidly among community residents. They then went to yet another police station, assaulted five PNTL officers there (including the station commander) and took them to an F-FDTL compound.

When the news of the incidents reached UNMISET, UNPOL Police Commissioner Sandra Peisley immediately gave instructions to UNPOL advisers in Los Palos to prevent any further incident. PKF Force Commander Khairuddin contacted Brigadier-General TMR, who sent his instructions to the F-FDTL battalion in Los Palos. As a result, the situation calmed down around midnight. A special flight to Los Palos was arranged to transport several officials for a first-hand survey of the situation. The special envoy included the PNTL Commissioner, the Chief of Staff of the President's Office, the Chief of Staff of F-FDTL and the UN Deputy Police Commissioner.

Hundreds of fearful Los Palos residents reportedly turned out to meet the team visiting from Dili, demanding punishment for the troops who committed abuses. On behalf of SRSG Sharma, who was abroad, attending a conference on UN peacekeeping, and in company with UNMIT Chief of Staff Atul Khare, I met President Gusmão just before his departure on official visits to Sweden and Belgium. President Gusmão indicated his clear disapproval of F-FDTL actions. At the same time, he pointed out that the events were a manifestation of deep-seated problems related to motivation, command and control of F-FDTL. He also pointed to the rivalry among factions within the armed forces, and the appalling rivalry with PNTL. Many military personnel felt that the international community, particularly the United Nations, had supported the PNTL at the expense of F-FDTL. They were not aware that the United Nations had not been given a mandate to assist them formally.

Two months later, a smaller security incident involving F-FDTL soldiers took place at the UN House. On 11 March 2004, three off-duty members of F-FDTL in civilian clothing caused a public disturbance in front of the gate of the UN House compound. They argued among themselves, and then with UNDP security guards, after the guards politely requested that they move from the gate to allow the UN shuttle bus to pass. The soldiers reportedly refused and threatened the UN guards. When the UNDP informed the UNMIST and PNTL, about 20 PNTL officers, including a few from the RIU, arrived at the scene.

The three F-FDTL members allegedly refused to be brought to the police station and challenged the police by trying to assault the police officers, as well as residents in the neighbourhood. One of the F-FDTL reportedly assaulted a local citizen before leaving the scene. All three appeared to be under the influence of alcohol, displaying violent and rowdy behaviour, and the police were not able to apprehend them.

These incidents reflected the need for institutional reform. From an institutional perspective and our discussions with Timorese government leaders, we shared a common view about the need for the government to adopt:

guidelines on the relationship between the two security agencies, PNTL and F-FDTL; and

a clear policy on the roles and functions of F-FDTL in the broad national security framework, particularly in the absence of organic laws for either PNTL or F-FDTL.

More importantly, we needed to understand and recognize the F-FDTL's reasons for lack of discipline and inability to behave properly in public. As President Gusmão pointed out repeatedly, there was a deep sense of frustration and genuine grievances among F-FDTL personnel for the perceived lack of respect in which they were held by the public. The military personnel had a feeling of loss in a new country where they were not sure how to play a constructive role. The international community was preoccupied with establishing the rule of law, and forgot to pay sufficient attention to the humane aspect of helping ex-combatants groups find their role in a new society. Viewed from this perspective, I felt it essential that they should be helped to change their mentality and mindset. Those who had fought for their independence, or simply for power in conflict-prone countries, were ready to use guns to settle their differences. When I met with one of the former guerrilla fighters, L7, in his town, I emphasized to him the constructive role he had the chance to play in democracy. I told him that if he became a politician he could achieve what he wanted. I was glad he chose to do so in 2007, when he won a seat in the National Parliament.

Peaceful end to church-inspired demonstrations

The crisis of 2002 was followed by relative stability in 2003 and 2004. This emboldened Prime Minister Alkatiri and his government ministers. The government gradually tightened its control of the education system and decided to discontinue its support of religious teaching in schools. In early 2005, the government then planned to start a pilot project in primary schools, making the study of religious education an optional subject in schools, rather than the compulsory subject it had been since 2001. Alarmed by the government's move, the Bishops of Dili and Baucau, representing the church, called upon the government to rescind the decision. However, the government insisted on the appropriateness of the measure based on the principles of separation of church and state. After numerous lengthy debates and negotiations, the church issued a statement claiming that people had lost faith in the government, and sought the removal of Prime Minister Alkatiri. This "church demonstration" then became the second serious internal political challenge to the first constitutional government.

Several hundred people, mostly youths, gathered on 19 April 2005 in Dili. Many more had embarked on the trip to Dili from outlying districts, although the PNTL had erected roadblocks and tried to prevent them from proceeding to Dili. Some were carrying religious icons; many more carried banners printed with such anti-government slogans as "Government Not Eradicating Hunger", "Government Should Not Intimidate or Cheat the People", "Establish an International Tribunal" and "Jobs for the People". The protest signs were a significant reflection of the people's feelings, not just about the importance of supporting religious practice, but also of the need to address the economic requirements of Timor-Leste.

The church demonstrators remained peaceful, and PNTL held the group in an orderly manner some 150 metres away from the government building. The protesters received meals from the church, with the message that there was a plenty of food for everybody. There were varying indications of the likely length of the protest, with some saying it could continue for a long time. The protesters sought a meeting with Prime Minister Alkatiri or the President of the National Parliament, Francisco Lú-Olo Guterres, and wanted a retraction of the government's "anti-religious" position on education. However, to begin with no government officials made themselves available to meet with the protesters. Unofficially, the government's national security adviser indicated that the government had a solution to this problem, which included the formation of a joint commission to discuss the issue. Reports from outlying districts indicated that many more protesters had gathered in district capitals with the intention of travelling to Dili to join in the protest. However, following orders apparently given by Interior Minister Lobato, the PNTL had prevented these groups from converging upon the capital. They had placed a number of road blocks on main routes from Bobonaro, Ermera, Covalima, Ainaro and Manufahi districts in the west and from Baucau in the east.

As the church demonstrations became large and demanding, I convened a meeting with senior mission managers, including the Force Commander, Chief of Staff, HRU, Political Affairs and UNMISET Security, to discuss possible steps to ensure the security of UNMISET staff and installations. The Force Commander explained to the participants that a decision had already been made to put the International Response Unit (IRU) in Dili on standby. It was ready to bring in additional backup from Maliana, should such a need arise. UNMISET staff members were also informed of the planned events and advised to remain alert, being told to stay away from areas where large groups were likely to congregate. The Heads of UN agencies and members of the diplomatic community were advised to take similar security precautions. Meanwhile, Timorese sources reported to us that the church was sending a strong anti-government message through its radio.

As the confrontation between the church and the government continued to escalate, I took an initiative to bring the two sides together by organizing a colloquium on "Religious Education in State Schools of Timor-Leste" on 28 April 2005. The Minister of Education and Chief of Staff of the President's Office joined representatives of the church and the academic community. There was a general consensus that the government should have had more consultations with the church and civil society, before making a decision on such a sensitive issue as religious education. The fact that all sides were willing to have a dialogue was a positive development that could lead to a peaceful resolution. The stated objective was to examine the subject of religious education in greater depth, although the real aim was to produce proposals that could bridge the differences between the church and the government.

To make the discussion substantive and fruitful, I requested the Minister for Education, Culture and Youth, Maia, and Father Goncalves, Chancellor of the Baucau Diocese, to make presentations of their cases. I also asked several key persons to provide their views as panellists. The participants included Ágio Pereira, Chief of Staff of the Office of the President; Valentin Ximenes, the Dean of the Faculty of Political and Social

Sciences, National University of Timor-Leste; Faustino Cordoso Gomes, the Director of the National Centre for Scientific Investigation; and Marcelino Magno of the East Timor Institute of Development Studies. Furthermore, I invited representatives of diplomatic missions and heads of UN agencies to attend.

Minister Armindo Maia admitted that the current government had moved away from the practice when religious education was a compulsory subject during the Indonesian occupation. Children could now make their own choices, from Christianity, Islam, Hinduism and other religions. Maia explained that the constitution of Timor-Leste provided for the separation of the church and the state, so obliging the government to make religious education a "facultative" subject. In other words, religious teaching would no longer be part of the regular curriculum as an obligatory subject, but should be taught optionally outside the regular school hours. Although this method of implementing the constitutional provision was theoretically correct, it did not appease the feeling of the overwhelming majority of the Timorese people, who were Catholics. Furthermore, the government measure left unanswered the question of who would pay for such education outside of the regular curriculum. The church felt that state schools should be obligated to have religious education as a part of the regular curriculum. Parents would have the option to decide whether to opt out of religious instruction or seek alternative religious instruction.

In the discussions that followed, there was a general consensus that the government had not consulted properly with the church on this issue before making such a serious decision. Also discussed was the need to have a mechanism for a dialogue between the government, the church, and civil society in general, including parliament. Due to the lack of proper consultation, there was a general perception that the government was trying to marginalize the church. In the rural areas especially there was criticism that the government was not reaching out to the people, and that power was centralized in Dili. The colloquium provided a forum for a frank exchange of views by all sides. The persistence shown by the demonstrators was a signal to the government that it could not ignore the church's views on religious education.

In spite of a conciliatory attitude shown by Education Minister Maia, a few days later a rumour started to spread, alleging that the police had given an ultimatum that the demonstrations should end on 3 May. When this unconfirmed report circulated through town, the banks and several stores closed their doors, creating fear and uncertainty. Some UN staff members became anxious about their own safety in the light of these developments. I organized a Town Hall briefing on 3 May for UNMISET staff and all UN agencies.

PNTL General Commander Paulo Martins was invited to speak to the staff. He assured all that the situation was under control, and that the police was not planning to use force to break up the church demonstrators. He also explained that the government had initiated discussions with the church to ensure that no incidents of violence would take place, and indicated that a peaceful end to the demonstrations was being sought. UN Police Training Adviser Malik told the UN staff that he was also in constant contact with the PNTL General Commander. Upon the conclusion of the meeting, I still advised all staff to stay away from the vicinity of the demonstrations as a precautionary measure, and I also told them not to venture out in the evening unless necessary.

On 4 May, I organized a similar meeting of a more consultative nature for the Heads of Diplomatic Missions in Dili and Heads of UN Agencies. I not only invited Father Filomeno Jacob, private secretary to the bishop of Dili, who was accompanied by Fernanda Borges, the adviser to the bishop, but also PNTL General Commander Paulo Martins.

At the meeting, the PNTL General Commander reiterated the points he had made the day before to UNMISET staff, namely that the authorities were not going to use force to end the demonstrations, and that the general security situation in the country was under control. He said that a dialogue with the church was ongoing. The police were present at the demonstrations, not as enemies but as protectors of the people. Father Filomeno agreed that the police had become more cooperative, and that lines of communication had been opened with them, although at the start of the demonstrations they had erected roadblocks to prevent people from the districts from reaching Dili. However, he questioned the legal basis of the General Commander's assertion that insufficient notice had been given to the police to hold demonstrations, and claimed that official permission had been denied.

US Ambassador Grover Joseph Rees complemented both sides on the peaceful and orderly manner in which the demonstrations had generally been conducted. However, he also raised concerns about the legal basis for not allowing free speech, which he said was fundamental in a democracy.

The church also received a few queries, if not criticisms. Despite the overall peaceful nature of the demonstrations, the Portuguese Ambassador expressed concerns about an incident in which demonstrators injured two Portuguese nationals. They had been held for several hours at the Bishop's residence before being turned over to the Portuguese Embassy. Father Filomeno was very defensive of the conduct of the demonstrators, claiming that the church had taken them into the Bishop's compound only to prevent any further violence from the protesters. He stressed that the individuals appeared to be under the influence of alcohol and drove in a dangerous manner in the direction of the protesters and the statues of the Virgin Mary.

Father Filomeno also denied that the protesters had thrown stones at vehicles. I clarified that one vehicle was indeed damaged extensively as shown in the photographs distributed at the meeting. Also, that a UNPOL officer was injured with a broken nose. I also informed the meeting that I had requested the PNTL investigate the incident. Meanwhile, the United Nations would also launch its own investigations.

Following the discussions, Father Filomeno took a more conciliatory approach and said that going forward the church would be strict with the protesters and anyone who behaved improperly would be handed over to the police. He admitted that some protestors had made inflammatory statements during the demonstrations, but denied that the church had organized its own "security groups" as was reported in some quarters, or that it had taken the law into its own hands. Finally, referring to the demands made by the church, Father Filomeno said that they reflected people's genuine concerns.

These concerns were addressed to parliament and the FRETILIN party, which held the majority there. He said the church was acting within the law both in terms of the content of the demands and the form of action taken to express and convey them. Discussions were ongoing with the President, who was in a position to act as mediator. Furthermore, the Bishops had met with both the President and Prime Minister for a "constructive" dialogue, and Father Filomeno was optimistic that an agreement between the two sides would be reached quickly. In the meantime, the protests would continue, but in a peaceful manner.

The meeting ended on a positive note with several issues and misunderstandings of the past few days clarified. I closed the meeting by complimenting both sides for the restraint that had been demonstrated so far, and I expressed my hope that there would soon be a peaceful resolution.

A violent confrontation between the church and the government was avoided due to three positive developments. First, the leaders of the church ensured that the demonstration did not become violent. Second, the government was willing to recognize the need for a compromise. Third, President Gusmão acted deftly as a mediator between the church and the government. He met with the Bishops of Dili and Baucau the day before the colloquium was held to discuss the issue, and commended the demonstration for being peaceful and state institutions for conducting themselves well.

However, the President did suggest that more genuine debate and discussion had to take place in Timor-Leste as in any democracy, so that a consensus could be built. He insisted that the government be more sensitive to the peoples' views. The demonstrators' demands that the Prime Minister should step down were only mentioned in passing by some of the speakers, and hardly elicited any discussion. I recall that during the colloquium did the President's Chief of Staff even suggest that the Prime Minister should stay in office until the next election.

As reported in the Secretary-General's report to the Security Council, a peaceful resolution of the crisis was achieved following several days of negotiations carried out by both sides. President Gusmão acted as mediator, and the Bishops and Prime Minister signed a joint declaration on 7 May 2005.

The agreement recognized that the teaching of religion must be included as a regular discipline in the curriculum. Attendance at classes on religion was subject to a decision at the time of enrolment, in accordance with freely expressed parental wishes. The declaration also called for the establishment of a joint working group to address matters of concern. The demonstrators subsequently dispersed peacefully.[31]

This peaceful resolution of the church demonstration had a major impact on the perception of the international community about the progress that had been made in post-conflict peacebuilding in Timor-Leste. It left the impression that Timor-Leste had achieved maturity in its democratic governance, whereby disputes could be resolved peacefully without resorting to violence.

The Security Council members praised the Timorese leadership for having successfully overcome the crisis with confidence. US Ambassador Holliday, for example, commended UNMISET, as well as the Timorese leadership and the people of Timor-Leste, for having accomplished a major achievement.[32]

After the church demonstration, key members of the Security Council were convinced that the presence and structure of United Nations' involvement should be transformed into that of "a development assistance framework", whereby UN agencies and the World Bank could assist the country in nation-building. A small political office could be maintained to monitor and report on the political developments in the country.

I visited London, Paris and Washington and talked to policymakers of the three key Security Council members. They were emphatic that the time had come for the United Nations to hand over its task to a group of agencies specialized in development. It was undoubtedly an optimistic perception of a post-conflict country that had just succeeded in resolving one of the challenges of establishing stability. The international community was to see yet another root cause of conflict – the struggle for power – which was to emerge and dominate the fragile environment of this new nation.

Notes

1. The number of resistance fighters numbered as many as 15,000 after the Indonesian invasion in 1975.
2. For an insightful and ground-breaking analysis of emotional intelligence in leadership see Daniel Goleman, Richard Boyatzis and Annie McKee, *Primal Leadership: Learning to Lead with Emotional Intelligence*, Boston: Harvard Business School Press, 2002; and Daniel Goleman, *Emotional Intelligence: Why it can matter more than IQ*, New York: Bentham Books, 1994.
3. In the first few months following my arrival, I found the Timorese leaders and people to be open and communicative. In particular, Xanana Gusmão was friendly and ready to discuss any issue in depth, expressing his anxiety when the situation became tense.
4. 3rd Summit of African, Caribbean and Pacific (ACP) Heads of State and Government, Fiji, 17–18 July 2002.
5. The international donor community occupied a large space in the minds of Timorese leaders in these early years of independence. However, as I had previously witnessed in the Rwanda crisis, the Timorese leadership also became increasingly confident and asserted its views and positions.
6. On 28 November 1975, FRETILIN made a unilateral declaration of the independence of the Democratic Republic of East Timor (in Portuguese, Republica Democrática de Timor-Leste). Even though this was not recognized by either Portugal or Indonesia, the Timorese consider their country to have achieved its political independence on this date, although it was occupied by invading Indonesians for the following 24 years until 1999. On 28 November 2002, President Gusmão demanded the dismissal of Rogério Lobato who was in China undergoing medical treatment.
7. Nicolau dos Reis Lobato had been named Prime Minister by President do Amaral when the Timorese declared independence on 28 November 1975. He established the Democratic Republic of Timor-Leste. Just before the Indonesian military launched a full-scale invasion on 7 December, three cabinet ministers fled abroad to seek diplomatic and material support for their armed struggle. One was Rogério Lobato, who was the then Defence Minister. The others were Mari Alkatiri, Economic and Political Affairs Minister, and José Ramos-Horta, the foreign minister at the time. Nicolau dos Reis Lobato was killed by the Indonesian military in 1978 when he was president of FRETILIN.
8. Lasama Araújo was known for his spirit of independence and sacrifice. He was born in the Ainaro District in 1963. He told me that he was only 12 years old when the Indonesian Army killed all of his family members. As the former leader of an East Timorese Students National Resistance (Renetil, Resistência Nacional dos Estudantes de Timor-Leste) he devoted much of his time to resistance activities, which resulted in his imprisonment for six years.
9. In the eyes of diplomatic observers in Timor-Leste, one of the remarkable performances of the Timorese leaders was the friendly manner in which they talk to each other in public at receptions and other functions. In Alkatiri's case he must have subconsciously felt that he could gain absolute power without destroying his cordial relationship with Gusmão.
10. Atauro Island was located near the capital, Dili, but had been neglected, and its several thousand inhabitants lived in very primitive conditions. They needed a water and power supply. In an open governance meeting (a "Town Meeting"), the inhabitants also stressed the need for roads to connect the villages. I agreed to provide funds from the Japanese human security funds to address these needs.

11. For the official version of the Prime Minister's speech, see Prime Minister and Cabinet Timor-Leste Government Speeches, Timor-Leste and the Development Partners Meeting, Opening Statement, 3–5 December 2003. http://www.pm.gov.tp/3decopening.htm, accessed on 20 February 2011.
12. KKN refers to Corruption, Collusion and Nepotism (Korupusi, Kolusi and Nepotisme in the Indonesian language).
13. PSD formed an alliance with ASDT and together received the combined total votes of 15.73 per cent. Meanwhile, the PD received 11.70 per cent of the total votes.
14. This point was addressed in the national public opinion poll conducted in 2009 by IRI which specifically asked the respondents if they considered that democracy will "reform" Timor-Leste and solve the problems they face. The response was positive as 11 per cent of respondents said they were "very optimistic" and 57 per cent said they were "optimistic."
15. The threat of being sued became an effective tool for the government to scare most people in Timor-Leste. However, it did not stop activists from launching attacks. The reputed author of the op-ed, Vicente Ximenes, was one of approximately 20 discontented members of the FRETILIN Central Committee (CCF). The group included Vicente Da Costa, who had been dismissed as the Director of Public Service. Members had signed and circulated a letter calling for a re-examination of CCF operations. Despite the media attention the party received, there was no evidence of a growing internal schism. Rather, there appeared to be a stable number of individuals who had agitated within the party for two years. Many were members due to their perceived slights in treatment by government, such as the aforementioned dismissal, and another issue was the government's lack of success in its tendering processes. Their strategy was to draw on the discontent over the supposed privileges of the Timorese leadership. From their perspective, these leaders had enjoyed an easy life in exile and now monopolized senior government positions.
16. The case was taken up first by the US District Court in Washington DC, and then transferred to the Texas District Court. On 16 April 2008, Judge Hughes of the Texas District Court dismissed the entire case on lack of clear evidence. However, Oceanic Exploration and Petrotimor filed notice on 15 May 2008. They appealed the decision to the US Fifth Circuit Court of Appeals. See La'o Hamutuk (http://www.laohamutuk.org/Oil/Oceanic/OcexConocoLawsuit.htm, accessed on 21 January 2013).
17. Interior Minister Rogério Lobato stated that FRETILIN had evidence that some East Timorese politicians were behind the suit. Although he did not give names, the public was led to believe that Pedro Carrascalão, the son of one of the key opposition leaders, Mario Carrascalão, was behind the legal suit. He was a representative of Petrotimor, a subsidiary almost wholly owned by the Oceanic Exploration.
18. Report of the Special Rapporteur on the promotion and protection of the right to freedom of opinion and expression, E/CN.4/1999/64 para.28, E/CN.4/2000/63 para.52, E/CN.4/2001/64 para.64.
19. Security sector reform became a major issue after the riot that erupted and spread on 4 December 2002. It was preceded by the Independence Day celebrations on 27 November. Timor-Leste has two independence days: one on 27 November when independence was declared in 1975, and another on 20 May 2002, which is called the "Restoration of Independence Day".
20. Group of disaffected, politically motivated individuals with grievances that include jobs for veterans and government assistance.
21. They and villagers from Gariwai, Wailili, Vermasse and Laga apparently came to the police station in Baucau to protest about an incident on 18 November involving police officers in Wailili, in which one offender was shot in the shoulder. Police then attempted

to arrest a man in Baucau in connection with the Wailili incident, which triggered the violent attacks by more than 1,000 people against the police station.

22. United Nations, Special Report of the Secretary-General on the United Nations Mission of Support to East Timor, (S/2003/243) (March 2003), para. 6.

23. At the instruction of the Prime Minister, Minister of State Administration Ana Pessoa and Secretary of Defence Roque Rodriques spoke to me heatedly about the event. They criticized the lack of action taken by UNPOL and even stated that it was intentional on the part of the UN Police Commissioner. I countered the accusation and said that it was not at all intentional, and that UNPOL wanted to secure strategic posts such as power plants and airports.

24. UNMISET, Executive Summary of Investigations of Police Response to the Riots on 4 December 2002, 14 November 2003, attached to a letter from SRSG Kamalesh Sharma to Prime Minister Alkatiri of the Democratic Republic of Timor-Leste dated 14 November 2003, http://www.eastimorlawjournal.org/Miscellaneous/unmiset-dec-2004-riot-report.pdf accessed on 21 February 2011.

25. Ibid, paragraph 18.

26. Ibid, paragraphs 12–24.

27. Ibid, paragraph 49. See also UNMISET media briefing note on the Special Mission Assesses Needs of Timor-Leste Police, Dili, 14 November 2002 and UNMISET spokesperson's note the Police Needs Assessment Mission Issues Report, Dili, 30 November 2002.

28. Ibid, paragraph 54.

29. Ibid, paragraphs 55–57.

30. Ibid, paragraph 58.

31. Report of the Secretary-General on the United Nations Mission of Support in East Timor (for the period from 17 February to 11 May 2005), 12 May 2005, S/2005/310.

32. The statement made by US Representative Holliday to the Security Council at its 5180th meeting on16 May 2005 reads:

> "UNMISET has done an outstanding job and we would like to commend all who have contributed. In particular, we wish to thank Special Representative Hasegawa for his leadership and commitment. The people and the Government of Timor-Leste have come a remarkable distance in the short time since independence. Their spirit and determination is admirable. We would also like to recognize the substantial achievement on the part of the international community, which clearly demonstrates a model for successful peacekeeping." See Security Council document S/PV.5180, p. 11.

IV

Internal conflicts, confrontations and clashes in 2006

Appearances to the mind are of four kinds.
Things either are what they appear to be; or they neither are, nor appear to be;
or they are and do not appear to be; or they are not, and yet appear to be.
Rightly to aim in all these is the wise man's task.[1]

Epictetus

When clashes of armed groups and violent acts occur, people on opposing sides perceive events through their own prisms, interpret how these events took place and reach conclusions that are different from each other. The gap between appearance and reality becomes critical in addressing the causes of conflict and finding solutions. The armed conflicts that occurred in Timor-Leste since the withdrawal of Indonesian troops in 1999 were relatively minor, in comparison with the large-scale massacres and genocide that had taken place in other parts of the world. However, it is worth reviewing the security incidents of April and May 2006, to understand the complexity of behaviours and actions that reflected the motives and intentions of various players. This will also allow recognition of the prudent decisions national leaders took in order to stop the escalation of violence, which would have taken the country into a civil war.

With the completion of the United Nations Mission of Support in East Timor (UNMISET) mandate in May 2005, the Security Council decided to keep only a handful of unarmed military observers and police trainers as part of a newly established peacebuilding office in Timor-Leste. They

Primordial leadership: Peacebuilding and national ownership in Timor-Leste, Hasegawa,
United Nations University Press, 2013, ISBN 978-92-808-1224-4

called it the United Nations Office in Timor-Leste (UNOTIL). As late as March 2006, the Security Council was to close this mission, and leave behind a small political office to monitor political and institutional development. The Head of Mission was to advise the Timorese political leaders on governance issues, particularly the forthcoming presidential and parliamentary elections in 2012. Meanwhile, the UN country team headed by the UN Resident Coordinator was to extend technical support to government and other republican institutions.

The security incidents of April and May 2006 compelled the Security Council to reverse its decision, reinstituting a peacekeeping mission known as the United Nations Integrated Mission in Timor-Leste (UNMIT) in August 2006.

Petitioners' peaceful demonstrations turn violent

The first sign of internal stress within the FALINTIL (Forças Armadas de Libertação Nacional de Timor-Leste) – Forças Armadas de Defesa de Timor-Leste) (F-FDTL)² surfaced when Lieutenant Gastão Salsinha and his group known as "the petitioners" appeared in front of the President's office on 8 February 2006. Numbering as many as 400 F-FDTL members, they had submitted a petition on 15 January signed by nearly 160 mostly *loromonu* officers, who felt that they had been discriminated against within the F-FDTL. The petition was addressed to President Gusmão; copies were also sent to Brigadier General Taur Matan Ruak (TMR), the Commander of the armed forces, and Minister of Defence Rodrigues. Having received no response from either the F-FDTL commander or the Minister of Defence, they went to the presidential office and asked for the President's intervention.

Defence Minister Rodrigues came to the office at the President's request, but TMR did not appear. The following day, the President's Chief of Staff Ágio Pereira told me the petitioners had stayed into the early morning hours in front of the President's office, until the President told them that a commission would be established to investigate their allegations. Subsequently the commission was created within F-FDTL. It did carry out an investigation, but the petitioners did not find the internally established commission was sufficiently independent of the F-FDTL leadership. Dissatisfied with its outcome, the petitioners again left their barracks on 17 February. More soldiers joined them, and their total number increased to nearly 600.

Noting the seriousness of the emerging dispute, on 10 March I invited both TMR and Roque Rodrigues to my residence first, to hear their side of the story. I then planned to advise them on the need to find a way to defuse the tension to prevent any confrontation with the petitioners. As we started our lunch, TMR told me how the whole thing had started. According to him, Gastão Salsinha, the leader of the petitioners' group, had complained that he had not been promoted to the rank of a captain, in spite of the fact that he had earned second place in the competency examination. TMR said that Salsinha was not promoted because he had been caught smuggling sandalwood for export to Indonesia. TMR also pointed out that many of the newly recruited soldiers demanded comparatively easy treatment; this contrasted with the severe hardship he and other guerrilla fighters had endured, without any reward, during the independence struggle. He felt the need for more discipline among young soldiers.

While acknowledging the hardship that TMR had experienced during the era of Indonesian occupation, I advised him on the need to manage the F-FDTL as a fully-fledged national defence agency. I pointed out that he was no longer a commander of a guerrilla army and then offered him UN assistance. The United Nations should be able to provide as many as ten advisers in the fields of human resources management, strategic planning and administration of F-FDTL as the national armed forces. Although I made this offer, the provision of ten international advisers would have to be approved by the Department of Peacekeeping Operations (DPKO) Headquarters, then by the Security Council and the General Assembly Advisory Committee on Administrative and Budgetary Questions (ACABQ). I did this as I felt strongly that the United Nations should be able to respond to the need for institutional capacity-building of the national armed forces, lest peacebuilding fail. The task of building F-FDTL had been left to the bilateral partners such as Australia, Malaysia, Portugal and the United States. The mandate given by the Security Council did not include the institution-building of F-FDTL, but gave a mandate to UNMISET and UNOTIL to train Timorese police officers, and build up the Polícia Nacional de Timor-Leste (PNTL, National Police of Timor-Leste) as an agency for democratic policing. I was convinced that F-FDTL could no longer be left to the bilateral agencies. TMR and Roque Rodrigues appreciated my offer of technical assistance, and told me that they would provide me with a list of required advisers. I then advised them that a request needed to be sent to New York by the President. They were pleased to receive this offer and asked the President to send a letter to the Secretary-General, requesting advisers to help reform and improve the institutional capacity of F-FDTL, as follows:

There is a need to secure the service of international advisers to strengthen the prosecution services, as well as to build the operational foundation and the institutional capacity of the Ministry of Defence and F-FDTL in light of recent developments. Therefore, we would appreciate it very much if you could kindly request the Security Council to authorize the deployment of 8 to 10 civilian advisers for institutional capacity building in the areas of defence and public prosecution.[3]

With regards to the petitioners, TMR said that he had no choice but to dismiss the petitioners as they had left the barracks on their own. He was emphatic that in any other country this kind of desertion could not be allowed to take place without disciplinary action. In the military, desertion was considered a most serious offence.

A few weeks later, on 16 March, TMR went ahead with announcing the dismissal of 594 soldiers. He had contacted the Prime Minister, but apparently could not reach President Gusmão, who was abroad. Gusmão was dismayed, and upon his return to Dili he made a televised speech on 23 March. He stated that in his capacity as the Commander-in-Chief of the armed forces, he respected the decision made by Brigadier General TMR as the Commander of the armed forces to dismiss the protesting soldiers. However, in his capacity as the President of a Democratic Republic, he found that "it focused more on military discipline and failed to address the root causes of the problems within the F-FDTL".[4] Furthermore, the President inadvertently acknowledged the existence of the differences between easterners (*lorosae*) and westerners (*loromonu*). Many Timorese interpreted the President's remark as admission that a division existed between the two highest-ranking military officers, and also between the easterners and the westerners, and led to the burning of houses in and around the capital city of Dili.[5] Surprised by the unintended outcome of his remark, the President retracted his statement the following day. It is noteworthy that President Gusmão, Prime Minister Alkatiri and Minister for Foreign Affairs Ramos-Horta then showed their unity, and repeatedly appealed to the public for calm during the subsequent weeks. Furthermore, on 12 April, the President met with the Prime Minister and Brigadier General Ruak. They all agreed to take steps to end the impasse regarding the dismissed F-FDTL soldiers. This included the possibility of undertaking a formal legal process to examine their contracts, and continuing payment of their salaries until that process had been completed.

Meanwhile, the petitioners moved to Taci Tolo and on 17 April announced their intention of holding a five-day demonstration from 24 to 28 April. They negotiated with senior PNTL officials on their plan, assuring them that it would be done in a non-violent, peaceful manner. Gastão Salsinha was to maintain control of the demonstration and would contact the PNTL district commander about any incident that might occur. PNTL General Commander Paul Martin issued a written instruction concerning the modality of PNTL deployment, including two Unidade Intervenção

Rápida (UIR, Rapid Response Unit)[6] platoons. On 23 April, following the agreement reached with PNTL, Salsinha announced that the demonstrations would be peaceful, and Paul Martin stated that the demonstrators would be stopped immediately if they became violent. On the same day, I had to leave for New York to participate in the meeting of the UN Security Council which had been scheduled for 21 April. My Deputy, Annis Bajwa, took over the UN mission until my return on 10 May.

On Monday, 24 April, the petitioners, also known as the "Group of 594" assembled at the Carantina in Taci Tolo, then started to march towards the Government Palace. The demonstrators remained peaceful as they demanded the establishment of a totally independent commission to address their grievances, including the alleged discrimination. The petitioners wore military uniforms, but were unarmed. On the second day of the protest, the petitioners were joined by outside groups including members of Comando de Libertação do Povo Maubere (Colimau 2000), a politically oriented regional activist group. Isolated incidents of violence started taking place around Dili, and increased in frequency during the week of the demonstration.

On 25 April a kiosk and goods were destroyed in the Lecidere beach area, and market stalls belonging to *lorosae* easterners were burned in the Taibessi area. Two youths were reportedly assaulted. The spokesman for Colimau 2000, Ozório Leki, then made a speech at the protest site in which he threatened to unleash the crowd if the police failed to stop the attack on market stallholders, and stated further that violence would be used to secure a change of government. Market stalls in Taibessi were burned again on 26 April, and an off-duty PNTL member in the area was attacked. According to the finding of the Independent Commission of Inquiry,[7] Salsinha allowed Leki to make a further speech on 26 April in which he used inflammatory anti-eastern language. Prime Minister Alkatiri was informed about the presence of Ozório Leki among the petitioners and the expression of anti-government rhetoric.[8]

On 27 April, Prime Minister Alkatiri called Salsinha to his office, although it was rather late at night. Foreign Minister Ramos-Horta was reportedly present with the Prime Minister. The Prime Minister then indicated his intention to meet the demands of the petitioners for an independent commission and to establish a government commission to look into petitioners' issues. He promised to report back to Salsinha within 90 days with the commission's own recommendations. Salsinha might have regarded this as a reasonable response on the part of the Prime Minister. Nevertheless he told him that the demonstrators, particularly youth supporters, would not be satisfied with the establishment of a yet another commission, and one which would be given three months before its findings were published. He felt that the Prime Minister should come out of his office and meet with the petitioners. Alkatiri, however, was unwilling to meet with the demonstrators on site, and Foreign Minister Ramos-Horta agreed to address them the following day.

On 28 April, as the demonstrators continued their protest into the fifth and final day, a small group of no more than 200 gathered in the early morning. Their numbers increased to more than 1000 by noon, their behaviour gradually turning aggressive as the speakers had become belligerent. It was noted that the original petition delivered to the state leaders had indicated 1:00 p.m. on 28 April as the time for the resolution of issues and the end of the demonstration. By 1:15 p.m., the tension had heightened, and Salsinha started losing control of the protesters, particularly a group of unidentified youths who had joined the demonstrations. The youths then broke away and ran towards the main gate of the major government building, the Palácio do Governo.

PNTL officers, including some from the UIR, retreated and fled the scene. As the demonstrators entered the area in front of the government building, a UIR commander ordered his men to stop the crowd from entering the building. However, it was apparently not possible for them to counter the intruders, as a large number of UIR officers had been redeployed from the Government Palace to Becora and Comoro without the knowledge of the Polícia Nacional de Timor-Leste (PNTL, National Police of Timor-Leste) general commander. Tear gas was used but no shots were fired at first. The rioters set alight three cars parked in front of the main government building, where the Prime Minister had his office. Some of the demonstrators then entered the government buildings without any major police intervention.

There were varying versions of what had happened prior to the outbreak of violence. According to the findings of the UN Independent Commission of Inquiry, the following series of events took place.[9]

On the morning of 28 April, President Gusmão, Prime Minister Alkatiri and Interior Minister Lobato were attending a business forum meeting at the nearby Hotel Timor with representatives from the private sector, while Foreign Minister Ramos-Horta was lunching with my Deputy, Bajwa. The deteriorating conditions at the demonstration site were reported to the Prime Minister, who apparently gave instructions by mobile phone to the Minister of the Interior, to send reinforcements to the government building. He then spoke to President Gusmão who agreed to telephone Salsinha. At about 10:00 a.m. Prime Minister Alkatiri telephoned F-FDTL Chief of Staff Colonel Lere, in the absence of F-FDTL Commander TMR, and ordered him to have the armed forces ready for deployment. Two platoons of the F-FDTL 1st Battalion in Baucau were prepared. At about 11:00 a.m. the Prime Minister again telephoned Colonel Lere to inform him that the situation had deteriorated further and instructed him to send military police (MP) officers to support PNTL. Colonel Lere ordered six MP officers to the site of the demonstration. At about 11:45 a.m. Prime Minister Alkatiri received a telephone call from the President informing him that he had met with Lieutenant Salsinha, who had promised to control the crowd and remove the petitioners from the site. Close to midday, Prime Minister Alkatiri, President Gusmão and Interior Minister Lobato spoke to each other at the Hotel Timor at the close of the conference. According to the Commission of Inquiry, the President was not made fully aware of the order that the Prime Minister had given to the armed forces to intervene in the situation. President Gusmão in fact told the Commission that there had been no discussion concerning the need for calling in the armed forces.

After leaving the main government building, the petitioners returned to Taci Tolo, escorted by PNTL and United Nations Police (UNPOL) officers. En route they passed through Comoro, a community of people of mixed eastern and western origin, and were joined by a platoon of 21 UIR police officers. The petitioners were then engaged in clashes with a crowd which attacked them. A weapon fired at long range killed one civilian; eight civilians suffered firearm injuries; and two police officers and two civilians suffered other serious injuries. After passing through Comoro, the retreating demonstrators continued towards Taci Tolo, some of them returning to their base in the Carantina and others dispersing into the hills.

As the mob moved through the area, in excess of 100 houses, owned mainly by easterners, were burned. Violence escalated shortly after 5:00 p.m. F-FDTL vehicles carrying 14 soldiers travelled past this group en route from the MP Headquarters in Caicoli towards the F-FDTL head-quarters in Taci Tolo. The demonstrators threw grenades at the F-FDTL vehicles; 14 F-FDTL soldiers responded with gunfire and approximately 100 shots were fired in 5 minutes. One civilian was killed as a result of the confrontation and one soldier sustained a minor injury to his finger as a result of a grenade explosion.

In the evening, Prime Minister Alkatiri met with Interior Minister Lobato, State Administration Minister Ana Pessoa and Defence Minister Roque Rodrigues, as well as Acting Chief of the Defence Force Colonel Lere and PNTL General Commander Paulo Martins. According to the Commission of Inquiry, there were different versions of what was dis-cussed at this meeting. There was no conclusive evidence that Prime Min-ister Alkatiri personally authorized F-FDTL to use force against the petitioners. The meeting, however, resulted in the deployment of F-FDTL soldiers to assist PNTL in restoring law and order. The meeting also authorized the security agencies to contain the petitioners. The geographic areas of responsibility of both PNTL and F-FDTL were established; significantly, F-FDTL was given responsibility for Taci Tolo.[10]

As the UN Commission of Inquiry states in its report, in making such a grave decision to deploy military forces, "No formal declaration of the state of crisis was made. During the meeting no contact was made or attempted with the president."[11] This decision had a serious implication as apparently neither President Gusmão nor Foreign Minister Ramos-Horta was informed of the decision until the following day when Prime Minister Alkatiri called the President to inform him of the decision to deploy F-FDTL troops to restore order. In all, five persons were reported killed and more than 40 injured in the violence that spread throughout the city. There was even a rumour that there were dozens of dead bodies lying in the "no-go" area at Taci Tolo and that more bodies had been thrown in the sea. Thousands of people started taking refuge in churches and other public buildings, including the UN facilities in Dili.[12]

Both PNTL and F-FDTL patrolled Dili and its outskirts during the night of 28 April into the daylight hours of 29 April 2006. The main purpose of these patrols was said to control the movement of the petitioners. However, as noted by the Commission of Inquiry, F-FDTL and PNTL had differing understandings of the exercise. The PNTL perspective articulated to the Commission was that petitioners only were to be arrested and handed to PNTL if they were moving about. No operations to capture petitioners were authorized. On the other hand, F-FDTL soldiers understood that they had been ordered to search for petitioners and shoot them if they attempted to escape.

The residents, including an ambassador whose residence was located in the western area of Dili, where F-FDTL had established positions at Rai Kotu, Taci Tolo and Beduku, heard gunfire throughout the night. Rumours spread that F-FDTL had massacred as many as 60 people in the early morning of 29 April. One claim even cited the licence plate number of the F-FDTL truck said to have been used to transport the corpses, either in boxes or a shipping container from Taci Tolo to Viqueque District on 1 May 2006. This rumour reached New York where I was about to report on the situation to the Security Council.

I asked my Deputy, Anis Bajwa, to do everything possible to verify if there was any evidence to support these rumours. He dispatched human rights monitors and police advisers to Taci Tolo. He informed me that after an extensive search they had not found any indications of mass killings. I had full confidence in the integrity of UN human rights monitors, and informed the Security Council that UNOTIL human rights officers and police advisers had not found any credible evidence to support allegations that a large number of people had been killed. The Commission of Inquiry later endorsed this conclusion, and stated that the rumour of a massacre was unfounded. While it recognized the possibility that several deaths might have occurred, it referred to the fact that extensive efforts by a variety of individuals and agencies had failed to find any evidence of a massacre. The Office of the Provedor appealed on both radio and television for families with missing persons to come forward. He made a similar appeal in leaflets distributed in internally displaced persons (IDP) camps. However, apparently nobody spoke of missing relatives. Interestingly, Salsinha confirmed that no petitioners were missing.[13]

On 29 April, Foreign Minister Ramos-Horta commendably held a briefing for resident ambassadors in Timor-Leste, as he did on numerous occasions, to keep the international community informed of what was happening. F-FDTL Chief of Staff Colonel Lere Anan and PNTL Commander Paulo Martins joined the Foreign Minister in explaining how the government had responded to the violence in the aftermath of the petitioners' demonstration. Both Martins and Lere spoke freely and without hesitation. According to Deputy Special Representative of the Secretary-General (DSRSG) Bajwa, who attended the briefing, Ramos-Horta explained that the leader of the Group of 594 had lost control over the demonstrators by the morning of 28 April. Police Commander Martins added that it was a group of youths that had joined the demonstration which had started rioting. He also noted that the rioting youths walked ahead of the Group of 594 and engaged in looting and burning houses and buildings along the way from the government building to Taci Tolo.

Colonel Lere Anan then provided a detailed explanation of what had happened during the previous 36 hours. He informed the ambassadors that the F-FDTL had carried out "joint activities" with PNTL, following the Prime Minister's instructions. He had proposed the definition of specific areas for F-FDTL and PNTL to operate along clear command and control lines. The Prime Minister and the Interior Minister, who assigned F-FDTL the area leading to Taci Tolo from the airport roundabout, accepted this proposal. Ramos-Horta indicated that this became a "no-go" area. Lere Anan also briefed the ambassadors on F-FDTL's mission. This was to protect the F-FDTL headquarters in West Dili, and to secure the passage of F-FDTL between locations, including from the Dili F-FDTL headquarters to PNTL's Dili District headquarters and from the F-FDTL Metinaro facility to Dili. Additionally, they were to contain and detain all demonstrators in the defined area. He estimated that as many as 1,000 people might be detained and turned over to PNTL. Lere Anan further indicated that in late afternoon of 28 April, four military police officers were ambushed while driving on the road in Taci Tolo. Shots were fired, stones thrown and two hand grenades were launched at them, one of which exploded. The military police reacted, and in the ensuing firefight,

Lere Anan estimated three or four persons might have been killed by the military police. The Colonel added that no deaths occurred otherwise since F-FDTL had joined the PNTL operation. He reported that one company, or roughly 100 armed soldiers, was involved in the operation, and that over the course of the afternoon the soldiers would be replaced by PNTL. He noted that five persons had been detained on the previous day, and five more were detained by F-FDTL on 29 April, and indicated that all detainees had been handed over to PNTL.

The ambassadors were eager to know the reasons for arresting members of the Group of 594, and wanted to know whether the Investigation Commission would go ahead in light of the violent developments. They were also interested in knowing how the humanitarian management of displaced persons would be handled. The ambassadors also made personal reports on their embassy staff. One mentioned hearing gunshots and grenade explosions around Taci Tolo in the early morning of 29 April. Colonel Lere Anan responded and explained that while the government knew that the Group of 594 was not engaged in violent acts, he had received complaints from the community along the way to Taci Tolo that non-uniformed members of the Group of 594 had participated in looting and other crimes. Foreign Minister Horta assured the diplomatic corps that the Investigation Commission established by Prime Minister Alkatiri would go forward as planned, and that the Prime Minister would urge the Commission to complete its work within one month. With regard to the humanitarian situation, Minister Horta informed us that the government was providing immediate food and shelter. He stated they did not yet require assistance from UN agencies, which would be sought in case national resources fell short.

Escalation of conflicts and breakdown of political processes

The consequences of the events on 28 and 29 April were grave and far-reaching, and three events emerged as most serious:

The Prime Minister's decision to mobilize F-FDTL troops to control a volatile situation, at the centre of which was a large group of dismissed soldiers and their supporters. This was widely criticized and its legal basis challenged.

The action of F-FDTL soldiers to prevent President Gusmão from entering the "no-go" area of Taci Tolo on the morning of 29 April. This resulted in a loss of trust and confidence of the President in the Prime Minister, and led to a breakdown in communication between the two top leaders of the country.

The desertion of Major Alfredo Reinado, the commander of the MP from F-FDTL. On the afternoon of 29 April, F-FDTL Commander Brigadier General Ruak went to Prime Minister Alkatiri's residence as soon as he returned from abroad. He participated in a meeting with all of the most senior government officials who had been there the previous day. The meeting resulted in a decision to withdraw F-FDTL forces from the city to the outskirts of Dili, but to continue joint patrols by F-FDTL MP and PNTL. The withdrawal of the military forces took until 4 May, when all of the F-FDTL troops returned to their bases in Taci Tolo and Metinaro. Joint MP and PNTL patrols started on 30 April and operated throughout Dili until 3 May when Major Alfredo Reinado abandoned his post and left F-FDTL. The desertion of the major and his followers had major ramifications not only for the security, but also for the political equilibrium among contested groups within the country. Unlike Lieutenant Salsinha, Reinaldo took weapons with him and used them without hesitation.

On the evening of 30 April, Prime Minister Alkatiri addressed the nation on television in an effort to extricate himself and F-FDTL from their predicament. He expressed his regret that Salsinha had lost control over the crowd, which was then taken over by Colimau 2000. Regarding the involvement of F-FDTL in the situation, Alkatiri explained that PNTL had asked F-FDTL for assistance in controlling the situation: it was not F-FDTL that had wanted to intervene. He then assured the public that the situation was under control.

Nevertheless, he said, four people had reportedly died and many others were injured, with thousands leaving their homes to seek refuge. Many houses had also been destroyed. The government was distributing food to the affected people and trying to see how it could help them more. He stated that he had already met with UNOTIL and other UN agencies to discuss how together they could help the people affected. The Prime Minister then asserted that a third party was behind the violence and destruction with the intention of dividing the nation into *lorosae* and *loromonu*. He indicated that this party sought to dissolve the government and National Parliament, in order to take over power and govern the country. He further stated that some people had even reportedly gone to talk to F-FDTL, attempting to gain their support to launch a coup against the government. The Prime Minister alleged that the same people also used the issue of *lorosae* and *loromonu* to set F-FDTL against PNTL. He claimed that the rumours about a possible confrontation and war between PNTL and F-FDTL were false.

Prime Minister Alkatiri then called on F-FDTL, PNTL, all institutions and the people to maintain unity and peace, so as to establish law and order in Timor-Leste. He asked them to build a country based on law, in which there was only one way to change the government: that is, to change parliament through elections. He appealed to all the petitioners to return from the surrounding hills, and to engage in a discussion with the government to find an acceptable solution to the problem. The Prime Minister encouraged the petitioners who did not commit any crimes to turn themselves in so that the police could hear their voices. He also called on the people to turn in those who had committed violence, such as burning houses, killing people and stealing goods, so they could be processed through the legal system. He guaranteed that if the petitioners returned, the Commission of Investigation he had established would go ahead with its investigation into the problem. All people should return to their districts, as they would also be entitled to receive an amount of money equivalent to their salaries in F-FDTL. The main interest of the government, the Prime Minister said, was to solve the problem of alleged discrimination within F-FDTL, of which the petitioners had complained.

The Prime Minister took a logical and conciliatory stance in his address to the people. He made it clear that those who violated the law would be punished, but also made known his intention to address the managerial problem within F-FDTL. Despite the violence that had taken place in the previous few days, he showed his willingness to have a dialogue with the petitioners. It was not made clear to whom he was referring when he alluded to "some people" who had ill intentions of dividing the nation by plotting a coup against the government and pitting F-FDTL against PNTL. The speech provided international observers with a different perspective and interpretation of what was happening.[14]

Prime Minister Alkatiri's appeals to the petitioners to return to dialogue with the state were received with scepticism, given the strong antigovernment sentiment that remained among the Group of 594. This group believed that F-FDTL soldiers had committed a massacre in the Taci Tolo area. In the early hours of 30 April, sporadic shooting was heard from the hills south of Dili, pointing to the possibility of a worstcase scenario in which, instead of surrendering or engaging in dialogue, the petitioners had initiated low-scale armed opposition from the mountains, a strategy that the former FALINTIL were familiar with. The leader of the petitioners, Salsinha, had stated several times in the preceding week that he and his group were prepared to die for their cause.

The desertion of Major Reinado, F-FDTL MP officers and UIR PNTL officers on 3 May 2006 created a new dynamic in the security situation. Unlike Salsinha, Reinado and his group took their arms and ammunition, travelling to Ermera District and meeting with the petitioners. The two groups did not merge, but Major Reinado and his group increased in number, as URP PNTL members joined them on 4 May. They were also joined by some additional regular F-FDTL soldiers later. However, the members of the Reinado group fell when 7 of the 11 UIR PNTL officers, who had originally left with Major Reinado, returned to PNTL on 5 or 6 May. Their return followed a telephone call from General Commander Martins to one of them, threatening dismissal if they did not return to PNTL.

The security incidents in Dili on 28 and 29 April brought about heightened tension in other parts of the country. For instance, in Gleno on 8 May, several hundred people gathered to protest the massacre which they believed had taken place in Taci Tolo. The demonstration led to the death of a Rapid Intervention Unit (RIU) police officer and in the serious injury of another police officer from the east. This incident resulted in increased antagonism among the eastern police officers, who blamed PNTL General Commander Martins and Deputy Commander Babo. Thus, it became apparent that the crisis contributed to enlarging consciousness of ethnic divisions among the people, a factor that had not hitherto been significant in the political discourse of the country. There had been indications that there was popular anger with the government for sending F-FDTL into the Taci Tolo area, and so pitting the eastern troops against the petitioners (mainly from the west), with many wondering why PNTL had not been deployed instead. This action aggravated the latent feelings of victimization already felt by those from the west.

The situation in Dili remained tense. Shops and businesses closed as rumours of retaliatory action by the petitioners grew. As tension mounted and security incidents rose, people became increasingly fearful of the conflicts intensifying, and some became concerned about possible civil war between *lorosae* and *loromonu*. Their fears were exacerbated by reports that some members of the Group of 594 had telephoned their friends and relatives, warning them to leave Dili so that operations could commence. Residents of Dili were continuing to leave the city in truckloads, seeking refuge in their home districts. Some also observed that military trucks were transporting soldiers' families to the districts.

Fear and anxiety led several family members of UNOTIL national Staff to begin entering the Obrigado Barracks,[15] as they did not feel safe in their homes. In the midst of the 4 May tumult, about 1,200 people were seeking refuge in the UNOTIL compound, while 17 local UNOTIL Staff did not report for work. Similarly, we noted that a majority of staff in the government ministries did not report for work either. UNOTIL civilian advisers, who had been located in various government buildings, had been brought to the Obrigado Barracks.

Meanwhile, the PNTL General Commander confirmed with my Deputy Senior Police Training Adviser that between 7 and 12 PNTL had abandoned their units, as had 18 F-FDTL military police. There were also reports of PNTL on the ground telling people to leave Dili, and of weapons being held by civilians there. The UN agencies held an emergency meeting with government representatives and international NGOs to discuss the need for humanitarian assistance. In the early afternoon they dispatched an assessment team to 14 locations where displaced persons had taken refuge. Based on the assessment, UN agencies took the necessary measures to provide the humanitarian assistance required.

In a conversation that my Deputy Bajwa had with Minister of State Administration Pessoa, the minister confirmed that the fact that people were leaving Dili exacerbated the general feelings of insecurity. She informed Bajwa that the fear and panic were not confined to Dili, but were also evident in the districts. People believed that there was going to be civil war. She emphasized, however, that this belief was based on unfounded rumours. She also mentioned that, fortunately, the F-FDTL and its senior command were not politicized; otherwise, there could have been a coup during the weekend of 29–30 April.

Given the erosion of trust and confidence among the Timorese leaders, it is noteworthy that President Gusmão, Prime Minister Alkatiri, Interior Minister Lobato and Defence Minister Rodrigues held a joint press conference on 4 May in an attempt to reassure the people. This was a commendable show of unity. The President appealed for calm, and said the four leaders had made a decision to convince the people to return to their homes. He asked that the people should trust them. The Prime Minister himself acknowledged that the only problem that existed at the moment was how to stop the alarmist rumours. He announced that F-FDTL soldiers, who had been controlling a part of the capital city since 28 April, were returning to their military barracks. Members of the PNTL, who had carried out patrols with automatic rifles, were also withdrawing.

In a press release from the Prime Minister's Office later in the day, it was stated that

> the presence of the armed military in the streets has been contributing towards the fear on the part of a significant part of the population living in Dili, and considering that the situation is under Government control, namely the ex-military who did not yet return to their districts of origin, the presence in the streets of-FDTL members and special PNTL units is no longer justified.[16]

It was then learned that a formal swearing-in ceremony for the Commission of Investigation would be held on Friday 5 May. The Ministry of Foreign Affairs, in a press release of 4 May, declared that the Commission had already started working. The government representative in the Commission, Minister Pessoa, had appointed the district administrators to help reach ex-F-FDTL members. All district administrators, with local representatives of both PNTL and the Ministry of Labour and Community Reinsertion, would make their best efforts to identify each of the so-called "petitioners". This would enable them to be registered either directly or through their families, and allow the payment of a subsidy until such time as the Commission completed its investigation. The process would also help each of the ex-F-FDTL members to be reintegrated into civilian life, with the government making its best endeavours to find them appropriate jobs. Their identification and registration would also be useful in determining if any had died or were injured during the violence and rampage of Friday 28 April.

On 6 May, Timorese police and military sources confirmed that 17 F-FDTL MP had deserted with their weapons, and were still missing. In addition, 12 PNTL officers, including 6 UIR agents carrying long-barrelled weapons, who had patrolled Dili with the MPs, had also left their units. The General Commander informed my Deputy Senior Police Adviser that these police and military personnel had been located in Suai, but that they did not want to speak to him. The PNTL was not clear about what the group's intentions were. These reports, which were circulating widely in Dili, included stories that weapons were in civilian hands. They contributed to the fear and sense of insecurity still prevalent among many in the country's capital.

It was learned that many government offices were not able to function, as staff had not showed up for work. The Prime Minister's Office then officially quoted the Prime Minister as saying that the government expected all public servants to return to work by Monday 8 May, and that anyone still absent then would be subject to disciplinary action. On the positive side, as of the afternoon of 6 May, UN Police confirmed that the five posts that had been manned by F-FDTL were all found to be deserted. DSRSG Bajwa visited four checkpoints on the outskirts of Dili between 4:00 and 5:00 p.m. He found them to be no longer jointly manned by police and military, with only a PNTL presence. PNTL were following orders to stop government vehicles transporting families outside of Dili, in order to limit the public appearance of government officials evacuating their families from the city.

The PNTL also provided a more visible, though still inadequate, presence in the city that day through foot and mobile patrols. These developments, and the redeployment of all F-FDTL to their barracks, contributed to restoring some degree of normalcy. Nevertheless, at three of the four checkpoints, PNTL still reported more vehicles leaving than returning to Dili. At the checkpoint in Taci Tolo, West Dili, PNTL reported that vehicles leaving Dili earlier in the day seemed to be returning later with families inside.

On 6 May, President Gusmão and Prime Minister Alkatiri again met with the Timorese media. This off-the-record meeting was aimed at discussing how the media could help to restore peace and calm after the panic in Dili the day before. The President told all media representatives that they had the responsibility to restore calm among the people. He and the Prime Minister agreed that as people still fled from Dili, it was proof that the population was still traumatized. The Prime Minister was asked about the number of MP officers who had deserted after patrolling in Ermera District. He downplayed the matter by responding that the MPs, along with some other UIR members, were not going to join the petitioners.

The Prime Minister then took the opportunity to announce that work was under way to see how the government could help to rebuild the 45 houses that had burned down and to repair 116 which were partly destroyed. He also said that there would be a new project to reconstruct Taibessi market, which was also largely destroyed. Meanwhile, the swearing-in ceremony for the members of the High Level Commission was held the same morning. In his opening remarks, the Prime Minister said that the work of the Commission was not to investigate the incident of 28 April, but to investigate the problems presented by the 594 F-FDTL petitioners, as set out in their petition. He also said that the Commission would start its work on Monday 8 May. It would review documents from the two previous Commissions, established to examine issues in previous incidents involving F-FDTL in Los Palos and Becora, and would also review other documents from F-FDTL and the petitioners.

The commission had ten members, comprising two from the government (Minister Pessoa and Vice-Minister of Interior Barris); two nominated by the President (Prosecutor-General Monteiro and Provedor Ximenes); two nominated by the National Parliament (Francisco Branco, a Frente Revolucionária do Timor-Leste Independente (FRETILIN, Revolutionary Front for an Independent East Timor) MP, and Pedro da Costa, a Timor Socialist Party (PST) MP); a representative of the church (Fr Antonio Goncalves); two representatives of civil society (Aniceto da Neves and Tiago Sarmento); and one representative from the judiciary (Judge Natercia). The Commission was to present its findings within 90 days.

In the midst of the crisis, the US and Australian governments began to issue travel advice to their citizens. The US Embassy in Dili sent a message to US citizens in Timor-Leste to inform them that if they wanted to leave the country, they could register for a chartered flight that the US State Department was sending to Dili, to pick up US Peace Corps volunteers and other Americans there.

The intensity of the animosity held by the *loromonu* against the *lorosae* erupted in Gleno on 8 May. About 500 persons, including some petitioners, surrounded the office of the Regional Secretary of State in Gleno, the district capital of Ermera, to prevent that official from leaving the building. The demonstrators attacked two unarmed PNTL officers of eastern origin, who had been persuaded to disarm by a commander of western origin, causing the death of one and serious injury to the other. The incident exacerbated tensions within PNTL, setting easterners against westerners and officers loyal to the Minister of the Interior, Rogério Lobato, against those who opposed him. As the clashes escalated, Lobato started arming two groups of civilians, Rai Los and Lima Lima, with weapons and ammunition belonging to the Border Patrol Unit (BPU) of PNTL.

The Security Council's initial response: 5 May 2006

On 5 May 2006, the Security Council reconvened the meeting with the participation of Foreign Minister Ramos-Horta, who had arrived in New York the previous day. His eloquent speech helped the Security Council and members of the core group to appreciate the fragility of the nascent country.[17]

Ramos-Horta told the Security Council that the security incidents in Dili had been a wake-up call for the Timorese leadership as well as the international community. He provided a detailed account of the disturbances, which had started several months earlier. He said that he had personally spent many days talking to leaders on all sides. The petitioners had intended to present their message in a peaceful demonstration, but had lost control of the demonstration when it was taken over by a mob of youths and hooligans. Horta expressed his intention to invite UN Human Rights Rapporteurs to carry out a thorough investigation, specifically into the allegations that many more than five individuals had been killed during the incidents of 28 and 29 April 2006.

He stated that the government and the Timorese leaders were determined to overcome the challenge. Horta further urged the Council Members and all stakeholders not to take the appearance of successful achievements and tranquillity for granted, and proposed that preventive measures be taken to stop any relapse into conflict and violence. He reminded the Council that in 1999 the Council had acted swiftly on the Secretary-General's advice to end the violence in Timor-Leste, expressing his hope that the Security Council would maintain a robust UN presence for another year.[18]

In my presentation, I also warned the Council Members that internal stability should not be taken for granted, as many had, by telling them: *"The latest developments have reminded us that not only is democracy in Timor-Leste still fragile, but also the internal security situation is easily assailable."* [19] I also told the Council participants that the extent of physical damage caused to property was minuscule in comparison with the destruction that took place in 1999. However, the psychological impact on the people had proved to be immense. I then underlined the importance of the Security Council responding swiftly to the most recent security incidents and requested continued United Nations assistance.

As the situation in Timor-Leste was undergoing a rapid change since the Secretary-General's report was issued two weeks before, I called upon the participants of the Security Council to adjust their perceptions and assumptions. While recognizing the need for an eventual transition to a sustainable development assistance framework, I presented to the Council a rationale for establishing an integrated office after UNOTIL had completed its mandate. The new mission must be able to meet the newly emerging security and political requirements to enable elections that were not only free and fair, but also credible; all essential elements for a peaceful transfer of power.

In my oral report to the Security Council, I also explained how the dismissed soldiers staged a demonstration, demanding that an independent commission be established to address the issue of discrimination and to seek a fair investigation into their grievances. I underlined the fact that the 594 former members of F-FDTL remained peaceful throughout the four-day demonstrations. I also explained how a mob of "non-594" youths and some political elements broke off from the camping group and attacked the government office building. The Council participants were informed that, according to a UNOTIL estimate, five people had been killed and at least 60 injured by firearms, stone throwing or stabbing. At the same time, I referred to the repeated assertions by the leader of the Group of 594 that the number of deaths caused by the deployment of F-FDTL on 28 and 29 April was far larger than officially announced. With regard to what might have happened in Taci Tolo during the night of 28 April, I informed the Security Council that the UNOTIL Human Rights Unit and police advisers had visited and checked the site carefully. They did not find any credible evidence to support the allegations of any mass killings. I insisted, however, that UNOTIL human rights officers would continue to monitor the human rights situation.

Mindful of the need to address the institutional weakness of F-FDTL, I also took the opportunity to stress the need for international advisers on the management of a security agency. I had discussed this issue with both the F-FDTL Commander and the Defence Secretary at my residence in March and it was subsequently mentioned by President Gusmão in his letter to the Secretary-General of 2 April.[20] These advisers, I emphasized, were needed to address grievances through the Independent Commission, and to strengthen the institutional foundations of the Ministry of

Defence and F-FDTL, improving their capacity to manage their human resources development. For that reason, I advised the Council to respond swiftly to the President's request and provide ten civilian advisers to assist in drafting and implementation of the organic law. They were also needed to support the Ministry of Defence and armed forces in developing policies, rules and regulations, procedures and principles governing all areas of defence.[21]

I then took the opportunity to present the rationale for establishing an integrated office after the completion of UNOTIL's mandate, in view of the importance of preparing for the 2007 parliamentary and Presidential elections. I noted that as little time was left for the first post-independence national elections, additional support should be provided in a systematic manner to all state institutions involved in the electoral process, including the Secretariat for the Technical Administration of the Elections, the independent Comissão Nacional de Eleições (CNE, National Electoral Commission), the Court of Appeal and other organs. In order to ensure a credible process, I referred to the particular needs of the CNE for adequate resources – both human and material – for monitoring purposes and voter education throughout the 13 districts. It was of utmost concern that the electoral process should be transparent, as this would directly affect the legitimacy of the outcome of the elections. Furthermore, a clear process would affect the prospects for the development of a healthy, multiparty democratic system in Timor-Leste. In aspiring to free and fair elections, I emphasized that the presence of the UN police was essential, to ensure that law and respect for human rights were maintained before and during the electoral campaign period. I felt the need to express our concern that the impartiality of the Timorese police could not be guaranteed in a tense political electoral environment.

In concluding my report, I provided my assessment of the situation in Timor-Leste as a conflict-prone, post-conflict country. The leaders and the people of Timor-Leste had made significant progress in consolidating peace and democracy over the previous five years. However, at the same time, national leaders and institutions were too fragile to address all the grievances of various groups for increased employment and participation in government to promote better livelihoods. As people had been led to expect these in a democracy, their leaders were increasingly faced with more demanding challenges in governing society. The country was facing the potential risks associated with the conduct of the first post-independence presidential and parliamentary elections in 2007. I drew upon the latest security incidents as reflecting the complex dynamics of political, economic and social factors at work in a nascent democracy.

Quoting Einstein, who once said that the significant problems we faced could not be solved at the same level of thinking that existed when the problems were created, I drew a parallel with regard to Timor-Leste. The country that was given its birth by the United Nations in 1999 was calling upon the international community to change its perceptions and assumptions. At very least, it was a call for help to change the lens through which the international community viewed the country in crisis. I underlined the issue, which was that the leaders and people were calling for continued international assistance to help them solve the problems – which we had not intended to create – that began when the United Nations helped restore their political independence in 2002.

Following Foreign Minister Ramos-Horta's speech and my presentation of the Secretary-General's report, members of the Security Council and other interested countries reacted positively to our calls for a continued presence of the United Nations, while recognizing the achievements that the United Nations and Timor-Leste had made since its independence. The majority of the speakers mentioned the nature of UN presence in terms of a political office to monitor human rights, transitional justice and preparatory works for presidential and parliamentary elections in 2007. In addition, many of the speakers expressed their alarm at the latest security incidents, but did not make any clear statements of support for the need to send back a fully-fledged peacekeeping mission to Timor-Leste. Some countries, such as Australia, France, Japan, New Zealand and Portugal, found the latest security situation developing in Timor-Leste as most alarming, and requiring more serious attention from the Security Council. Ambassador to Great Britain, Emyr Jones Parry made the most realistic response, recalling what Foreign Minister Ramos-Horta had said about Timor-Leste being on the edge, and expressing his extreme concern over the violence in Dili. In the end, Council Members agreed to the suggestion made by Mr William J. Brencick of the United States for a one-month extension of UNOTIL to enable that body to consider the most appropriate manner in which to respond to the emerging crisis.[22]

As it often does in similar situations, the Security Council responded to the newly emerging security situation by extending the existing mandate temporarily, in order to assess the situation. It then allowed informal consultations to take place outside of the chamber of the Security Council. This arrangement proved an effective way of allowing Member States to discuss how they wanted the Secretary-General to assess the latest situation. It also allowed time to propose the structure and composition of a future mission for consideration by the Council.

Following the 5 May Security Council meeting on Timor-Leste, Japan, as coordinator of the Council and Core Group members on the Timor-Leste issue, convened a meeting for 8 May. This was to discuss the US proposal to extend the mandate of UNOTIL for 30 days until 20 June. The Department of Peacekeeping Operations (DPKO) sent its Staff to accompany me to the meeting, which affirmed the willingness of Security Council and Core Group members to respond to the emerging needs for the United Nations' continued and enhanced presence.

A review of the Security Council and its follow-up meetings showed three pertinent points:

Security Council members and other interested countries appreciated the progress made in Timor-Leste by successive UN missions and by Timor-Leste itself.

Most of the delegates to the Security Council felt firmly that the international community, and the United Nations in particular, needed to remain in the country to ensure its peaceful transition to a framework of sustainable democratic governance and development.

They were not yet aware that the culture of violence could easily worsen the struggle for power. Timorese leaders had not attained sufficient maturity to fully assume their responsibility to manage the national security forces in a peaceful manner, and this necessitated the return of international security forces to Timor-Leste.

Escalating conflicts between the Gusmão and Alkatiri camps

FRETILIN National Congress results in loss of public confidence

Upon the completion of the Security Council deliberations, I returned to Timor-Leste. I found FRETILIN busy preparing for its National Congress from 17 to 19 May, and for the election of its leadership. One of the founders of FRETILIN, and the incumbent Timorese Ambassador to the United Nations, José Luis Guterres decided to challenge the party leadership of Mari Alkatiri. It was understood that the voting was to be carried out by secret ballot in accordance with political party law. However, at the last moment, the voting procedure was changed to "show of hands". Everybody immediately realized that it was done so to force the participants to vote for the existing leadership. José Luis Guterres decided to withdraw from the race.[23]

The FRETILIN National Congress re-elected Francisco "Lú-Olo" Guterres as its chairman and Mari Alkatiri the Secretary-General. FRETILIN reformists took the case to the Court of Appeal and contested that the vote by "a show of hands" violated the Law on Political Parties 3/2004.[24] They then called for a special convention for new elections. Mari Alkatiri and his FRETILIN leadership, however, made a counterargument. They insisted that the voting by "a show of hands" was more transparent, because the delegates would be better held accountable to the members who had selected them; members would be able to know how the delegates voted. They also pointed out that, although the vote was cast by secret ballot in FRETILIN's first convention in 2000, FRETILIN held a national conference in Sydney, Australia in 1998, where the voting was done by a "show of hands".

The FRETILIN leadership responded further with the legal arguments that the petition was filed after the ten-day period allowed under the law and that, upon the expiry of the limitation period, the election became final and could not be challenged. They also argued that, if the intention of the legislator under law 3/2004 was to limit the election of the organs of leadership to a system of direct and secret vote, it would not have permitted an election in a convention (congress) through a representative assembly which is, by its own nature, an indirect vote. Article 17 of FRETILIN's by-laws stipulated that, as a general rule, when the by-laws require a "personal, direct and secret" vote, then the whole membership votes in that manner, as in the selection of delegates to the convention. However, once the membership has selected delegates to represent them, it would be up to the delegates to choose whether to hold a secret ballot or to vote by "a show of hands".

The Court of Appeal dealt with all the arguments made in the petition, rejecting those put forward by the petitioners and accepting in full the arguments of the respondent, the FRETILIN leadership. The court first addressed the issue concerning Article 29 of the Law on Political Parties 3/2004, which required that the court must be constituted exclusively by national judges.[25] The court decided the case based on the expiry of the limitation period for an application under Law 3/2004, holding that, even though Law 3/2004 did not provide a limitation period, the court could look at the civil procedure code (codigo de processo civil) where Article 119 provided that when there was no limitation period provided in a statute to apply to the court for a remedy, then the limitation period was ten days. The court then held that the FRETILIN convention ended on 19 May 2006, and the petition was filed only on 6 July 2006 (48 days later). The court held that, even though it was during a period of political instability, the courts were open during that period. Therefore, there was no satisfactory justification for the 48-day delay in filing the petition. Once the limitation period had expired, the petitioners could not challenge the results of the election of the President and of the General Secretary of FRETILIN.

Francisco Lú-Olo Guterres and Mari Alkatiri won the re-election and kept their leadership positions in FRETILIN through the "a show of hands" voting procedure, and also defeated the reformist challengers on legal grounds. However, the credibility of their elections was left in doubt. Many considered that they would have lost if the voting had been done through a secret ballot. When I discussed this issue with Alkatiri before the FRETILIN Congress, I urged him to keep the secret ballot procedure so that his re-election would have more credibility. After the election was held, he told me that he would have accepted a secret ballot; it was his followers who insisted on "a show of hands". I feel that this event convinced Gusmão that Alkatiri would keep his position of power by any means, even if this meant betraying the trust of the people.

Armed confrontation among security personnel

The security crisis had by then fully transformed a security-sector issue into a larger political tumult. The lack of institutional capacity to deal with the managerial issue shed light on the pressing need for reforming F-FDTL, as well as PNTL. Mutual suspicion between these two rival security agencies was in fact a manifestation of the deteriorating relationship between the two top national leaders. It resulted in the multiplication of conflicts into a larger realm of east (*lorosae*) and west (*loromonu*), struggling for their perceived interests. The security crisis that followed the petitioners' demonstration also exposed the fragility of the governance structure for peaceful resolution of the emerging struggle for power between the Prime Minister and the President.

On 23 May, an armed group led by Major Alfredo Reinado, who had come down to Dili from his base in the hill town of Aileu, engaged F-FDTL soldiers and PNTL officers in a protracted exchange of fire that resulted in five deaths and more than ten seriously injured on both sides. The following day, the Rai Los group, joined by some of the petitioners, PNTL officers and civilians, attacked the F-FDTL headquarters in Taci Tolo. F-FDTL headquarters called in support from the F-FDTL naval component to repel the assault, which lasted several hours and resulted in two deaths. At around the same time, the residence of TMR came under attack, reportedly by an armed group of PNTL officers and armed civilians. While these serious incidents were taking place, a number of PNTL officers of eastern origin threw in their lot with F-FDTL, taking refuge at the F-FDTL training centre at Metinaro to the east of Dili.

Against this background, on 24 May President Gusmão, Prime Minister Alkatiri and President of the National Parliament Guterres decided to ask the Governments of Australia, New Zealand, Malaysia and Portugal for both military and police security assistance. The combination of these four countries reflected a careful balance of forces considered by the top Timorese leaders. I immediately transmitted this news to the Secretary-General. He sent a letter to the Security Council on the same day, appealing to the Council Members to give favourable consideration to the request of the Government of Timor-Leste for international security assistance. Following an informative and insightful briefing by Under-Secretary-General Jean-Marie Guéhenno, the Security Council expressed its full support for the deployment of defence and security forces from the four countries to assist Timor-Leste in restoring and maintaining internal security.

Australia and the three other countries made preparations to dispatch their troops. In the meantime, the confrontation between the two Timorese security agencies reached its climax when F-FDTL soldiers assaulted PNTL Headquarters on 25 May, exchanging fire early in the morning in Comoro. Each side believed the other had attacked it. At about 11:00 a.m., following a warning shot fired by a PNTL officer, F-FDTL launched an attack on the PNTL headquarters building in Caicoli. F-FDTL soldiers also launched attacks around noon against the Ministry of Interior, which was located just across the road from the UNOTIL compound in Caicoli. Intense gunfire was heard in UNOTIL's offices, causing international and national Staff to seek cover in buildings away from the perimeter wall of the compound.

UNPOL officers, who were present within the building that came under attack, contacted UNPOL Senior Adviser Saif Malik, who reported to me. He sought my authorization to help rescue the UNPOL and PNTL officers from the PNTL Headquarters. Shortly afterwards, UN Military Training Adviser Colonel Reis entered my office, and asked for my authorization to meet the F-FDTL commander to seek cessation of fire. I was first concerned about their safety, as both the UNPOL officers and UN military observers were no longer carrying any weapons to protect themselves from assault. However, as the situation required an urgent decision, I authorized not only Malik to rescue the besieged UNPOL and PNTL personnel, but also Reis to stop the shooting by contacting TMR. I also told Malik to use the only bulletproof vehicle available in UNOTIL. My gut reaction was based on my prior experiences in Rwanda, where the United Nations had been accused of inaction when an imminent slaughter of a countless number of people was impending. My deputy Anis Bajwa and Chief of Staff Michiko Kuroda were with me in the office when Saif Malik came to see me. Bajwa then left my office before Colonel Reis came and sought my permission to go to see the F-FDTL commander. I sanctioned both Malik and Reis to proceed with their plans on my own authority.

Colonel Fernando Reis succeeded in establishing contact with TMR to order the F-FDTL troops to stop firing. TMR agreed to the ceasefire on condition that PNTL officers stopped firing and dropped their weapons. Reis and Malik then proceeded to inform the PNTL officers in the police headquarters of the conditions offered by TMR. After their agreement to those conditions, Reis and Malik began the evacuation of police officers from PNTL Headquarters to the neighbouring UN compound. As the unarmed PNTL officers left the building in a column, marching slowly and accompanied by Reis, Malik and several unarmed UNPOL officers with the UN flag, F-FDTL soldiers opened fire on the convoy. They killed eight PNTL officers, and injured two UNPOL officers as well as 16 PNTL personnel.

F-FDTL soldiers avoided shooting at UN officers, but two of these were injured. The casualties were immediately taken in UN vehicles to the UN clinic in the UNOTIL compound. Two of the PNTL agents died in the clinic. One UNPOL officer was treated locally, while the other had to be transported to Darwin and hospitalized for treatment in Australia. Australia was magnanimous in extending its medical assistance. One of the injured Timorese police officers was then sent to South Australia where she received advanced medical treatment. She became a quadriplegic through spinal cord injury and lost the ability to move her body. Australia has reportedly given her and her family the right to become Australian citizens if they choose to do so.

The decision I took to authorize the intervention by the two unarmed UN military and police training advisers became a source of controversy. However, the UN Commission of Inquiry recognized that the responsibility for the shooting of the PNTL officers could not be placed on UNOTIL. The actions of Reis and Malik were based on the agreement reached with TMR that he had ordered his F-FDTL troops to cease firing. It was clear that Reis and Malik disarmed the PNTL officers and escorted them out of the building under UN auspices in accordance with the agreement reached with TMR, and that the two UN military and police advisers acted to the best of their judgment at the time.

The UN Commission of Inquiry, however, did point out that too much reliance was placed on the personal experience of the UN military and police officers. The Commission then raised several organizational and managerial issues, such as the need for pooling of relevant information and identification of a clear strategy, including a communications strategy with domestic authorities. The Commission also pointed out the desirability of developing a collective plan for intervention and establishing channels of communication to enable effective control to be exercised by senior UNOTIL leadership. These and many other issues could indeed be raised. However, it should be pointed out that the situation at that time was extremely volatile, requiring an immediate decision on my part. There simply was no time for lengthy consultations and formulation of an intervention strategy.

The more important issue that should have been raised was the absence of any armed UN troops available for me to dispatch and take control of the situation. The Members of the Security Council and the Core Group, particularly the United States and Australia, did keep the developments in Timor-Leste under close scrutiny, and made their own security threat assessments. The capitals of these countries received the results of assessments directly from their embassies or investigative missions they had sent. However, they misjudged the overall security situation prevailing in 2006. They had insisted on withdrawing all international armed personnel, both military and police, from Timor-Leste, leaving behind only unarmed training officers. Had there been a few companies of armed UN peacekeeping soldiers at my disposal, they could have deterred armed groups from engaging in shooting incidents in April and May 2006.

Ian Martin, whom the Secretary-General appointed as his Special Envoy, arrived in Dili on 29 May. He was there to meet with national and international interlocutors to assess the situation first-hand, and to foster reconciliation until his departure on 7 June. For my part, I went with José Ramos-Horta, who had just become Defence Minister as well as Foreign Minister, to meet with Major Reinado in Maubisse, Aileu District and the petitioners in Gleno, Ermera. We also met with F-FDTL leaders in Dili with a view to promoting reconciliation between F-FDTL and PNTL.

After a meeting with Gusmão the following week, Major Reinado handed over the weapons under his control to the international forces on 16 June in Maubisse, Aileu District. Minister Ramos-Horta acted swiftly to inform former FALINTIL fighter Vincente da Conceição, commonly known as Rai Los, to also hand over the weapons under his control. In doing so, the Rai Los group leader stated that he and his men had received their weapons in early May, on the orders of Prime Minister Alkatiri and former Interior Minister Lobato. They had been told to use them against FRETILIN's political opponents. They demanded that the Prime Minister be arrested and tried by an international tribunal before they were willing to surrender their weapons. The next day, the Prime Minister's Office issued a press release denying the allegations made by Rai Los. While there was no concrete evidence for the Prime Minister's involvement, there was sufficient evidence that Interior Minister Lobato distributed the weapons that were in the possession of Rai Los.

As Lobato became aware of what could happen to him when the public learned his role in the distribution of weapons, he made an attempt to escape the country. I seized this critical opportunity to enhance the rule of law. I suggested to the President that he needed to obtain a court order for the arrest of the former Interior Minister as he was trying to board a plane for Malaysia. The President was perplexed, but agreed to my suggestion. I immediately asked one of the Portuguese prosecutors to come to my office and draft the arrest warrant for Lobato; this was typed by my assistant and delivered to the court. The court approved the arrest warrant for the former Minister of the Interior for alleged involvement in the distribution of weapons to civilians. He was later put on trial and found guilty of illegally distributing weapons.

Gusmão moved with determination to end his confrontation with Alkatiri, making it clear that the responsibility for the security crisis had to be assumed by the government. However, Alkatiri did not agree with the rationale for the government being solely responsible. Nonetheless, the Prime Minister eventually agreed to the resignation of Minister of Interior Lobato and Minister of Defence Rodrigues, who were held responsible for the breakdown of law and order in the country. The resignation of the two ministers was followed by the broadcasting of a televised report by the Australian Broadcasting Corporation (ABC), which depicted Mari Alkatiri and Lobato authorizing the distribution of weapons to civilian groups. At a meeting of the Council of State on 21 June, Gusmão pressed the Prime Minister to either resign, or be dismissed, as there was evidence for his role in the illegal distribution of weapons. According to Gusmão, there was a call for a change of government and the dissolution of parliament. This, however, turned out to be impossible constitutionally, as the President did not have the power to dismiss the government and remove the Prime Minister.

The power struggle between Gusmão and Alkatiri reached its climax when José Ramos-Horta resigned as Foreign Minister on 25 June 2006, stating that the government was not functioning properly. The turmoil spread to the whole government, as eight ministers threatened to resign the following day. Gusmão insisted that either the Prime Minister or the President had to take responsibility. Gusmão then made the decisive announcement that he would resign as President of the República Democrática de Timor Leste (RDTL, Democratic Republic of Timor-Leste) if Mari Alkatri did not resign as its Prime Minister. Gusmão's determination and Ramos-Horta's resignation, along with threat of resignation by other ministers, left Alkatiri no choice but to resign as Prime Minister. At a press conference on 26 June 2006, Prime Minister Alkatiri insisted that he was resigning from the office of Prime Minister only to avoid the resignation of the President and any further conflict and possible civil war in Timor-Leste.[26]

The resignation of Mari Alkatiri as the Prime Minister was a turning point in the post-independence history of Timor-Leste and was expected to ease the tension. However, as the Secretary-General's report to the Security Council noted, it left a period of continued insecurity in Dili. Several thousand supporters of FRETILIN, mostly from the eastern districts, gathered just outside the capital, showing support for their party. Alkatiri addressed them, and the broadcasting of part of his address on television sparked several hours of street protests. Houses and public buildings in Dili were even set alight, and there was fear of clashes between pro- and anti-Alkatiri groups.

However, anti-Alkatiri groups from the western districts were withdrawn from the city to avoid any confrontation when the pro-FRETILIN demonstrators from the east entered Dili. Newly arrived international forces were also there by then, to control the situation. As a result of this, some have said that Alkatiri did not have the chance to incite his followers to armed struggle against the group led by Gusmão. However, from my perspective, Alkatiri could have incited his followers to engage in violent acts, but showed prudence in recognizing the need for self-discipline. I recall Mari Alkatiri repeatedly telling me that he still had the power to destabilize the country and plunge it into a civil war if he had wanted to do so in June 2006. The Timorese leaders, including Mari Alkatiri, proved themselves committed to the national interest, and capable of subordinating their personal interests to the need for national stability.

According to the Constitution, the resignation of the Prime Minister should have resulted in the dissolution of the government as a whole, and a new government with a new Prime Minister should have been formed. It required the President to consider the nomination of a majority party in the parliament, with the constitutional right to propose a new Prime Minister, who would form a new government. FRETILIN started to develop a formula which would satisfy the President. During my contact with FRETILIN leaders, I thought of Ana Pessoa as well qualified for the post, as she was someone whose integrity was unquestioned. However, President Gusmão initially refused to receive any proposal from FRETILIN. He stated that the then FRETILIN leadership lacked legitimacy since it had been elected during the party's May congress by "a show of hands" rather than by secret ballots. He called on the party to hold an extraordinary congress to elect new leaders within a month, failing which he threatened to dissolve the parliament, appoint a caretaker government and call for early elections.

Gusmão eventually agreed to enter into discussions with the FRETILIN Party representatives, after the President of the party made a public appeal for the return of weapons. FRETILIN agreed to discuss the objectives of a government of transition as proposed by President Gusmão, together with possible candidates for the post of Prime Minister and two Deputy Prime Ministers.

On 8 July, after extensive consultations with the FRETILIN leadership and other political parties represented in parliament, President Gusmão announced that Ramos-Horta would be the new Prime Minister, and swore him in on 10 July. Also sworn in were two Deputy Prime Ministers, Estanislau da Silva and Rui Araújo. On 14 July, the new Council of Ministers was announced, with most of its members being reappointed to their previous portfolios. Two FRETILIN "reformers" entered the cabinet for the first time, one being José Luis Guterres, the then Permanent Representative of Timor-Leste to the United Nations, who succeeded Minister Ramos-Horta as Minister for Foreign Affairs. The four other new ministers had been deputy ministers in the same ministries under the previous government.

The manner in which the new Prime Minister was chosen, and the new government formed, showed the Timorese leaders' commitment to work out their differences. It also demonstrated their willingness to accommodate newly emerging conditions. The security crisis of April–June 2006 also revealed the supremacy of primordial leadership in transcending administrative and legal constraints imposed on their political behaviour.

Call for international security assistance and independent investigation

In April, in one of the weekly meetings with Prime Minister Alkatiri, I had discussed the need to have international military forces in case the security situation become out of control. Alkatiri agreed and proposed to bring in Portuguese soldiers. I then took up this idea with President Gusmão. Contrary to my expectations, Gusmão was reluctant at the time to have Portuguese forces on hand, although he recognized the need to seek international security assistance should the security situation worsen. As a result, this idea did not move forward. The differing positions taken by the Prime Minister and the President on the need for international forces reflected their views on the impact of international forces on the structure of governance at that time.[27] It was not until the eruption of violence, during the third week of May 2006, that the national leaders agreed jointly to seek assistance in stationing international armed forces to handle outbursts by armed groups.

Tensions were heightened during the FRETILIN Party National Congress held from 17 to 19 May. This marked the beginning of armed clashes throughout the city. As mentioned previously and confirmed by the UN Commission of Inquiry,[28] Interior Minister Lobato started to distribute additional Unidade Patrulhamento Fronteira (UPF, Timor-Leste Border Patrol Unit) weapons to the Rai Los group on 21 May.

On 23 May Major Reinado and his group ambushed F-FDTL and PNTL officers, resulting in the death of five people and the serious injury of ten others. The Rai Los group, petitioners and PNTL personnel, attacked ten F-FDTL soldiers in Taci Tolo and Tibar areas, causing the death of five people and serious injury to two. Even the residence of

TMR was attacked and one person killed. Faced with new security incidents, F-FDTL apparently started arming civilians.

In view of the deterioration in security conditions, the Timorese leaders discussed various alternative means of securing international security assistance. They were aware of the impossibility of securing the return of UN peacekeeping forces within a short period of time. Therefore, as indicated in a letter to the Secretary-General and signed by the three national leaders,[29] they decided to make a direct request that Australia, Malaysia, New Zealand and Portugal should send security forces to Timor-Leste as soon as possible.

They explained that the request had been made in order to establish some measure of security and confidence among the population. The strategy was to restore tranquillity throughout the national territory, and to promote a climate of dialogue among the various sectors of society. They added that the request had been made to those countries in a bilateral framework, as securing security forces under the UN mandate would incur delays. In view of the importance they attached to the role of peacekeeping and peacebuilding efforts in Timor-Leste, they requested that the Secretary-General obtain international support in addition to the assistance it was hoped would be extended by the four countries.[30] Their request had in fact mandated that the Secretary-General obtain the legitimacy of the security assistance by the four countries through the Security Council.

As soon as I obtained the signed original letter in the afternoon of 24 May, I faxed it to DPKO Headquarters in New York. I requested that the letter be brought to the urgent attention of the Secretary-General and the Security Council, and that the Security Council should meet and respond to the request immediately. The 13-hour time difference between Dili and New York helped us to process this request. Within the same day, DPKO was able to arrange for the Secretary-General to send a letter to the President of the Security Council. He expressed the hope that, on the understanding that the four countries were ready to provide security, the Security Council would consider the request favourably.

Under-Secretary-General (USG) Jean-Marie Guéhenno attended from DPKO. He first made informative and insightful briefings to an informal meeting of the Core Group, and then to the Security Council on 24 and 25 May 2006, noting that the overall security situation had begun to deteriorate since I reported to the Security Council on 5 May. USG Guéhenno explained in detail the security incidents that had taken place, including those that occurred in Gleno on 8 May, Becora on 21–22 May, Fatu Ahi on 23 May and Taci Tolo on 24 May. This series of events had culminated in the submission of a request made jointly by President Gusmão, Prime

Minister Alkatiri and National Parliament President Lú-Olo Guterres for security assistance from Australia, Malaysia, New Zealand and Portugal.

Guéhenno not only supported the Timorese authorities' request, but also pointed out the need for the United Nations and the international community to:

> help Timor-Leste address the underlying causes of the current crisis, beyond the immediate containment of the present very volatile situation.... Such efforts should aim not only to prevent any further deterioration of the situation, but to also bring all interested parties together to engage in a constructive dialogue in order to discuss steps for addressing outstanding grievances of all groups concerned and to resolve the deeper underlying problems in order to overcome the current impasse.

Guéhenno also indicated his readiness to dispatch a senior UN official who was familiar with the situation in Timor-Leste, who could facilitate a dialogue among warring groups without being involved in dealing on a day-to-day basis of the ongoing political and security situation.[31]

By the end of 25 May, it was possible for the President of the Security Council to issue a statement acknowledging the request made by the Government of Timor-Leste. He welcomed the positive responses made by the selected partner countries in deploying their security forces to assist Timor-Leste in restoring and maintaining security forces.[32] The manner in which the UN system acted on this request can be cited as an example of efficiency and unity in international security assistance, for within two days, the Secretary-General and the Security Council had taken all necessary measures.

Call for an Independent Special Commission of Inquiry

In early May, Ramos-Horta had suggested that the UN High Commissioner for Human Rights should send a Rapporteur to investigate human rights violations during the incidents of 28 and 29 April. I then discussed with him the idea of bringing in an independent UN Commission of Inquiry, whose purpose would be to investigate the incidents that took place in late April and May 2006. He agreed, and on 13 June Ramos-Horta officially called for the establishment of an Independent Special Commission of Inquiry, acknowledging that any domestic inquiry would lack credibility. In order to overcome the ongoing crisis and achieve reconciliation, he emphasized the critical importance of establishing the facts and circumstances through an international investigation. Ramos-Horta suggested that the UN commission should specifically review the incidents of 28 and 29 April and 23, 24 and 25 May, and other related events that had contributed to the crisis. He expressed his hope that the international inquiry could assist the reconstitution of Timor-Leste's security sector, and that it would assign accountability for criminal and human rights violations committed during the crisis period.

In doing so, it would re-establish public confidence in the government and security institutions, essentially promoting democratic governance. The government considered that the domestic justice system should be the primary avenue of accountability for any criminal and human rights violations that the Special Commission of Inquiry deemed had been committed. It was critical that such a commission be established as quickly as possible, so it could submit its findings and recommendations to both the Secretary-General of the United Nations and the National Parliament of Timor-Leste within a period of three months.[33]

In a letter from Minister Ramos-Horta to me dated 8 June,[34] the Government of Timor-Leste officially invited the United Nations to "establish an independent Special Inquiry Commission" to "review the incidents of 28 and 29 April, 23, 24 and 25 May and other related events or issues which contributed to the crisis". In this letter he expressed his genuine concern about the need for Timorese society to find a way to restore its stability on the basis of truth, justice and democratic principles. It also demonstrated his conviction that these goals could best be achieved with international assistance through the United Nations. I was both pleased and proud of the fact that the Timorese leaders accepted my suggestion of asking the United Nations to establish an independent, international commission.

In response, the Secretary-General on 12 June requested the United Nations High Commissioner for Human Rights to take the lead in establishing this commission. On 27 June, the Secretary-General then wrote to President Gusmão to inform him of the appointment of Paulo Sergio Pinheiro of Brazil, Zelda Holtzman of South Africa and Ralph Zacklin of the United Kingdom and Northern Ireland to the Independent Special Commission of Inquiry (COI) for Timor-Leste.

The mandate of the Commission included clarifying responsibility for the events, and recommending measures to ensure accountability for crimes and serious violations of human rights allegedly committed during the period. It meant that the Commission would identify specific persons. The Commission, which began its work in July, was asked to submit its report to the Secretary-General via the High Commissioner for Human Rights and to the National Parliament of Timor-Leste, within three months of its deployment to Timor-Leste, meaning that the report was due by 7 October 2006. The Secretary-General noted the request I had made to the Timorese government for an investigation into the 25 May incident in which two UNOTIL police training advisers were injured and nine PNTL officers had died. Foreign Minister Ramos-Horta informed the Secretary-General that the Office of the Prosecutor-General had initiated an investigation into the incident.[35] The Minister requested UNOTIL to *"make available any testimonies, any autopsy records and any other material evidence to the Office of the Prosecutor-General"*, and sought *"additional human and material resources to enable the Office to carry out its investigations"* into the incidents on 28–29 April and 25 May.[36]

Responding to the Timorese Government's request, the Secretary-General appointed an Independent Special Commission of Inquiry to establish the facts and circumstances relevant to incidents that took place on 28–29 April and 23–25 May 2006. The Commission was not only to identify events that contributed to the crisis, but also to clarify responsibility for them. After three months of deliberation, the Commission concluded that:[37]

- the violent events of April and May were more than a series of criminal acts, and reflected the deep-rooted culture of violence and impunity as well as the fragility of state institutions that need to uphold democratic principles and the culture of governance;
- the national judicial institutions with the support of the international community should take measures to ensure the accountability for crimes and serious violation of human rights committed in April–May 2006;
- prosecution and trials of criminal cases should be handled by the Timorese domestic judicial system;
- trials should be carried out by a panel consisting of two international judges and one national judge, or a single international judge;
- an international prosecutor should be appointed as Deputy Prosecutor General with a clear mandate to investigate and prosecute cases impartially and without political interference;
- former Interior Minister Lobato and several others should be prosecuted and brought to trial, and former Prime Minister Alkatiri be investigated with regard to his possible involvement in the distribution of weapons among unauthorized groups of personnel.

The Dili District Court tried former Minister of Interior Lobato and in its judgment sentenced him to seven and a half years of imprisonment. The Court of Appeal upheld this, signifying that the national judicial system was functioning reasonably well. However, Rogério Lobato was discharged because of ill health.

Another issue that came up was the possible role played by Rogério Lobato in distributing weapons and hiring civilians to replace the police. Rogério Lobato contacted the Rai Los group known as Lai Los. According to Lai Los, Lobato contacted him and took the group to the Prime Minister's residence, and in the latter's presence, the decision was made to form a hit squad and distribute weapons. Mari Alkatiri totally denied his involvement. Rogério Lobato at first insisted that the Prime Minister asked him to do this, but changed his mind following advice from his lawyers, and accepted all the blame himself. President Gusmão's decision not to pursue the matter demonstrated his reluctance to exact any revenge, but there was much debate about the appropriateness of his decision, which was made immediately before the change of government.

Divergent views on the direct and root causes of the 2006 crisis

The security crisis of 2006 was triggered physically by "petitioners" or dissatisfied soldiers who complained about the discrimination within F-FDTL, and escalated into a wider conflict between *lorosae* and *loromonu* groups. The complexity of the conflict increased because of the animosity between PNTL police officers and F-FDTL soldiers. Nevertheless, diagnosis shows three root causes. The first was the struggle between the two top leaders, Gusmão and Alkatiri, for power and authority. The second was the mentality and mindset of Timorese people, who readily resorted to violent acts to prove their loyalty to one of the two leaders, or through fear for their own safety. The third was the expectation of marginalized groups for inclusion in the political, economic and social structures of society.

The clashes of security personnel exposed not only the differences in dealing with these issues, but also the identical intentions of the two national leaders, Gusmão and Alkatiri. As the International Crisis Group (ICG) points out, the rivalry between the two had roots in ideological and political disputes in the 1980s and 1990s: "*particularly between FRETILIN central committee members and Xanana Gusmão, then commander of the guerrilla army FALINTIL, carried over into the post-conflict government.*"[38] While the ICG's emphasis was the ideological differences between the two men, in my view, these are secondary to the prime cause of conflict: their desire for power and authority.

It was Mari Alkatiri's insatiable desire for more power and authority that tipped the delicate balance that previously existed between him and Xanana Gusmão. Gusmão had been willing to tolerate Mari Alkatiri in order to pursue his centrally planned economic policy and authoritarian rule by dominating government and parliament.

It is significant to note that Gusmão did not act to stop Mari Alkatiri until three events took place, revealing Alkatiri's intention to take away power from Gusmão, and beginning to pulling the country apart. The first event was Alkatiri's unilateral decision to deploy F-FDTL soldiers on 28 April 2006. The second was the act of disloyalty of his own soldiers on the morning of 29 April, when they stopped him, as Commander-in-Chief, from entering the no-go area of Taci Tolo, where a massacre had reportedly taken place in the previous night. The third event occurred when José Luis Guterres, then the Timorese ambassador to the United Nations and reformist member of FRETILIN, challenged Mari Alkatiri's leadership of that party. The decision was made to change the method of electing party leaders from the secret ballot to an open show of hands at the FRETILIN party congress in May 2006. This convinced Gusmão that Alkatiri would do anything to gain and strengthen his power in the pursuit of domination. These events forced Gusmão to conclude that he himself must prevail, lest the country fall into the hands of Alkatiri. In Gusmão's view, Alkatiri would eventually become a dictator and would disregard the principles of democratic governance.

According to DSRSG Bajwa, who acted on my behalf during my participation in the Security Council sessions in New York, he met separately with the Prime Minister and the President on 29 April. Both of them confirmed the understanding that Salsinha, leader of the Group of 594, had lost control over the youths who had joined the demonstrators. Other than the fact that the youths triggered the violent clashes, the concerns of the Prime Minister and the President differed. The Prime Minister wished to take immediate countermeasures, while the President was more concerned with the ramifications of the eruption of violence. Alkatiri had no doubt that the youths would resort to violence and immediately asked Lobato to increase the number of police personnel. He reportedly told Bajwa that he had ordered the deployment of military police at the Government Palace, followed by the deployment of F-FDTL soldiers to take control of Taci Tolo. The Prime Minister insisted that he had decided to do that in order to avoid overlapping control between F-FDTL and PNTL. According to Bajwa, Alkatiri seemed confident that the situation would be under control in a few days.

Reflecting his legal mindset, Alkatiri's intention was to counter the Group of 594 at two levels: through the criminal procedures and through the investigation commission. He dismissed the idea that the F-FDTL operation was creating anxiety among the people, but agreed with the need for visible PNTL presence throughout the city. The Prime Minister then went on to say that the situation provided an opportunity for citizens' political education, which he considered a part of nation-building. With regard to the causes of the incidents, the Prime Minister asserted that the latest developments were influenced by some politically motivated elements, but cleared the main opposition parties from that blame. He would not rule out the involvement of some foreigners.

Xanana Gusmão's main concern was the manner in which the F-FDTL soldiers had been deployed. He was also troubled about the fact that F-FDTL was given the authority to control the Taci Tolo area completely, and prevented anyone from entering that area. When the President tried to verify a rumour that spread on the morning of 29 April, that mass killings had taken place the previous night, F-FDTL soldiers prevented him from entering the area. This was a major blow to his authority. Gusmão complained to Bajwa that he had neither been consulted nor informed of the Prime Minister's decision to call in F-FDTL, and had learned about it only after the operation had already commenced. The President raged that the government had made a seriously wrong decision without having consulted him. He repeatedly said that had he been consulted, he would never have allowed the use of F-FDTL. Gusmão was angry that the excuse given by the Prime Minister for lack of timely consultation with him was the jammed mobile telephone communications. The President emphasized to Bajwa that he was the Supreme Commander of the Armed Forces and that the troops had been deployed in this operation without his orders or even his knowledge.

It is worth assessing further the psychological impact the Prime Minister's decision to deploy F-FDTL had on President Gusmão. When Bajwa met the President on 29 April, he looked and sounded very unhappy, expressing disgust over the situation. The President lamented that although the government had promised him that the army would be recalled by the afternoon of Saturday, it was still in control of Taci Tolo on Sunday. Referring to the continued patrolling of the city by armed F-FDTL and PNTL, the President said that instead of having a good effect, the practice was scaring and harassing the people.

The President perceived that by seeing PNTL working with armed F-FDTL soldiers, the people's confidence in PNTL was eroded. He thought that the relationship between the F-FDTL and PNTL had become that of "cat and mouse", and deplored that all this happened at the time when he was attempting to solve the problem of discrimination inside F-FDTL. The President told Bajwa that the Prime Minister had come to see him, and had insisted that his decision on using F-FDTL had been right. The President repeated to Bajwa that, if he had been asked, he would never have allowed this to happen.

The manipulation of the FRETILIN congress by its incumbent leadership also deepened Gusmão's mistrust in Alkatiri. It created a polluted environment, where the grievances became a primary reason for eventual armed confrontation between forces aligned to the President and those of the Prime Minister. The breach of democratic principle for electing leaders of FRETILIN, and the government's inability to address the deepening socio-economic issues – particularly unemployment – were as critical as its failure to address the institutional management issues within F-FDTL. It could be further construed that, in spite of the rational efforts made by Xanana Gusmão and Mari Alkatiri to resolve their personal differences and forge national unity, the mutual struggle for power had intensified. It became the fundamental cause of the crisis itself.

The rivalry between the two men preceded the 2006 crisis; its origins were many years ago during the period of Indonesian occupation. The onslaught of the Indonesian army was massive and brutal. Most of the FRETILIN activists and fighters, including its President Lobato, lost their lives within a few years. Although Gusmão started as a relatively junior officer of FRETILIN in 1975, he emerged as one of the few remaining resistance fighters, and was elected in 1981 to become the leader of FALINTIL. He then became disenchanted with the ideology pursued by FRETILIN, and left the political party to form the Concelho Nacional da Resistência Maubere (CNRM, National Council of Maubere Resistance) which included the União Democrática Timorense (UDT, Timorese Democratic Union) and the Resistência Nacional dos Estudantes de Timor Leste (RENETIL)[39] as well as some FRETILIN members.

By 1986, FRETILIN recognized FALINTIL as a non-partisan force with Gusmão as its commander. He established himself as the most visible commander in the independence struggle against Indonesia, until he was captured by the Indonesian army and imprisoned in late 1992. It is important to observe that even a decade later, after the departure of Indonesian troops and the establishment of an independent sovereign country, the ideological and political disputes between FRETILIN central committee members and Xanana Gusmão continued. I recall him telling me that he could not continue fighting for independence with FRETILIN enshrining Marxism–Leninism as its political ideology.

Once Mari Alkatiri became the Prime Minister of the first Constitutional Government, his inclination to acquire power propelled him to take total control of the entire government system. He sought control of all institutions of governance, including the security agencies, PNTL and F-FDTL, and achieved this through legal and institutional means as head of the government from 2002 to 2006. Significantly, during the first few years Gusmão was relatively accommodating, and not particularly opposed to Alkatiri. In this way he strengthened Alkatiri's position until the latter posed an imminent threat to his own authority as President.

For instance, on 20 May 2004, Gusmão was not concerned with Alkatiri's demand to be one of the two signatories to a document formalizing the transfer of power to command the defence forces, during the ceremonial transfer of command and control. According to UNMISET, which was preparing the document for executive policing authority transferral for the ceremony, it was to be signed by UN Police Commissioner Sandra

Peisley and PNTL General Commander Paulo Martins. SRSG Kamalesh Sharma and Prime Minister Alkatiri then signed a supplementary document on the defence power transferral.

Then, a similar but a more important document on power transferral was to be signed by SRSG Sharma, on behalf of the Secretary-General of the United Nations, and Xanana Gusmão, as Head of State and Commander in Chief of the Timorese national defence forces. However, as the date for the ceremony approached, Prime Minister Alkatiri insisted that he should be the one to sign the document. His argument was that he was head of the Government of Timor-Leste, to which the Minister of Defence reported, along with the Commander of F-FDTL. When this proposal was raised with Xanana Gusmão, he was surprisingly relaxed and did not object to the Prime Minister sitting alongside him and signing the document. He said that it would be him, and not Mari Alkatiri, who would stay in the country and fight again in its defence if any foreign troops invaded Timor-Leste.

It may still not be fair to label Mari Alkatiri as one who disregarded the presidential authority over the armed forces as their Commander-in-Chief. While Mari Alkatiri wanted the public to recognize that he had authority over the security forces, he told me that he nonetheless thought that F-FDTL remained in the President's domain of control. When Lieutenant Salsinha and his soldiers knocked on the President's office door in January 2006, Xanana Gusmão as the President and the Supreme Commander initially admitted the existence of a difference between officers from the eastern part of the country (*lorosae*) and those from the west (*loromonu*). As more soldiers from the west joined the petitioners, personal and institutional tensions grew between the President on one hand, and the government and F-FDTL on the other. The President advocated mutual accommodation and tolerance between *lorosae* and *loromonu*. At the same time, the government supported the enforcement of military rules and disciplines by F-FDTL leadership. Both sides began to protect and increase their own power base, and this encouraged the security forces to become political.

The political and institutional dimensions of the 2006 crisis were widened by the imbalance in power between the institutions of state; these allowed the government to operate with few constraints. The President and opposition parties became critical of Mari Alkatiri and his FRETILIN subgroup, for having used their dominant position and superior political machinery to limit the time available for genuine political debate in the National Parliament, and even within FRETILIN itself. Their use of the overwhelming parliamentary majority, and the weakness of the small and fragmented opposition parties, meant that there was no chance for the National Parliament to be able to function as an effective check on the executive. Outside of parliament, there was growing tension between the governing elite on the one hand, and the church and much of civil society on the other. The government was also seen as attempting to further politicize the security agencies, F-FDTL and PNTL, allowing these institutions to disintegrate instead of developing an integrated strategy for the security sector.

The government faced almost impossible challenges. It needed to fulfil people's expectations for the fruition of political independence, while at the same time developing the human and institutional capacities for democratic governance suited to Timorese conditions. Both required time and resources. Furthermore, as the spirit of democracy slowly but steadily spread, the public began to expect the civil service to be politically independent, and government officials to be accountable to the population at large. During the first three years, however, the institutions of governance had suffered from the centralization of decision-making and the politicization of many issues. The absence of regulatory frameworks was particularly detrimental in the security sector, where the government had not been able to develop sufficient managerial capacity and staff development plans.

It should also be noted that capacity deficits in such areas as management and administration went hand in hand with unused capacity. In particular, at the local level, there were unemployed youths, women, traditional leaders, middle managers and those with technical skills. The failure to use available capacity, and its concentration in Dili, were associated with the highly centralized system of financial control. During one of my field trips to rural districts, a sub-district administrator lamented that he had received absolutely no funds to spend on repairing schools and clinics, not to speak of roads and bridges. People, he said, would not take him seriously as he had nothing to offer.

High urban unemployment and rural poverty are the main economic reasons for a populace becoming disenchanted with any government, including the first constitutional Government of Timor-Leste. Many people were alienated by the perception that government leaders were enjoying the material and political benefits of independence, while they themselves continued to suffer from lack of food and gainful employment. Furthermore, the absence of any prospect of meaningful involvement in public service and employment opportunities led young people to protest whenever an opportunity arose.

It is crucially important to understand and appreciate the mindset of national and local actors in post-conflict countries; I feel it is vital to prevent them from falling into the black hole of conflict. To help resolve the ongoing crisis in Timor-Leste, I made several suggestions, as noted in my end-of-assignment report submitted before the completion of my assignment as SRSG on 30 September 2006. The key recommendations are as follows:[40]

The publication of the report of the Independent Commission of Inquiry should be followed vigorously through a judicial process. The court should constitute a special panel and a special prosecutor, as the United Nations had done for the serious crimes committed in 1999. The United Nations should recruit and hire new international judicial personnel to augment professional competence and integrity. The Chief Justice of the Court of Appeal and the Prosecutor General should be relieved of their supervisory responsibility over the judges and prosecutors, who handled the cases originating from security incidents in April and May. UNMIT should provide both substantive and operational support to enable the judicial personnel to maintain their integrity.

It was incumbent upon the international community to ensure that free, fair and credible elections were held in 2007 as scheduled, and in a secure environment. For this purpose, the international community should provide support for all electoral activities, such as drafting electoral laws, voter registration, voter education, electoral campaigns and vote counting, as well as verification and certification of these processes. Additionally, it should also ensure that the Technical Secretariat for Electoral Administration (STAE) be overseen by CNE, the independent national electoral commission.

Both Xanana Gusmão and Mari Alkatiri should be allowed to run for political leadership positions in 2007, in spite of calls for them to step down due to their involvement in the security crisis of 2006. The people of Timor-Leste should exercise their right to choose their leaders. The incumbent President, former Prime Minister and the leaders of any political party should indeed be available for the people to choose if they wished. My suggestion was based on the premise that both the President and the former Prime Minister were entitled to know if their own people approved or disapproved of their behaviour and conduct. The international security forces and UN police would be responsible for protecting Gusmão and Alkatiri, along with all other candidates, to enable them to exercise their right to participate in the electoral process without fear for their safety.

The arrival and presence of the international security forces helped to stabilize the country, but the calm on the surface did not reflect the intensity of the continued underlying power struggle. Nor should one underestimate the strength of feeling that various actors have about their right to be in power and govern the country. To maintain control over such strong feelings and prevent them from erupting into violent acts, it is essential for a full international military to back up UN police forces, until the elections are over.

The Security Council should provide a mandate for a comprehensive security sector review to clearly define the respective roles of F-FDTL and PNTL. However, the review should not be undertaken solely by foreign experts. This reflects the major decision taken by the United Nations to create a special police unit in 2003, without a full assessment of its consequence on various segments of Timorese society. We had learned an important lesson. The process of consultation among different segments of Timorese society was essential to secure their ownership of any proposal for change. The government ministries and agencies concerned should take a lead in formulating the security sector reform proposal, with the assistance of UNMIT and other international partners. However, thorough consultations should take place within and between the Council of Ministers, the Superior Council on Defence and Security, the National Parliament, and ultimately the civil society organizations including the church. If all segments of Timorese society were involved in the process of consultations on key components of security sector reform, they would feel ownership and accountability of the security sector framework being developed for the nation.

With regard to the root causes of the security crisis, on 10 October 2006 the International Crisis Group published its Asia Report No 120 which critically commented on what the Timorese government and the international actors had or had not done. The United Nations Transitional Administration in East Timor (UNTAET), according to the report, failed to deal quickly with the cantoned FALINTIL fighters. UNMISET was criticized for not having questioned or even understood the implications of politicization of the police by Rogério Lobato and FRETILIN's accumulation of power. Both UNTAET and UNMISET were accused of having been responsible for lapses that led to a politicized and inept court system.

These criticisms, I found, lacked perspective in assessing critical factors at work in post-conflict countries. Concerning the judiciary, the United Nations and the international community had been preoccupied with the implementation of transitional justice at the expense of the national judiciary. Shortly after my arrival in Timor-Leste, I found a large unit of more than 30 international staff investigating serious crimes and prosecuting perpetrators. They were paid from resources provided by the Security Council. Yet there was little budget for defence lawyers, who were mostly UN volunteers. It was a clear violation of the principle of "equal arms".

Furthermore, UNMISET had no budget for building the national judiciary, except for prisons. As a result, the United Nations Development Programme (UNDP) and bilateral donor agencies used financial resources contributed to them voluntarily in order to help build the capacity of national judiciary institutions and personnel. Transitional justice needed to be carried out, but the national judiciary needed material and training support from the international community including the UN system. One of the difficulties encountered in building the cadre of competent national judiciary personnel was the decision made by the political leaders to adopt Portuguese as the official language of governance. Initially, national judiciary personnel showed their reluctance to learn and use this language, as they had been trained in Indonesian laws in the language known as Bahasa Indonesia. As the controversy lasted several months, I intervened in one of the crucially important meetings to persuade the national judiciary personnel to accept the Portuguese language and use it, along with Tetum, in court.

Sharma and I were acutely aware of the implications of FRETILIN's accumulation of power, and discussed these in depth between us, as well as with Timorese colleagues. I remember that in April 2004 we suggested to Gusmão that the President should not approve the inclusion of Prime Minister Mari Alkatiri as a signatory to the document transferring the power to manage national defence from the United Nations to the State of Timor-Leste. We agreed to the Prime Minister signing it only after Gusmão said that he did not view this as a major threat to his authority, for he saw things differently. He told us that we should not be concerned as it would be he, and not Alkatiri, who would stay in Timor-Leste to command F-FDTL if there was a need to resist an attack on the Timorese people's independence and freedom. Had Gusmão taken a firm position against any encroachment of his Presidential power by Alkatiri, he might not have pushed so hard to challenge Gusmão in 2006.

I discovered to my dismay that the mandate of UNMISET and UNOTIL missions did not authorize us to be directly involved in the institutional capacity-building of F-FDTL in order to establish its proper management capacity. The Security Council wanted UN missions to build the national police force, but not the national defence forces. The military was left to bilateral partners such as Australia, Malaysia, Portugal and the United States. Despite the UN's inability to support F-FDTL institutional capacity-building, in March 2006 I told the key Timorese security leaders that I would request the United Nations to provide ten advisers for improvement of F-FDTL management.

The training provided by the United Nations and other international agencies emphasized operational, administrative and managerial issues, but the training of police officers needed to have a more psychological, anthropological, sociological and cultural approach. The mindset and mentality of Timorese security officers headed by Minister of Interior,

Rogério Lobato, interpreted any development in terms of being for or against them. This needed to be changed.

The ICG report created another misleading impression about the crucial decision made to establish the special police unit to deal with armed groups in 2003. The report referred to a statement that the Unidade de Reserva da Polícia (URP, Police Reserve Unit) had been created after the F-FDTL's failure to handle militia incursions in early 2003. This did not reflect what had actually occurred. Timorese soldiers did not fail in this task, but they had to leave the area at the insistence of PKF Sector West Command that the F-FDTL not be maintained in the same area of responsibility as the PKF in Bobonaro and Ermera Districts. To fill the gap, a heavily armed national police force was created and tasked with guarding the border areas. In February 2003, I visited Atsabe and Hatolia and met with local inhabitants who appreciated and pleaded for continued stationing of the F-FDTL soldiers in their area. Admittedly, this decision to create a special unit armed with long-range weapons eventually resulted in importing a large number of high-powered weapons for various special units created to deal with armed violence.

With reference to the ICG reports comments about my own role, it is pertinent to note specific actions I took to address several issues of concern to key actors in Timor-Leste:

As the petitioners stepped up their demand for fair treatment in March, I took up the issue not only with Prime Minister Alkatiri, but also with Defence Minister Roque Rodrigues and F-FDTL Commander Brigadier General TMR. As noted already, on 10 March I invited both of them to my residence and advised them to take into account the political implications of any steps they proposed. I also advised of the need to address management and personnel issues, such as the promotion of security personnel, by establishing the institutional capacity and mechanisms to deal with them. They told me they had not received appropriate assistance in this area from bilateral partners. My suggestions of UN assistance were welcomed, as they were eager to build the institutional capacity to manage their agency.

The Security Council had never given any mandate to UNMISET and UNOTIL to be formally involved in institutional capacity-building of the defence agency. However, I told the Defence Minister and F-FDTL commander that I would do everything to secure UN advisory assistance in terms of legal, management and training experts. We then discussed the specific requirements for advisory services. This laid the ground for a subsequent review by the needs assessment team. A further result was the Secretary-General's proposal for advisory services for security sector reform, as reflected in his report to the Security Council.

As soon as I returned to Dili from the Security Council meetings in New York on 11 May, I suggested that an independent UN-led investigation be conducted into the events of 28–29 April. My suggestion was accepted and later emerged as a consolidated request by the Timorese leaders for an independent UN inquiry into the key incidents of both April and May.

In order to arrest the proliferation of weapons, I took an initiative to meet with Lieutenant Gastão Salsinha in Gleno in mid-May, and followed up the matter with both the President and the Prime Minister on 16–17 May. During the meetings, I emphasized to both that it was their responsibility to collect the missing weapons. They agreed to make a joint appeal for their return, although the Prime Minister stressed it would not be an easy task. The joint declaration, however, did not materialize, as the outcome of the FRETILIN congress from 17 to 19 May widened the gap in communication between the two leaders. Here, again, it should be noted that I had no international forces to back me up and collect the weapons; the international security forces subsequently did this after their arrival.

I invited national and international prosecutors to my residence on 14 June, and judges on the following day, and stressed the importance of their acting independently in this time of crisis. The judges and prosecutors thanked me for giving them strong moral support. It was as a result of this encouragement that they acted expeditiously in issuing arrest warrants for former Interior Minister Rogério Lobato, Major Alfredo Reinaldo, Deputy Commander Abilio Mesquita (Mausoko) and others. I believe these judicial actions had a lasting, positive impact on increasing public confidence that no one was above the law in Timor-Leste; no doubt, the people began to feel ownership of the national judiciary.

In July 2006, newly appointed Prime Minister Ramos-Horta and I travelled extensively to many parts of the country in order to hold meetings and dialogues with local leaders and people. UNOTIL's daily situation reports indicated that I visited Alieu, Baucau, Gleno, Los Palos, Maliana, Viqueque and Suai, as well as Ermera, during and since the crisis of April–May. My findings and recommendations were brought to the attention of the President and the Prime Minister, along with other ministers. In contacting Ramos-Horta at every step, Janelle Suffin provided invaluable help in conveying key points of my messages to him and reverted to me expeditiously. Having served as senior political adviser to the Foreign Minister for three years since 2004, she moved to Australia in 2007 and was elected a member of the Australian Parliament for Page, New South Wales, in 2007.

In spite of my active involvement, as well as that of my deputy and other senior staff of UNOTIL, the lack of international armed troops and police did not allow me to exercise the necessary authority in dealing with my Timorese colleagues. The trust and confidence that the Timorese leaders placed in me made it possible to influence their policies and conduct, but not their behaviour and actions, which were triggered by fear of their own security. It should be noted that the report of the ICG was too simplistic in insisting that the SRSG should merely pressure, confront and dictate national leaders to accept what the SRSG wanted, lest the country is put under Chapter VII status.

The Timorese leaders took my views and opinions seriously. In a letter dated 5 June 2006 to Secretary-General Kofi Annan, President Xanana Gusmão, Prime Minister Mari Alkatiri, Foreign Minister Ramos-Horta and National Parliament President Lú-Olo Guterres jointly reiterated their appreciation of the constructive engagement undertaken by me and other UNOTIL staff. President Gusmão even asked me to remain in Timor-Leste. I am pleased to note that, after my departure, my former deputy Atul Khare was appointed the new SRSG and continued to maintain the relationship of mutual respect and confidence with the Timorese leaders.

Notes

1. Discourses. Chapter xxvii. http://ancienthistory.about.com/od/stoicism/a/121510-Epictetus-Quotes.htm accessed on 1 September 2012.
2. F-FDTL stands for FALINTIL-FDTL. "FDTL" is an acronym of Forcas Defesa Timor Lorosae in Tetum and Forças de Defesa de Timor Leste in Portuguese. As it was formed from "FALINTIL" (Forças Armadas de Libertação Nacional de Timor-Leste in Portuguese or Armed Forces for the National Liberation of East Timor in English), it is often referred to as F-FDTL.
3. Letter dated 2 April 2006 sent by President Gusmão to the Secretary-General. See the Secretary-General's report to the Security Council (S/2006/230), annex.
4. United Nations, *Report of the Secretary-General to the Security Council*, S/2006/251 of 20 April 2006, paragraph 3.
5. The Timorese national police officers responded to various incidents and arrested a total of 48 suspects, 8 of whom were reportedly dismissed F-FDTL soldiers.
6. UIR was created in 2003 with the task of responding rapidly to violent demonstrations in urban areas.
7. Report of the Independent Special Commission of Inquiry for Timor-Leste (S/2006/822), 17 October 2006, Paragraph 41.
8. Leki's presence and his behaviour could be one of the reasons why Alkatiri decided not to go out of his office to meet the petitioners when he was asked later by Salsinha to speak to them.
9. Report of the Independent Special Commission of Inquiry for Timor-Leste, *op. cit.*, paragraphs 43–48.

10. Ibid, paragraph 52.
11. Ibid, paragraph 53.
12. Ibid, paragraph 56.
13. Ibid, paragraph 57.
14. FRETILIN later publicly stated that the government was toppled by a *coup d'état* following the resignation of Mari Alkatiri on 26 June 2006.
15. 'Obrigado Barracks' was the name given to the UN Mission Headquarters compound in Dili.
16. Press release issued on 4 June 2006 by the Government of the Democratic Republic of Timor-Leste.
17. For the official record of the statements made during the 5432th meeting of the Security Council, see UN Security Council document S/PV.5432, 5 May 2006.
18. For a summary record of the meeting of the Security Council, including the statement made by Foreign Minister Ramos-Horta, see UN Department of Public Information Press Release SC/8712 on Security Council 5432 Meeting of 5 May 2006.
19. UN News Centre, "Timor Leste: 5 dead in recent riot, UN official tells Council, urging that UN stay," UN News Service, 5 May 2006.
20. Letter dated 10 April 2006 from the *chargé d'affaires ad interim* of the Permanent Mission of Timor-Leste to the United Nations addressed to the Secretary-General, S/2006/230.
21. UN Department of Public Information Press Release SC/8712 on Security Council 5432 Meeting of 5 May 2006.
22. UN Department of Public Information Press Release SC/8712 on Security Council 5432 Meeting of 5 May 2006.
23. In a subsequent meeting held with Mari Alkatiri, he explained to me he was not in favour of the change of voting procedure, but it was proposed and decided by the FREITLIN Party Congress.
24. The Law on Political Parties (No. 3/2004) provided that "*the candidates to the organs of leadership can only be elected, by direct and secret vote of all members, or by an assembly made up of the representatives of the membership*".
25. The Court of Appeal consisted of Chief Justice Claudio Ximenes, Justice Jacinta Correia da Costa and Justice Maria Natercia Gusmão Pereira.
26. In announcing his resignation, Alkatiri said, "I declare I am ready to resign my position as Prime Minister of the government ... so as to avoid the resignation of His Excellency the President of the Republic, Xanana Gusmão." See Agence France-Presse, 26 June 2006.
27. Had the Portuguese troops had been stationed in Timor-Leste in April or even early May, they would have solidified the position of the government. They would have made it impossible for any dissident groups to demand by force any changes in not only the governance structure but also in its policies.
28. Report of the UN Independent Special Commission of Inquiry for Timor-Leste *op. cit.*, paragraphs 64–70.
29. These were Kay Rala Xanana Gusmão, President of the Republic; Mari Bin Amude Alkatiri, Prime Minister; and Francisco "Lú-Olo" Guterres, Speaker of the National Parliament.
30. Letter dated 24 May 2006 from the President, Prime Minister and Speaker of the National Parliament of Timor-Leste addressed to the Secretary-General.
31. Statement made by Under-Secretary-General Jean Marie Guéhenno to the Security Council on 24 May 2006.
32. Statement made by the President of the Security Council, S/PRST/2006/25, 2 May 2006.
33. Annex to the letter dated 13 June 2006 from the Permanent Representative of Timor-Leste to the United Nations addressed to the Secretary-General, S/2006/391.

34. See S/2006/391, annex.

35. See S/2006/411, annex.

36. Report of the Secretary-General on Timor-Leste pursuant to Security Council Resolution 1690 (2006) of 8 August 2006, S/2006/628, paras. 24–25.

37. Report of the United Nations Independent Special Commission of Inquiry for Timor-Leste (Geneva: 2 October 2006), paragraphs 221–245.

38. International Crisis Group, *Resolving Timor-Leste's Crisis: Asia Report N°120* (10 October 2006). See its Executive Summary, p. i.

39. RENETIL is a youth and student organization that has been involved in the struggle for freedom since 1988. It began as an organization of East Timorese students attending universities in Java, and its work organizing the resistance there led to many of its leaders being jailed during the period of Indonesian occupation. It is now working to secure a democratic future for East Timor through participation in the election process and other nation-building programmes. Its headquarters are in Dili. http://www.wiser.org/organization/view/09eeb70a6872cd84ed61a80fa43dba04 accessed on 3 September 2012.

40. These recommendations were mine and did not necessarily reflect the views of the United Nations.

V

Transitional justice: Primacy of truth or justice for reconciliation and peace

Justice is the first virtue of social institutions, as truth is of systems of thought. Being the first virtues of human activities, truth and justice are uncompromising.[1]

John Rawls

Truth was seminal to the quest for justice and for victims. Reconciliation, however, had been a long-standing process enabling the people of Timor-Leste to endorse the principles of tolerance and forgiveness as the true basis for the coexistence of diverging opinions in society.... It was the result of efforts at reconciliation that there had not been a single revenge killing of suspected elements implicated in the occupation of Timor-Leste.[2]

Kay Rala Xanana Gusmão

An international doctrine advocated that any lasting success in peace-building in post-conflict countries depends on achieving truth, justice and reconciliation aimed at strengthening the rule of law.[3] In Timor-Leste, the leaders worked with the international community in establishing truth and then in carrying out judicial processes. The truth-seeking exercise covered the 25 years from 1974 to 1999, a period when as many as 200,000 people were estimated to have been killed in armed conflict, or to have died under the debilitating conditions related to the conflict. A judicial process was conducted concerning the killings of about 1,400 civilians in 1999, before and after the United Nations conducted a popular consultation.

Primordial leadership: Peacebuilding and national ownership in Timor-Leste, Hasegawa, United Nations University Press, 2013, ISBN 978-92-808-1224-4

The UN and Timorese authorities established the following main institutions to address the issues of truth, justice and reconciliation:

- The Comissão de Acolhimento, Verdade e Reconciliação (CAVR, Commission for Reception, Truth and Reconciliation).
- The Serious Crimes Process (SCP).
- The Commission of Experts (COE).
- The Commission of Truth and Friendship (CTF).

Truth and reconciliation first

The Timor-Leste CAVR was established on 13 July 2001 by UNTAET. This was an independent entity with the objective of investigating human rights violations committed by both sides, i.e. both Indonesian and Timorese entities. The period of investigation was a total of 25 years from April 1974 to October 1999. CAVR was also tasked with facilitating community reconciliation for those who had committed less serious offences.[4] In doing so, it was to help establish the truth about these violations, and carry out the process of reconciliation aimed at restoring the human dignity of victims. It was not a prosecutorial mechanism. CAVR was, however, empowered to refer serious crimes of human rights violations for prosecution.

Through community hearings organized by CAVR, thousands of Timorese from all parts of the country came and gave personal accounts of what had happened. They gave the names of those who had killed people and committed other crimes. CAVR documented detailed accounts of serious and less serious human rights violations based on more than 8,000 of these testimonies, communal consultations and field research. Its voluminous report of 2,800 pages entitled *Chega* (meaning "stop" or "enough" in Portuguese) was published and submitted to President Gusmão on 31 October 2005. The President provided copies to the National Parliament on 28 November and to the Prime Minister on 30 November. President Gusmão then took the report to New York and handed it to Secretary-General Kofi Annan on 20 January 2006.[5]

The CAVR exercise is considered to have been fruitful in healing the psychological wounds of many local communities through its reconciliation programme, yet there remained a strong feeling among the population that those who were behind the atrocities remained free. CAVR had established trends, patterns and factors in the acts of repeated human rights violations. While recognizing that the Commission was not empowered with any judicial authority, its chairman emphasized that it felt compelled to identify persons, authorities and organizations that held ultimate responsibility for the serious crimes committed during the 25-year period.

CAVR recommended that the United Nations should continue its serious crimes prosecution process. Furthermore, it suggested that the Security Council should establish an international tribunal to investigate human rights violations if other methods failed to bring about justice. The Commission emphasized its view that lasting reconciliation could not be achieved without establishing the truth, striving for justice and providing reparations to the victims. Reparations were regarded as necessary to restore the dignity of victims and to repair damaged relationships within society. In East Timorese society, the institution of *kasu sala*[6] is the foundation for community reconciliation and peacebuilding.

However, Gusmão did not want to distribute the report widely in public,[7] for he was concerned that CAVR would perpetuate negative feelings and animosity. His conception of justice and peace was different from that of the international community. He felt that the report should not be used to turn the people who died into victims, but rather into heroes who gave their lives for the independence struggle. Therefore, when he submitted the report to UN Secretary-General Kofi Annan, Gusmão affirmed that as far as he was concerned he would not pursue the process, as he felt there would be less to gain from continuing it. The bottom line of his thinking was that it was the final, tragic phase of the independence struggle: these people had made the ultimate sacrifice in their quest for peace. His view was that the Timorese people should now move on and build their future, instead of examining the scars of the past atrocity.

From the beginning, Gusmão was adroit in handling this sensitive report. He went through several processes, attaching much importance to each of them. In particular, I recall a special sitting I attended in late 2005, in the National Parliament of Timor-Leste. The occasion was the presentation of the CAVR report to the Speaker of the National Parliament, Francisco "Lú-Olo" Guterres. The handover was part of the celebrations for the 30th anniversary of the proclamation of independence in 1975. In presenting the report, Gusmão as President made a public statement before the members of parliament, remarking that it was incumbent upon the sovereign state institutions to make a political decision on the entire process.

He affirmed that CAVR addressed its recommendations both to the state and to the general public, stressing that "there are many valuable recommendations that deserve to be studied in-depth by the Timorese society and, particularly, by the political forces of our Nation."

Gusmão then quoted from the report:

The Commission is of the opinion that it is not possible to achieve long-lasting reconciliation without establishing the truth, obtaining justice, and providing compensation to the victims. Compensation is necessary in order to restore the dignity of victims and to amend the damaged relations throughout our society.

Significantly, he did not evaluate the CAVR report solely from the narrow perspective of denouncing the human rights violations that it contained. He raised concerns with respect to the recommendations on justice put forward by the Commission, which he considered "very ambitious". From my perspective, he appeared to make the report an historical account of what had happened and not a presidential tool for revenge killing or for the punishing of Indonesians.

The launch of the Serious Crimes Process

In Resolution 1272, the UN Security Council recognized that serious crimes had been committed before and after the popular consultations in 1999 and demanded "that those responsible for such violence be brought to justice".[8] In response to this call, UNTAET established the Serious Crimes Unit (SCU) to investigate and prosecute war crimes, crimes against humanity and individual offences of murder, torture and rape, committed between 1 January and 25 October 1999. All charges brought by the SCU were to be tried before one of the Special Panels of Serious Crimes, each panel consisting of two international judges and one East Timorese judge.

Since the independence of Timor-Leste on 20 May 2002, the SCU, which continues to be staffed by the United Nations, has worked under the legal authority of the Prosecutor-General of the República Democrática de Timor Leste (RDTL, Democratic Republic of East Timor), Longuinhos Monteiro. From 2002 to 2005, with the support of international judiciary personnel, the national judicial institutions carried out the SCP. They also managed the Serious Crimes Prosecution Unit, the Public Defenders and the Special Panels for Serious Crimes, which included both international and national judges. The SCU received ample funds from the budgetary allocation of the United Nations Mission of Support in East Timor (UNMISET) for the UN peacekeeping mission and expanded its investigative capability by creating an investigation unit.

A strong team of capable investigators and prosecutors was assembled in a relatively short period of time. A senior Norwegian prosecutor, Siri Frigaard, who carried the official title of Deputy Prosecutor General for Serious Crimes, headed the prosecution team. International judges were recruited from countries that practised Civil Law, notably from Portugal and Brazil; from two other European countries, Germany and Italy; and from two African countries, Burundi and Cape Verde. One senior American judge of Portuguese origin, Phillip Rapoza, was recruited, although he came from a country ruled by Common Law. The appointment of Judge Rapoza was very much in line with my desire to diversify the composition of international judges and other judiciary personnel; I felt strongly that it should reflect the diversity of views held by the international community. Therefore, I was delighted to receive from then US Ambassador Grover Joseph Rees, who himself was a legal expert and had once been a judge in American Samoa, a proposal to consider Judge Rapoza's availability.

Judge Rapoza spoke Portuguese and was knowledgeable in Portuguese law, having headed a bilateral judicial exchange programme between Portugal and the United States for a number of years. He came strongly recommended by several high-ranking Portuguese authorities, including that country's former Prosecutor-General. Judge Rapoza turned out to be a tower of strength. He managed the Special Panels in a most professional manner for nearly two years from 2003 to 2005. Upon his return to the United States, he was appointed Chief Justice of the Appeals Court of the State of Massachusetts.

In addition to their national service, both Siri Frigaard and Judge Rapoza have continued to provide their services in other countries that have been affected by conflict, such as Cambodia, Haiti and Sri Lanka. In Timor-Leste, they demonstrated how the international community could help the people in post-conflict countries to learn to live on the basis of the rule of law. They also enabled the United Nations to uphold a sense of justice and dignity.

Tangible accomplishments and shortcomings

In my view, the SCP achieved tangible results in investigation, prosecution and trials. However, it suffered from a compromise mandate that did not authorize the pursuit and arrest of suspects who had fled to Indonesia. Its accomplishments and shortcomings are shown below.

Accomplishments

The SCU completed investigations and indictment of 391 persons for 684 out of an estimated total of 1,339 murders committed in 1999. Trial proceedings achieved the basic international standard of fairness, with the Special Panels conducting trials of 87 defendants, dismissing charges against another 13 defendants and finding one defendant not fit to stand trial. Of those tried, 85 defendants were convicted of either all or some of the charges brought against them and 2 defendants were acquitted of all charges.

Shortcomings

Only 87 of 285 suspects (about one-third) were put on trial. Furthermore, an additional 303 suspects had reportedly escaped to Indonesia, including many "big fish" who remained at large. It was not possible to bring any of those in Indonesia to trials in Timor-Leste. The Ad Hoc Tribunal created in Jakarta proved totally ineffective, as the Court found only Eurico Guterres, a Timorese, guilty.

As the SCP had been established as an independent institution, UNMISET was not mandated to manage it, but only to provide administrative support and report on its progress. When I took up the position of Deputy Special Representative of the Secretary-General (DSRSG) in 2002, I was assigned the task of simply monitoring the exercise. However, I soon discovered that the defence team was very small in comparison with the prosecution unit; the latter had more than 100 staff, including approximately 30 professional investigators and prosecutors. Siri Frigaard, who headed the team, was a very well-known prosecutor from Norway. Her prosecution staff included almost 40 international professional experts. On the defence side, there were only four UN volunteers from Australia and Bangladesh. This "inequality of arms", I felt, should be rectified.[9]

In any transitional justice, the composition of judicial personnel reflects the perception of a country or the international community as to how the trials should run. In contrast to the Timorese SCP, the Ad Hoc Tribunal in Jakarta had the completely opposite arrangement. A tiny prosecution team acted in a feeble manner, while a group of strong defence lawyers dominated the scene.

The dismal outcome of the Ad Hoc Tribunal reinforced the feeling that the United Nations had an obligation to help realize a credible process in Timor-Leste. I therefore asked for an increase in the budget for defence lawyers, to improve the credibility of the SCP. I also asked for an increase in the number of judges, as we only had enough judges for one panel, and I felt it was essential to have two fully staffed panels of judges to carry out trials efficiently and effectively.

I must say that this judicial process went quite smoothly. The initial sentencing was rather harsh, as I recall the first defendant found guilty was sentenced to 24 years in prison. Later on, the number of years of imprisonment ranged between 10 and 15 years. There was, however, a major shortcoming in the process. In theory, it was possible to arrest and put on trial the key individuals who had planned and organized the killings. In practice, however, this approach was fraught with the impossible political reality. Although arrest warrants were issued for 20 Indonesian senior officials who were implicated, none of the Indonesian military commanders could be found guilty, starting with President Suharto's man, General Wiranto, at their head. General Wiranto was popular among the Indonesian public as he played a moderating role and took care of the difficult transition period in 1998 when President Suharto was forced to resign and was succeeded by Vice-President B. J. Habibie as the new president.

There was a sense of frustration among the victims and human rights organizations when they considered the inability or unwillingness of the United Nations to find and arrest the Indonesian generals and military commanders. As the accusations increased, I thought it in everyone's best interest to bring in independent legal experts, who would assess the situation in a professional and dispassionate manner. UN Headquarters agreed to this suggestion, and decided to hire a team of three experts.

Secretary-General Kofi Annan appointed the three experts for the independent commission in January 2005. They visited Timor-Leste first and were ready to proceed to Jakarta, but the Indonesian Government was reluctant to receive them. I thought it would be futile to continue if the COE could not at least hear the Indonesian authorities' views. Without the other side's input, whatever the commission concluded and recommended would have little or no credibility.

It was my hope that the experts would assess the legal implications against the wider requirements for fostering lasting peace. This was very much in line with the more realistic approach adopted by the Security Council. Against this background, I talked to then Foreign Minister Ramos-Horta who agreed to speak to his counterpart in Jakarta. It took a few weeks, but in the end the Indonesian Government agreed to receive the three experts.[10] The Independent Commission felt that my hopes, and those of the Security Council, were unrealistic. In its report to Secretary-General Kofi Annan, the Commission members insisted that Indonesia should retry accused war criminals acquitted by a special court in Jakarta. This was because the due process had been manifestly inadequate, and had not met the relevant international standards of justice. The report even suggested that Indonesia be given six months to prepare credible trials. If it did not comply, the experts argued, the United Nations should invoke its charter to set up an international war crimes court for Timor-Leste.

The Security Council debated for hours, but could not reach any agreement on the COE recommendations, and asked the Secretary-General to make his suggestions on how to proceed with the recommendations of the Commission. The Department of Political Affairs took the lead in drafting a Secretary-General's recommendation for a feasible plan as the Security Council wanted. It was a rather time-consuming process and took almost one year to complete and submit to the Security Council on 26 July 2006. The Secretary-General's recommendation called for the establishment of an experienced investigation team, led by an international serious crimes investigator, with sufficient resources to resume the investigative functions of the SCU and to complete investigations into outstanding cases of serious crimes in 1999 in a timely fashion.[11]

The United Nations wanted to strengthen the judicial process, although Gusmão did not share this desire. Ramos-Horta felt the same as Gusmão, feeling there was less to gain by trying to find and punish killers than by establishing friendship with Indonesia. Therefore, neither of them insisted on continuing the SCP any further. There was, however, one influential person who remained adamant about keeping alight the torch for justice. This was US Ambassador Grover Joseph Rees, who felt that the justice process should not be abandoned. He made a strong plea suggesting that the process of fact-finding and investigation should be continued, with a view to assembling as much evidence and factual information as possible for use in future judicial process. This suggestion was followed up by the US delegation by including a clause for retention of an investigation process in the Security Council. The Council then adopted a Resolution on 25 August 2006, which, *inter alia*, mandated the new UN Mission in Timor-Leste (UNMIT) to continue the fact-finding and investigative activities.[12]

In understanding the establishment of the formal judicial process to prosecute serious crimes, it is important to recall that the UN Security Council emphasized the importance of establishing a formal judicial process to bring to justice perpetrators of serious crimes that occurred between January and October 1999.[13] This was based on the findings and recommendations of the United Nations International Commission of Inquiry on East Timor (ICIET). ICIET had visited Timor-Leste in the wake of major militia violence following the UN-organized popular consultation on 30 August 1999. The Commission reportedly found evidence of "a pattern of serious violations of fundamental human rights" by the Indonesian security forces and Timorese militias, expressing a view that "ultimately the Indonesian Army was responsible for the intimidation, terror, killings and other acts of violence". Its report called, *inter alia*, for the United Nations to "establish an international human rights tribunal consisting of judges appointed by the United Nations". In the identical letters accompanying the transmission of the ICIET report to the Security Council, the Secretary-General recognized the determination of the Government of Indonesia to act against impunity, and the national investigation process under way in Indonesia. This subsequently led to the establishment of the Indonesian Ad Hoc Tribunal for Human Rights with regard to human rights violations in East Timor mentioned above. The Secretary-General also indicated that the UNTAET transitional administration would be strengthened to conduct investigation "[w]ith a view to bringing justice to the people of East Timor".[14]

In conclusion, it should be noted that the Security Council raised an expectation that all major perpetrators of serious crimes would be brought to justice through the SCP. This expectation was reinforced when the Special Panels for Serious Crimes and the SCU were established in Timor-Leste under UNTAET regulation.[15] The populace thought that the United Nations had envisaged the extradition of suspects between both jurisdictions as agreed in a Memorandum of Understanding from April 2000, signed by the UN Transitional Administrator, the late Sérgio Vieira de Mello and the former Attorney-General of Indonesia. However, as the Indonesian Parliament never ratified the agreement, no suspects were extradited between the two countries.

Key organs of the Serious Crimes Process

The SCP consisted of judicial activities undertaken by three units: the Special Panels for Serious Crimes (Court), the SCU (Prosecution) and the Defence Lawyers Unit (Defence). All units had national and international professional staff.

The Special Panels were established in the early phase of peacekeeping in Timor-Leste under UNTAET transitional authority. UNTAET regulations borrowed heavily from the Rome Statue of the International Criminal Court with jurisdiction over war crimes, crimes against humanity and international violations of humanitarian law. The Special Panels have often been described as "hybrid", as each comprised two international judges and one Timorese judge.[16] The establishment of Special Panels for Serious Crimes represented a significant step in Timor-Leste, as much in delivering formal justice as in supporting the institution-building of the national justice sector in the country. Many observers considered those convicted as being the "small fish". However, at the national level and particularly in the victim communities, these convictions were significant. They represented formal justice being carried out, as there were convictions of some East Timorese members of the Indonesian military. Many East Timorese district and sub-district militia commanders were included, as well as one Indonesian militia company commander.

The SCU was officially established in 2000 but did not start functioning until September 2002, and only began operating in April 2003. Its responsibility included investigation and prosecution of serious crimes committed in 1999, and it was also tasked with preparing and filing indictments with the Special Panels. The SCU was located within the Office of the Prosecutor-General of Timor-Leste, headed by a Deputy Prosecutor-General for Serious Crimes. The Defence Lawyers Unit, given people's often very limited financial means, provided legal services for virtually every defendant who came before the Court. It was a long time before the Unit could evolve into a fully fledged entity, and it was never able to counter the prosecution effectively.

In 2004, by Resolution 1543 the Security Council ordered the SCU to stop all investigations by November 2004, and directed the Special Panels to complete all trials by 20 May 2005.[17] During its tenure, the SCU filed

95 indictments charging 391 persons with serious crimes. As some of the accused were included in more than one indictment, the total number of defendants numbered 440. Following the indictments, the Special Panels called before the court 101 defendants, 13 of whom had had their cases withdrawn or dismissed and 1 was found mentally incompetent. Thus, 87 defendants, mostly Timorese members of the local militia, were brought to justice. 85 were convicted of either all or some of the charges brought against them, and 2 acquitted of all charges. This meant that 339 defendants have not come before the court, presumably because they were outside the country, and Timorese law did not permit trials *in absentia*. In the absence of an extradition treaty with Indonesia, where the overwhelming majority of defendants resided, no prosecutions could proceed in these cases.

It was widely accepted that approximately 1,400 persons were killed in the 1999 violence, yet the 95 indictments that have been filed only accounted for 579 of those murders. This meant that over 800 killings remained to be accounted for by way of indictment. In addition, the Special Panels have issued 284 arrest warrants, including for General Wiranto. Most of the warrants were still in the hands of the Prosecutor-General of Timor-Leste who had not yet forwarded them to Interpol.

In accordance with paragraph 9 of Security Council Resolution 1599 (2005), UNOTIL made a complete copy of all records compiled by the SCU, including forensic photographs.[18] As previously reported to the Security Council,[19] the Unit's records, including the copies made by UNOTIL, were placed under the authority of the Prosecutor-General of Timor-Leste. However, an agreement had been reached with the Government of Timor-Leste on the preservation and management of the serious crimes records. While the original records were formally handed over to the Prosecutor-General, a complete duplicate copy of the records was prepared and shipped to UN Headquarters in New York for preservation.

Challenges faced by the Serious Crimes Process

The SCP encountered several obstacles and challenges, some anticipated, while others were totally unexpected. The major obstacle was the demand of investigation termination by the end of 2000, which had been made on political grounds. Additionally, the trials were to be completed by May 2005, which was the end date of UNMISET's second phase. The ensuing manner with which judicial and administrative personnel from the world over dealt with these obstacles demonstrated a solidarity that showed care about what had happened in Timor-Leste. It also showed consideration for what would be left behind for the people of this conflict-prone country.

Since the trials' commencement in 2001, the Special Panels for Serious Crimes had moved steadily. The Unit examined available evidence, testimonies and witness accounts. Both prosecution and defence lawyers made presentations, and within a period of 2 years they completed 33 trials and made 39 judgments. During the early months of 2004, the Special Panels finished 3 additional cases, but 15 were still pending. The SCU continued carrying out investigations in several districts where a large number of atrocious murders had been committed. In Bobanaro, 209 murders had reportedly been committed; and in Liquica and Ermera there had apparently been 156 and 107 killings, respectively. When its mandate was extended by 1 year, along with that of UNMISET, the SCU was able to file an additional 15–20 cases (depending upon the rate of disposition) against some organisers of violence, and some of the worst individual perpetrators. The scheduled termination of the SCP by the end of December 2004 became a major source of concern for the staff concerned. They thought it impossible to complete their investigations and file these additional cases for trial, a process which would take at least several more months and meant the SCP had to continue until May 2005.

In assessing these implications, it became clear that:

The scheduled termination of the SCP would have required the immediate suspension of any further investigations. There was widespread expectation throughout Timor-Leste that the United Nations would provide justice for the atrocities committed in 1999. Any suspension of the trials was thought to increase the frustration of victim families, and risked acts of vengeance.

Many UN staff felt strongly that the violence was intended to disrupt the process mandated by the UN Security Council, as it eventually forced the withdrawal of the entire UNTAET staff to Darwin. In 2004, the SCU was still receiving a large volume of documents and expected to indict several key individuals involved in the killings.

It could jeopardize the successful work carried out by CAVR. The Timorese had great emotional investment in the assumption that the perpetrators from outside the jurisdiction of CAVR would be handled by the SCU. There was a genuine fear that instability and tension could emerge in district communities if the efforts of the SCU and Special Panels to bring perpetrators to justice were discontinued. Militia suspects had been living in the community for a protracted period of time, and a large number of killings had taken place in areas that had not yet had a proper SCU investigation.

While a 12-month extension would allow the SCU staff to develop a handover strategy, there was still the need to develop national capacity within the Timorese prosecution, courts and defence, to enable them to handle cases if any of the almost 300 indictees returned to Timor-Leste.

The SCU had planned a series of lectures intended to train Timorese prosecutors on all aspects of criminal prosecution, but in particular for those who would have to handle cases of crimes against humanity. It would also allow the voluminous evidence, including hundreds of hours of video and audiotape, to be digitized and translated. This was to make knowledge accessible to the Timorese prosecutors for the purpose of continued investigation and prosecution, as well as for public information.

In addition to completing investigations, writing indictments and litigating cases, the SCU needed to devote significant resources to ensure that the court had a useful summary of the evidence for complex cases. This was particularly necessary in cases where the accused were outside of Timor-Leste.

In order to address these concerns, it was considered best to bring together as many interested parties as possible, so that the issues could be discussed frankly. In February 2003, I convened a coordination meeting of section chiefs of UNMISET's SCP, as well as other staff members. This meeting proved most useful in establishing facts and sharing a common understanding of what was at stake, regardless of status and ranking, as international or national officials.

Two national judges (who sat on the Special Panels at the Dili District Court), and the national judge sitting in the Court of Appeal (which heard appeals from the Special Panels), also attended. We started by establishing a common understanding of UNMISET's mandate with respect to the SCP, and the achievability of the goals set by the Security Council.

To start the discussion in a productive manner, I underscored the need to ensure that coordination of SCP activities was conducted with an eye on the time and budget-limited nature of UNMISET's mandated support for the programme. In that regard, I outlined three possible options:

To continue at the current less than swift pace, which meant that not all of the priority cases would be tried by June 2004.

To expedite the process by increasing human and material resources.

To decide that UNMISET should simply suspend its support for the trial process of some cases, even if they had been investigated and indictments had been filed.

As some of the participants were not familiar with the status of trials, I asked the Section Chiefs to explain their understanding of how we were doing in meeting targets, with respect to the entire trial process. Ms Siri Frigaard of Norway, who had been appointed Deputy Prosecutor General for Serious Crimes as Head of the SCU, provided a summary of the obstacles facing it, including difficulties in locating witnesses given the isolation of many communities and the rough terrain. Although we had referred to ten priority cases, each case actually resulted in more than one indictment. She added that many of the significant suspects were not within the reach of the prosecution and probably would never be brought to trial under the SCP. She then insisted that it would be politically beneficial for UNMISET to be seen to be investigating some atrocities in each district. She stressed her expectation that indictments could be filed in respect of two further cases by March 2004, and anticipated an indictment for a third case by the end of June 2004.

According to the judges at the Special Panels, 49 indictments had so far been filed with the Court, and 24 judgments delivered. They pointed out that half of the cases before the Special Panels were still pending. It was a fact that the pace of delivering justice had been slow, due to the limited resources and the unavailability of judges. The judges indicated that all of the pending cases could be finished by the end of the year, although the feasibility of this would depend on the availability of international judges and defence witnesses. Helder Viana do Carmo, a national judge, underscored the importance of ensuring that vacancies on the Special Panels were filled quickly, especially given UNMISET's time-limited support to the SCP. He also stressed the importance of making appointments to the Special Panels swiftly, according to the existing law. The absence of a legal procedure to appoint prosecutors under the law of Timor-Leste was also discussed. Given the urgency, I asked the Office of Legal Affairs to examine the issue with a view to formulating suggestions for the government to resolve the impasse.

It was noted that an earlier draft of the Statute of Magistrates had contained a provision, which authorized the Superior Council of the Judiciary to recommend candidates for appointment as prosecutors under the law to the President of the Republic. However, at the insistence of the Minister of Justice, this provision was removed from the final version of the law. Judge Jacinta Correia da Costa requested me to bring to the attention of the Advisory Committee on Administrative and Budgetary Questions (ACABQ) the dichotomy of UNMISET's support to the Special Panels at the "first instance" level, while leaving the "appellate" level under-resourced. In response, I told her that while I was willing to bring this issue to the attention of the ACABQ, it was my understanding that UNMISET's mandate was limited. UNMISET's support for the SCP had expanded from an initial commitment to support the investigation and prosecution of those accused of serious crimes, to support their defence, and also to provide support to the Court itself. I told her that UNMISET had not been expected to provide extensive support to meet all of the costs of strengthening the entire national judicial organs. This was a subject for the United Nations Development Programme (UNDP) and bilateral donors to consider, as it would be a capacity-building programme. Other issues raised throughout the SCP included:

- The amount of space accorded to the Special Panels, both for an additional trial chamber and for administration.
- The need to improve and coordinate the Court calendar.
- The possibility of hearing cases in districts, which might expedite the trial process by ensuring fewer deferrals due to non-appearance of witnesses.
- The need to ensure that prosecutorial policy accords with SCP's management policy with respect to the ten priority cases.

Clearly, there was a need for a successor mission to contemplate any further support to the SCP, albeit on a reduced scale. This would be possible if management were to decide on the scale of resources made available to support the Timorese Government's investigation and prosecution efforts. The management of the SCP also needed to focus on the need to coordinate all of the Units within the Programme to achieve the mandate with respect to the ten priority cases of serious crimes.

In September 2003, the Special Representative of the Secretary-General (SRSG) Sharma and I participated in a meeting of the Justice Council of Coordination with judges, prosecutors and defence lawyers involved in the SCP. All international and national judges working at the Court of Appeal and Special Panels attended the meeting. Additionally, key international and national staff from the Serious Crimes Unit and the Defence Lawyers' Unit came. In the meeting the adoption of new administrative arrangements for the SCP was discussed. I heard a presentation of the three post-UNMISET options for the SCP, and conducted preparatory works for the upcoming Consultation Meeting on Justice Stability Requirements in Timor-Leste, scheduled for 30 September 2003.

Regarding the three post-UNMISET options, the President of the Court of Appeal indicated that there might be some constitutional restriction to the continuation of the special instance of international judges on the Special Panels. This was because of the constitutional phrase "shall remain operational for the time deemed strictly necessary to conclude the cases under investigation" being seen as determinative, as at 20 May 2002. The acting Head of SCU argued against this restrictive interpretation. He noted that as exclusive jurisdiction for serious crimes in the period 1 January–25 October 1999 rested with the Special Panels, not a court in the land would have jurisdiction to hear those serious crimes cases. Although they had occurred between 1 January and 25 October 1999, they were not "under investigation" prior to 20 May 2002. It was further noted that this was unlikely to be the intention of the drafters of the constitution. This position was understood to be reflected in the *travaux preparatoire* to this Article of the Constitution.

The meeting also turned its attention to the achievements of the SCP. The New Deputy Prosecutor General for Serious Crimes, Mr Essa Faal, who had replaced Siri Firgaard, described the achievements of the

Serious Crimes Investigation and Prosecution Unit to date. He indicated that the prosecution unit had been successful in investigating and prosecuting 1,422 recorded cases of murder which had occurred in 1999. He then underscored the need for investigative support from United Nations Police (UNPOL) officers working as investigators, if significant further progress was be made with respect to the remaining recorded cases of murder. The President of the Court of Appeal, Judge Claudio Ximenes, suggested that it was important to keep in mind the need to strike a balance between what should be done and what can be done.

The meeting revealed other interesting issues of common concern. Judge Siegfried Blunk of Germany indicated that the cost of the SCP in Timor-Leste was estimated at only $6.3 million a year with more than 30 cases handled in 2 years. This compared with the International Criminal Tribunal for Rwanda (ICTR), which was costing the United Nations, or the international community, as much as $100 million year, with an output of ten cases in eight years. He went on to indicate that the International Criminal Tribunal for former Yugoslavia (ICTY) was also costing $100 million a year, and the Special Court for Sierra Leone, which was set up jointly by the Government of Sierra Leone and the United Nations, still cost approximately $20 million a year. It was indicated that the United Nations had spent a total of $1.6 billion so far to operate international tribunals. This highlighted the need to look at the SCP on a global level.

A subsequent discussion then highlighted the need for capacity-building of Timorese judges and legal personnel, rather than the need to complete all cases before the termination of the process. Timorese Judges Maria Natercia Pereira and Antonio Helder Viana do Carmo pointed out that continued support from the international community to the SCP was required, due to the lack of skilled national staff. Michael Lackner and James McGovern then made informative presentations of what needed to be changed to achieve desirable results.

McGovern suggested a rethinking of the indicators of success used to measure the progress of the SCP. He said that instead of focusing on the number of cases processed by a particular date, we should focus on a measure of the skills of national staff working in the SCP, as they ultimately had to take responsibility for running the process. I felt it was clearly a challenge to our thinking as we moved forward.

Timorese Judge Jacinta Correia da Costa reinforced the notion that while the international staff could leave the process on the final day of UNMISET, 19 May 2004, Timorese national staff could not just abandon the process. Judge Dora de Morais of Brazil emphasized that the international community ran the risk of a patronizing approach to the SCP when it spoke of leaving the process half-finished. She said what was needed was a participatory approach, to continue working with sovereign authorities.

Judge Sylver Ntukamazina of Burundi underscored the need to develop a new policy on the issue of how long the SCP should continue, and the Head of the Defence Lawyers' Unit, Regunathan Thamburan, stressed the need to have more resources for defence, given the disparity of arms that still existed.

The informal and frank sharing of ideas led to general understanding on several subjects. For example, the issue of prosecutorial discretion with regard to the number of serious crimes cases, which rested with the national Prosecutor-General, could be separated from the policy question facing the Security Council on the extent to which the United Nations should continue to support SCP. It was noted that a sufficient number of Timor-Leste prosecutors, investigators and defence lawyers had been trained. However, the process should continue for as long as the competent sovereign authorities deemed it appropriate to do so, requiring much less support from the United Nations. To this end, if SCP were to be extended beyond 19 May 2004, we should focus on developing national competencies in the justice sector in general, rather than on a simple identification of the number of serious crimes cases processed. This would allow the formulation of an appropriate exit strategy for the United Nations. The SCP was ultimately a part of and dependent upon the national justice system, which unfortunately remained fragile.

All participants agreed to do their best to reduce case scheduling administrative irregularities through the mechanism of a Special Panels Administrative Working Group. There was a genuine spirit of collaboration: all judges, prosecutors and defence lawyers agreed not to take any leave until 12 December 2003, and to return to work by 11 January 2004. I examined the possibility of an administrative accommodation in order to synchronize leave for international staff (including judges) working in the SCP, so that the courts could continue to function for three months without any break. It was thought that such a rationalization could achieve better trial scheduling and greater efficiency in the functioning of the courts.

In a closing remark, SRSG Sharma emphasized to the participants that the international community and the national authorities owed an obligation to the relatives of victims of crimes against humanity that had occurred in 1999. It was important to bring to justice not only so-called "small fish" who had been already put in jail, but also those who remained beyond the reach of the jurisdiction of the Special Panels. He also underscored the usefulness of presenting a clear picture to the Security Council of the needs of the SCP and of the Timor-Leste justice system, when the question came up for discussion by the Security Council on 14 October 2003. He then informed the participants that Prime Minister Alkatiri essentially wanted the international community to do some innovative thinking on how to take forward the SCP.

A series of consultations produced possible scenarios and options for the SCP from the point at which the Security Council mandate expired on 19 May 2004. The range of alternative scenarios was limited, and there were only three options to choose from.

Option 1

The SCP finishes pending cases by 30 June 2004. Under this option, UNMISET begins the process of withdrawing budgetary support to the SCU and "first instance" Special Panels between the end of May and June 2004. UNMISET-funded judges at the Special Panels complete the pending cases by June 2004. UNMISET-funded SCU investigators and prosecutors complete investigating cases and filing indictments at this time.

This arrangement, however, would have left a major administrative question unresolved. If the SCP were to conclude its work on 20 May 2004, a considerable number of those "first-instance" cases already begun would remain unfinished. The largest portion of the appeal cases would also remain unheard. Accordingly, it was assumed that if the SCP was to complete its work on 20 May 2004, given the current level of competencies of the national justice system, it was highly unlikely that any further serious crimes proceedings could take place.

Completion of the pending "first instance" cases before 30 June 2004 would require overcoming administrative obstacles which had plagued the process to date, including recruitment and procedural delays and legal issues (such as decisions on the applicable law and retrospectivity). Given the current administrative constraints of the system, it was highly unlikely that pending "first instance" cases could be completed by 20 May 2004. Therefore, under the first option, it was suggested that the SCP would need to be staffed at its current level in all three units (Special Panels, SCU, Defence Lawyers' Unit) until 30 June 2004. By 30 September 2004, it would be possible to reduce staffing for the Defence Lawyers' Unit and the SCU by 40 per cent. The Court of Appeal would, however, need to be at least fully staffed until June 2005.

Option 2

The SCP would continue to operate until 30 June 2005. According to this scenario, UNMISET continues budgetary support to the SCU and to the "first instance" Special Panels up to 20 May 2005, under the auspices of a follow-on mission. Then UNMISET-funded judges at the Special Panels complete the pending cases by June 2004 and continue hearing additional cases. UNMISET-funded SCU investigators and prosecutors continue investigating cases and filing indictments up to 20 May 2005. Meanwhile, a supplementary arrangement is concluded with the government, which provides for continuation of the SCP beyond 20 May 2004. To ensure the quality of work, the agreement would describe the types of assistance which the international community would deliver. Donor countries would be asked to contribute to the process, including budgetary support and technical advice.

This second option would see all pending cases through to completion, and give the SCU an opportunity to continue investigation and trials of those accused in about 700 murder cases. The majority of the appeal cases from the current pending cases would also be completed prior to June 2005. Appeals could also be filed in respect of final decisions handed down up to June 2005. The requirements for the appeal procedures for pending cases would be similar to those for Option 1.

Completion of all currently pending cases, both "first" and "second instance" cases, would depend on the number of additional indictments filed by the SCU. All three units would require a continuation of the current budgetary support for staff and resources until 30 June 2005. The second option would also provide sufficient lead time to develop an effective exit plan to come into operation on 30 June 2005. Early notification of a decision on the part of the United Nations not to continue support beyond 30 June 2005 would facilitate transfer of case management and files.

The second scenario would also enable the negotiation of a supplementary arrangement between the United Nations and the Government of Timor-Leste. This would provide functioning administrative support and avoid administrative flaws. Such an arrangement could also serve as a useful vehicle to solve the posited "unconstitutionality" of the retroactive application of UNTAET Regulation No. 2000/15, as raised in the Dos Santos Case. As noted in the ICTJ report, the applicability or inapplicability of any transitional administrative rule and national laws in a post-conflict situation was to create a great deal of confusion.[20]

If the National Parliament did not move to clarify the situation with respect to the applicable law, continuation of the SCP to 30 June 2005 would provide an opportunity to solve this issue via alternate appeal decisions. A continuation could also assist efforts towards greater national ownership of the process.

Option 3

The SCP continues beyond 20 May 2005 on the basis of an agreed strategy to deal with "absent" indictees. The United Nations, through a possible successor mission to UNMISET, continues its support to the SCP beyond 20 May 2005. Although budgetary and logistic support would remain as in the second option, efforts would be made to process cases where the accused was outside the jurisdiction, under a procedure akin to the ICTY's Rule 61 Procedure. If the SCP was continued beyond 20 May 2004, with a view to extending it until June 2005, there was a possibility to develop a strategy to deal with cases involving absent indictees. The combination of the current legal framework and the refusal on the part of Indonesia to process requests meant there was no realistic means to conduct proceedings against indictees who were absent from Timor-Leste. However, with additional time, and depending upon the collective will of the Security Council, the executive, judicial and legislative organs of Timor-Leste could establish a procedure for dealing with absent indictees, similar to the Rule 61 Procedure adopted by the ICTY. This would, of course, have an implication for resources requirement. If such a procedure was adopted, the extent of resources, and staffing at the same level, would be required for at least one year beyond 20 May 2005.

The next step was to formalize the arrangement that had been worked out by the series of consultations. The Office of the High Commissioner for Human Rights (OHCHR) agreed to the recommendations drawn up by UN players in Dili. On 15 April 2004, OHCHR published a report indicating the priority areas for the consolidation phase. It reflected the shift in the focus of what had already been made towards the institutional capacity-building and the functioning of the national court system. The OHCHR report proposed:

- Placing four international judges to work as mentors and sit as judges in the consolidation phase, providing on-the-job training. In order for the work of these international judges to be efficient, they should have sufficient infrastructure at their disposal, including electricity, computers, interpreters and translators.
- SCU staff would provide support for the development of national prosecutor trainees, case manager trainees, information management officer trainees and IT assistant trainees, who had been undergoing training since 2002.
- A similar training programme should also start under the UNMISET Public Defenders Unit, by hiring national trainees and a legal officer to organize their training programme once the follow-up mission budget was approved by UN Headquarters.
- Job training of national judges should be provided in the Special Panels, where two international judges sit together with one national judge.

The proposed measures were in line with our thinking at UNMISET. We were already working closely with the Timorese Government to ensure the continuation of the Special Panels process by the Timorese judicial institutions. The intake of trainees was one way of ensuring the sustainability of the process. Other measures were also taken, such as translation of evidence and training of both interpreters and translators, for the process to continue after May 2004.

Issuance of an arrest warrant for General Wiranto

A major development occurred on 10 May 2004 at 3:35 p.m., when Judge Phillip Rapoza of the Special Panels for Serious Crimes issued an arrest warrant for retired General Wiranto, who was then running for President in Indonesia. The former Minister of Defence and Security of Indonesia, and Commander of the armed forces, had previously been indicted on 24 February 2003. General Wiranto, along with several high-level military officers and the former Governor of East Timor, had been accused of crimes against humanity committed in Timor-Leste in 1999. The indictment charged Wiranto with command responsibility for murder, deportation and persecution committed in connection with widespread and systematic attacks on the civilian population in Timor-Leste. Although the prosecution had requested an arrest warrant when the indictment was originally filed with the court, no action was taken on the request until Judge Rapoza joined the Special Panels in late 2003.

The arrest warrant issued by Judge Rapoza was a 20-page document outlining the facts in support of the indictment against Wiranto. As described in the warrant, the prosecution supported the charges with 21 volumes of evidence amounting to over 15,000 pages and included statements from over 1,500 witnesses. In his judicial findings, Judge Rapoza stated that reasonable grounds existed to believe that Wiranto had committed crimes against humanity in the course of a widespread and systematic attack against the civilian population of East Timor. Wiranto had used Indonesian military forces, police and pro-autonomy militia groups. He also asserted that, as Wiranto effectively had command authority over those forces, he bore criminal responsibility for their actions. Judge Rapoza further concluded that Wiranto knew, or had reason to know, of the ongoing criminal violence in East Timor. However, he had failed to prevent the commission of such crimes by those over whom he had command authority, or to punish the perpetrators of those crimes.

While the issuance of the arrest warrant had been expected in diplomatic circles, it put the Government of Timor-Leste, particularly the national Prosecutor-General, in an awkward position. Immediately after the arrest warrant was issued, Prosecutor-General Linguino Monteiro filed a motion with the Special Panels for Serious Crimes to allow him to "review the indictment and file an amended indictment after removing the defects when found under UNTAET Regulation 2000/30, section 32 paragraph 32.1 and under UNTAET Regulation 2001/25, section 27 paragraph 27.1 subpara-1". Some doubted that the Prosecutor-General could legally make such a request; nevertheless, the court had to reach a decision. Until the ruling of the court was made, however, the arrest warrant for Wiranto remained technically valid.

As the atmosphere became charged, the national leaders pondered its political implications. It was clear that Prosecutor-General Monteiro was acting in line with the national leadership, as he took a step to make an announcement in a press conference the same day. He explained that the motion was part of his overall strategy to work with the government and other institutions of state, for the good of the nation as a whole. He claimed that certain individuals who were politically motivated had been hasty in filing the indictment with the Special Panels. Speaking in Tetum, Monteiro repeatedly claimed that he was not answerable to external pressure or interest (referring to the United Nations), but rather to the national interests of Timor-Leste. He criticized the United Nations for promoting the idea of justice, and then not defending justice by claiming not to have enough resources. He appealed to the public to have confidence in him and his work, as he intended to achieve a positive outcome for the future of all East Timorese. There was no doubt that the higher authority simply told Monteiro to file this motion with the court. This step was consistent with statements he had made in preceding weeks; he had already earlier confirmed his intention to withdraw the Wiranto indictment by 19 May 2004 if the Special Panel did not issue an arrest warrant.

What was rather surprising to me was that Nicholas Koumjian, the new Deputy-General-Prosecutor for Serious Crimes, also spoke at the same press conference, where he explained that the indictment was not politically motivated. The indictment had been lodged with the courts back in March 2003, before Wiranto became a presidential candidate. He argued that his office assisted the courts by providing a 15,000-page summary of evidence supporting the indictment in March 2003, such that it could expedite its decision to issue the warrant. His office made the decision to work on the Wiranto case first, because Wiranto was the Commander of the armed forces at the time the alleged crimes against humanity took place.

Earlier that day Monteiro postponed a press conference in order to meet with President Gusmão, who was a strong advocate of reconciliation with Indonesia and had generally taken a critical view of any such legal steps that could antagonize Jakarta. Such views were echoed by numerous members of the National Parliament, who proclaimed that it was the responsibility of the United Nations, not Timor-Leste, to arrest and prosecute Wiranto, if the United Nations wanted to do so. Members called upon the President of the National Parliament to meet with the other organs of sovereignty, and to resolve the issue of the arrest warrant, such that it did not jeopardize good relations with Indonesia. Late that morning, about 100 people participated in a demonstration organized by a coalition of NGOs called the Alliance for an International Tribunal, and by Universidade Nacional Timor Lorosa'e (UNTL, National University of East Timor), students. They passed the Indonesian Embassy and then proceeded to the street in front of the Palacio do Governo where various speeches were made.

The demonstration had already been planned to take place sometime in the future, but was rescheduled for that day in light of the issuance of the arrest warrant. The speeches generally called on the international community to take responsibility for prosecution of war crimes committed in 1999, and more specifically for the creation of an international tribunal. Despite initial information to the contrary, the organisers did not request to speak with UNMISET representatives. However, the Alliance did formally present a statement that generally denounced the actions of the Tentara Nasional Indonesia (TNI, Indonesian National Armed Forces). The Alliance lamented that many suspected of involvement in violations in Timor-Leste were at large in Indonesia, seemingly out of reach of the SCP. The Alliance statement called for the establishment of an international tribunal, and for the international community, including the United Nations, to challenge Wiranto's candidacy for president. It sought international support to bring the "main perpetrators to justice".

Within a few days, it became known publicly that the Prosecutor-General's request to rescind the Wiranto indictment was due to his eagerness to concur with the wish of the highest levels of Timorese leadership and avoid any confrontation with Wiranto, and by extension, the Indonesian authorities. Many international experts felt that Timor-Leste could no longer be expected to take responsibility for the SCP, placing in jeopardy the pursuit of justice for the crimes against humanity committed in 1999. The Prosecutor-General's change in position was ironic, as earlier in January 2004 he criticized the judges on the Special Panels for not issuing an arrest warrant and accused the United Nations of slowing the process down.

On 17 May, Judge Rapoza issued a decision on the Prosecutor-General's motion to withdraw the indictment for review and to file an amended version. Rapoza stated that after a prosecutor filed an indictment with the court, it could not be withdrawn or amended without the court's permission, which he declined to give. He pointed out that the prosecutor had not specified any alleged defects in the indictment and had failed to present any proposed amendments for which he was seeking approval. Concluding that it was without foundation, Judge Rapoza denied the

Prosecutor-General's motion and the indictment and warrant remained in effect.

In retrospect, however, there was indeed a need to balance strict adherence to legal procedure against the quest for peace with the giant neighbouring country. The Timorese leadership perceived that the issuance of a warrant against the Indonesian presidential candidate would be viewed as provocative. It had to be mindful of a broad perception within Indonesia that judges could not be neutral. Therefore, the issuance of the arrest warrant during the period of electoral campaigning would be viewed as politically motivated.

The attitude of the Timorese leadership did not reflect the desire of ordinary people for realizing justice. The former had supported the serious crimes process as long as it did not have to take responsibility in public. The difference then was that the political pressure had become too strong. The leadership was fearful of damaging its relationship with Indonesia, which it believed could have serious security, economic and political implications for Timor-Leste in the future. In a public meeting held on 13 May 2005 in Maliana, which UNMISET staff witnessed, the community representatives expressed strong concern that perpetrators of the 1999 violence were not being held fully to account, and specifically mentioned Wiranto. The crowd loudly applauded those calling for the continuation of investigations and trials.

One last extension before closure

On 24 May 2004, the Security Council took a decision to extend the SCU to May 2005. Extending the SCP for one year would allow for indictment of at least half of the serious crimes investigated.

This would undoubtedly contribute to consolidation of the earlier productive efforts made to address the atrocities committed in East Timor in 1999. Moreover, it would allow completion of investigations and indictments in the districts not yet investigated, including the five widespread patterns, such as the killing of the two UN staff members in Ermera. It would also allow completion of all trials, and appeals of those charged with serious crimes.

There were still several significant investigations outstanding in districts where no investigation had taken place and many were murdered, in particular Bobanaro (209 known killings), Liquica (156) and Ermera (107). With a one-year extension of its mandate, SCU could pursue filing cases against some of the organizers or commanders of the violence and some of the worst individual perpetrators. The last case would be in November 2004, in order to allow the court at least six months to handle it.

The additional 12 months was indeed sufficient for developing a handover strategy, so that after the United Nations terminated its involvement in the SCP, there would be capacity within the Timorese prosecution, courts and defence to handle cases. This self-sufficiency would be valuable if any of the almost 300 indicted who remained free returned to Timor-Leste. The SCU had planned a series of lectures intended to train Timorese prosecutors on all aspects of criminal prosecution, and in particular they provided training on how to handle a case of a crime against humanity. The mandate's extension also allowed time for digitization and translation of the extensive evidence collected to date, which included hundreds of hours of video and audiotape recordings. These would be made accessible to the Timorese prosecutors for continued investigation and prosecution, and potentially for the public records. The SCU devoted considerable resources to ensure that the court had useful summaries of the evidence for complicated cases, where the accused were outside of Timor-Leste and the prosecution had requested an arrest warrant, in order to facilitate a ruling on the application.

The SCP then followed its course despite some setbacks. During a field visit to Oecussi on 6 September 2004, I held intermittent conversations with Prime Minister Alkatiri. I pointed out to him our position that there was a need for a unified approach towards ascertaining the best arrangement for dealing with the SCP. It was easier to point out such a need than to find a proper answer and to establish a satisfactory arrangement.

In September 2004, I received a visit from Mr Grant Niemann, who was preparing a technical report to the High Commissioner for Human Rights. This concerned the judicial processes in Jakarta and Dili in relation to the crimes committed in 1999, and possible options for the way forward. I met with Niemann on 10 September and briefly on 13 September when I invited him to lunch with diplomatic representatives from Finland and Thailand. He agreed with me that an independent COE should indeed be established in order to further assess the two processes that took place in Jakarta and Dili, in relation to the serious crimes committed in 1999 in Timor-Leste. On the subject of the Jakarta trials and the SCP in Timor-Leste, Niemann was of the opinion that the Jakarta Ad Hoc human rights tribunal had been severely compromised in its outcome. He considered that the work of SCP in Timor-Leste had operated effectively and successfully.

On the subject of the future of the SCP, Niemann suggested that the outstanding indictments of 279 accused believed to be at large outside Timor-Leste be preserved, rather than allowed to be withdrawn. He felt that the SCP in Timor-Leste was part of the new direction in international justice, and that what the United Nations and the international community had achieved through its work should not be disregarded. According to his thinking, the international community could not allow those in power to commit such serious crimes as murder with impunity, and he saw the need for an international judicial mechanism to ensure justice.

In regard to the way forward, we agreed that Niemann would recommend in his report the continuation of the judicial process through some sort of an international mechanism, which would relieve Timor-Leste of the responsibility for the process. He was also of the opinion that progress would best be achieved by finding a solution where Indonesia could also participate in the process. It was also possible that his report might recommend some alternative international mechanisms as options for consideration.

One suggestion envisaged was that further trials in Jakarta be conducted by "mixed" panels of Indonesian and international judges. Another was that trials be conducted in a third regional state, which might be receptive to an arrangement whereby national courts would exercise universal jurisdiction. New Zealand was mentioned as a possibility. Other options were the establishment of an international territory or arrangement under UN jurisdiction in Timor-Leste, and an international tribunal service using the resources and facilities of the International Criminal Court (ICC) on a cost-effective basis. Niemann also indicated that he could include the recommendation of an International Truth Commission, although he remained sceptical in terms of ensuring accountability for the crimes. He submitted his report to the Secretary-General and the High Commissioner on 30 September 2005.

It is of significance that, around the time of Niemann's visit to Timor-Leste, Mario Carrascalao, President of Partido Social Democrata (PSD), was reported in the national media to have said that he would be for a referendum to be held concerning the establishment of an international tribunal for the crimes committed in 1999. He was eager to establish accountability of national leaders and institutions before the people whether they were in Timor-Leste or Indonesia. Carrascalao was once the governor of East Timor during the Indonesian occupation but still had a considerable degree of popular support among the Timorese people.

Engaging the Commission of Experts (COE)

The Secretary-General established the Commission of Experts (COE) in January 2005 and appointed three members. A highly respected judge, Prafullachandra Bhagwati of India, headed it. Professor Yozo Yokota of Japan and Shaista Shameem of Fiji supported the judge. The Commission had six specific tasks to carry out:

To review the judicial processes of the work of the Indonesian Ad Hoc Human Rights Court on East Timor in Jakarta, and the SCU and Special Panels for Serious Crimes in Dili.

To assess the effective functioning of both the Jakarta and Dili processes.

To identify the obstacles and difficulties encountered by the two entities.

To evaluate the extent to which the two institutions had been able to achieve justice and accountability for the crimes committed in Timor-Leste.

To recommend legally sound and practically feasible measures, so that those responsible were held accountable, and justice secured and reconciliation promoted for the victims and people of Timor-Leste.

To find ways in which its analysis could be of assistance to the CTF that the Governments of Indonesia and Timor-Leste had agreed to establish, and to make appropriate recommendations to the Secretary-General in this regard.[21]

The three experts analysed the two judicial processes in Jakarta and Dili and submitted a set of recommendations. In my view, their findings were strictly in line with their legal interpretation of the judicial processes carried out in Jakarta and Dili. The measures they recommended turned out to be neither practical nor feasible.

The SCP carried out in Timor-Leste was considered credible, and accountable to "a notable degree" but as "having not yet achieved full accountability for those who bear greatest responsibility for serious violations". The Commission recommended a continuation of the SCP until it could complete all of the remaining cases, which numbered more than 500 out of nearly 1,500 civilians killed in 1999. The Commission, however, also raised concerns about the lack of political will in Timor-Leste and the independence of the Prosecutor-General.

The Ad Hoc Human Rights Court for Timor-Leste in Indonesia was considered "manifestly inadequate" and not in conformity with international standards. From the list of 22 suspects, 18 were indicted, 17 of which had been acquitted. The Commission recommended the reopening of all cases and suggested that SCU evidence and files be delivered to the Indonesian Attorney-General so as to accept international assistance to build judicial and prosecutorial capacity. Indonesia was requested to report to the Secretary-General on the implementation of the Commission's recommendations after six months.

The COE also commented on the CTF. The COE expressed its grave reservations about some of the provisions in the terms of reference (TOR), though recognizing that the CTF could contribute to rebuilding relations between Indonesia and Timor-Leste. The experts recommended that the international community should not provide finance or advisory assistance until the two governments reviewed the TOR and the Secretary-General was satisfied that the terms met international standards.

The Commission concluded its report with the proposal that if the Governments of Indonesia and Timor-Leste did not initiate the recommended actions within the given time frame, then the Security Council was recommended to adopt a Resolution under Chapter VII, to establish an ad hoc international criminal tribunal for Timor-Leste, to be located in a third state. Alternatively, the ICC could be charged to investigate and prosecute the serious crimes committed in Timor-Leste in 1999. Furthermore, Member States might exercise universal jurisdiction, and initiate investigations and prosecution of those responsible for serious crimes.

The Governments of Indonesia and Timor-Leste both immediately rejected the COE report and its recommendations. The COE received strong support from international and national NGOs. In light of the political context, Timorese political leaders raised questions about the effectiveness of such an international judicial arrangement as an international tribunal. They also questioned the appropriateness of exerting political pressure or potential sanctions against Indonesia, as the country still remained in a fragile state of democracy. Gusmão and Ramos-Horta were particularly concerned about the impact of the approach advocated by COE on the progress made in bilateral relations and international reconciliation between Timor-Leste and Indonesia. There were significant improvements in bilateral relations as a result of regular meetings held by the Joint Ministerial Commission for Bilateral Cooperation and, most prominently, by the State Visit to Timor-Leste by President Susilo Bambang Yudhoyono in early April 2005.[22]

To recapitulate the key points, the COE found that the SCP had accomplished a great deal, but did not achieve full accountability for those who were truly responsible for the serious crimes committed in 1999. After visiting sites of massacres and interviewing victims, the Commission found it essential that the judicial process should not be terminated as planned by the Security Council, and specifically recommended that: the SCP should continue beyond May 2005;

Indonesia be provided with legal experts in international criminal law, international humanitarian law and international human rights law;

the Indonesian prosecution authorities be persuaded to reopen the cases against those already found not guilty in the Jakarta tribunal;

SCU staff and evidential documentation be provided to the Indonesian prosecution unit to determine any involvement of former General Wiranto and other high officials; and

the United Nations should establish an international tribunal in a third country or refer the remaining cases of serious crimes committed in 1999 to the ICC.[23]

These findings and recommendations of the COE were considered not only by both Timorese and Indonesian leaders, but also by some members of the Security Council, as not being as practical as they should have been. Reflecting this view, the President of the Security Council asked the Secretary-General to provide a proposal that would be practical and feasible. The UN Department of Political Affairs started to draft a report on justice and reconciliation with a practical, feasible approach. The Department of Political Affairs (DPA) was asked to take into account not only the recommendations of the COE, but also the views expressed by government officials and other actors in Indonesia and Timor-Leste. DPA was also asked specifically to consult with me.[24]

At this juncture, I should comment on my discussions about this issue with various parties in the UN system. A few weeks before the COE report was made public, I held a series of informal discussions and meetings with Special Panel judges and Serious Crimes lawyers from the Prosecution and Defence Unit. Additionally, I met with senior mission managers from Legal Affairs, Political and Human Rights Units, in order to take stock of various opinions on the COE recommendations. There was general consensus that the establishment of the COE was a logical step towards the conclusion of the SCP, as there was a need to assess the concurrent processes in Jakarta and Dili to allow progress to continue.

However, many thought there was no chance that the Timorese leadership would agree to the drastic measures the COE recommended. With regard to the timing of the COE report's publication, it was a predominant view that the United Nations should wait for the Indonesian presidential election process to finish before proceeding further. On the topic of the future of the SCP, it was a mutually shared understanding that the Timor-Leste leadership had made clear: it would take neither ownership nor responsibility for the SCP beyond May 2005. It was also clear that there were many different expectations of the outcome of the COE. They ranged from COE being a step towards the establishment of an international tribunal, to the COE being a practical mechanism to consider the creation of a Truth Commission. Propositions on the future of the SCP ranged from the continuation of the judicial process in its existing form to an independent judicial process similar to the Sierra Leone model. There was also a suggestion that a clear exit strategy should be prepared, and a memorial archive established to provide public access to the collected evidence.

With respect to the COE proposal, I advised the diplomatic corps of the discussions I had held with Under-Secretary-General (USG) Prendergast in New York and Acting High Commissioner for Human Rights Ranchevan in Geneva. In my view, there was a need to await completion of the presidential elections in Indonesia. I also indicated the need for the COE to have clearly defined objectives, especially in view of the differing expectations. Most UN and diplomatic staff agreed on the need to proceed on this issue, but after the conclusion of the Indonesian presidential elections. One of UN Mission Staff raised the lack of consensus or clarity on the part of the Timor-Leste leadership with regard to the mechanisms in the post-May 2005 period. Another was emphatic that the

United Nations should not be pressured to act on recommendations from external groups, referring to a letter from a coalition of NGOs urging the Secretary-General to take early action on the COE. In discussing the Secretary-General's response to this letter, I suggested that he consider highlighting the importance of justice and acting against impunity, at the same time recognizing the available options and different expectations held by various stakeholders over this sensitive matter.

In reviewing various understandings of the significance of transitional justice, I should also note President Gusmão's reaction to the COE exercise. When I told him that the COE was likely to recommend to the Secretary-General of the United Nations the continuation of both the Jakarta Ad Hoc Tribunal and the SCP in Timor-Leste, he wanted to know the specific steps being recommended. I explained that three options were mentioned for consideration:

a handover to national judges, prosecutors and defence lawyers;

continuation of the current process; and

having the United Nations take over the entire process with international judicial personnel.

As always, Gusmão listened to me in a courteous and friendly manner, but he then firmly said that we should move forward and think more about the future of the relationship between the two countries, rather than looking back on what had happened in the past.

The United Nations rebuffs the Commission of Truth and Friendship (CTF)

Both the Governments of Indonesia and Timor-Leste wanted to set aside the past and move on to the future. For this purpose, they agreed to create a unique body, the Commission of Truth and Friendship (CTF) in August 2005, in order to establish conclusive truth, with a view to promoting reconciliation and friendship between the two countries. This also signified that, for the first time, the two countries had decided to create and own a truth-seeking mechanism instead of following the advice of the United Nations and the international community. The emphasis was on reconciliation. Truth was to be established so that it could be a foundation for building a friendly relationship between the two countries. The bilateral Commission commenced its work almost immediately, embarking upon the analysis of documents provided by the Ad Hoc Human Rights Tribunal in Jakarta and the records compiled by the SCU in Dili.

The mandate of the CTF, initially extending over a period of one year, reflected the forward-looking and reconciliatory approach taken by Timor-

Leste and Indonesia. Ten Commissioners – five Indonesians and five Timorese – were appointed to:

reveal the factual truth of the nature, causes and extent of reported violations of human rights that occurred in 1999;

issue a report establishing the shared historical record of the reported human rights violations; and

devise ways and means as well as recommend appropriate measures to heal the wounds of the past, and to restore human dignity, by recommending *inter alia* amnesty, rehabilitation measures, means to promote reconciliation and innovative approaches to enhance intra- and inter-communal cooperation.

The controversial provision contained in the CTF's charter was a clause granting immunity from prosecution based on the testimony to any person testifying before the Commission. This was in line with the approach taken in South Africa. The UN Legal Office maintained that it would not approve the CTF or provide it with support as long as the immunity clause remained in its charter. The leaders of Indonesia and Timor-Leste eventually decided to launch the Commission without the support of the United Nations.

On 31 May 2005 I met with President Gusmão, who was confident that the CTF would establish the truth, and that it could complement the work of the SCP. He clarified that it would not be holding trials. He then emphatically stated that the revelation of truth was, under the prevailing circumstances, the best approach towards the development of the country, given that the State of Timor-Leste assumed the principle that this was a way of achieving justice. Gusmão insisted that the key lesson learned was not to allow the recurrence of political violence in the country under any circumstances. He added that, if the SCP were to continue in Timor-Leste, it would complicate matters. Therefore, he suggested that, if the international community wished to continue the process, it should be held outside of Timor-Leste. President Gusmão was also of the view that it was futile to prosecute and indict individuals. He then informed me that the Timorese Commissioners of the CTF had been identified and would include Aniceto Guterres, Head of CAVR, and Jacinto Alves, a CAVR Commissioner. The President hoped to have the CTF functioning no later than August 2005. He then said that he would welcome international legal and human rights advisers attached to the CTF, and expressed the hope that the United Nations and the international community could provide advisers to support its work.

During the subsequent weeks, further consultations took place concerning the membership of the CTF. On 1 August 2005, Foreign Minister Ramos-Horta convened a meeting with the diplomatic corps and announced the final list of five Timorese members of the CTF. Ramos-Horta emphasized that in accordance with paragraph 16 of the TOR, Timor-Leste selected personalities of "high standing and competence". They were:

- Mr Aniceto Lopez Gutierrez, a lawyer, former Head of CAVR, and an outspoken human rights advocate;
- Mr Deonisio Babo Soares, lawyer and anthropologist, and former Programme Director of the Asia Foundation;
- Mr Jacinto Alves, CAVR staff member and human rights activist;
- Ms Felicidade Guterres, resistance activist, former member of the Conselho Nacional de Reconstrução de Timor (CNRT, National Congress for Timorese Reconstruction) and World Bank staff member; and
- Mr Cerilio Christopho Varadales, lawyer, and one of the country's leading judges.

The Minister also announced the names of three alternative Commissioners. Although the TOR for the CTF did not provide for alternative members, both countries had agreed on their appointment in case of illness or absence of the original five Commissioners.

The Foreign Minister insisted that the selected members reflected integrity and full independence from both governments. They would exercise the greatest efforts to get to "the bottom of the truth" in fulfilment of their mandate, while staying within the respective constitutional contexts. Referring to the need for technical assistance and research support, Ramos-Horta stated his intention to recruit two international advisers, and sought support from the international community. I proposed that the Minister send an official letter for my attention so that I could officially follow up on the request. The diplomatic corps was then given an opportunity to pose questions in order to clarify a number of issues, including the physical location of the joint Secretariat; this was to be established in Bali. We also discussed the submission of a progress report to the governments and heads of state every three months.

Ramos-Horta explained that with the official announcement of the members of the Commission, the CTF was to begin by establishing its organizational structures, including staffing, office allocation and administrative procedures; a detailed work programme for the duration of its mandate was also to be established. He further emphasized that while the Commission operated independently, the two Foreign Ministers would observe the work of the Commission closely in order to provide advisory or other assistance as required. The Governments of Timor-Leste and Indonesia were contributing $500,000 and $1 million, respectively, to the CTF budget.

The CTF would conduct its work using the material gathered by CAVR, the SCU and the Ad Hoc Human Rights Court in Jakarta. The American Ambassador, Grover Joseph Rees, congratulated the Foreign

Minister on his choice of Commissioners, as they were people of great integrity and intelligence. In order to facilitate contact, I asked the five Commissioners to identify a focal point for interacting with the United Nations and diplomatic corps. I felt reassured by the Foreign Minister's emphasis on the importance of upholding transparency throughout implementation of the entire mandate, and by his confirmation that the Commissioners would remain at the disposal of the international community for any future queries pertaining to the work of the CTF.

On 2 August 2005, Ramos-Horta came to visit me. As usual we began by talking about a variety of issues of mutual interest, and then discussed in depth the need for international assistance to implement the mandate of the CTF. He handed me a letter inquiring about potential UN support, and pointed out the need for recruiting two international advisers to assist the CTF. He stressed that the "institutional memory" of the two advisers, and their experience in the field of human rights and justice in the country, would be indispensable for effective and successful implementation of the CTF mandate. I agreed, and told him that I recognized the need for international advisers to maintain the professionalism of CTF's work, assuring him that I would forward the request to UN Headquarters.

I then mentioned to Ramos-Horta the need to complement the Commission's mandate with an effort to deal with the return of former militia members who had been indicted under the SCP. I explained that in my opinion this would greatly contribute to greater national ownership of the process. Ramos-Horta understood my reasoning and told me that he would discuss this possibility with the Prime Minister and the President.

He also noted that follow-up decisions, taking into account the constitutional provisions of both countries, had to be made by the National Parliaments of both Timor-Leste and Indonesia. Referring to concerns raised about the provision of amnesty to ex-militia, he was cautious that amnesty would only be recommended in case of collaboration with the truth-seeking process. The actual amnesty would be granted only with Parliament's approval.

On my part, I emphasized the importance of conducting a credible process. The CTF had to prove that it was not meant to gloss over the past, but to prepare the two countries for an amicable relationship. I told him that some sources in the international community were indeed concerned that the CTF process would avoid naming names in favour of ascertaining "institutional accountability".

Taking note of this concern, Ramos-Horta spent much time elaborating on how he had impressed upon Indonesian Foreign Minister Wirajuda and other Indonesian authorities the importance of carrying out a credible process. He referred to the appointment of the Indonesian

Commissioners as reflecting the good intention of the Indonesian state. Furthermore, he stated that as the reputation of Heads of State was at stake, both sides would make every effort to bring the CTF's mandate to a successful completion. As we were finishing the meeting, I commended Ramos-Horta for his relentless efforts in building the cordial relationship between the two countries. I urged him to ensure that Timor-Leste and Indonesia serve as a leading example for achieving reconciliation between two formerly hostile states, based on truth and justice.

Contrasting concepts of truth, justice and peace

There was no doubt that international advisory assistance could have allowed CTF to carry out its work more credibly. Almost all of the members of the Security Council, including China, France, Russia and the United States, supported the CTF. However, most unexpectedly, the UN Secretariat, particularly the Office of Legal Affairs and the High Commissioner for Human Rights, opposed the provision of UN support for the Commission, considering the approach would compromise justice in favour of reconciliation and friendship. Their position was that truth should be established not just to achieve reconciliation, but more importantly, justice. It was also felt that this truth and friendship approach would be counterproductive to achieving sustainable peace in the long run. Their concern was to ensure also that similar human rights violations would not occur again.[25]

On 29 August, prior to and following participation in a closed meeting of the Security Council,[26] I took the opportunity to hold a series of consultations with senior officials of the Department of Peacekeeping Operations (DPKO), the Department of Political Affairs and the Office of Legal Affairs on issues related to the COE recommendations and CTF requirements. I wanted to understand clearly where they stood on the proposal being drawn up for the Secretary-General's report on the complex issue of truth, justice, reconciliation and peace. Ms Shraga from the Office of Legal Affairs had serious reservations about an amnesty clause. She asked for my input on possible approaches that the Secretary-General could recommend with respect to the COE and the CTF. USG Ibrahim Gambari, who had replaced Kieran Prendergast, encouraged me to engage in further consultations with the Governments of Indonesia and Timor-Leste on the CTF.

In a meeting at the US Permanent Mission to the United Nations in New York, the staff reiterated the US position, confirming interest in ensuring the credibility of the CTF process, adequate witness protection and strengthening the national judicial systems as a long-term institutional capacity-building initiative. Ambassadors of both Indonesia and Timor-Leste expressed their hope that I could find a solution that was feasible within the historical and current political context. I felt that the meetings were repetitive in covering the legal grounds, although they were held in an atmosphere of mutual trust. They resulted in a constructive exchange of views and possible ways on how to proceed with the follow-up of the SCP and the Secretary-General's response to the COE and the CTF.

During my meeting with the Office of Legal Affairs, I stressed the importance of reconciling legal interpretations with reference to the wider political requirements in both Timor-Leste and Indonesia. I first touched upon the TOR of CTF, outlining that paragraph 14 c (i) of the TOR was not authorizing the Commission to grant amnesty, but merely recommending it. Furthermore, paragraph 13 (e) provided that the CTF did not prejudice the judicial process. Ms Shraga indicated that the recommendations presented by the COE did not constitute "feasible measures". In order to meet international legal standards, she stressed that two key provisions in the Commission's TOR needed to be revisited, namely the references to instituting accountability mechanisms and amnesty. In order to ensure accountability, the two countries should stress the complementary nature of the CTF – their commitment to ensure a formal judicial process, if not at present, then at some point in the future.

With respect to the amnesty provisions, Ms Shraga emphasized that according to legal standards, amnesty was barred for three serious crimes: genocide, crimes against humanity and war crimes. On the topic of international assistance to the CTF, I stressed that international advisory and technical support could induce adherence to international legal standards and norms. Additionally, international guidance would enable greater independence from the respective governments, allowing the Commission's work to gain more credibility and legitimacy.

We discussed two measures to enhance adherence to international legal standards. One was to institute an investigative unit within the CTF. The second was to provide institutional capacity-building support for Indonesia's prosecutorial bodies. Ms Shraga stated that she would welcome my insights into the complexity of the legal and political situation on the ground. This was to facilitate consideration of possible approaches that the Secretary-General could recommend to the COE and the CTF.

Mindful of the need to consult further with senior UN officials on the CTF process, I met with USG Gambari and briefed him on recent political and judicial developments. He was supportive of the judicial process for indictees to be continued by the Timorese judicial authorities with international assistance. Referring to the CTF, USG Gambari emphasized that the wider political picture should be taken into consideration when deciding on the legality of the Commission and the provision of international assistance.

Moreover, USG Gambari informed me that he had met with Ambassador Rezlan Ishar Jenie of Indonesia and they had discussed the possibility of revisiting the TOR. He encouraged me to follow up on this issue, and I assured him that I would keep him abreast of any further discussions I had with anyone on this matter. Additionally, I referred to one of my meetings with the US mission, during which Mission Staff stressed the importance of ensuring the credibility of the CTF process. They also stressed the institutionalization of strong witness protection measures and pointed out the need to strengthen the judicial system to improve long-term institutional capacity-building, thus reiterating the US government's opinion that Indonesia should be engaged in a dialogue to accept international assistance to strengthen its judicial organs. There was an urgent need to safeguard and protect statements that would be gathered in the CTF truth-seeking process.

It was apparent that both Timor-Leste and Indonesia had a pressing need to enhance the legitimacy of the consultation, and that the United Nations had to find a way out of this stalemate. I recommended, therefore, that the Security Council be asked to express its view, through a presidential statement, that it wished to receive a report from the Secretary-General on the follow-up of the COE recommendations. I would then provide UN Headquarters with the views and opinions of respective stakeholders, which could be used as input for the Secretary-General's report. I thought that the Secretary-General in his report could then recommend legally sound and practically feasible ways to bring justice, peace and reconciliation.

Following my consultations with USG Gambari and other senior UN officials, I had a working dinner with Ambassador José Luis Guterres of Timor-Leste and Indonesian Ambassador Rezlan Ishar Jenie. I informed them that the Secretary-General had agreed to submit a report on the COE recommendations, if formally requested to do so by the Security Council. I maintained that the controversy over the provision of international assistance to the CTF had to be addressed, and explained the implications of the TOR provisions that recommended amnesty for those who cooperated. I noted that they fully understood that the CTF was not intended to replace the ongoing judicial processes in both countries. They referred to the position taken by Foreign Minister Ramos-Horta that the CTF's TOR should restrict its mandate sufficiently to respond to the concerns expressed by the Secretary-General in his statement. In light of the possibility of CTF going ahead with its work without any UN participation, they considered that the strong backing of the Security Council could provide the requisite strength needed to influence the opinion of authorities both in Dili and in Jakarta.

The Indonesian and Timorese Ambassadors expressed their disappointment with the COE report, and criticized those who questioned the legitimacy of the CTF. They felt others should accept the Commission, as it was a bilateral initiative to which both Indonesia and Timor-Leste had agreed. I told them that in this globalizing world it was the business of everyone to assess the legitimacy of any undertaking, and they accepted my explanation. They agreed to continue the dialogue in order to find a feasible solution within the historical and current global political context.

When I met Foreign Minister Ramos-Horta on 6 and 7 September, I informed him of the outcome of the consultations held in New York, in particular explaining the reservations held by the Office of Legal Affairs about amnesty. Foreign Minister Ramos-Horta reiterated that the CTF had not been constituted to replace any judicial process. The CTF had been empowered only to "recommend" immunity from prosecution to those who cooperated and spoke the "truth" wholeheartedly. He said that he would welcome the engagement of international advisers to assist the CTF as investigators, to ensure that the whole truth would be revealed and recorded by the CTF. I thought at the time that the meetings were most productive, and had provided valuable insights to be taken into consideration.

On 19 September 2005, I met with Indonesian and Timorese authorities. We shared our differing views and understanding of what constituted legally sound and practically feasible ways to address the issues faced by the SCP, in order to follow up the Security Council's decision on the recommendations of the COE report.

We agreed to take into account the Secretary-General's remarks made at the monthly luncheon of the Security Council ten days earlier. He had stated that the United Nations could not endorse any process leading to amnesty for acts of genocide, war crimes and crimes against humanity. The United Nations would therefore have difficulty in accepting the TOR of the CTF as they had been formulated. This was in line with the explanation I had received from the Office of Legal Affairs at UN Headquarters. Having accepted their reasoning, I explored with the Office of Legal Affairs any possibility for making another interpretation of the TOR. I insisted that international advisers be recruited and assigned to CTF, not to help carry out the task with which it had been entrusted, but to add credibility to its deliberations by providing professional research and investigation activities.

Furthermore, to reconcile the various understandings of CTF's TOR and their implications, it could be asked to review its own TOR, and then issue its interpretation in order to clarify what it was required to do. This would underlie the commitment made in the world summit declaration to protect civilians against genocide, war crimes and crimes against humanity.

We felt that this could stress that the CTF had not been empowered to replace the judicial process: that although it had no right to grant amnesty, it could recommend it.

On 20 September 2005, I met separately with Indonesian Ambassador Makarim Wibisono and UN High Commissioner for Human Rights Louise Arbour in Geneva. We informally shared views and ideas on what the international community could or could not do with regard to the serious crimes committed in Timor-Leste in 1999. Their views differed significantly on the validity of the recommendations made by the COE, and on what constituted legally sound and practically feasible measures to ensure justice and promote reconciliation.

High Commissioner Arbour stressed that the COE affirmed the importance of pursuing justice and accountability. Her position, I found, was straightforward and stringent in support of the COE experts:

- That the diagnosis of the COE (and many other analyses of the justice processes in Jakarta and Dili) was solid, whatever one might think of its recommendations.
- That truth and justice were not inimical to each other.
- That assistance should continue to be provided to the Dili process.
- That assistance to the Jakarta trials would require some evidence of genuine commitment to reform.
- That the argument concerning the need to "support the democratic process" (thus requiring the suppression of a call for justice) was specious.
- That the United Nations could not support the CTF in its current form.
- That she anticipated a possible call from the Security Council to the Secretary-General to develop a proposed plan of action, in which the Office of High Commissioner for Human Rights stood ready to play a central role, together with other concerned parts of the system, to develop proposals on how best to move forward.

She emphasized that the United Nations had to make clear that amnesty could not be granted under any shape or arrangement, whether by the CTF or by any other authorities. In her view, no institution had legitimate power to grant amnesty to those who had committed "certain" serious crimes such as genocide, war crimes and crimes against humanity. She felt that the South African model of truth and reconciliation was an exceptional case and should no longer be considered applicable, as the international community had moved away from such an approach. Referring to the case of Sierra Leone, the High Commissioner stressed that the judicial as well as the truth-seeking process must be carried out in a credible and transparent manner. The perpetrators of crimes against humanity, and other serious crimes, must be held accountable through not only the truth and reconciliation body, but also the proper judicial process.

Arbour then asked me what Indonesia and Timor-Leste wanted from the United Nations. I clarified that not only these two countries, but the international community also that wanted the CTF to undertake its task in a credible manner. I then added my own view that the United Nations should provide international advisory services to enhance the credibility and legitimacy of the CTF. It was possible for the CTF to continue its work without any involvement of the United Nations, but the result would be a superficial exercise. Therefore, I suggested that the United Nations assist it in reconciling the need for seeking justice and truth. If the amnesty clause was taken out, most Indonesian military personnel and Timorese militia would not testify before the CTF. Contrary to my expectation, Arbour did not reject my suggestion outright. Instead, she thought that the "compellability mechanisms" in the TOR should be examined carefully. She said that the absence of an amnesty clause did not necessarily preclude persons from giving testimony. Nevertheless, Arbour did not waiver and stated that there were only two options, either:

the amnesty clause is removed completely (for crimes giving rise to universal jurisdiction – genocide, crimes against humanity and war crimes); or

both Timor-Leste and Indonesia pass legislation stipulating that no amnesty would be granted for the above-mentioned crimes.

With regard to the idea of supporting the Indonesians in improving their judicial system, Arbour thought it might be possible only if "the ethical deficit" was eliminated, namely, that the national framework was ready to bring about genuine change in the attitude of authorities towards justice. She stated clearly that the problem with the Jakarta process was not so much the lack of competence in the judiciary, but rather a lack of political will, not least on the part of the prosecution. She thought mere training of judicial personnel would remain palliative. She then asked for my views on how the judicial system in Timor-Leste was carried out. I told her that many of the former militia members had been put on trial and received sentences that were found reasonable. Nobody complained about the qualitative aspects of the judicial process in Timor-Leste. What remained problematic was the inability of the international community to bring to trial those who had fled to Indonesia.

The conversations that I had with Wibisono and Arbour showed the difference in their conceptions of the relative importance attached to pursuing truth, justice and reconciliation. They also revealed the difficulty in formulating a legally sound and practically feasible approach. Wibisono placed emphasis on the political reality that existed in Indonesia, and the need to nurture the democratic process that he believed the international community should support: truth provided a better chance for sustainable peace to flourish. Arbour was convinced that the international community should place the highest importance on securing "true accountability" of both persons and institutions responsible for serious crimes such as war crimes, genocide and crimes against humanity. Wibisono was concerned about potential backlash in Indonesia by military and fundamentalist groups against what they perceived as undue pressure on the sovereignty of Indonesia. Arbour was more concerned about the failure of any nation to transform its ethical and moral standards. It was clear that both of them were genuinely interested in realising justice, truth and reconciliation.

By the time I met Ramos-Horta back in Timor-Leste, he was deeply disappointed and frustrated with the unexpected position taken by the UN Legal Office. Rather than allow his request to be declined, he decided to withdraw it on 10 October 2005, by issuing a letter critical of the UN approach. He stated that he knew how each and every member of the Security Council feels about the initiative taken by the Timorese leaders and found with much distress that the views of the UN secretariat was quite different from the views held by the international community.

The letter was another reflection of the emotional intelligence that Ramos-Horta did not hesitate to display in expressing his feelings. Upon receipt of his letter, I asked him to elaborate on what he knew about the feeling of "each and every member" of the international community. He told me that, according to meetings and consultations he had held in New York and Washington, DC, he found that the United States, France and Japan were in support of the CTF. In addition, most of other Security Council members including Brazil, China, Russia and the Philippines were supportive. He then pointed out that the only member of the Security Council questioning the CTF was Denmark.

The decision of the United Nations not to approve the CTF left an impression that the United Nations was interested in punishment and retribution rather than reconciliation and peacebuilding. This was, however, a simplistic view of differing opinions of the relationship among the concepts truth, justice and peace. Legal and judicial experts tend to reason rationally that the United Nations should most importantly be committed to eradication of the culture of impunity. It was and still is their conviction that those accused of committing very serious crimes should not be excused or freed, and should be held to account for their crimes.

In my view, the United Nations should have supported the CTF between Timor-Leste and Indonesia, because it aimed at ascertaining the truth of what had actually happened, and then acknowledging crimes that had been committed with a view to forgiving them.[27] As I felt strongly on this point, I impressed upon the Office of Legal Affairs that it should find a way to allow international assistance. It advised me then that the only way I could do this was through the Security Council passing a new Resolution. This is a very interesting legal approach, as a Security Council decision automatically constitutes a part of international law. In other words, according to the legal experts, the Security Council was the supreme organ of the international community that can adopt resolutions that then become the international law. But, in my view, what is right and wrong exists even outside of the realm of the Security Council. The role and effectiveness of the pursuit of truth and justice should be to bring about sustainable peace among individuals and communities.

The CTF carried out its task without support from the United Nations and completed its deliberations, and its findings and recommendations were published on 31 March 2008. Despite what critics of the Commission TOR had feared, the CTF was harsh in its fact-finding and concluding remarks concerning Indonesian responsibility for what had happened in 1999. Indonesian and East Timorese leaders jointly accepted the findings of the CTF blaming Indonesian security forces for committing "gross human rights violations" in a failed attempt to prevent the secession of East Timor from Indonesia in 1999. The President of Indonesia Susilo Bambang Yudhoyono, President of Timor-Leste José Ramos-Horta and Prime Minister Gusmão issued a joint statement that expressed "deep regret to all parties and victims, who directly or indirectly suffered physical and psychological wounds" due to the affair, in which hundreds of people died.[28]

It was previously thought that the absence of international involvement and support of the Commission, particularly from the United Nations, would make it too weak to conduct its business in a vigorous and effective manner. This interpretation was reinforced when in April 2007 retired General Wiranto, the former armed forces Commander of Indonesia, declared that it was an absurd allegation that the Indonesian military and police officers had committed grave human rights violations in 1999. He claimed there was no policy and plan to attack civilians and commit any crimes against humanity. It is true that President Ramos-Horta wanted international advisory support to enable the Commission to act at the highest standard of professionalism. However, the UN Legal Office denied any UN involvement as long as the amnesty clause was maintained. Some international journalists were questioning the credibility of the Commission as an instrument to ascertain the truth and achieve justice.[29]

Many leaders of civil society and NGOs expressed their reservations about the proposed Commission when the CTF was established. The main argument was that neither the SCP in Timor-Leste, nor the Ad Hoc Tribunal in Indonesia, had brought to justice those most responsible for the serious crimes that had been committed. The CTF was not considered to be a vehicle capable of achieving any more justice for the victims.

Further criticism targeted the TOR of the Commission. Critics pointed out the lack of distinction between lesser and serious crimes, amnesty provisions for crimes for which amnesty is unacceptable in international law, questionable independence of the CTF, contradictions to human rights law and inadequate provisions for reparations. Furthermore, the CTF emphasized institutional responsibilities, rather than individual accountability for their crimes. These were legitimate concerns. A successful conclusion by the CTF did not mean it was not necessary to deal with these issues of justice. At the same time, the need for justice should not deter the process of seeking truth and reconciliation.

A solution to these complex issues needs to be found: the question of how to deal with the remaining cases of crimes against humanity remains. Continuation of the process of national and international reconciliation, while ensuring good cooperation between Timor-Leste and Indonesia, will most likely remain on the agenda for many years to come. Durable solutions to these difficult issues and ensuring sustainable peace for Timor-Leste will require careful dialogue. It will need much consultation in order to reach mutually beneficial positions, without allowing impunity and ignoring human rights violations, as recognized in the United Nations Charter.

In Resolution 1599, Member States reaffirmed the need for credible accountability for the serious human rights violations.[30] UNOTIL therefore sought to further assist the Timorese authorities, to ensure the adequate archiving of all records compiled by the SCU, and in the implementation of the recommendations made by the COE, including possible ways of assisting the CTF.

Assessment of UN involvement in the transitional justice process in Timor-Leste

As indicated at the outset, it should be noted that various theorists and practitioners have interpreted the role of transitional justice differently in armed conflict and war. Transitional justice started as a temporary mechanism to respond to large-scale violations of human rights, primarily aimed at addressing the need for establishing justice and rule of law in post-conflict situations. The international community resorted to both judicial and non-judicial processes intended to prevent the recurrence of such violations.

The first generation of transitional justice was launched by international military tribunals to hold trials of German and Japanese political and military leaders for their war crimes committed during World War II. The intention was to punish those leaders, with the expectation that this

would deter similar acts of aggression and serious human rights violations. Following the end of the Cold War, internal conflicts and civil wars
in some former communist and developing countries were accompanied
by massive human rights violations, involving atrocity and even genocide.
This led to a growing recognition in the international community that
criminal prosecutions alone do not serve the purpose of rebuilding a war-
torn society.

A second generation of transitional justice was constituted by the
United Nations when the Security Council established the ICTY and the
ICTR. These institutions turned out to be costly, and were characterized
by slowness and remoteness in their deliberation of justice. To overcome
these shortcomings, the United Nations adopted hybrid courts, which
were managed by national and international judiciary personnel. The Security Council then authorized the establishment of such hybrid courts in
such countries as Sierra Leone, Timor-Leste and Cambodia. They proved
not only cost-effective, but also instrumental in enhancing the capacity of
national and local judiciary institutions and personnel.

The third generation of transitional justice activities advocated a significant role in establishing linkage between truth and reconciliation. The
outcome of the Truth Commission in South Africa was successful, and
emulated by other countries. Yet, by the end of the 1990s, both scholars
and practitioners began to feel that over-reliance on the truth and reconciliation approach would undermine the establishment of justice and rule
of law. A new approach to transitional justice experiences stressed both
truth and justice, based on the recognition that a single method may be
inadequate. Intended specifically for societies rebuilding after a period of
conflict and violence, the idea was to balance the quest for justice with
the need for reconciliation, for the ultimate purpose of achieving a just
and peaceful society.

The fourth generation of transitional justice has followed the emergence of a peacebuilding doctrine. The doctrine necessitated the transformation of transitional justice as a means to secure genuine commitment
from the political leaders of a conflict-prone society: namely, to rebuild
their society based on mutual trust, respect for basic human rights and
the dignity of individuals. This approach is political. The role of transitional justice is regarded as achieving a transition from the conflict-prone
society into a form of democratic governance, anchored on the principles
of the rule of law, human rights and democracy.

In the post-conflict country of Timor-Leste, the fourth transitional
justice mechanism was employed to address the demand for truth and
justice, as well as the desire for reconciliation and sustainable peace. It
was aimed at fostering the quest for truth, justice (both retributive and
restorative), reconciliation (at community, national and international

levels) and a peaceful society based on the principles and practices of democratic governance.

The CAVR was established as an independent entity. It succeeded in establishing what had actually happened with respect to human rights violations and in carrying out the process of reconciliation. The CAVR exercise was carried out in a credible manner and was considered successful in healing many local communities through its reconciliation programme, by sometimes bringing together victims and offenders. The Commission also referred those who had caused atrocities and committed serious crimes to the formal judicial process.

The SCP addressed these serious crimes through the formal retributive justice mechanism. Offenders were tried and imprisoned if found guilty. As the controversy increased over the appropriateness of continuing the retributive justice mechanism, the Secretary-General established the COE, which affirmed the centrality and imperativeness of maintaining the formal justice approach. The national leaders of Timor-Leste, however, opted for a more reconciliatory approach with their Indonesian counterparts and founded the CTF, aimed at ascertaining what had happened and building a friendship between the two countries.

When the Timorese and Indonesian leaders established the CTF, many leaders of civil society and NGOs expressed their reservations. Their main argument for their hesitation was that the CTF was not considered to be capable of achieving justice for the victims of serious crimes. Further criticism targeted the TOR of the CTF, pointing out the lack of distinction between lesser and serious crimes, the amnesty provisions for crimes for which amnesty is unacceptable in international law, questionable independence of the CTF, contradictions to human rights law and the inadequate provisions for reparations.

Furthermore, the CTF emphasized institutional responsibilities, rather than individual accountability for crimes. These were and are legitimate concerns. However, the outcome of the CTF deliberations revealed a sense of transition in people's minds towards a better future, although the need for justice did not disappear in the process of seeking truth and reconciliation.

The Timorese people's experience with transitional justice made me reflect on its role in healing the past as well as in building the future for the people. What matters is the outcome of the transitional justice process as much as the manner in which the process was carried out. The truth can be found and used to establish either justice or reconciliation. In post-conflict countries, there is a need to balance our efforts in pursuing the objectives of both justice and peace. The net result of these efforts will result in the creation of a society in which people respect each other's fundamental rights as stipulated in the Universal Declaration of Human Rights.

Notes

1. John Rawls, *A Theory of Justice*, (Cambridge, MA: Belknap Press of Harvard University Press, 1971), pp. 3–4.
2. Excerpt from the statement made by President Gusmão to the 5351st Meeting of the Security Council. See United Nations Department of Public Information press release SC/8615, 23 January 2006.
3. For example, see Simon Chesterman, "Justice and Reconciliation: The Rule of Law in Post-Conflict Territories," in *You, the People: The United Nations, Transitional Adminis-tration, and State-Building* (New York: Oxford University Press, 2004), pp. 154–182; Neil J. Kritz, "The Rule of Law in Conflict Management," in Chester A. Crocker, Fen Osler Hampson and Pamela Aall (eds), *Leasing the Dogs of War* (Washington, DC: United States Institute of Peace Press, 2007) pp. 401–424.
4. UNTAET Regulation 2001/10 on the Establishment of a Commission for Reception, Truth and Reconciliation in East Timor, 13 July 2001 UNTAET/REG/2001/10.
5. Mr Aniceto Guterres, Chairman of the Commission, submitted the Report of the Com-mission on Reception, Truth and Reconciliation to President Gusmão on 25 October 2005 pursuant to regulation No. 2001/10 of the United Nations Transitional Administra-tion in East Timor (UNTAET) and as amended by the National Parliament.
6. A traditional mediation process which determined who had been wronged by whom and what compensation should be given to the wronged party.
7. Nonetheless, some human rights NGOs such as the International Centre for Transi-tional Justice have obtained and published it.
8. Security Council Resolution 1272 (1999) adopted by the Security Council at its 4057th meeting on 25 October 1999.
9. Professor David Cohen also points out in his report for the East–West Center "the lack of equality of arms" along with the failure of the UN Security Council to provide a clear mandate and political will to pursue the perpetrators of serious crimes who fled to Indonesia. See David Cohen, *Indifference and Accountability: The United Nations and the Politics of International Justice in East Timor* (East–West Center Special Report Number 9, June 2006), p. 4.
10. It should also be noted that the Security Council in its Resolution 1599 (2005) called on all parties (including Indonesia) to cooperate fully with the work of the Commission of Experts.
11. United Nations Security Council document S/2005/458, dated 15 July 2005, *The Report to the Secretary-General of the Commission of Experts to Review the Prosecution of Serious Violations of Human Rights in Timor-Leste (then East Timor) in 1999.*
12. UN Security Council Resolution 1704 (2006) authorized the resumption of the investi-gative functions of the former Serious Crimes Unit.
13. UN Security Council 1272 (1999), (S/RES/1272 25) October 1999.
14. United Nations, *Report of the International Commission of Inquiry on East Timor* (A/54/26 and S/2000/59), 31 January 2000.
15. UNTAET Regulation 2000/15 on the Establishment of Panels with Exclusive Jurisdic-tion over Serious Criminal Offences in East Timor, 6 June 2000, UNTAET/REG/2000/15.

16. UNTAET Regulation 2000/15 on the Establishment of Panels with Exclusive Jurisdiction over Serious Criminal Offences in East Timor, para. 4 art. 22.1, 6 June 2000, UNTAET/REG/2000/15.

17. Security Council Resolution 1543 adopted at its 4968th meeting, para. 8 S/RES/1543 (2004).

18. Security Council Resolution 1599 adopted at its 5171st meeting, para. 9 S/RES/1599 (2005).

19. Progress report of the Secretary-General on the United Nations Office in Timor-Leste, para.13, S/2005/1533 (2005).

20. See Caitlin Reiger and Marieke Wierda, *The Serious Crimes Process in Timor-Leste: In Retrospect*, March 2006, written for the ICTJ, p. 30.

21. The key task of the Commission was to produce "legally sound and practically feasible measures", but the Commission did not delineate measures that were legally sound and practically feasible. To the members of the Commission, justice could not be secured for the victims and people of Timor-Leste, and reconciliation promoted, unless all those perpetrators of injustice who had been indicted, including Indonesian military personnel, were brought to trial.

22. The Governments of Timor-Leste and Indonesia then officially expressed their sense of disappointment at the report of the COE, stressing that it did not promote the process of reconciliation. They emphasized that the political leadership in both countries was committed to pursuing reconciliation.

23. United Nations, *Report of the Commission of Experts* (15 July 2005), S/2005/458.

24. The Security Council found it necessary to ask the UN Secretariat to find a practical and feasible way to deal with the issues raised by the COE. See UN document S/2005/613 dated 12 September 2005.

25. The causal relationship that many legal experts consider exists between truth, justice and reconciliation, is not as clear as they claim. Also, we need to assess the hierarchy of importance that should be attached to each of these. The Japanese consider that the Tokyo International War Tribunal conducted trials, established facts (the truth) and executed key military leaders or carried out justice. Yet, there remains lack of reconciliation between Japan and its neighbours, i.e. China and Korea.

26. This was the time when the overall situation in Timor-Leste was relatively calm and stable, since the dispute in May 2003 between church and government had been resolved peacefully. The international community had the impression that Timor-Leste had reached maturity in its democratic governance, but I told the Security Council that it still needed all forms of assistance from the United Nations, as suggested by the Secretary-General's report (S/2005/533), until presidential and parliamentary elections were held in a free and fair manner in 2007, allowing a peaceful transition of power. I also informed the Council that after four years of work, CAVR was nearing completion of its final report, which would include comprehensive recommendations, among other things on further action on the issue of justice, reconciliation and assistance to victims of past human rights violations. As for the Serious Crimes Process, I said UNOTIL had produced a copy of all records compiled by the SCU, and added that the national judicial system had demonstrated its capacity to act upon the return of a former militia member who had been indicted under the Serious Crimes Process. Finally, I emphasized that in the absence of a UN security force, the security and safety of UN personnel remained a major concern and challenge to UNOTIL. See United Nations Department of Public Information press release SC/8484 on Security Council 5251 Meeting of 29 August 2005.

27. I vividly recall how the Indonesian officials, accompanied by their President Susilo Banbang Yurdiono, were in tears when the Timorese people welcomed them en route to the

residence of Timorese President Gusmão. It was the Timorese way of showing their spirit of forgiveness that touched the Indonesians.
28. Commission of Truth and Friendship Report, 31 March 2008.
29. The effectiveness of the CTF was questioned by human rights advocates and legal experts for its inability to perform "professionally". An association of human rights groups was reported to have sent letters to the Presidents of both Indonesia and Timor-Leste to close the Commission.
30. United Nations Security Council Resolution 1599 of its 5171st meeting (S/RES/1599 (2005), paragraph 9).

VI

Premature withdrawal of peacekeepers and transition to a sustainable development framework

The Security Council insists on rapid transition: SRSG asked to consult with all stakeholders

In the Secretary-General's report presented to the Security Council on 20 February 2004, Under-Secretary-General Guéhenno noted that no nation had ever advanced more rapidly along the path to self-sufficiency than Timor-Leste. However, at the same time, he stressed that there were always limits to what could be achieved in such a short time frame. He insisted that continuation of peacekeeping operations in Timor-Leste for one additional year was essential to strengthen what had been achieved. Guéhenno then made a strong appeal for continued UN security presence in Timor-Leste beyond May 2004, as the country faced "a paradoxical challenge". He proposed that a military presence, with aviation and the support of 310 personnel, be retained in order to protect a small group of military advisers and UN civilian staff after May 2004.[1]

Three months later, in his last address to the Security Council as Head of the United Nations Mission of Support in East Timor (UNMISET), the Special Representative of the Secretary-General (SRSG) Sharma called for continued UN assistance to ensure sustained development and strengthening of key sectors, mainly justice, public administration and the Polícia Nacional de Timor-Leste (PNTL, National Police of Timor-Leste). Furthermore, Sharma stated the continued need to provide support for maintenance security and stability in Timor-Leste.[2]

Primordial leadership: Peacebuilding and national ownership in Timor-Leste, Hasegawa,
United Nations University Press, 2013, ISBN 978-92-808-1224-4

It is significant to note that following the strong pleas made by Guéhenno and Sharma, the Security Council recognized the need for continued UN military and police personnel presence. It decided to maintain 42 military liaison officers, 310 formed police personnel and a 125-person international military response unit to provide the necessary support to Timor-Leste; an additional 58 civilian advisers and 157 police advisers were also provided. The presence of trained international police and a rapid response unit was key to the continued stability of the country. The Security Council made it clear that it was authorizing the extension of the UNMISET mandate only for six months, "with a view to extending it for a further final period of six months until May 20, 2005."[3]

Three months later, in August 2004, Hedi Annabi, Assistant Secretary-General for Peacekeeping Operations, made a comprehensive report on the extended phase of UNMISET to the Security Council.[4] He informed the Council that Timor-Leste had successfully taken over responsibility for external and internal security. Annabi also stated that Timor-Leste still required international security assistance, because of the fragility of law enforcement institutions. He referred to the peaceful resolution, on 19 and 20 July, of demonstrations by veterans and former combatants who felt marginalized and neglected. Annabi thought a national dialogue organized by President Gusmão, with the support of UNMISET, was instrumental in bringing about a peaceful resolution of the dispute.

Annabi then reiterated the need for addressing the issue of veterans and ex-combatants. He found that tangible progress had been achieved in democratisation processes such as village chief elections, border demarcations, and negotiations between Australia and Timor-Leste on natural resources. He thought it possible for the majority of the 58 most critical civilian advisers to implement their exit strategies. However, it was incumbent on the government to identify and assign counterparts to take over functions currently carried out by the international civilian advisers. It was also necessary to find a sustainable manner to secure professional services carried out by the 15 advisers in the justice sector, including judges for the district courts. Annabi found that the PNTL continued to face problems such as insufficient professional skills, misconduct and the need for further training of anti-riot rapid intervention police officers.[5]

The Security Council members discussed the proposal put forward by Annabi. After a lengthy consultation, they decided to recognize only the need to maintain UNMISET's current tasks, configuration and size, in order to allow the mission to complete key tasks of its mandate and consolidate gains made thus far. This reflected the views of key Council Members and security partners such as Australia. The Australian Ambassador, John Dauth, stated that he agreed with the assessment of the need for further training of PNTL police officers, including the Rapid Intervention Unit (RIU) members. Furthermore, he saw the need for an international emergency police response unit to remain in Timor-Leste until May 2005.

Taking into account the views of Australia and other key members such as the United States, the Security Council stressed the need to focus increasingly on its exit strategy by increasing Timorese involvement and ownership. In addition, it insisted that UN development, humanitarian agencies, and multilateral financial institutions such as the World Bank and the Asian Development Bank, needed to start planning immediately for "a smooth transition" in Timor-Leste: that is, transition from a peacekeeping operation to a sustainable development assistance framework. To make its expectation for completion of UN peace operations in the country very clear, the Council asked the Secretary-General to submit "a final report" in May 2005.[6]

Security Council members remain divided over security perceptions

On 28 February 2005, I reported to the Security Council on how tangible progress had been made to achieve a smooth transition to a sustainable development framework. I provided detailed proposals that had been worked out in consultation with all stakeholders. This time, I also provided the Security Council with an explanation of the two most demanding challenges:

the pending challenge was to stabilize the situation around the border
    with Indonesia by concluding the land border demarcation negotiations;
the further challenge was to establish a harmonious relationship between
    the two Timorese security agencies, the F-FDTL (FALINTIL (Forças
    Armadas de Libertação Nacional de Timor-Leste) – Forças Armadas
    de Defesa de Timor-Leste) (F-FDTL) and PNTL.

The first task had become urgent as incursion by ex-militia groups continued around the border areas. The second was a real challenge for not only the personnel, but also both security agencies and the Timorese leadership.[7]

Following my introductory statement, there was a great deal of debate in the Security Council due to different perceptions of the security situation. Brazil was seriously concerned about stability in Timor-Leste and supported my observation. The Brazilian Ambassador, Henrique Rodrigues Valle, stressed that Timor-Leste had not yet achieved the level required for its people to enjoy their complete potential. He did not expect that Timor-Leste would be in a position to assume the principles and practices of democracy without outside help. The Ambassador urged the Security

Council to reaffirm its commitment to a continued presence of an integrated mission, with a comprehensive long-term strategy.

Mr Cesar Mayoral, the Argentinian representative, agreed with this perspective. He stated that Timor-Leste had not yet reached the required critical threshold of an independent sovereign country. He felt that the hasty withdrawal of UNMISET might jeopardize all that had been achieved, and that such a move would have serious repercussions for the well-being of Timor-Leste. Mayoral urged the United Nations to continue to lend its support to Timor-Leste, as a premature withdrawal of the mission would derail the country's efforts invested thus far.

Portugal was also cautious about the situation in Timor-Leste. The Portuguese Ambassador, João Salgueiro, identified a number of areas in need of international assistance beyond UNMISET's mandate. In the area of police training, he considered that much work still needed to be done in border management. The porous border remained a source of illegal incursions and illegal trade. Noting that security on the border was a key factor for the political and social stability of Timor-Leste, Ambassador Salgueiro expressed his concern that the land border demarcation remained incomplete.

Ending the UN peacekeeping mission: The United States prevails

In spite of the concerns expressed by the representatives of Portugal and South American countries, Mr Reed Fendrick of the United States made it clear that, in the view of his country a peacekeeping mission was no longer required, and that UNMISET should conclude its mandate in May 2005. The United States was convinced that the peacekeeping phase was past, and that Timor-Leste could safely enter its path to self-reliance. An alternative way to fill the gaps should be found, he suggested, such as a political mission. It was important that the Government of Timor-Leste increasingly take more responsibility for the nation's future. In particular, attention should be paid to constitutional development, continued police training and the building of a diverse political party system.

Other key members of the Security Council such as France, the United Kingdom and Japan essentially supported the judgement of the United States, while they differed slightly in their expressions. The Japanese Ambassador, Kenzo Oshima, said Japan was prepared to support the proposal to retain some form of UN presence in Timor-Leste upon the expiration of UNMISET's mandate in May 2005, noting that leaving unmet requirements unresolved could threaten the important gains made. A small UN mission dedicated to peacebuilding, with the minimum number of personnel required, could be a useful solution to remaining problems.[8]

The message from the most dominant member of the Security Council was clear: we must now abandon any hope of keeping any security forces in Timor-Leste, and should start to prepare for a peace- and nation-building mission. I shared my misgivings about the security risk with the then Foreign Minister Ramos-Horta. Ramos-Horta and I made a last effort to convince the key members of the Security Council at their capital cities. Foreign Minister Ramos-Horta visited Washington, DC, where he met with US political leaders and government officials indicated his views on the future UN presence beyond the end of the United Nations Office in Timor-Leste (UNOTIL) mandate. He then received a clear message that the United States did not find it necessary to continue any additional peacekeeping or peacebuilding mission, but only a small political office to monitor and support the electoral process.[9]

Nobody should question the solid ground for peace that had been laid in Timor-Leste. I was told during my visits to London, Paris and Washington, that it was time that I left the country, as the Timorese were fully capable of taking care of themselves. Similar views were expressed during my own consultations in the capitals of key Security Council members. In London, Paris and Washington, I was also told politely but firmly that the United Nations had done a good job in Timor-Leste and should now close its mission. In one place, I was even reminded in a joking manner that I had stayed in Timor-Leste for nearly four years, and that the time had come for me to leave the country.[10]

By April 2005, contrary to the advice of the Secretary-General, the Security Council as a whole accepted the judgment of the United States. It concluded that there was no longer any serious threat to external and internal security, and decided to remove all armed personnel. In place of the peacekeeping mission, the Security Council found it sufficient to maintain a special political mission, with a view to transferring the capacity-building task to the United Nations Development Programme (UNDP) and other UN agencies. The newly created UNOTIL was then mandated to transfer administrative and technical skills from international advisers to their national counterparts. This represented a logical progression in the transition from peacekeeping to peacebuilding and then to a development assistance framework.

Furthermore, the Security Council found it imperative to accelerate the mission transition in order to facilitate the new country's ability to achieve democratic governance and sustainable development. The key members of the Security Council also considered that such a transition to a development framework should be possible, as the Timorese had achieved adequate internal security and stability. With this logical perception of the local situation, the Security Council went on to not only withdraw all armed military and policy personnel, but also to reduce the number of civilian advisers assigned to all state institutions including the parliament, the courts and the Office of the President.[11]

On 28 April 2005, the Security Council recognized that the state institutions were still in the process of consolidation. Further support was required in key sectors, particularly with respect to the rule of law, justice, human rights and the police. The Council then adopted Resolution 1599 (2005) establishing UNOTIL as a one-year, follow-on, special political mission that would remain in the country until 20 May 2006. For this final phase of the transition process, reflecting the views of the United States and other key members, the Council insisted that the UNOTIL mission should be a small UN political office, to provide support for the consolidation of police, border patrol and other critical institutions. The Security Council members, at the same time, showed appreciation of the need for their support in the development of critical state institutions. For this purpose, the Council decided to provide up to 45 civilian advisers. It also supported further development of the police through the provision of up to 40 police advisers, 10 of whom might be military advisers. UNOTIL was also mandated to undertake training in observance of democratic governance and human rights by providing up to ten human rights officers.[12]

The Security Council also became reluctant to provide any more funds, and urged the donor community, including UN agencies and multilateral financial institutions, to provide more resources and assistance to enable the implementation of development projects to promote sustainable peacebuilding in Timor-Leste. It also decided that UNOTIL should emphasize proper transfer of skills and knowledge. This was in order to build the capacity of Timorese public institutions, so that they could deliver their services in accordance with the principles of the rule of law, justice, human rights, democratic governance, transparency, accountability and professionalism. The Council encouraged the Government of Timor-Leste, UNOTIL, the UN Secretariat, UN development, humanitarian agencies and multilateral financial institutions to start immediate planning for a smooth and rapid transition from a special political mission to a sustainable development assistance framework.

Sharma establishes a transitional working group

The Security Council also asked me to establish and chair a consultative group, made up of stakeholders in Timor-Leste, to advance the transfer of necessary skills to Timorese institutions and personnel. We would meet regularly for the purpose of coordinating various assistance programmes provided by bilateral and multilateral donors, regional mechanisms, NGOs, private sector organizations and other international actors.

Consequently, I convened a meeting of the heads of diplomatic missions based in Dili, which took place on 20 September 2004. I explained to the stakeholders that I had constituted a Transition Working Group (TWG) to establish a concrete transitional framework. It would allow the transition of Timor-Leste from the existing peacekeeping and peacebuilding phase to a sustainable development phase when the UNMISET mission was completed in May 2005.

The Transition Working Group (TWG) undertakes a needs assessment for progress to a sustainable framework

The TWG was tasked to clearly delineate what the international community should do to fill any needs for continuing international assistance after the departure of UNMISET. We constituted eight groups which would take stock of progress in their respective areas, identify remaining challenges and propose how to meet the remaining requirements after the end of UNMISET's mandate. In other words, the TWG's recommendations were to constitute the core elements of UNMISET's exit strategy, providing for a smooth transition from peacekeeping to a sustainable development assistance framework.

On 15 November 2004, I participated in the Security Council for the first time. The atmosphere was so congenial that I felt relaxed and comfortable in the chamber. This time, the meeting was held under the chairmanship of Ambassador Danforth of the United States. I exchanged a few words with him before the meeting started, recalling that he had visited Mogadishu, the capital city of Somalia, in 1994 when I was Director of Policy and Planning of the United Nations Operations in Somalia II (UNOSOM II). He was a member of the Security Council mission to assess the local situation before the Council decided on the termination of UN peacekeeping operation in Somalia.[13]

In my opening statement, I gave a report on the situation in Timor-Leste, and detailed specific arrangements that needed to be made for a smooth transition from the peacekeeping to the peacebuilding phase. The successive UN peacekeeping operations in Timor-Leste were indeed recognized as major, successful undertakings of the international community. However, I also reminded the Council that much of the success was due to the determination of Timor-Leste's leaders and people to build peace and stability anchored on the principles of democratic governance.

The Timorese leaders had been alert and expeditious in taking necessary action whenever threats to stability had emerged, as when PNTL had made use of excessive force in arresting peaceful demonstrators of mostly former independence fighters in July, causing widespread concern. Also, realizing the urgency and seriousness of the veterans issue, the Timorese leadership had taken initiatives to address the grievances of former resistance fighters and other disgruntled groups. I explained to the Council that the significance of the National Dialogue organized by President Gusmão on 21 August had brought veterans and government leaders together.

Timor-Leste had made steady progress in its peace- and nation-building efforts. This demonstrated what could be achieved by constructive partnership between a newly independent country and the international community. Much remained to be done, however, within the remaining period of UMMISET's consolidation phase. I then reminded members of the Security Council that, in accordance with Security Council Resolution 1543 adopted earlier in May 2004,[14] an integrated assessment mission headed by Director Lisa Buttenheim of the Department of Peacekeeping Operations had visited Timor-Leste in October 2004. It reviewed the situation on the ground in order to determine the feasibility of modifying UNMISET's size, composition and tasks, including the configuration of its police and military components. The mission sought the views of all stakeholders and also travelled to the border districts. I then stressed the conclusions of the mission that, despite the notable advances achieved during the UNMISET consolidation phase, Timor-Leste had not yet reached the critical threshold of self-sufficiency.[15]

The task of identifying specific measures for transition to a sustainable development framework was huge and time-consuming, and required consultations with all stakeholders. In my statement to the Security Council, I advised that I had constituted eight TWGs to address the concerns raised by the Member States.

The TWGs were to take stock of achievements so far in their respective areas, identify remaining needs and requirements, then propose options and solutions to fulfil them. Included were recommendations for training and capacity-building, the legal framework, the institutional system and procedures, and organizational norms and customs. These would have to put in place to enable the institutions concerned to function in a viable and sustainable manner, and to identify the "responsible hands" that would provide any further external assistance upon completion of the consolidation phase of UNMISET in May 2005.[16]

For respective working groups, I assigned executive responsibility to coordinators to convene and manage meetings, and ensure that the groups would make reasonable progress towards the goals of the TWGs as a whole. They should assist chairpersons, who could be ministers and ambassadors, to chair and direct meetings. They would then represent the working groups at meetings of the central steering group headed by the SRSG. This arrangement proved to be reasonable in managing numerous groups and partners with vested interests. The TWGs were also asked to present an overview of progress to date in their areas, and identify the remaining challenges, in order to achieve some coherence among the proposals. Finally, they also were asked to identify means to meet remaining requirements after the withdrawal of UNMISET. I then asked the secretariat of the CSG to compile the recommendations of each group, which would be submitted to the three stakeholders as background material. The key stakeholders were the Government of Timor-Leste; the development partners (some of whom were also members of the Security Council and the Core Group in New York);[17] and the UN agencies. They were to receive the materials before their next meeting of the Timor-Leste development partners in March 2005.

The 8 working groups had more than 150 participants. These included ambassadors, diplomatic representatives and Timorese leaders based in Dili, including President Gusmão, who had agreed to chair the working group on security issues. The final reports from the working groups were to be ready in January 2005, and their conclusions and recommendations would be reflected in the next report by the Secretary-General. I emphasized that national ownership was a primary determining factor for any successful nation-building effort in a post-conflict country.

It was indeed a major exercise with so many people involved. Each of the working groups held four to six meetings over countless hours and days between August and December 2004. Their pace of work intensified following the adoption of Resolution 1573 on 16 November 2004, the focus of which was on implementing an exit strategy. To reflect the spirit of partnership in the process of consultation, I requested that ambassadors and senior officials of partner countries actively participate in TWGs and chair some of their sessions. TWG participants included ambassadors from Australia, Brazil, China, Indonesia, Japan, Malaysia, Portugal, Republic of Korea, Thailand, United Kingdom and United States, as well as UN agencies and the Bretton Woods institutions.

Perhaps because I was a former UNDP Staff member, I was particularly conscious of the intent of Resolution 1573, which was to ensure increasing Timorese involvement and ownership. In order to ensure Timorese ownership of the process at the highest level, I requested that the President, the Prime Minister, the Foreign Minister and other ministers chair some of the meetings of the TWGs. The Prime Minister chaired working group meetings on Institutional Capacity-Building of State Administration, Enhancement of Transparency and Accountability, and Institution Building of the Justice Sector. He also co-chaired two meetings on the Roles and Responsibilities of the National Security Agencies; the President himself chaired one meeting of this TWG. The Minister of Foreign Affairs chaired one meeting on the Serious Crimes Process.

Meanwhile, the Minister of Interior chaired the final meeting on the development of PNTL.

Ambassadors and heads of diplomatic missions complemented UNMISET on its initiative, welcoming the participation of government representatives in the working groups. They also appreciated the efforts made to avoid any duplication of the process already put in place to identify the country's medium- and long-term development requirements. They agreed that, by focusing the attention of the TWGs on identifying the means to meet Timor-Leste's continuing needs after the withdrawal of UNMISET, they could perform a useful role.

Transition Working Groups (TWGs) recommend comprehensive transition measures[18]

I was very pleased that the findings and recommendations of the TWGs reflected the results of inclusive and comprehensive discussions held by all stakeholders in the eight areas.

In order of TWG numbers, these areas were:

TWG 1. Institutional capacity-building of state administration.
TWG 2. Enhancement of transparency and accountability.
TWG 3. Institution-building of the justice sector.
TWG 4. Future of the Serious Crimes Process.
TWG 5. Professional development of the PNTL.
TWG 6. Roles and working relationships of national security agencies.
TWG 7. Support to marginalized groups: veterans and youth.
TWG 8. Transition from peacekeeping to the development phase.

After numerous TWG meetings, a conclusive consultation was held on 10 January at the Office of the President. President Gusmão and Prime Minister Alkatiri chaired the final TWG meeting on the roles of national security agencies. Alkatiri presented a detailed discussion on various issues identified in the TWG's matrix, declaring that there were plans to transform the Secretariat for Defence into a Ministry. He further emphasized that the Secretary of Defence reported directly to him as Prime Minister. His statement signalled his intention to establish clearly the line of command that was to flow from the Commander of the F-FDTL to the Defence Secretary and then to the Prime Minister. He then acknowledged that F-FDTL soldiers needed more training. In regards to the management structure for defence and security, Alkatiri noted that draft law for the Superior Council for Defence and Security was before parliament.

Alkatiri was forthright when he indicated the need to clearly define the roles and responsibilities of the security agencies, and his government endeavoured to do so in the following months. He then pointed out the lack of staff in his own office as a major reason for not being able to hold more committee meetings focusing on security-related issues. He asked for at least three international advisors in his own office to whom he could address security issues. This request received some sympathetic response from the diplomatic corps, but it was felt that the first priority should be to strengthen the Secretariat of Defence with more trained civilian nationals, as 14 of 18 designated positions had not yet been filled. Secretary of Defence Roque Rodrigues pointed out that more time was needed to find suitable candidates for these positions. The US Ambassador reminded everyone that the recruitment of these civilian officers would help strengthen civilian control of the military. With the agreement of both Gusmão and Alkatiri, the consultation meeting adopted a recommendation for the government to identify several civilian candidates who could start training without further delay.

The working group took note of the most urgent and explosive issue faced by the newly formed Government of Timor-Leste. This was the support for marginalized groups, particularly veterans and ex-combatants who demanded due recognition for their contributions made in the country's fight for independence. The government also had to find the means to provide gainful employment for them, and solutions for the youths who had learned that they had the right to demand education and jobs. The working group also took note of the fact that President Gusmão was deeply concerned about the plight of former independence fighters; he had established the Veterans Commissions in order to compile a list of veterans.

Along with the initiative taken by the President, the government had made two proposals to address the veterans' issues:

the campaign of recognition would recognize all veterans through a public act whereby certificates would be conferred upon them indicating their category and classification, in line with a law to be approved by parliament; and

the programme of valorization would be carried out based on a National Plan of Inclusion into Active Life. As the government had these proposals in place, the international community could support these proposals at its request.

The international community showed its interest in helping to mitigate the problems faced by veterans and ex-combatants. As noted in earlier chapters, two major programmes had offered support without targeting them specifically. Once the veterans were identified and clear definitions made, it was hoped sufficient programmes were in place to ensure that the veteran issues would be addressed.

The working group recognized that the youth support programmes lacked the high profile of the veterans' issues. Additionally, they were grossly underfunded. Although programmes were in place to provide youth training, due to the large numbers involved, these programmes were still relatively small. Yet, the funds that could be made available was limited. The Ministry of Education, Youth, Culture and Sports had made some plans aimed at developing a youth policy, which represented a promising start. As in the case of "veterans" the Ministry had to formulate a definition of "youth" before it could develop and implement a policy.

The working group adopted a pragmatic approach to enable a smooth transition from a phase of peacekeeping and peacebuilding to one of development. As the first step, the TWG established a sub-group to prepare an inventory of the work done by UNMISET. This would allow development partners and the government to continue with their programmes. They addressed areas that were not being examined by any other group. The sub-group produced a matrix provided a description and approximate costing for all areas of support, including security, human rights monitoring, communications, medical, logistics and aviation.

The group also considered options for ensuring that UNMISET provided coordinated and coherent assistance to Timor-Leste. It then assessed emerging needs where other mechanisms were unavailable beyond 20 May 2005. In this endeavour the group recalled the stated position of the Government of the República Democrática de Timor Leste (RDTL, Democratic Republic of Timor-Leste) as preferring the continuation of some level of military observer capacity, a human rights monitoring function, and additional police training and mentoring functions. Additionally, they had a preference for continued technical assistance in public administration. The group then examined several specific options:

- The continuation of a peacekeeping mission, albeit considerably reduced in size. It meant that the UN mission would continue to maintain security forces not only to protect its own personnel, but also to intervene in case of militia incursions and domestic security conflicts. This was considered highly desirable by both the UN Secretariat and Mission Staff on the ground. The Timorese authorities also thought the presence of UN security staff would provide a sense of certainty for the presidential and parliamentary elections to be held in 2007. However, given the perceived conditions of peace, the representatives of the Security Council and the Core Group members – particularly Australia and the United States – insisted that there was no need for a peacekeeping mission to continue.

Given the rejection of the first option by the key partner countries, TWG examined other options:

- A peacebuilding operation with a range of different funding options, including assessed and voluntary contributions or a combination thereof. This still envisaged a multidimensional mission consisting of civilian political, judicial, human rights and security advisers. Furthermore, capacity-building experts and development advisers supported by voluntary contributions would be hired.

- Constituting a separate UN Military Observer Mission and retention of UN police advisers. This meant that the security advisers would be independent of other UN activities, signifying a return to an old arrangement. The TWG found this approach contrary to the need for an integrated and holistic approach.
- To dispense of any special UN political and security operations. Instead, the United Nations would undertake coordination of institution-building functions, including training activities carried out by UN police advisers. These activities would be being entrusted to the Resident Co-ordinator of the United Nations System's Operational Activities for Development (RC), who would coordinate all development assistance provided and carried out by the UN system and the Transitional Support Programme. Bilateral assistance was coordinated in the context of the Development Partners Meetings. It was also felt that retention of Timor-Leste on the agenda of the Security Council should also be considered, in conjunction with a peace-building operation or a UN Military Observer Mission with the presence of UN Police Advisers.

The findings and recommendations of the TWGs demonstrated clearly that Timor-Leste would require the continued, integrated assistance of the international community in many vital areas to enable it to reach the critical threshold of self-sufficiency. The active participation in TWG deliberations by development partner countries, UN agencies and the World Bank attested to their keen interest in continuing and increasing their assistance to Timor-Leste. Indeed, they were already at different stages of discussion with the Government of Timor-Leste on their bilateral assistance programmes.

Implementation of practical transition measures

We then faced the challenge of establishing an institutional mechanism to secure financial resources and advisers, engaging people who could continue to perform the functions that the Timorese had not mastered. In practical terms, these two came together. In other words, interested bilateral and multilateral agencies were expected to provide both funds and experts. This was also true of most of the remaining functions of UNOTIL that were required beyond completion of the mandate, as UNOTIL would probably be replaced by UNDP or the RC, and act as a team leader for the UN development system of operational activities. A large number of positions and programmes needed to be redefined to fit the new objectives for a sustainable assistance framework. On this point, both UN and bilateral partners showed their readiness to extend their support to continue most UNOTIL programmes in the next framework.

This began with analysis of the working structure that supported the UNOTIL apparatus. By the end of the UNOTIL mandate, 5 of 45 civilian adviser positions were envisaged with regard to supporting institution-building of critical state institutions. Eventually, 40 UNOTIL civilian advisory positions were identified as requiring international support in the post-UNOTIL period., and a number of bilateral and multilateral partners were identified to take over most of these functions. UN agencies involved in former UNOTIL areas of support filled the vacant positions, according to their capacity and plans for the post-UNOTIL period:

UNDP agreed to take over all 17 positions in the justice sector. UNDP's support projects and multi-donor programmes filled three positions in the National Parliament and one in the Office of the President. Also, Australia, the World Bank and other donors were committed to support the Ministry of Planning and Finance. The International Monetary Fund (IMF) agreed to provide an adviser for the Director of the Treasury. Among the bilateral development partners, Australia indicated its intention to assist in strengthening the Office of the Prosecutor-General. Brazil, Portugal, Australia and others expressed their readiness to support the development of the justice sector with funds and advisers through UNDP programmes. The United States and Japan brought their support for two positions in the Office of the Inspector-General related to transparency and accountability. Japan offered support for a position in the areas of small and medium industries development, and civil aviation. New Zealand showed interest in providing one Human Rights adviser to the Office of the Prime Minister, while Cape Verde offered to make available six legal advisers to different state institutions.

UNOTIL had been putting emphasis on the further development of PNTL, which was playing a crucial role in the reconstruction process. The United Nations Police (UNPOL) would complete most of the capacity-building objectives within the given time frame of the mandate. However, there were intensive negotiations about continued bilateral support for the eight specialized units and the Immigration Unit. The United Nations Educational, Scientific and Cultural Organization (UNESCO) expressed willingness to continue its support for the PNTL Public Information Unit. Two areas, however, required longer-term bi- and multilateral support: assistance to the Minister of Interior, and the further development of logistical and management skills of the Border Patrol Unit (BPU).

In light of training in the Observance of Democratic Governance and Human Rights, functions that required post-UNOTIL support were revealed. These included the Office of the Provedor, the Office of the Adviser on Human Rights to the Prime Minister, the Ministry of Education, the Ministry of Interior and the National Parliament. Such support was mainly to be ensured through the takeover of National Professional Officers by respective state institutions. Additional support activities to be continued were in capacity-building of civil society organizations, and in monitoring and reporting functions.

Three additional substantive areas required post-UNOTIL attention:

- political affairs, including the monitoring of the political and security situation in the period leading up to the 2007 elections, and electoral assistance, political advice and strengthening of key state institutions and democratic processes;
- legal affairs, including the maintenance of RDTL legislation online content, finalization of the Tetum legal dictionary, indexing of G-RDTL–UN agreements, archiving of documentation and the transfer of legal library books; and
- public information, including the continuation of the daily media review and regular press releases for continued public awareness and correct information dissemination on UN system activities. These functions were to either be taken over by the government, by bilateral partners or to be subsumed under the RC Unit.

Restructuring of the RC Unit in order to meet the post-UNOTIL requirements. Discussions brought out possible elements to be added, including human rights, political affairs, legal affairs and public information. Further areas of development were identified, included operational aspects such as security and medical services.

The above efforts were developed in consultation and coordination with development partners and other multilateral partners, such as UN agencies, but were nonetheless subject to funding availability.

Assessment of the transition process: Benchmarking mission responsibilities

International assistance was directed primarily at supporting development. There was lack of full recognition of the need for a post-conflict country to have a balance of both peacebuilding activities and peacekeeping operations, before it could be placed in a self-sustainable development framework. As early as February 2004, the Security Council urged the UN development and humanitarian agencies and multilateral financial institutions to start immediately planning for a smooth transition, in Timor-Leste, from a peacekeeping mission to a sustainable development assistance framework.[19]

This signified the absence of the link between peacekeeping and peace-building phases prior to sustainable development. In recognition of the need to build the capacity of state institutions, on 28 April 2005 the Security Council authorized the continued presence of a UN mission in the form of UNOTIL. It was designed solely to undertake systematic state institution-building activities. The SRSG was requested to direct the operations of the mission and coordinate all UN activities in Timor-Leste.[20]

This showed the Security Council's full acceptance of the report of the Secretary-General's High-Level Panel issued at the end of 2004 regarding threats and challenges faced by the international community and a necessary change that must be brought about in the UN system to realize a more secure world. The Secretary-General acknowledged that it was indeed a necessary step to undertake peacebuilding activities after the completion of a peacekeeping operation, before the phase of sustainable development could begin. It also recognized the need for the SRSG to "have the authority ... as well as the resources to perform coordination functions effectively, including ensuring that the sequencing of UN assessments and activities are consistent with Timorese government priorities."[21]

A major focus of the new mandate became institutional capacity-building within the state organs, agencies and government ministries that were responsible for security, law and order, justice and civil administration. These eventually enabled a smooth and rapid transition from a special political mission to a sustainable development assistance framework.

My own extensive experience with nation-building assistance led me to believe that the new nation-building process was a time-consuming exercise that required growth of solid institutional capacity. It also meant that the culture of democracy, based on respect for human rights and freedom, needed to be attained. These processes required not only transfer of technical know-how and skills to individuals, but also Timorese understanding of democratic norms and standards. However, institutionalization of administrative procedures, systems, democratic norms and principles were still not sufficiently internalized in the minds of local people. This would be a long and difficult process, as it was not easy to find common ground for democratic norms because of the diversity of the people, some having spent many years in different societies. There was also a desire for individual power and wealth. Furthermore, the quest for democracy would no doubt become a destabilizing factor, as people learned to voice their demands for participation in governance of their affairs.[22]

At this juncture, it should be noted that the roles of the United Nations for the maintenance of peace and security changed dramatically over the period 1999–2006. Peace- and nation-building began to occupy an increasingly significant part of the attention and efforts of UN peace operations. The nature and composition of threats to peace had also become complex and inter-connected, and managing them required extensive, coordinated efforts by multilateral and bilateral agencies, and by both state and civil society organizations.

Thus, the notion of security had become more comprehensive, and as it was not confined to the military, we had to deal with diverse threats. We needed to pay attention not only to the safety and well-being of individuals, but also to their protection from a multitude of threats. These ranged from former antagonists to newly emerging groups. Neither state nor specialized international agencies could solve the threats. The role of the United Nations, the sole universal organization, which conducts activities in a wide range of fields, became increasingly critical in mobilizing a multitude of players, for the purpose of addressing the complexity of challenges and threats in a comprehensive and integrated manner.

Divergent views expressed by international stakeholders

Among the bilateral partners, Indonesia was one of the most important. Both the UN mission and the Government of Timor-Leste paid special attention to Indonesia and engaged in constant dialogue. When I took up my assignment with UNMISET in July 2002, the mission maintained its liaison office in Jakarta, which reported to us daily. After this office was closed in 2004, SRSG Sharma and I visited Jakarta periodically to brief ambassadors of interested countries and the Government of Indonesia. Once I became SRSG, I also kept a close working relationship with Indonesian Ambassador Ahmed Bey Sofwan in Dili. He was also willing to share information and consult with me, and we agreed to visit each other often.

On his return from Jakarta in September 2004, Sofwan visited me, accompanied by Counsellor Primanto Hendrasmono. Sofwan stressed the importance President Megawati and Foreign Minister Wirayuda placed on building a relationship between Indonesia and Timor-Leste. The Ambassador gave concrete evidence by stating that the government had pushed hard for his appointment as Indonesian Ambassador to Timor-Leste by the House of Representatives (the Dewan Perwakilan Rakyat).

Referring to the border negotiation, I emphasized the importance of Indonesia and Timor-Leste resolving the remaining differences on border lines. The time had come for political dialogue and to complete the decision-making process by signing the agreement before the end of the year. Both the Indonesian Ambassador and Counsellor agreed. They added that Foreign Minister Wirayuda wanted to conclude the final agreement before the new Indonesian Government was formed after the conclusion of the presidential elections on 20 September. Sofwan was convinced that it would constitute a major personal achievement for the Foreign Minister.

Regarding the future of the Ad Hoc Tribunal in Jakarta and the Serious Crimes Process in Dili, I explained that the Secretary-General would only decide on any specific steps after receipt of a comprehensive report from the High Commissioner for Human Rights. Sofwan asked me if the Secretary-General would establish the COE so it could begin work in the field. I answered that it was a possibility, but that no decision had been made. He then emphatically conveyed to me the message that Indonesia would not allow it to enter the country, or even allow it to pass through Indonesian territory to reach Timor-Leste. This would mean that the COE would have to reach Dili via Darwin. Sofwan emphasized that it had become an issue of national sovereignty that many Indonesians now felt should be protected.

This was a most alarming message to me as I had worked hard to bring about this Commission. I explained to him how and why this commission had come about, talking about the decision of the Court of Appeal of Jakarta to overturn the ruling made previously by the Ad-Hoc Tribunal. This disappointment had compelled the international community to explore an alternative means of achieving justice. Furthermore, I brought to his attention that the task of executing justice, and the eradication of the culture of impunity, had become a major concern of the global community. During the course of the succeeding several weeks, Foreign Minister Ramos-Horta joined me in persuading the Government of Indonesia to accept the COE.

In my encounters with Indonesian officials in Dili, Jakarta and New York, I found a genuine desire to build a friendly relationship between the two countries. Director-General of the Ministry of Foreign Affairs Makarov Wibisono, and Ambassador Rezlan Ishar Jenie in New York, were both emphatic that the Indonesians only invaded Timor-Leste after US Secretary of State Henry Kissinger gave his consent. In my view, Indonesia's genuine acceptance of the independence of Timor-Leste was one of the key elements in Timor-Leste's stability and progress.

Australia was the only country that maintained its diplomatic presence in the territory during the period of Indonesian occupation. As a major country with military capability located adjacent to Timor-Leste, Australia not only influenced the situation in the Timor-Leste, but also played a decisive role in restoring security and stability in 1999 and 2006.

The relationship between Australia and Timor-Leste was complex due to the conflict of interests concerning the exploitation of natural gas resources. There was also tension due to ideological and cultural differences between the two countries. Australia balanced its desire to play a leading role in the UN peacekeeping missions with its wish not to appear as a neocolonial power. It also found itself competing with Portugal, which wanted to maintain its strong historical and cultural ties with the Timorese people. The Australian press was most active in covering the activities of UN missions and political development in Timor-Leste.

Portugal was no longer a major economic power in the world. However, as a former colonial power, it sustained its influential position in Timor-Leste. Although its economy was small and stagnant by any European standard, Portugal provided a relatively large sum of reconstruction and development aid, in addition to security assistance. As Ambassador Joao Salgueiro claimed in his speech to the Security Council on 5 May 2006, Portugal had contributed more than €400 million since 1999; it thereby remained "the largest donor". Portugal was also the major contributor to the UNDP programme, as it aimed at strengthening the na-tional capacity in justice and electoral process.

It is significant to note that, along with Brazil, Portugal remained consistent in insisting on the continuation of a strong UN presence, and an active engagement in security and capacity-building, particularly justice and finance. The statement that Ambassador Salgueiro made several months earlier, in January 2006, was significant, as it was an early recognition that Timor-Leste had achieved lasting peace and stability. I felt he was most insightful in his call for UN assistance in addressing systemic problems within the security sector, as "an approach solely based on bilateral programs of assistance will not be sufficient, given the political sensitivity of this issue."[23]

The United States had little strategic interest, but it remained a most influential pivotal country as it played a decisive role in the Security Council of the United Nations. Its ambassador, Grover Joseph Rees, was active in shaping the approach of the diplomatic community in Dili. He took a leading role in examining various issues and posing incisive questions at meetings convened by the UN missions and the Government of Timor-Leste. Ambassador Rees was particularly vocal on justice issues; prior to his appointment as Ambassador to Timor-Leste, he had been a law professor at the University of Texas in Austin, and a judge in American Samoa. He had been engaged in matters related to Timor-Leste for several years prior to his arrival in Dili. In 1998, four days after the fall of President Suharto, he visited Xanana Gusmão at Cipinang prison in Jakarta, as part of Congressman Smith's delegation. Rees again visited Gusmão when the latter was transferred to house arrest in Salemba in 1999. Whenever consultation meetings were held with the diplomatic corps, Ambassador Grover Joseph Rees spoke articulately and made insightful interventions.

Shortly after the eruption of violence in Dili, I visited Washington on 3 May 2006, where I held a series of meetings with senior officials of the National Security Council at the White House and the State Department. I thought it was highly desirable to consult with them in view of the dominant position held by the United States in the Security Council. Ms Lisa Buttenheim, Director of the Asia and Middle East Division, and Mr Antero Lopes from the Police Division at the Department of Peace-keeping Operations (DPKO), also joined me in meeting with American officials. The US government had maintained that the UN presence in Timor-Leste should be scaled down to a small political liaison office, and other institutional capacity-development support activities should be taken over by UNDP and other UN agencies. This process was called "a smooth transition to a development assistance framework".

I felt that this approach was premature, as both political and security conditions were considered volatile even before the incidents of 28–29 April. My task, therefore, was to convince the relevant American officials at the National Security Council and the State Department of the need to maintain an integrated UN mission with police and military advisers, even after the completion of the UNOTIL mandate. When I met relevant US government officials, most of them were still sceptical of the need for the continued presence of police and military advisers. Yet, as we alerted them of the emerging situation, they began to see the need to revisit the issue, although they did not say so explicitly.

At the Executive Office building adjacent to the White House, I met first with Ms Patricia Davis, Director of Democracy and Human Rights, and Ms Holly Morrow, Regional Director for Southeast Asia in the National Security Council Secretariat. Referring to the deterioration of the security situation in Timor-Leste, I stressed the fact that the demonstrations staged by the dismissed F-FDTL had been hijacked by youths and disgruntled groups who were dissatisfied with the government. The event signified the unpredictability of developments in post-conflict countries. In this context, I explained the need for an holistic approach and identified key components of the proposed follow-on Integrated UN Office. In doing so, I particularly emphasized the importance of continued support by UN police to ensure law and order. I also told them about the need to protect the security of campaigners and voters during the forthcoming electoral campaign.

I then asked for US support for a solid UN presence, as members of civil society and the church all feared the events of 1975 might repeat themselves. Mr Lopes found my explanations to be plausible. I called for a careful consideration of the proposed deployment of UN police, as an impartial UN presence would be crucial to assist the government in the planning and implementation of an electoral policing strategy. In addition, the United Nations needed to pre-empt a possible failure of the PNTL during the electoral process. In particular, the concerns of the US officials were about the possibility of abuse of force, and the respect for human rights. On the topic of civilian advisory posts, I elaborated that the proposed advisers would further support institutional capacity-building efforts in a number of key areas. These areas included the justice sector, in particular public prosecution; the Ministry of Defence and F-FDTL; the Office of the Provedor for Human Rights and Justice; and the National Parliament.

The White House officials were clearly puzzled by the latest development, as their embassy staff in Timor-Leste had informed them that the country had achieved most of its post-conflict goals and said that Timor-Leste was ready to transit to a peaceful democratic society. Therefore, Ms Davis simply asked if there was any more need for additional international human rights officers, or whether national staff could possibly undertake this task. In response, I pointed out that national human rights officers had often only been granted access to detention facilities and prisons after intervention by international staff. Therefore, we needed international human rights staff to remain. I also told her of the need for police advisers to ensure the safety of electoral campaigners.

At the State Department, I met with a large number of officials starting with Ambassador Tim Carney, Interim Coordinator for Resource Management; and Ms Ciara Knudsen, International Relations Officer of the US Department of State Office of the Coordinator for Reconstruction and Stabilization (S/CRS). Separately, I also met with Ms Angela Dickey, Director for Southeast Asian Affairs, who played a key role in formulating the US policy towards Timor-Leste. Following a detailed explanation of the causes for the departure of the 594 soldiers from the F-FDTL, and the subsequent involvement of youths and political elements, I noted the need to understand the mentality and mindset of national leaders as constituting a key factor in response to the demands of a crisis situation.

I emphasized that these people simply think and act differently from those in a mature democracy. Ms Dickey acknowledged that while the US government had been urging for the downsizing of the UN mission in Timor-Leste, recent developments clearly indicated the potential for violence in the country. She then agreed with me that a robust and impartial security presence would be required to ensure a free and fair electoral process. Ms Dickey maintained that the key was to make the Timorese Government feel that the international community was closely monitoring the transparency of the process. To build on this understanding, I further elaborated on the other elements contained in the Secretary-General's recommendations on a follow-on Integrated Office. I emphasized the need for police and military support, and also for ten civilian advisory positions for security sector reform. On the latter, I reiterated the importance of strengthening the institutional foundations of the Ministry of Defence and F-FDTL through organic laws and effective management structures, weakness in these being the root causes of the current problem within the F-FDTL. On the US position in the forthcoming Security Council meeting, Ms Dickey affirmed that the United States would reassess the situation in light of recent developments and revisit its position on the establishment of an Integrated UN Office prior to the Security Council meeting on 5 May. It was the first time that US officials recognized the need for more than a token political liaison office to be kept after the completion of the UNOTIL mandate.

The United Kingdom played a visible role in shaping the international response to the Timor crisis situation during the first few years of its presence. However, it decided to close its embassy in 2005 as part of cost-cutting measures. On 17 November 2005, I met with UK Ambassador Tina Redshaw, to discuss the anticipated closure of the UK Embassy in Timor-Leste. I also discussed other issues of interest to us, including the provision of international assistance to the electoral process, the follow-up to the COE report and post-UNOTIL scenarios, including political and security developments. Tina was a lovely lady, married to a Mongolian gentleman, and in the past she had worked with a civil society organization. Our consultations took place in a friendly atmosphere and were characterized by mutual trust.

Ambassador Redshaw first briefed me on the expected closure of the Embassy of the United Kingdom in Timor-Leste, which she said would take place in July 2006. I reiterated that her government was taking the wrong decision: Timor-Leste still needed the strong presence of many embassies. Their presence would not only give legitimacy to its political independence, but also necessary pressure to the national leaders to perform well. The Ambassador agreed with me and emphasized that the United Kingdom would retain a UK representation in the country until after the National Parliament passed the electoral law. She expressed her hope that an exceptional extension would be granted for keeping the Embassy until December 2006. I responded by proposing that the United Kingdom should maintain the Embassy in Dili until the presidential and parliamentary elections were held in 2007. She shared my views personally, but stated that as Timor-Leste was not one of the UK's priority countries, and considering that the UK Embassy in Jakarta could cover Timor-Leste, she said that London was firm in closing the Embassy by the end of 2006.

We then talked about the forthcoming presidential and parliamentary elections. I first outlined a number of options for the provision of electoral assistance or combinations thereof, including:

the placement of up to 500 UNVs as electoral observers throughout the country to assist in and ensure a fair and transparent electoral process;

sound voter education to be carried out by national NGOs;

support for the drafting of the electoral law, establishment of database and electoral management systems and capacity-building; and

electoral monitoring during the election period only.

Ambassador Redshaw placed particular emphasis on sound voter education to ensure high voter participation. She emphasized capacity-building of local staff and adequate women's participation during the national elections, and also focused on the topic of female representation in the National Parliament. She mentioned that equal support should be granted to smaller parties, as lack of financial and human resources might hamper their electoral campaigning and outreach. In regards to international assistance for the electoral process, Ambassador Redshaw indicated that the United Kingdom would not be in a position to provide bilateral support, but could offer assistance through EU- or UN-led initiatives, such as electoral observer missions.

Subsequently, we discussed various post-UNOTIL scenarios, including the retention of a human rights component and a political affairs office under the umbrella of the RC Unit. The Ambassador was very interested in retaining a human rights element aimed at the need to continue to provide human rights training and monitoring. Placing international human rights officers in Timorese state institutions would fill this need. In this context, I informed Ambassador Redshaw about the division within the government regarding the presence of the UN mission in Timor-Leste. While Foreign Minister Ramos-Horta and President Gusmão both supported a mandate extension, Prime Minister Alkatiri strongly advocated that the UN mission should end by May 2006. The President of the National Parliament, Francisco "Lú-Olo" Guterres, was closer to the Prime Minister's point of view, even though his insistence on a UN departure was not as strong. We also talked about the need to follow up on the COE recommendation on the Serious Crimes Process. The British Ambassador indicated that her government had not taken any clear position or given any specific instructions on the COE report, having decided to await the Secretary-General's comments. This was one of my last formal meetings with Ambassador Tina Redshaw, which had served a good purpose in enabling an exchange of our views and opinions. Indeed, our meetings were very insightful and useful. In my memory, Tina remains warm and caring of Timor-Leste.

Japan was prominently represented in Timor-Leste by its first Ambassador, Mr Hideaki Asahi, who had substantial historical knowledge of Timor-Leste. He was keenly interested in greater national ownership in rehabilitation works supported by donor countries and was active in enhancing civil–military collaboration. He provided his support to infrastructure rehabilitation works carried out by the Japanese defence force personnel, officially known as the Japan Engineering Group of the Japan Self-Defence Force (JEG). Ambassador Asahi was also keen to help community recovery and supported the organization Recovery, Employment and Stability Programme for Ex-combatants and Communities in Timor-Leste (RESPECT), which provided employment opportunities to community inhabitants, including former combatants. As a strong advocate of human rights and human security, he pursued the task of refining the concept of human security in a conflict-prone society such as Timor-Leste.[24]

The UN mission relationship with Japan was also maintained at the level of DSRSG. For example, in September 2005 DSRSG Bajwa discussed with Counsellor Takashi Koizumi (of the Japanese Embassy) the possibility of Japan providing bilateral assistance to Timor-Leste during the drawdown of UNOTIL, and Koizumi confirmed Japan's intention to collaborate with UNOTIL. He further informed Bajwa of Japan's plan to take over four civilian advisers' positions from UNOTIL during its drawdown phase, in the areas of investigation and in small enterprise. Koizumi noted the possibility of further assistance in the governance area, notwithstanding that Japan's assistance has traditionally been in the development and construction of infrastructure.

Koizumi then pointed out to Bajwa the need for coordination of the police training activities provided by various stakeholders. Koizumi rightly noted that while one country might provide training in a particular style of policing, another country might follow with training in another method. Bajwa agreed to address this issue with his UNPOL team, in order to effect proper coordination of police training activities. His remit was not only among stakeholders, but also in the overall policy of the Ministry of Interior in this regard. Bajwa then drew to Koizumi's attention that the Japanese Government had donated a significant amount of equipment, which was nevertheless not being used optimally, apparently due to a lack of generators with the right voltage. Koizumi believed that the problem lay with the lack of management and administration skills of Timor-Leste's electricity authority, as the voltage issue had been analysed prior to the handover of the equipment. Nonetheless, he agreed to look into the possibility of liaising with this authority in order to resolve the situation.

During my visit to Japan in September 2005, I held a series of meetings with senior officials of Ministry of Foreign Affairs. On 2 and 5 September, I discussed several issues including:

the procedure of the Serious Crimes Process and the Commission of Truth and Friendship (CTF);

the possibility of Japan providing further support to Timor-Leste, especially in the area of governance and to the proposed projects submitted by UNDP-Timor-Leste; and

the likelihood of the Japanese Government taking an initiative to hold a Consultative Group meeting for assessment of the involvement of international society in Timor-Leste. I was pleased to find that the officials I met were basically in support of the approach taken by the United Nations.[25]

On the CTF, Director of Southeast Asia Division Shigeki Takizaki stated that the Government of Japan considered that CTF should ideally work most effectively to promote reconciliation between Indonesia and Timor-Leste. Therefore, the Government of Japan would be willing to support the CTF, if requested. Takizaki further referred to a discussion held between Ramos-Horta and Foreign Minister Machimura, when Ramos-Horta indicated that he was proud of Timor-Leste for having established the CTF, as it showed that Timor-Leste was in the position of forgiving sins committed by others, rather than being accused of them in the courts.

Referring to Ramos-Horta's suggestion that this could become a model for different conflict resolutions, I mentioned that it would enable the CTF to maintain greater independence from the Governments of Timor-Leste and Indonesia; this would enhance the credibility and legitimacy of the work of the CTF itself. I suggested that Japan should explore the possibility of taking an initiative to support the CTF process. With Ramos-Horta's agreement, I further suggested that the Japanese Government take the initiative to hold a consultative meeting, with the participation of all relevant stakeholders, in Tokyo in March or April 2006. The main objective would be to assess accomplishments made in Timor-Leste during the past five years. Both Vice-Minister Yachi and Director-General Nishida welcomed the idea, and stated that the meeting could be held as a coming-of-age ceremony for Timor-Leste. It would mark the start of a new phase of Timor-Leste as an independent country, moving from being a post-conflict society to that of one achieving sustainable development. It was agreed that this meeting would provide not only an ideal occasion for the international community to evaluate the accomplishments made, but also for Timor-Leste to maintain a sense of ownership for moving the country forward.

Stressing the need for a Peacebuilding Commission and a Peacebuilding Support Office, to provide further support for nation-building of post-conflict societies, I suggested that the Government of Japan demonstrate its leadership in instituting such a Commission or Office. Yachi supported the idea, stating that Japan was in an ideal position to support peacebuilding activities in international society, given its own rich experiences of nation-building. Moreover, it was noted that there was a need for creating a course on Peace Studies at the United Nations University (UNU) in Tokyo. Foreign press centre chief Terada mentioned that it would be possible to launch a seminar and lecture series at UNU, for which facilities and equipment would willingly be provided.

In New York, the Permanent Mission of Japan played a key role in co-ordinating the international approach to Timor-Leste. For example, it convened a consultation meeting on 29 April 2006 for Member States of the Security Council, the Core Group and Association of Southeast Asian Nations (ASEAN) countries, as well as the UN Secretariat (Department of Peacekeeping Operations (DPKO) and Department of Political Affairs (DPA)), UNDP and the World Bank.

The purpose of the meeting was to solicit the views of international stakeholders on the recommendations of the Secretary-General in establishing a new mission in Timor-Leste, following UNOTIL. It is noteworthy that, while Australia, the United States and New Zealand insisted that there was no need for police and military components, Argentina, Brazil, Portugal and Singapore strongly advocated a continued fully fledged UN presence. The following indicates the views of UN member states based on comments made by their representatives. They are listed according to the order of their taking the floor.[26]

- Australia stated that it remained committed to assisting Timor-Leste, including in the area of police training. However, with respect to a post-UNOTIL presence, Australia considered UN Security Council Resolution 1599 as the last extension of a UN political and security presence in the country, and argued that international assistance should continue to be provided by UN agencies, the World Bank and other bi- and multilateral partners.
- New Zealand supported a continued UN presence, including civilian advisory support. However, military and police advisers went beyond what New Zealand had envisaged. New Zealand stood ready to support the Secretary-General's recommendations to assist Timor-Leste, in agreement with other partners.
- The United States took note of the recommendations contained in the report of the Secretary-General and recognized the rationale for a follow-on mission. While the United States was supportive of the

international community in focusing on electoral assistance, voluntary bi- and multilateral assistance should be increased. Although the representative noted that acknowledging the need for a follow-on mission was a major advance in comparison with the earlier stand taken by the United States, he stated officially that the UN presence in Timor-Leste should end. The representative, however, questioned the need for the continued stationing of police and military advisers.[27]

- Portugal warned that Member States should not lose sight of what was really happening on the ground and emphasized the volatility of the security situation. The representative stated that the perseverance of the Timorese leadership was commendable, and that Portugal remained committed to assisting the young nation. Portugal was strongly supported the analysis of the Secretary-General's report, and underscored that the recommendations, outlining the minimum support requirements. With respect to the proposed role of the Military Liaison Officers (MLO), Portugal advocated an expansion of the mandate, including both monitoring of the security situation along the border and capacity-building in the defence sector, maintaining that merely bilateral partners could not provide the latter, and that an impartial UN presence would be crucial.[28]

- Brazil stated that concerns about the security situation remained. It wholeheartedly embraced the remarks made by Portugal, in particular the need for continued monitoring of the security situation along the border and further capacity-building of the BPU. Brazil recognized that elections in a post-conflict environment very often led to a deterioration of the political and security situation. Brazil remained committed to supporting institution-building efforts, in particular the police and judiciary, in order to uphold internal security and the rule of law; these would provide the Timorese with the necessary peace and tranquillity to render Timor-Leste economically viable. The representative reminded the meeting that the United Nations had played an important role in assisting Timor-Leste to restore its independence and argued that the United Nations should continue to provide unconstrained support, especially prior to the 2007 elections.

- Argentina strongly supported the Secretary-General's recommendations for the establishment of an Integrated UN Office, given the security concerns along the border and the need for a peaceful environment during the electoral period. Argentina supported the Timorese Ambassador's view that the Secretary-General's recommendations were the minimum of what the United Nations should provide.

- Indonesia commented on the excellent bilateral relationship established between Indonesia and Timor-Leste, which Indonesia planned to expand further. Indonesia commended the democratization process in

Timor-Leste and recognized that UN assistance would be valuable in the preparation for and during the 2007 elections. Indonesia assured that security along the border would be upheld to enable a free and fair electoral process.

- Singapore fully supported the recommendations outlined in the Secretary-General's report. While acknowledging the sentiments of Australia, New Zealand and the United States, Singapore did not think that UN agencies would be able to absorb the full scope of assistance required in the post-UNOTIL era. The security situation remained quite precarious and Singapore warned against jeopardizing the achievements made thus far. In order to render the role of the proposed UN civilian advisers most effective, the Singaporean representative then suggested that the advisers should undertake an assessment of the achievements made by international advisers in various sectors, and specify why advisers in some areas were more effective than in others.

- France shared the views expressed by the Secretary-General and agreed with the need for an Integrated Office, which should be of a political nature, and include a security dimension as well as a human rights section. In the context of justice and human rights, France raised the question of the submission of the Secretary-General's report on justice and reconciliation to the Security Council, and whether the recommendations could be integrated as part of the mandate of the follow-on UN office.

- Japan commended Timor-Leste for its achievements and called upon the international community to support peacebuilding efforts. After termination of the UNOTIL mandate, the combination of both bi- and multilateral assistance would be critically important in ensuring national ownership and sustainable assistance. Japan reiterated its willingness to continue providing bilateral assistance. The representative then stated that in view of the importance of presidential and parliamentary elections in 2007 in advancing the democratization process of the young nation, Japan was supportive of a small UN office, to provide mainly electoral support.

- Germany considered the Timorese case a story of success. While hoping that international support would eventually move away from Security Council assistance, Germany acknowledged the merits of the Secretary-General's recommendations and pointed in particular at the need for continued assistance in the areas of justice, law enforcement and human rights.

- The representative of China stated that it fully supported the Secretary-General's recommendations and recognized the different views of Member States. China was looking forward to further discussions on the issue in order to find a compromise, and supported the notion of the Timorese Ambassador that the Secretary-General's recommendations constituted the bare minimum of assistance required.

Acknowledging the views expressed by Member States and the questions they raised, I reminded participants that, given the latest security development, any positive outcome could only be achieved if the international community remained committed to continuing to assist Timor-Leste in making a success of the process of transition from one style of government to another. I affirmed that both the political and security situation remained fragile, and that, if the United Nations left at this critical juncture, political hardliners and opportunists would possibly take advantage of the situation. In this regard, as most of the participants of the meeting were not fully familiar with the latest political developments in Timor-Leste, I reported to them that Timorese Ambassador Guterres had decided to challenge the current leadership of the Frente Revolucionária do Timor-Leste Independente (FRETELIN, Revolutionary Front for an Independent East Timor) during the forthcoming National Congress of the political party in May. I explained the significance of such a step towards greater legitimization in the struggle for political power and influence, and emphasized that the United Nations should foster a political and security environment conducive to a free, fair and credible electoral process. I also insisted that the Timorese people felt an indisputable sense of danger, and reminded participants that according to the Timorese Government, the international community had failed to see and act during the riots of 4 December 2002. Referring to the Timorese call for a continued, modest UN presence, I stressed that the support outlined in the Secretary-General's report was indeed the minimum required for the country to achieve peaceful transfer of power through elections.

DPKO Director Lisa Buttenheim then clarified that the new mission or office should not be considered a continuation of UNOTIL, as the UNOTIL mandate had been largely fulfilled. She then joined me in emphasizing that the first post-independence national elections scheduled for 2007 were extremely important in fostering the democratization process and, therefore, the DPKO fully supported the Timorese Ambassador's view that the recommendations by the Secretary-General met only the minimum requirements. As concerned police training and advisory support, member states should acknowledge that PNTL was a 5-year "young" institution. It was still growing in maturity and impartiality, and it lacked adequate accountability mechanisms to monitor the electoral process. The international community needed to ensure that there were no gaps between bilateral and UN assistance. Under the follow-on office, UNPOL was to focus on creating a secure electoral environment, through both training and advising on strategic planning, in cooperation with other bilateral partners. This was equally true for the border region, and this required the engagement of impartial UN military liaison officers to monitor and advise on the security situation, and to liaise with the Unidade Patrulhamento Fronteira (UPF, Timor-Leste Border Patrol Unit) and the Tentara Nasional Indonesia (TNI, Indonesian national armed forces).

Finally, the representative of DPA stated that the date of the presidential and parliamentary elections, being an issue of great political contention, had not yet been decided upon. On this point, the Electoral Assistance Division of the Department of Political Affairs (EAD) participant advised that the elections would have to be held prior to 20 May, as stipulated by the Timorese Constitution.

The coordination meeting proved most useful to ascertain the perception of key Security Council members and other international supporters about the conditions in which Timor-Leste evolved. Their perception, which reflected the assessment of local situations based on the understanding of their ambassadors and representatives, was that Timor-Leste had successfully achieved maturity in its governance and that all that was needed was a small office to monitor political developments and assist in electoral processes. Such were the views of key members of the Security Council, particularly France, the United Kingdom and the United States, as they had been communicated to me during my previous visits to Paris, London and Washington, DC.

Kofi Annan presides over policy committee discussion on post-UNOTIL custodianship

As the closure of the UN peacekeeping mission became imminent, the custodianship of a successor mission became of major interest and concern to various units at UN Headquarters. Secretary-General Kofi Annan convened a meeting of senior officials of DPA, DPKO, Department of Public Information (DPI), Office of Legal Affairs (OLA) and UNDP in March 2006, to review options available for the post-UNOTIL structure of the UN system in Timor-Leste.

As the exercise would no longer be a peacekeeping mission, management was to be handed over from DPKO to some other appropriate department. DPA claimed that it was in the best position to take charge, as its primary function was to monitor political development and to provide political advice to host country leaders. Others considered that it should be managed by the UN Development Group represented by the UN RC on the ground; this would mean in practical terms that UNDP would become responsible for the management of the mission. Still others felt that DPKO should retain responsibility.

In opening the meeting, Secretary-General Kofi Annan said that there was an agreement to disagree on how the United Nations should proceed. He then asked for the views of Department Heads at Headquarters. He also asked for the opinions of the Regional Director of UNDP for Asia and the Pacific on the three options.

The first option

This would realize an effective transition to a full development assistance framework through the establishment of an office headed solely by the RC. It meant that UNDP would basically take over all management responsibilities of UN activities in Timor-Leste, including institutional support in electoral areas. The RC would be responsible for arranging and coordinating the technical support to be provided by the civilian advisers to the government, which would focus on the justice and finance sectors. Bilateral and multilateral donors, including the World Bank, were expected to commit themselves to finance all civilian advisers by the end of the UNOTIL mandate. If this option was chosen, the RC would also assist, primarily through DPA's EAD, in providing support to the government for the preparation of the 2007 elections. In addition, the RC's office would include a human rights officer funded by the Office of High Commissioner for Human Rights (OHCHR) to mainstream human rights within the work of the UN country team. The OHCHR officer would also oversee the implementation of OHCHR's technical cooperation programme with the government. While the government had earlier asked for the continuation of UN police trainers and military liaison personnel, this option ruled out any further UN assistance in security sector on the understanding that bilateral arrangements should be adequate to meet such requirements. DPKO and UNDP supported this option as it constituted a clear transition from the peacekeeping phase to a development assistance framework.

The second option

This envisaged the establishment of a UN Integrated Office in Timor-Leste. This represented an institutional arrangement that I personally considered appropriate, as I felt that the United Nations should respond to the government's request for continued assistance in police and military institution-building. Earlier in March, I had agreed with then F-FDTL Commander Taur Matan Ruak (TMR) that the United Nations should provide as many as ten advisers to strengthen the institutional capacity of F-FDTL. In my view, it was essential that the post-UNOTIL office should include all civilian, military and police elements, by establishing a UN Integrated Office in Timor-Leste. UN Headquarters staff considered it would be similar in structure and mandate to the office that had been created in Sierra Leone. There, my friend Victor da Silva Angelo of Portugal,[29] had been appointed in January 2006 by Secretary-General Kofi Annan as his Executive Representative for the United Nations Integrated Office in Sierra Leone (UNIOSIL). When I served as UNDP Resident Representative in Rwanda in 2005 and 2006, I met him on several occasions, and we developed a warm friendship.

Following the Sierra Leone model, the UN Integrated Office would support the Timorese Government in the preparation of the 2007 elections, in addition to further development of police force capacities, particularly electoral-related security functions. It would strengthen critical state institutions in the judicial and financial sectors. Senior officials at UN Headquarters regarded the Sierra Leone model as a good example of an Integrated Office. I explained that I was already acting as not only the SRSG, but also as the Resident Coordinator of the UN operational activities and the Resident Representative of UNDP in Timor-Leste. The only difference would be the nomenclature of its head, who might be called an Executive Representative rather than SRSG.

As with the first option, UNDP would be responsible for recruiting and managing the civilian advisers assigned to various Timorese institutions. The Integrated Office would more specifically provide the Government of Timor-Leste with several experts, including electoral advisers, civilian advisers in the justice and finance sectors and police training advisers to support the further development of the Timorese police. The focus there would be on electoral-related functions. Additionally, military liaison personnel would assist the government in pursuing enhanced dialogue and cooperation between Timorese and Indonesian security personnel, in order to prevent tensions arising along the border.

The Integrated Office would also include political and public information officers, who would focus on monitoring and reporting the electoral process, as well as being watchful advisors of the overall political situation. In coordination with OHCHR, it would include a human rights unit, comprising national and international staff who would work closely with state institutions and civil society. They would provide assistance in the electoral, justice and police training areas. The Secretary-General seemed inclined to entrust DPKO with the responsibility of managing this Integrated Office.

The third option

Proposed by DPA, this was the establishment of a UN Political Office. It would be a small and distinct UN Political Office funded through the

regular budget, as was the case for UNOTIL. It would have no more than ten international professionals, headed by a Director, to be limited to the duration of the 2007 electoral process. I understood that DPA had envisaged that the proposed Political Office should carry out core functions geared towards supporting the electoral process including:
electoral guidance;
political monitoring, facilitation and reconciliation;
human rights; and, possibly,
coordination of police training and military liaison personnel.

DPA had indicated that a provision would be made for senior officials at Headquarters to travel to Timor-Leste and provide reinforced political support as needed. Furthermore, DPA had indicated that the Head of Political Office would closely coordinate with the RC in the implementation of the electoral assistance project to be funded by UNDP. DPA argued that, under this option, civilian advisers in the justice and finance sectors, police training and military liaison personnel would be provided either through the Country Team or bilateral partners. It was DPA's selling point that the Office would meet the Government of Timor-Leste's requirement for support to the electoral process. This would keep the presence very small, which was desired by the United States and other key members of the Security Council. They felt strongly that the United Nations should complete its peacekeeping and peacebuilding mission.

When Kofi Annan asked for my view, I told him and other participants of the meeting that I was serving not only as SRSR, but also RC of UN agencies, funds and programmes in Timor-Leste. This made it possible for me to "enhance coordination and integration of activities between UNOTIL and UN agencies, funds and programmes in order to facilitate the transition to a sustainable development assistance framework."[30] I referred to my participation in a regional workshop on common country programming held in Nadi, Fiji. In March 2006, I had launched the process to formulate a common UN country programme for Timor-Leste for submission to the executive bodies of respective UN agencies, funds and programmes in 2007. It enabled me to ensure that UN agencies, funds and programmes actively participate in the "Timor-Leste and development partners" meeting to be jointly organized by the Government of Timor-Leste and the World Bank in Dili, in April 2006. It was my conviction that the political, security and development components of the UN system should work together in an integrated manner.

In conclusion, it was clear that the meeting reflected the eagerness of DPA to take over the UN mission in Timor-Leste. Based on a meeting with Ramos-Horta, Under-Secretary-General (USG) Ibrahim Gambari of DPA indicated that the Government of Timor-Leste was against the idea of handing over the UN mission to UNDP, as the main reason for the UN's continued presence was to support the Timorese in holding free and fair elections in 2007. In fact, Foreign Minister Ramos-Horta had written a letter to the Secretary-General on 2 March 2006. He stated:

the main purpose of our request is to ensure that Timor-Leste will continue to benefit from UN assistance in support of our political consolidation process leading to the 2007 elections ...

and

Fundamentally, therefore, Timor-Leste is looking to the UN for sound policy guidance in electoral matters as well as support and facilitation, as appropriate, in key areas relevant to our political consolidation, including in the areas of reconciliation and human rights.[31]

Preparing a new UN integrated mission in Timor-Leste: Kofi Annan's proposal

By its Resolution 1690 (2006) of 20 June 2006, the Security Council extended the mandate of UNOTIL until 20 August 2006. The Council requested the Secretary-General to submit a report by 7 August outlining the specific roles and responsibilities of the new UN mission in Timor-Leste. In order to do so, the Secretary-General engaged Jan Martin, former SRSG and head of the United Nations Assistance Mission in East Timor (UNAMET) as his special envoy, to assess the prevailing situation and the need for a strengthened UN presence.[32] Jan Martin and his team visited Timor-Leste from 26 June to 9 July 2006 and submitted their findings and recommendations. The Secretary-General's proposal was drawn up taking into account the needs assessment mission recommendations, and the request made by President Gusmão, President of the National Parliament Francisco Lú-Olo Guterres and Prime Minister Alkatiri in their 11 June letter addressed to the Secretary-General.[33]

Some of my staff complained to me that the Jan Martin mission was not absolutely necessary. They felt that as UNOTIL staff, they could have written a report with more detailed findings and recommendations. While I understood their sense of frustration, I fully recognized the necessity of entrusting a team of Headquarters staff and other knowledgeable experts to assess the situation. They could develop a framework for a new integrated mission without being preoccupied by daily security and political developments.[34] Mr Ian Martin was an experienced and knowledgeable former SRSG, who had prepared for and administered the critically important Popular Consultation in 1999. Nobody doubted his credentials for the task. He was highly respected within the United Nations and the Government of Timor-Leste. I appreciated his speaking to me at the end of each day during his stay in Timor-Leste on the outcome of his and his team's work during the day.

On 8 August, the Secretary-General issued a report on the future of the UN presence in Timor-Leste.[35] The report highlighted the need for a sustained, long-term commitment. It further proposed the creation of a compact between the Timorese Government and international donors, to improve coordination and setting priorities in peacebuilding. The new UN mission would operate within this framework of agreed priorities and roles, particularly in the following areas:

- Political good offices and reconciliation.
- Electoral support.
- Security sector support, including the provision of international advisers and assistance to the military and the police, as well as initial executive policing and support from a small UN military component composed of troops and military liaison officers.
- Institutional capacity-building, governance and development.
- Humanitarian support.
- Public information.
- Human rights and accountability for both the recent wave of violence and the violations that occurred in 1999, in particular through assisting in the implementation of the Secretary-General's recommendations on justice and reconciliation in Timor-Leste (especially the provision of serious crimes investigators).

Much of the anticipation surrounding the report focused on the size of the police component and the nature of the future international military presence. The Timorese Government, however, indicated its preference for forces under UN command and control. The Secretary-General recommended 1,608 police personnel backed up by 350 troops under UN command, with the progressive withdrawal or "blue-helmeting" of the current force. On justice matters, the report adopted many of the recommendations on justice and reconciliation made by the Jan Martin team.

The Secretary-General, however, did not recommend the reinstitution of the prosecutorial wing of the Serious Crimes Unit, but only the Unit's investigative capabilities. In addition, he recommended a programme of international assistance for community restoration and justice. The programme was to include the establishment of an investigative team and strengthening of the Timorese prosecutorial capacity. The programme would be funded through voluntary contributions. It was not clear whether, even with capacity-building, Timorese institutions would be willing and able to try serious crimes cases.

Debate over the command and control of new security forces

The Secretary-General recommended that the Australia-led force already stationed in Timor-Leste transfer progressively to a UN "blue helmet" operation under UN command and control. However, Australia wanted to keep its troops on the ground as part of the multilateral security assistance forces. The United States and the United Kingdom supported Australia's position, while Brazil and Portugal wanted the United Nations to maintain command and control of the international forces. Several other members, notably China, France and Russia, were also apprehensive about the possibility of rejecting UN command and control of the military force.

There were also divergent views in the Core Group on this issue. The firm support by the United States and the United Kingdom for the Australian position was interpreted in the Core Group and among Timor's regional neighbours as clear threats of vetoes. Japan, France and New Zealand reportedly tried to find a compromise approach but failed. Neither side, Australia, the United States and the United Kingdom on the one hand, and Portugal and Brazil on the other, seemed willing to seek middle ground.

The majority of the multinational forces deployed in Timor-Leste at the request of Timor-Leste since late May was Australian, and Australia insisted on keeping its soldiers under its own command. Timor-Leste, which had formally conveyed to the Council several times its wish that the military component be under UN command and control, was faced with the bleak alternative of accepting the Australian proposal which was supported by the United States and the United Kingdom. During the week of 14 August, there were apparently heated private discussions within the Security Council about Australia's desire to keep the military outside of the UN mission structure. Japan, as chair of the UN Core Group on Timor, drafted a Security Council Resolution reflecting the Australian position, which differed from the views of the Secretary-General and Timor-Leste.

The draft resolution generated more heated discussions, and Japan asked its ambassador in Dili to talk with Prime Minister Ramos-Horta. The ambassador then reported back that Ramos-Horta had changed his position. A letter from Ramos-Horta dated 18 August, but not officially circulated, revealed the difficult position he was placed in. It restated the content of the earlier letter dated 4 August, but added that the Japanese position had some merit. Some Security Council members took this to mean that Timor-Leste was backing down. Due to the confusion over Timor-Leste's position and continued disagreement among the major partner countries, the Security Council extended UNOTIL for five more days until 25 August, allowing another week to find a compromise.

On 25 August, the UN Security Council adopted Resolution 1704 creating a new United Nations Integrated Mission in Timor-Leste (UNMIT). The Resolution contained a compromise, which allowed Australia to continue leading the multinational Joint Task Force outside of UN command. However, it directed the Secretary-General to review this and report back to the Security Council within two months. The Council also asked the Secretary-General to present his views on any adjustment that might be made in the mission structure no later than 25 October 2006.

The Timorese leaders continued to hope that the United Nations would maintain part of the command and control of the international security force. On 26 October, the Parliament of Timor-Leste held a special session and approved a resolution concerning "The Security System in Timor-Leste" which called for all foreign troops in the country to be under a unified UN command. Meanwhile, the RDTL government became receptive of Australia's strong desire after a meeting between Prime Minister Ramos-Horta and Australian Prime Minister Howard on 12 October 2006. The Australian Prime Minister seemed to have informed Ramos-Horta that Australian troops would remain in Timor-Leste until the end of 2006 and beyond, as part of the existing multinational security force under Australian command.

Ramos-Horta conveyed the change in the Timorese position in a letter he sent to Secretary-General Kofi Annan on 19 October, which explained the rationale for keeping the multinational security forces under the existing arrangement. The multinational forces, he said, had quickly quelled the violence and stabilized the situation. The joint task forces furthermore provided a secure environment in which the Timorese leaders and UNMIT could undertake their respective governance and support and offices roles. The presence of the multilateral force enabled the Timorese leadership to focus on current priorities of nation- and institution-building activities. Ramos-Horta then concluded that the existing arrangement of the UN police in maintaining law and order, and the multinational military forces providing security, was working well and best suited the situation in Timor-Leste.[36]

On 27 October, the Security Council held a closed-door consultation. After reviewing the letter from the Prime Minister of Timor-Leste, the Security Council decided to continue the arrangement that had already been made to maintain the multilateral nature of the international forces, without the UN having a role in its command and control.

Notes

1. Security Council document S/PV.4913 on its 4913th meeting held on 20 February 2004.
2. Security Council record document S/PV.4965 on its 4965th meeting held on 10 May 2004.
3. Security Council Resolution 1543 (2004) adopted on 14 May 2004.
4. Hedi Annabi was an old friend of mine who helped launch a programme of engagement of UN volunteers as electoral supervisors in Cambodia in 1993. Then, as United Nations Volunteer (UNV) Deputy Executive Co-ordinator, I visited his office in New York asking for inclusion of funds for recruitment of 700 UNV electoral supervisors and technical support staff in the United Nations Transitional Authority for Cambodia (UNTAC) headed by Yasushi Akashi as the SRSG.
5. Security Council document S/PV.5024 on its 5024th meeting held on 24 August 2004.
6. Security Council Resolution 1573 (2004) adopted on 16 September 2004.
7. As stated in the Secretary-General's report, there was the reported incursion of an armed ex-militia group in January and clashes between the military and police, although the overall situation in Timor-Leste remained calm and stable. See *Report of the Secretary-General on the UN Mission of Support in East Timor*, S/2005, 18 February 2005, paragraph 2.
8. Mr Takahisa Kawakami, then Minister Counsellor of the Permanent Mission of Japan, was actively involved in the deliberation of the Security Council in 2004–2006. In September 2008, he was appointed Deputy Special Representative of the Secretary-General (DSRSG) for Security Sector Support and Rule of Law. On his way to Timor-Leste in October 2008, he told me that the Security Council should have assessed the local situation more carefully before it decided to withdraw UN peacekeeping security personnel.
9. This view that Timor-Leste was already on solid ground and ready to move into the development phase was repeated by the complimentary remarks made by US Secretary of State Condoleezza Rice and World Bank President Wolfowitz, when they met Prime Minister Alkatiri in Washington, DC, on Monday 26 September 2005. See the media release by the Government of Timor-Leste, 27 September 2005.
10. Due to the hardship and political nature of a peacekeeping mission, the Head of Mission tends to remain in office only several months to one year, or at most two years.
11. Security Council Resolution 1599 UN document S/RES/1599 (2005).
12. Security Council Resolution 1599 (2005) passed on 28 April 2005.
13. A Security Council assessment mission visited Mogadishu, Somalia, in 1994 while I was stationed in the country as Director of Policy and Planning of UN peacekeeping mission, United Nations Operation in Somalia II (UNOSOM II). For the contents of statements made by respective representatives to the Security Council, please refer to Security Council document S/PV.5076 on its 5076th meeting held on 15 November 2004.
14. Security Council Resolution 1543 of 14 May 2004.
15. Official record (S/PV.5076) of 5076th meeting of the Security Council held on 15 November 2004.
16. Terms of Reference (TOR) of the Transitional Working Group (TWG).
17. The Core Group in New York consisted of not only some of the Security Council Members, but also such countries as Australia, Brazil, Indonesia, Japan and Portugal, which were interested in Timor-Leste and met often to discuss issues of concern to them and the UN Secretariat.
18. For a detailed coverage of the TWG meetings, please refer to the reports of the Eight Transition Working Groups (UNMISET, January 2005).
19. See Security Council Resolution 1573 taken at its 5079th meeting in February 2004.
20. See Security Council Resolution 1599 taken at its 5171st meeting on 28 April 2005.

21. Report of the Secretary-General's High-level Panel on Threats, Challenges and Change, *A more secure world: Our shared responsibility* (United Nations, 2004), paragraph 226.
22. For detailed analysis of these issues, see UNDP Human Development Reports on *Human Rights and Human Development* (2000) and *Deepening Democracy in a Fragmented World* (2002).
23. Statement by Ambassador Joao Salgueiro of Portugal to the Security Council on 13 June 2006. See http://www.un.int/portugal/TIMORDOCSPORT.htm accessed on 31 January 2013.
24. Hideki Asahi, *Thinking about Peacebuilding on the Ground* (unpublished manuscript, 2006). Paper based on his diplomatic observation in Timor-Leste.
25. The officials I met included Mr Shotaro Yachi, Vice-Minister for Foreign Affairs; Mr Tsuneo Nishida, Deputy Minister for Foreign Affairs; Mr Kaoru Ishikawa, Director-General of the Economic Affairs Bureau; Mr Shigekazu Sato, Director-General of the Economic Cooperation Bureau; Mr Toshihisa Takata, Deputy Director-General of the Asian and Oceanic Affairs Bureau; Mr Shigeki Takizaki, Director of the Second Southeast Asia Division, Asian and Oceanian Affairs Bureau; Mr Masaharu Kouno, Deputy Vice-Minister for Foreign Policy, Foreign Policy Bureau; and Mr Teruyuki Terada, President of the Foreign Press Centre.
26. These comments are based on notes that my assistants and I took.
27. The convenor of the meeting, Counsellor Takahisa Kawakami of Japan, told me afterwards it was the first time that the US representative mentioned the term "a follow-on mission" and hinted at the possibility of including a police component in that mission.
28. I was pleased to hear this perception of the need for the UN to play a key role in security sector reform as it reflected the endorsement of the idea I put forward in March 2006.
29. Earlier in his career, Victor Angelo held several peacekeeping posts: Deputy Regional Director for Africa at UNDP in New York, Resident Co-ordinator/Resident Representative in Tanzania and the Gambia and Deputy Resident Representative in the Central African Republic.
30. Report of the Secretary-General on the United Nations Office in Timor-Leste, S/2006/251, 20 April 2006, paragraph 38.
31. Letter dated 2 March 2006 from Foreign Minister Ramos-Horta to Secretary-General Kofi Annan.
32. Jan Martin's recommendations were reflected in the report of the Secretary-General on the new United Nations Integrated Mission in Timor-Leste (UNMIT). This report is distributed as UN Security Council document, S/2006/628 of 8 August 2006.
33. See S/2006/383, which contains the letter dated 11 June 2006 addressed to the Secretary-General from the President of RDTL, the President of the National Parliament and the Prime Minister of Timor-Leste.
34. This process of assessing local conditions was to become a standard exercise envisaged in the Integrated Strategic Framework before the UN Security Council considered the possibility of establishing a new peacekeeping mission. See the report of the Secretary-General on peacebuilding in the immediate aftermath of conflict A/63/881-S/2009/304 11 June 2009.
35. Report of the Secretary-General on Timor-Leste S/2006/628 dated 8 August 2006 pursuant to Security Council Resolution 1690 (2006).
36. A letter dated 19 October 2006 from *chargé d'affaires ad interim* Sofia Borges of the Permanent Mission of Timor-Leste to the United Nations addressed to the Secretary-General transmitted this letter.

VII

UN Mission Management

Over the last 20 years, UN peacekeeping operations expanded in their scope, becoming an integrated complex of multidimensional activities, with an increasing emphasis on building sustainable and stability. This transformation of UN peace operations has increasingly required mission leaders to unite efforts on three levels:

maintaining unity of command, control and coordination of activities, not only encompassing all components of the UN mission, but also in relation to all UN agencies operating in the country;

working closely with partners and other stakeholders outside of the UN system; and

most importantly, enhancing the national ownership and accountability of peacebuilding efforts.

To achieve these new objectives, the mission structures and leadership roles have changed over the years. In Timor-Leste, the United Nations adjusted the mandates of five missions and their modalities of operations, as well as adjusting the roles and responsibilities of mission leaders.

The United Nations carried out a series of peace operations starting with Australian-led military intervention including multinational forces in September 1999. This multilateral military intervention lasted for only six months, until the arrival of UN peacekeeping forces and the establishment of a UN mission. The latter was tasked as administrator of the territory and to lay the foundation for democratic governance.[1]

The UN Transitional Administration for East Timor (UNTAET) succeeded in building a basic framework for four state institutions of governance, while maintaining security and stability until the Democratic

Primordial leadership: Peacebuilding and national ownership in Timor-Leste, Hasegawa,
United Nations University Press, 2013, ISBN 978-92-808-1224-4

Republic of Timor-Leste was established in May 2002. The Security Council then created a new peacekeeping mission, the UN Mission of Support to East Timor (UNMISET), and entrusted it with peacekeeping and peacebuilding mandates for an additional period of three years until May 2005. Key members of the Security Council, most notably the United States, became convinced by early 2005 that transition from the peace-building phase to a sustainable development assistance framework should take place.

It was frequently mentioned in Security Council sessions that these transition phases could and should take place in a sequential manner. In reality, however, the peacekeeping and peacebuilding phases were not distinct and separate entities that moved in a linear line manner. In fact, there were no clear demarcations of the end of one phase and the begin-ning of another. There were also significant differences between peace and nation-building activities.[2] It was necessary for the UN system to simultaneously carry out peacekeeping and peacebuilding operations. Also, it was neither desirable nor feasible to undertake only peacebuilding activities centred on state institution-building, instead of nation-building activities. Successful peacebuilding required the fostering of civil society and democratic culture.

In October 1999, as the first step in a series of transitions, the Security Council replaced the United Nations Assistance Mission in East Timor (UNAMET) that had carried out the Popular Consultation leading to the independence of Timor-Leste, with a new UN transitional administration, UNTAET. The latter agency was given a mandate to undertake all neces-sary military actions under Chapter VII. Furthermore, UNTAET was to provide all governmental services, including civil administration and maintenance of law and order. Under the leadership of Sérgio Vieira de Mello as the Transitional Administrator, the mission also laid the founda-tion for democratic governance through establishment of state organs such as the presidency, the government, the parliament and the judiciary.[3] There has been a great deal of debate concerning the speed with which the power of governance was transferred to national authorities. How-ever, as Simon Chesterman recognized, the role of the UN transitional administration was "precisely to undertake military, economic, and polit-ical tasks that are beyond existing local capacities".[4]

This major transition took place in May 2002, when UNTAET com-pleted its mandate and was replaced by the multidimensional UNMISET, combining the tasks of peacekeeping and peacebuilding activities. In May 2005, the Council then decided to constitute a UN political office known as the United Nations Office in Timor-Leste (UNOTIL) at the end of UNMISET's period. UNOTIL would undertake peacebuilding, and in-creasingly engage in state institution-building functions. More specifically, it was asked to carry out transfer of knowledge and skills. This was in order to build the capacities of public institutions of Timor-Leste to function properly, based on international principles of rule of law, justice, human rights, democratic governance, transparency, accountability and professionalism. UNOTIL was then given only one year to transform the entire external assistance activities into a development assistance framework. This framework consisted mostly of capacity-development activities supported by the UN development group, the World Bank, bilateral donor agencies and a small political office.

The successful settlement of the church demonstrations in April 2005 reinforced the notion held by both Timorese leaders and international observers, that the time had come to end the presence of UN peacekeeping forces, or any remnants thereof. The Security Council did not accept the proposal by the Department of Peacekeeping Operations (DPKO) to retain a small unit of armed personnel, and only authorized provision of 40 police advisors to train national police personnel. Also authorized were 35 additional advisers, including 15 military advisers to support the development of the Border Patrol Unit (BPU). The Security Council stressed that UNOTIL should concentrate on peacebuilding support during its year of operation, after which UN activities should be handed over to the UN development group headed by the Resident Co-ordinator. The Security Council envisioned such a sequential move to a sustainable development assistance framework in its Resolution 1599 in April 2005.[5]

This transformation of the UN mission's nature and mandate turned out to be logically sound but premature, and did not take into account the reality on the ground. Since the departure of Indonesian troops in 1999, the Timorese people and their leaders became free, but their mindset was slow to change. They remained captive within their old mentality of expressing their desires and grievances through violence. This became a critical factor when an internal discord within FALINTIL (Forças Armadas de Libertação Nacional de Timor-Leste) – Forças Armadas de Defesa de Timor-Leste (FDTL) (F-FDTL) surfaced in January 2006. This resulted in armed clashes among military, police and other elements in April and May 2006. Armed clashes between F-FDTL and the Polícia Nacional de Timor-Leste (PNTL, National Police of Timor-Leste) resulted in the loss of 37 lives in May 2006. This incident could have been prevented, had a UN military unit been present, or a police unit formed of just a few hundred armed personnel.

Changing configuration of the mission architecture

Shortly after the "popular consultation", UNTAET was established on 25 October by Security Council Resolution 1272 (1999), with a view to administering the territory temporarily and to laying the foundation for democratic governance. UNTAET was tasked with providing security, and maintaining law and order throughout the territory of East Timor. Special Representative of the Secretary-General (SRSG) de Mello held and exercised executive, legislative and judicial authority in administering the territory. UNTAET was also responsible for the coordination and delivery of humanitarian, rehabilitation and development assistance. UNTAET gradually transferred executive, legislative and judiciary authority to the Timorese institutions before its mandate expired in May 2002.

As noted in Fig. 7.1, the UN Peacekeeping Force (PKF) was part of UNTAET under the authority of SRSG. It was equipped with an authorized strength of 9,150 military personnel, to take over the security of the territory when the International Force for East Timor (INTERFET) departed in February 2000.

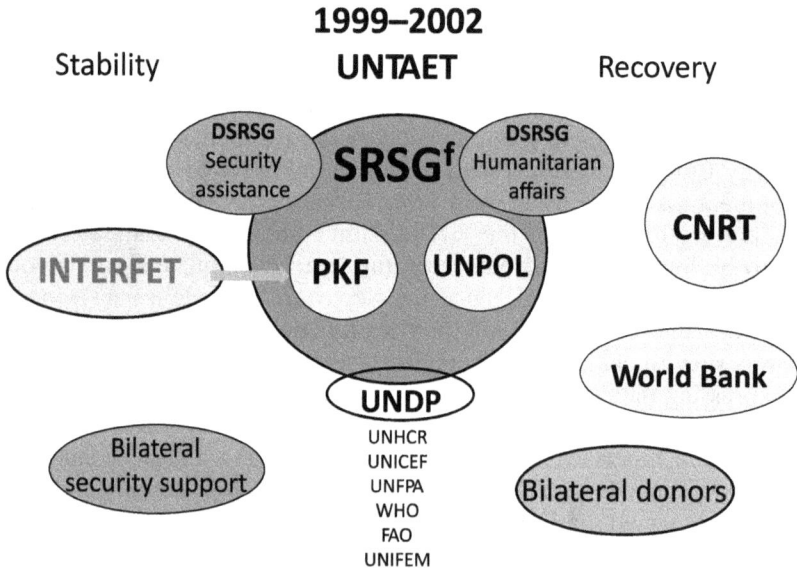

Figure 7.1 Architecture of UN Mission 1999–2002
Notes: CNRT, Conselho Nacional de Reconstrução de Timor (National Congress for Timorese Reconstruction); DSRSG, Deputy Special Representative of the Secretary-General; FAO, Food and Agriculture Organization; INTERFET, International Force for East Timor; PKF, Peacekeeping Force; SRSG, Special Representative of the Secretary-General; UNDP, United Nations Development Programme; UNFPA, United Nations Fund for Population Activities; UNHCR, United Nations High Commissioner for Refugees; UNICEF, United Nations Children's Fund; UNIFEM, United Nations Development Fund for Women; UNPOL, United Nations Police; UNTAET, United Nations Transitional Administration in East Timor; WHO, World Health Organization.

It was noteworthy that as many as 31 countries from all four continents contributed troops. The United Nations Police (UNPOL) was also deployed, with 1,640 civilian police personnel contributed by 39 countries. Both the force commander and the UN Police Commissioner reported to the SRSG.[6] The SRSG was assisted by two Deputy SRSGs: Christian Cady (France)[7] who was the second in the hierarchy and dealt with all issues pertaining to transitional administration, and Hiroshi Takahashi (Japan) who was made responsible for coordination of humanitarian affairs.

The World Bank was active. Sarah Cliff, the chief of the bank office in Dili, played a lead role in arranging the development partners' meeting for the coordination of donor assistance. Her active engagement in the recovery phase represented a major change from the previous World Bank approach of refraining from active engagement until a post-conflict country had been sufficiently stabilized. Typically, the World Bank helped rehabilitate physical infrastructure facilities. However, in Timor-Leste, the physical rehabilitation work was left for the Asian Development Bank and the European Union to undertake. The World Bank was more interested in coordinating donor assistance and building the national capacity for governance. The United Nations Development Programme (UNDP) was also concerned with institutional capacity-building. UNDP chief, Finn Reske-Nielsen, acted as Development Co-ordinator and worked in his office on the ground floor of the UN House. Deputy (D) SRSG Takahashi was on the second floor, carrying out the coordination of humanitarian activities.

By the time I arrived in Dili in July 2002, UNMISET had replaced UNTAET, and a new SRSG, Kamalesh Sharma, had taken over mission leadership. UNMISET had the mandate for both peacekeeping and peacebuilding tasks. I was, however, given the functions that had been carried out by two Deputies previously. Additionally, I was made responsible for humanitarian and development assistance works as the Humanitarian and Resident Co-ordinator of the UN system's operational activities for development. Having performed these functions before in Rwanda, it was possible for me to undertake the tasks immediately without much guidance from the SRSG; I was even able to take some initiatives in building the institutional capacity of national government and ministries.

In 2003, the government became functional and operationally active in starting schools and health clinics. The Prime Minister began to consolidate his control through the district administrators he had appointed. UN peacekeeping forces and UN police officers were first reduced in size and then withdrawn completely by the middle of 2004. The Security Council entrusted me with providing support for the public administration and justice system, with 58 civilian advisers, and to conduct training programmes for the development of PNTL. It also tasked me with providing support for the security and stability of Timor-Leste with only 157 civilian unarmed police advisers and 42 military liaison officers.[8] As SRSG, I was also entrusted with the responsibility to manage the mission as well as UN agencies, funds and programmes (Fig. 7.2).

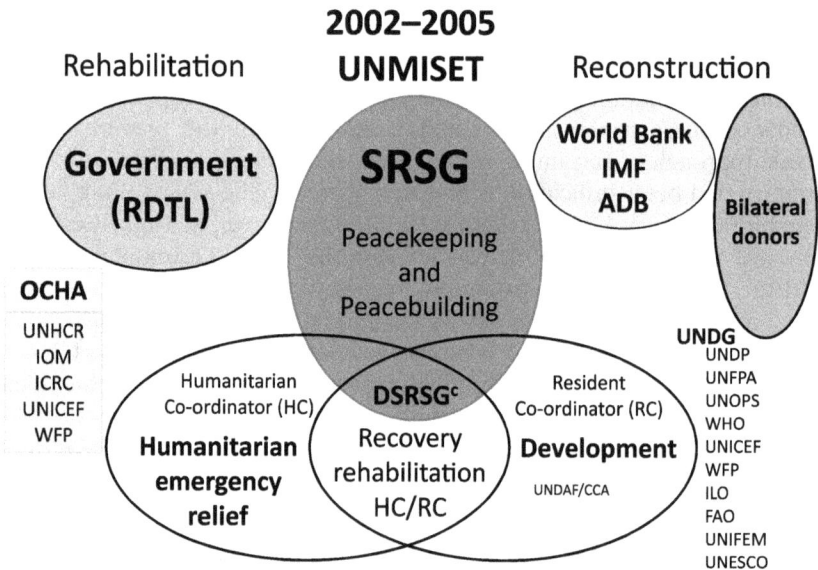

Figure 7.2 Architecture of UN Mission 2002–2005
Notes: ADB, Asian Development Bank; CCA, Common Country Assessment; SRSG, Deputy Special Representative of the Secretary-General; FAO, Food and Agriculture Organization; HC, Humanitarian Co-ordinator; ICRC, International Committee of the Red Cross; ILO, International Labour Organization; IMF, International Monetary Fund; IOM, International Organization for Migration; OCHA, Office for the Coordination of Humanitarian Affairs; RC, Resident Co-ordinator of the United Nations System's Operational Activities for Development; RDTL, República Democrática de Timor Leste (Democratic Republic of Timor-Leste); SRSG, Special Representative of the Secretary-General of the United Nations; UNDAF, United Nations Development Assistance Framework; UNDG, United Nations Development Group; UNDP, United Nations Development Programme; UNESCO, United Nations Educational, Scientific and Cultural Organization; UNFPA, United Nations Fund for Population Activities; UNHCR, United Nations High Commissioner for Refugees; UNICEF, United Nations Children's Fund; UNIFEM, United Nations Development Fund for Women; UNMISET, United Nations Mission of Support in East Timor; UNOPS, United Nations Office for Project Service; WFP, World Food Programme; WHO, World Health Organization.

A year later, in April 2005, the Security Council decided to establish a special political mission by the name of UNOTIL. As mentioned earlier, the Security Council provided UNOTIL with 45 civilian advisers to assist in the further development of critical state institutions engaged in the rule of law, justice, human rights and other public administration. UNOTIL also provided 40 police advisers to support further development of PNTL. Additionally, 35 advisers, including 15 military advisers for the development of the BPU, were provided by the agency.

The Security Council also entrusted UNOTIL with ten human rights officers to provide training in observance of democratic governance and human rights. UNOTIL was, in essence, constituted as a political advisory and capacity-development agency. As Fig. 7.3 shows, the structure and staff of UNOTIL became distinctively small in contrast to the state institutions of Timor-Leste.

On 25 August 2006, the Security Council established a follow-on mission and named it the United Nations Integrated Mission in Timor-Leste (UNMIT). The decision had four significant implications:

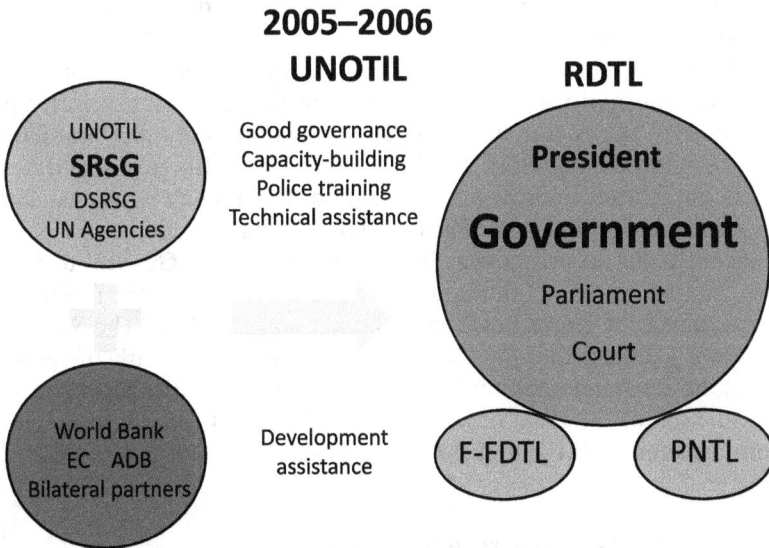

Figure 7.3 Architecture of UN Mission 2005–2006
Notes: ADB, Asian Development Bank; DSRSG, Deputy Special Representative of the Secretary-General of the United Nations; EC, European Commission; F-FDTL, FALINTIL – Forças Armadas de Defesa de Timor-Leste; PNTL, Polícia Nacional de Timor-Leste (National Police of Timor-Leste); RDTL, República Democrática de Timor Leste (Democratic Republic of Timor-Leste); SRSG, Special Representative of the Secretary-General of the United Nations; UNOTIL, United Nations Office in Timor-Leste.

Peacekeeping operations were to be reactivated with authority entrusted under Chapter VII of the UN Charter. For this purpose, UNMIT would have 1,608 police personnel and 34 military liaison and staff officers, who would support the government and relevant institutions in consolidating stability and preparing for the 2007 presidential and parliamentary election process. United Nations police officers were to realize the restoration and maintenance of public security in Timor-Leste by exercising executive policing authority and retraining PNTL personnel. This meant that UNPOL would again exercise interim law enforcement and public security until PNTL was reconstituted.

The Security Council authorized UNMIT to assist the government in conducting a comprehensive security sector review. International advisers were to be brought in to assess the role and needs of the security sector, including the F-FDTL, the Ministry of Defence, the PNTL and the Ministry of the Interior. The security sector review would be carried out in cooperation with other partners; it was expected to produce a series of comprehensive recommendations on how to strengthen institutional capacity-building of the security agencies. It was the first time that the UN mission took a lead in conducting a security sector reform in Timor-Leste.

UNMIT was empowered to promote a "compact" between Timor-Leste and the international community to coordinate the top priority programmes of the government, the United Nations and other multilateral and bilateral contributors. The Security Council also gave mandates to carry out further improvements in rule of law, human rights, assistance to vulnerable groups and almost all government functions.

Significantly the Security Council asked the Secretary-General to review the status of the International Security Forces (ISF) with the Government of Timor-Leste and all other stakeholders.[9] The Secretary-General assessed the implications, and in agreement with the government, he recommended that the ISF be kept out of the SRSG and the jurisdiction of the head of the UNMIT. Figure 7.4 reflects the relationship between UNMIT and ISF.

Mission leaders and strategic goals

The role of mission leaders is to focus on strategic goals mandated by the Security Council, and to achieve them by undertaking necessary operations in a timely and effective manner. For this to happen, mission leadership is expected to mobilize all mission staff as well as other stakeholders, to strive for common goals in an integrated manner. Developing a vision requires formulating and implementing a strategy to achieve an outcome for which the mission was created. To implement the strategy and realize

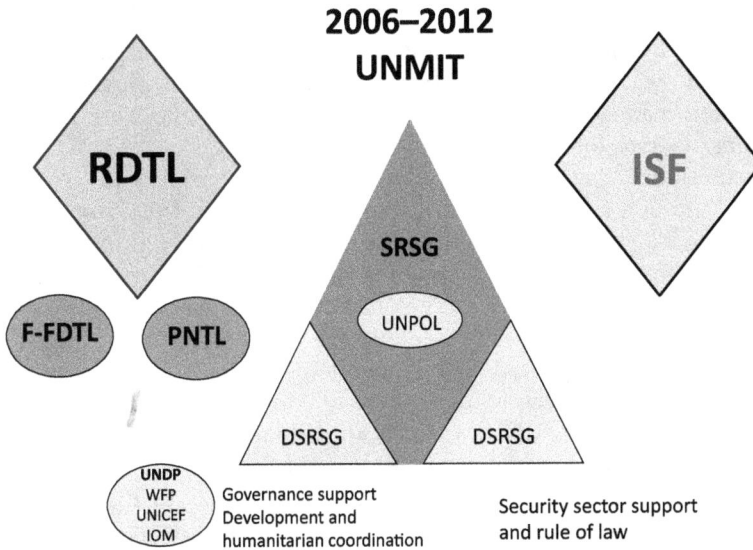

Figure 7.4 Architecture of UN Mission 2006–2012
Notes: DSRSG, Deputy Special Representative of the Secretary-General; F-FDTL, FALINTIL – Forças Armadas de Defesa de Timor-Leste; IOM, International Organization for Migration; ISF, International Security Forces; PNTL, Polícia Nacional de Timor-Leste (National Police of Timor-Leste); RDTL, República Democrática de Timor Leste (Democratic Republic of Timor-Leste); SRSG, Special Representative of the Secretary-General of the United Nations; UNDP, United Nations Development Programme; UNICEF, United Nations Children's Fund; UNMIT, United Nations Integrated Mission in Timor-Leste; UNPOL, United Nations Police; WFP, World Food Programme.

the vision, mission leaders need to refine the organizational structure and procedures of the UN mission. They must also understand the social structure, values and culture of a country or a community the mission is meant to assist. Achieving a strategic goal and realizing a vision in such a situation requires the participation of the United Nations, international players and national leadership. In order for this to happen, it is imperative for mission leaders to effectively communicate the vision of the mission to all stakeholders. These players include all UN mission and agency staff, international partners and national players.

To perform their roles, UN peace mission leaders are required to exercise strategic, managerial and situational leadership. I discovered that the most critical role of UN mission leaders was to develop a strategic vision and direction by interpreting the mandate of the Security Council, then turning it into operational tasks and implementing these efficiently and effectively. The mission leaders need to bring together a multitude of stakeholders. These players include not only the military, police and civilian components of the mission, but all UN funds, programmes and specialized agencies in the country of assignment. This is a daunting task as agencies have their own mandates, headquarters and governing bodies. The leaders must then manage the expectations of both the beneficiaries and stake-holders to strive for a common strategic goal.

Furthermore, the leaders must understand the social structure, values and culture of a country or a host community the mission is sent to assist. Achieving a strategic goal and realizing a vision also requires the partici-pation of the United Nations and other international actors. Additionally, buy-in is required by a wide-range of national actors such as the national authorities, political leaders (including the opposition), civil society, reli-gious leaders and the academia. In order to achieve this, it is imperative for the mission leaders to develop a common vision and manage all stakeholders' collaborative work. As the situation changes, so does the approach, to meet newly emerging requirements. In Timor-Leste's case, the United Nations organized five missions from 1999 to 2012. Each mis-sion received multifaceted mandates to carry out various tasks dependent on the prevailing local conditions, to achieve sustainable peace and sta-bility. Seven mission leaders exercised their leadership in situations that required different competencies and attributes.

The first SRSG was Ian Martin from the United Kingdom, who headed UNAMET from May to November 1999. Martin administered the Popu-lar Consultation. He is a human rights activist and previously was the Secretary-General of Amnesty International from 1986 to 1992. Martin strongly believed in and focused his attention on empowering the Timor-ese people to exercise their right to self-determination. During my time as UN Resident and Humanitarian Co-ordinator in Rwanda in 1995–1996, Martin was the Chief of the Human Rights Field Operation based in Kigali, Rwanda. The host countries appreciated Martin's diplomatic skills and professional expertise. He was later appointed SRSG and Head of the United Nations Mission to Nepal (UNMIN). Due to his remarkable negotiating skills and eloquent communication abilities, Martin has since become one of the few, very senior UN officials to act as Special Envoy of Secretaries-General Kofi Annan and Ban Ki-moon.

As Ian Martin once said:

> The key responsibility of the SRSG is to set a clear strategy for the mission, to make sure that everyone understands it and is on board with it and that the dif-ferent components of the mission cooperate in carrying out that strategy – rather than fight each other to pursue contradictory goals or even the same goal in con-tradictory or competitive ways. That's really the SRSG's job, but you are up against big cultural conflicts, between the military, police, electoral, civilian public information types.[10]

Sérgio Vieira de Mello from Brazil was not only the SRSG, but also the transitional administrator of Timor-Leste from November 1999 to May 2002. He was a dynamic leader who was respected and admired for his commitment to the principles of the United Nations. Like many of us, he had entered the United Nations at a young age, and worked for the organization in many duty stations for more than 30 years. I recall meeting him in Dili in January 2000, and finding him courteous, and at the same time determined to help the Timorese people in establishing their own governance. I never expected then that I would meet him again three years later in Geneva, myself being DSRSG and him the High Commissioner for Human Rights. It was very tragic that he was killed on 19 August 2003 in Bagdad, along with more than 20 other members of his staff. In my brief encounters with him, I felt, as biographer Samantha Power aptly described, that Sérgio was a world realist as well as an acolyte who believed in the United Nations. He was a fiercely disciplined UN official who had vast knowledge of the intricacies of the UN system, but who also knew how to make others feel relaxed in social occasions.[11] From my encounters with Sérgio, I sensed that his passion for excellence and his love of humanity were at the core of his leadership style.

Kamalesh Sharma from India succeeded Sérgio de Mello in May 2002, when Timor-Leste regained its political independence. He had served in the Indian Foreign Service from 1965 and became one of the most senior diplomats ever to master the art of diplomacy. He was a reserved gentleman who nevertheless was direct and effective in communicating his views to his counterparts. His mission was to make the Timorese leaders become self-reliant and accountable to their people, as well as to the international community, and they respected him for his integrity and impartiality. President Gusmão listened to SRSG Sharma. When there was a need for the Timorese leaders to show their unity in 2003, Sharma convinced the reluctant President to join other Timorese leaders in an independence celebration being held in a rural district. Upon completion of his assignment in Timor-Leste, Ambassador Sharma was appointed Indian High Commissioner in London in 2004 and then the Secretary-General of the Commonwealth of Nations in 2008. His moral integrity made him a strong and respected SRSG.

Atul Khare from India succeeded me as SRSG for Timor-Leste and Head of UNMIT in December 2006. He first served as Chief of Staff, and later as DSRSG with UNMISET from June 2002 until its completion in May 2005. He later returned to the Indian Foreign Service and worked as Director of the Nehru Centre and Minister (Culture) of the High Commission of India in London for a little more than one year until November 2006. He was called back by Secretary-General Kofi Annan to return to Timor-Leste, this time as his Special Representative. Like Kamalesh

Sharma, Khare was an Indian diplomat, and his career began in 1984. He had served in various capacities in the Indian Foreign Service, including as Deputy High Commissioner of India to Mauritius, and Counsellor at the Permanent Mission of India to the United Nations in New York. As the Special Representative, he nurtured self-confidence and pride among the Timorese leadership, who appreciated his care and understanding. Exerting his diplomatic and excellent managerial skills, Atul assisted the leaders' efforts to overcome a multitude of problems, including the re-integration of internally displaced persons (IDPs) into communities, addressing the grievances of "the petitioners". As President Ramos-Horta said in his farewell speech to SRSG Atul Khare, SRSGs "must be able to gain the respect and confidence of the receiving community and its leaders through discretion, humility, honesty, (and) hard-work. You have succeeded."[12]

Ameerah Haq from Bangladesh, who was appointed by Secretary-General Ban Ki-moon as his SRSG for Timor-Leste in December 2009, was an old friend of mine as we had both worked for the UNDP for more than 30 years. She served as UN Resident Co-ordinator and UNDP Resident Representative in Laos (1991–1994) and Malaysia (1994–1997) just as I did in the same capacity in the South Pacific (1985–1987), Rwanda (1995–1996) and Timor-Leste (2002–2006). Ameerah moved up steadily in her career and served as Deputy Assistant Administrator and Deputy Director of the Bureau for Crisis Prevention and Recovery at UNDP Headquarters in New York before she was appointed DSRSG and UN Resident and Humanitarian Co-ordinator for Afghanistan in 2004 and for Sudan three years later in 2007. In my association with Ameerah, I found her to be always clear-headed and disciplined in her conduct. Her fairness, impartiality and determination to strengthen national capacity gained her much respect from the Timorese leaders. It was also her excellent managerial capacity that made her successful in Afghanistan and the Sudan before her appointment as the SRSG for Timor-Leste. As a seasoned and skilled negotiator as well as consensus-builder, she quickly built strong relations with the country's leaders, and shifted their focus towards long-term socio-economic challenges. She also prepared the country for an orderly transition and departure of the UN mission in December 2012, by demonstrating her excellent managerial capability. These accomplishments were acknowledged by her colleagues for: "the thorough way in which your team is preparing for the departure of UNMIT and the necessary transition of the work of the international community".[13] Ameerah's superb managerial capacity and fairness appeared to be significant in leading Secretary-General Ban Ki-moon to appoint her Under-Secretary-General (USG) for the Department of Field Support at UN Headquarters in June 2012.

Finn Reske-Nielsen served in Timor-Leste longer than any other SRSG. Before his recent appointment as Acting SRSG in June 2012, he had served as DSRSG of UNMIT since 2006, ably acting as the head of the UN mission by filling a gap of several months following my departure and the arrival of Atul Khare. Like Ameerah, Finn also served as UN Resident Co-ordinator and UNDP Resident Representatives in Laos from 2002 to 2004. Earlier, from 1999 and 2002, he was UN Resident Co-ordinator and UNDP Resident Representative, respectively, in Timor-Leste. He had worked closely with the then SRSG, the late Sérgio de Mello. With more than 35 years of experience with the United Nations, and close to a decade of experience serving in Timor-Leste, he was well-experienced and trusted by the Timorese leaders. In my view, he was eminently qualified to complete the transition from a UN peacekeeping presence to a sustainable development assistance framework in Timor-Leste.

UN mission leaders in Timor-Leste had a central role in setting specific agendas and strategic goals. These goals were accomplished by building trust with internal and external stakeholders, and engaging senior staff in continuous planning and preparedness exercises, aimed at establishing varying responses to different hypothetical but possible scenarios, which kept them mentally prepared for eventualities. These practices allowed for more effective and adaptable responses. Even if the mission was unable to foresee and avoid all eventualities, such flexible approaches allowed key UN and international actors to turn unforeseen developments, such as the crisis of April–May 2006, into an opportunity to build a foundation for lasting peace. Mutual trust allowed SRSGs to undertake intimate consultations to help build peace and stability with key national leaders, such as the President, the Prime Minister and Speakers of the National Assembly. Additionally, the UN SRSGs were able to consult with the leaders of the opposition political parties and key international stakeholders as well. These stakeholders included permanent members of the Security Council and the Core Group, such as Australia, Indonesia and Portugal.

The leadership quality of SRSGs who served in Timor-Leste showed that the United Nations had carefully selected individuals who possessed critical competencies that were needed in various phases of peace operations. After the end of the Civil War, the increasing engagement of UN missions in peace and nation-building required professional expertise in not only conflict mediation, but also in human rights, rule of law and capacity-building of national institutions. In addition to diplomatic skills, these tasks required SRSGs to possess substantive knowledge about development requirements and managerial expertise. Managerial leaders were now needed to perform superior organization of peacekeeping and peacebuilding missions. There is also an increasing need for SRSGs who can help national leaders and actors to transform their political culture and structure, such that the political leaders can retain the trust and confidence of the people.[14]

Building an integrated and cohesive team

The task of building an integrated mission team in Timor-Leste required that the SRSG, DSRSG and their senior management staff work together as a cohesive group. As previously noted, SRSG Sharma and I ensured that we worked closely together with the force commander, the Police Commissioner, Chief of Staff, directors of administration, the political office and various other constituents and units of the mission. During my tenure as the SRSG from 2004 to 2006, I made concerted efforts to integrate the various UN agencies into a cohesive team. I regularly included the heads of the UN agencies in key senior mission staff meetings in which the force commander and the police commissioner also participated.[15] Senior mission staff and UN agency staff jointly formulated strategic plans for the capacity-building of national institutions and smooth takeover of functions, whether they were in the security sector or government services.

The relationship between the SRSG and the force commander is arguably a central factor in sustaining the effectiveness of the peacekeeping and peacebuilding mission. Yet, several peacekeeping missions have encountered major difficulty at the top, due to the inability of the SRSG and the force commander to work closely together. For instance, I had witnessed the collapse of the UN peacekeeping mission in Somalia in 1994, due to the SRSG and the force commander no longer working together.

In Timor-Leste, the SRSG and the force commander recognized the need for a close working relationship. The difficulty of this type of working relationship emerged in other peacekeeping operations, due to the lack of the force commanders' full acceptance of the SRSG's authority, but I found the three force commanders in Timor-Leste fully accepted this. In fact, they had no difficulty reporting to the SRSG. The fact that all three shared the commonality of coming from Asian countries could be part of the reason for the spirit of cooperation prevailing, rather than the desire to show their independence.[16] Lieutenant-General Winai Phattiyakul succeeded Lieutenant-General Boonsrang Niumpradit as force commander of UNTAET at the end of August 2001. General Winai had served in the Royal Thai Armed Forces for more than 30 years since 1969. He had held several appointments at the Royal Thai Armed Forces Headquarters, most notably in military intelligence as Director of the Directorate of Joint Intelligence, Supreme Command Headquarters of the Royal Thai Armed Forces. Yet, he was a mild-mannered gentleman who was extremely sensitive to the feelings and views of other persons. At the daily senior staff meetings chaired by the SRSG, he spoke gently, but also with authority.

General Eric Tan Huck Gim of Singapore was also a quiet person, but he spoke with precision. It was clear that he cherished the task of analysing any situation meticulously. Having served in the Singapore Armed Forces (SAF) for 30 years, General Tan joined UNMISET in August 2002. He acted as force commander for one year, leading a UN peacekeeping force of 3,000 troops. He then returned to Singapore to become the Commandant of SAF's Tri-Service Officer Training and Education Institute. He also held the position of Director of Administration at the Lee Kuan Yew School of Public Policy, National University of Singapore. In recognition of General Tan's managerial and intellectual capacity, Secretary-General Kofi Annan brought him back to Timor-Leste in November 2006 to serve as DSRSG, responsible for the security sector and rule of law. In announcing General Tan's appointment, Acting SRSG Finn Reske-Nielsen accurately said that UNMIT was fortunate to have someone of General Tan's calibre, and that with his leadership qualities he would do "a splendid job".[17]

The last UN force commander in Timor-Leste was Lieutenant-General Khairuddin Mat Yusof of Malaysia, who succeeded General Tan on 31 August 2003. Like General Winai and Tan, General Khairuddin had served in the Malaysian Armed Forces for over 30 years. However, unlike the others, he had previous UN peacekeeping experience as the Assistant Military Adviser at the Department of Peacekeeping Operations, New York (1991–1993). Like the two other generals, General Khairuddin was a team player. He was also a realistic manager who recognized that troops from several different countries could perform their duties based on mutually acceptable conditions. As General Tan once mentioned to him, he had to learn, to his sorrow, that various contingents acted almost independently and followed the command of the force commander to the extent that suited their interests. I fully shared the three generals' view that the UN peacekeeping force could not become effective unless its contingents were placed under a unified command.

The Police Commissioner, another key member of the UN peace mission, reported to the SRSG, and participated regularly in the daily meeting of the senior mission staff. During my tenure in Timor-Leste, we had two UN Police Commissioners with considerable prior experience with the UN peacekeeping operations. Peter Miller from Canada had been head of a UN police force in Western Sahara in 1997–1998. He had also served in other senior roles, including as deputy UN Police Commissioner of a

UN mission in Haiti in 1996–1997. Sandra Peisley of Canada succeeded Peter Miller in 2003. Before replacing Peter Miller, Sandra Peisley had served with the United Nations in Cyprus in 1994.

In Timor-Leste the Police Commissioner had two roles to play during the period of UNMISET. One was executive policing authority for internal security, which meant that UNPOL held the power to arrest and detain people. UNPOL had another responsibility, which was to train national PNTL officers. When I arrived in Dili, Peter Miller had already served as UN Police Commissioner before and after the restoration of independence in May 2002. Due to his prior experience with UN missions in Africa, he knew the importance of working as a team player in the context of UN peacekeeping operation. He consulted closely with SRSG Sharma when riots erupted in the morning of 4 December 2002. While he served the mission well, Miller came under severe criticism by the Timorese government for the failure of UNPOL to contain the riots.

Sandra Peisley had strong leadership qualities; she spoke and acted forcefully. She worked closely with SRSG Sharma and left Timor-Leste when the first phase of UNMISET came to its end in May 2003. I was still in my role of DSRSG when Miller and Peisley, respectively, served as UN Police Commissioner. They reported directly to and worked primarily with the SRSG. It was only when SRSG Sharma was out of the country that they dealt with me directly. I respected them both for their ability to accept decisions I made even as acting SRSG, even when there was a disagreement on how to deal with any particular issue. For example, Peisley and I disagreed on whether or not UNMISET should accept Prime Minister Alkatiri's proposal to have a convoy escorting Malaysian Prime Minister Mahathir and his delegation through the central Comoro Road, instead of the Beach Road. Peisley thought the latter was more suited for the protection of a visiting dignitary. After a heated discussion, she agreed that we should adopt the proposal made by the Timor-Leste government.

In every UN mission, the SRSG has a team of professional and technical staff providing close assistance. The Chief of Staff plays a key role in managing the work of the Executive Office of the SRSG, and in coordinating several mission offices for political, legal, human rights, humanitarian and administrative work. The Chief of Staff also liaises with the PKF and UNPOL, and coordinates with a large number of technical advisers in the case of UN Missions in Timor-Leste. Upon my arrival in Timor-Leste in Dili in July 2002, Atul Khare was Special Assistant to SRSG Kamalesh Sharma and became Chief of Staff upon departure of Sue Ingram in 2003. When Atul became my Deputy in 2004, we advertised the post, and in my view Sue Ingram appeared well qualified for the job out of a pool of about 20 potential candidates. She had already been the Acting Chief of Staff when I arrived in Timor-Leste. Atul found Sue experienced and knowledgeable of UN undertakings in Timor-Leste, but felt strongly that I should have someone with fresh perspectives and new ideas, who would understand me well and could also translate my ideas into action. The selection committee, headed by Atul, then reviewed all candidates and came up with Michiko Kuroda as being the most qualified. I was hesitant to recruiting her as my Chief of Staff, as she was Japanese, as am I. However, Atul insisted that I should not penalize her for her nationality. It turned out that Michiko was very familiar with UN Headquarters and was efficient in handling personnel and policy coordination matters.

Regarding the position of DSRSG, to my dismay, after a year Atul decided to return to the Indian Foreign Service. I felt that UNOTIL's mandate required vigorous institution-building support in the field of justice and the rule of law. Therefore, I thought it best to recruit Sri Frigaard, a Norwegian, who was Deputy Prosecutor General responsible for Serious Crimes. I called her and asked her to join in the mission as my Deputy. She already held a senior position as Prosecutor General in Norway, and told me that she was not available immediately. She did however indicate her interest at the prospect of returning to Timor-Leste. I conveyed this idea to Lisa Buttenheim, who was the Director of Asia, Europe and Middle East division of DPKO. After several weeks, I was informed that, given the need to fill the position, DPKO had decided to assign General Anis Bajwa who was Director of Change Management in the Office of Under-Secretary-General of DPKO. Anis turned out to be an exemplary Deputy, who possessed rich experience in security matters and political affairs. He was a forthright and conscientious person.

Neither Atul Khare nor Anis Bajwa was an expert on economic and social development. Their appointment as DSRSG meant that I had to continue functioning as UN Resident Co-ordinator for development assistance works, running from one meeting to another. Therefore, when Finn Reske-Nielsen was appointed as UN Resident Co-ordinator shortly in July 2006, it was a real relief for me, as I no longer had to carry out the triple duties of SRSG, Resident Co-ordinator, and Resident Representative. Finn had served in Timor-Leste as a UNDP Resident Representative from 2000 to 2002. He then went to Vientiane to become the UN Resident Coordinator in the Lao People's Democratic Republic. As previously mentioned, I respected him, as he was an experienced and conscientious UN professional who immediately could grasp the reality of the situation in Timor-Leste once he was back. His concurrent appointment as Deputy Special Representative made it possible for us to work as a cohesive team.

The integration of UN missions and all UN agencies into an integrated team had become a principal goal of the United Nations in its endeavour to carry out multidimensional peacekeeping and peacebuilding activities. As mentioned in a policy statement commonly known as the Capstone Doctrine, it requires the engagement of not only main UN peacekeeping and peacebuilding actors, but also humanitarian and development agencies of the UN system to achieve sustainable peace and stability in post-conflict countries. Ultimately, multidimensional peacebuilding requires the active involvement of national authorities and the local population. The integration of UN activities also better assists post-conflict countries to make a smooth transition from conflict to sustainable peace. In conflict-prone and post-conflict countries,

> [a] multi-dimensional United Nations peacekeeping operation is likely to be far more effective when it is deployed as part of a United Nations system-wide response based on a clear and shared understanding of priorities, and on a willingness on the part of all United Nations actors to contribute to the achievement of common objectives.[18]

Notoriously, many UN missions encounter the challenge of reconciling differences in views among senior management. However, UNMISET and UNOTIL maintained overall harmonious and well-integrated working relationships with UN agencies. I remember staff from UN Headquarters commenting on how well we all worked together as a team. This was the result of deliberate efforts made by Kamalesh Sharma, Atul Khare and myself. As SRSG, Khare ensured that senior management respect each other, even if views differed on any particular issue. From my perspective, staff members of the UN missions and UN agencies followed the spirit of their mission as expressed by their leaders. Teamwork, however, requires not only mutual trust, but also a shared understanding of the mission's goal, structure and operational modality, which is conducive for mutual consultation and successful collaboration. As we moved into the peacebuilding phase, we worked closer together. I was carrying out the triple roles of UN Resident Co-ordinator, UNDP Resident Representative and SRSG/ Head of UNMISET and UNOTIL, and this arrangement enabled me to bring both political, security, humanitarian and development staff together.

Security of UN staff

Most UN personnel travelled through Bali, as it was the main gateway to the outside world. It was also a restful place for people to spend their weekends. On 12 October 2002, a car bomb was detonated outside the Sari Club in the Kuta beach area in Bali, destroying the club and the Padi

Bar opposite. The explosion killed 182 persons. Both locations were popular sites for tourists, and UN personnel also frequented these places during their periods of leave. For every three months of work, personnel had the right to take three days off, which they usually combined with their own leave days.

In order to identify persons who were involved in the incident and learn the status of missing persons, we immediately activated our tracking system and made strenuous efforts to identify each and every member of UN staff who was thought to have been in Bali on that day. Eventually we knew where everybody was.

Among UN personnel who were in the area, we discovered that seven UN mission staff members were seriously injured, including two PKF and five UNPOL officers. Additionally, there were nine personnel for whom we could not immediately account. Two were PKF personnel, four UNPOL, two civilian mission staff and one UN agency staff member. It turned out that 115 UNMISET personnel were in Bali on the night of 12 October, consisting of 45 PKF members, 64 UNPOL officers (including 33 Chinese police officers in transit) and six civilian personnel. It was thought that an additional 19 PKF and 21 civilian personnel could have been in transit through Bali around that time. They may have stopped off for a few days without our records showing the transit stop.

Of the 45 PKF personnel in Bali, 43 had been accounted for, including two who had minor injuries and one had been seriously injured. Of the 64 UNPOL personnel known to be in Bali, 60 were accounted for, of whom two had sustained serious injuries, and three had minor injuries. Of the six civilian staff known to be in Bali, five were accounted for; one transiting passenger had not yet been contacted, but was assumed to be in Thailand. Among the UN agencies, the United Nations Volunteers (UNV) had the most efficient system of identifying the location of UNVs attached to UNMISET. Of three UNVs from the UN agencies, two were accounted for immediately and the third was in transit on Saturday or Sunday night.

The status of transiting personnel was less clear as we worked from the Movement of Personnel (MOP) forms, which did not show detailed itineraries, but only the dates of departure from and arrival in Dili and ultimate destinations. Following up on these turned out to be a time-consuming exercise. The data on civilian staff were taken from MOPs, which had been lodged with leave applications, supplemented by the flight manifests of Merpati (the Dili–Bali carrier) for the last week. Where we relied on flight manifest data, we obviously could not determine whether Bali was the destination or transit point only. Nonetheless, we managed to account for almost all of the civilian staff within 24 hours. We telephoned the families of those personnel still unaccounted for, in order to establish whether contact had been made in the wake of the bombing. Also, it was a gesture of concern and reassurance that we were following-up through our own channels. Where we had personal email addresses for the personnel, we also followed-up by this method.

The Bali bombing was the culmination of a series of attacks on various parts of Indonesia. There was a warning that Timor-Leste was not exempt from a potential terrorist attack. Shortly after my arrival in Timor-Leste, Osama Bin Laden issued a warning in one of his recorded messages, broadcast twice on Al-Jazeera television, that Australia and the United Nations should "be punished", for they had taken away Timor-Leste from Indonesia, the largest Muslim country in the world. This warning was taken seriously by diplomatic sources in Timor-Leste. Furthermore, UK and US embassy staff indicated that they had received warnings on potential attacks on their and our premises. In response, we took full precautions at two levels:

To brief all mission and UN staff about the potential attack, and to caution them that they had to behave in such a way as to avoid becoming the target of these potential threats. They were told that in places such as Bali, they should not go to nightclubs and similar places. They were also advised not to travel to Jakarta and other parts of Indonesia that were regarded as terrorist targets. Even within Timor-Leste, the mission and UN agency staff were cautioned not to expose themselves.

Senior mission staff fortified their residences with sandbags, piled up nearly 2 metres high, to prevent vehicles from breaking into the buildings. I was tasked on behalf of UNMISET to coordinate a precautionary erection of walls to be built in front of the premises of the United States and New Zealand Embassies. Additional premises to be provided with sandbag walls were those of the SRSG, DSRG and force commander; the adjacent residences of the World Bank Representative and the President of the National Parliament were also sandbagged for protection. There was an open space in front of their premises, adjacent to a road that led to the beach, so it could have been quite easy for a vehicle to ride into the open space and smash into any of the buildings. We placed sandbags around the buildings, but they did not appear sturdy enough to stop a vehicle from riding over them. For this reason, the US Embassy built concrete blocks in front of its building. The wall construction project took months of planning and execution, the cost being divided evenly among the international residents.

After the Bali bombings, we were greatly concerned that some of these suicide bombers might penetrate into Timor-Leste and bomb any of the cafés in Dili where many Western customers congregated. We maintained a high sense of alertness for about a year; after 9/11 and subsequent incidents, the attention of Al Qaeda and others must have moved to other places. The Bali bombing incident brought to realization the security issues for international personnel in Dili, particularly staff from the embassies. Indonesian authorities were also most determined to stop this kind of violence within Indonesia, and arrested many of the radicals.

After the Bali bombing came the banning of Merpati Airline flights. The officer responsible for civil aviation within UNMISET was uncertain about the safety of Merpati Airlines, and talked very informally to his counterpart at UN Headquarters in New York. Staff at UN Headquarters then took the decision to ban the use of Merpati Airlines, without any in-depth consultation with any others such as the International Civil Aviation Organization (ICAO). This turned out to be not only embarrassing, but also quite costly. Both Merpati Airlines and the Government of Timor-Leste asked for specific technical reasons for this decision, and air safety officers could not provide any serious explanation. As air movements of UN agency staff were governed by a separate system managed by the World Food Programme (WFP), most UN agencies continued to use Merpati Airlines for movement of their staff. UNMISET staff, however, had to travel from Dili to Darwin, Australia, in order to reach Europe or the United States, adding $1,000–2,000 to travel costs.

The officer in charge of air safety had acted to ensure that nothing would happen under his responsibility. His concern was justified, as the Indonesian airlines had the lowest credibility in terms of safety records. However, the most agonizing aspect was the length in time it took to reverse the decision. I had to request that the most authoritative UN agency, ICAO (based in Montreal), to conduct its own safety inspection and assessment. It took months before UN Headquarters agreed for ICAO to field an inspection team to Indonesia and Timor-Leste, which cost UNMISET between $50,000 and $60,000. In the end, the ICAO team certified Merpati for safety, and we resumed flying with the airline. However, as we were required to fly through Darwin for nearly a year, it cost the United Nations a considerable amount. The important lesson learned was that if any officer is concerned with the safety of an airline operation, he should propose conducting a full investigation before any drastic decision is taken to ban its use, unless the situation is too urgent to permit a delay.

Notes

1. The UN peacekeeping forces were first commanded by Lieutenant General Jaime de los Santos of the Philippines, and included contingents from Argentina, Brazil, Denmark, Fiji, Ireland, Japan, Malaysia, New Zealand, Philippines, Portugal, Russia, Singapore, South Korea, Sweden, Thailand and the United Kingdom. The United States did

not participate directly in the UN peacekeeping forces, but provided a contingent of American police officers.

2. Peacebuilding was often equated with state-building, and nation-building with physical reconstruction and development. It needs to be emphasized that societal norms and standards need to be built or rebuilt to meet the newly emerging requirement of any post-conflict society.

3. Security Council Resolution 1272 mandated the mission not only to maintain security but also to facilitate relief assistance and to help rehabilitate physical infrastructure facilities.

4. Simon Chesterman, *You, The People: The United Nations, Transitional Administration, and State-Building* (New York, NY: Oxford University Press, 2004), p. 143.

5. Paragraph 8 of Security Council Resolution 1599 adopted by its 5171st meeting on 28 April 2005 emphasized the need to effect "a smooth and rapid transition".

6. Contributing countries of military personnel were Australia, Bangladesh, Bolivia, Brazil, Chile, Denmark, Egypt, Fiji, Ireland, Japan, Jordan, Kenya, Malaysia, Nepal, New Zealand, Norway, Pakistan, Philippines, Portugal, Republic of Korea, Russian Federation, Singapore, Slovakia, Sweden, Thailand, Turkey, United Kingdom, United States and Uruguay. Contributors of civilian police personnel were Argentina, Australia, Austria, Bangladesh, Benin, Bosnia & Herzegovina, Brazil, Canada, China, Egypt, Gambia, Ghana, Jordan, Kenya, Malaysia, Mozambique, Namibia, Nepal, Niger, Nigeria, Norway, Pakistan, Philippines, Portugal, Russian Federation, Samoa, Senegal, Singapore, Slovenia, Spain, Sri Lanka, Sweden, Thailand, Turkey, Ukraine, United Kingdom, United States, Vanuatu and Zimbabwe. See www.un.org/peace/etimor/untaetF.htm accessed on 2 February 2013.

7. Dennis McNamara (New Zealand) replaced Cady in June 2001.

8. Security Council Resolution 1543 (2004) of 14 May 2004.

9. Security Council Resolution 1704 (2006) of 25 August 2006.

10. Connie Peck (ed.) *On Being a Special Representative of the Secretary-General* (Geneva: UNITAR, 2006), p. 116.

11. Samantha Power, *Chasing the Flame: Sérgio Vieira de Mello and the Fight to Save the World* (London: Penguin Books, 2008).

12. Speech delivered by President Ramos-Horta at a farewell ceremony for SRSG Atul Khare on 9 December 2009.

13. Statement made on 22 February 2012 by Mr Ioannis Vrailas, Deputy Head of the EU delegation to the Security Council.

14. To meet this new challenge of appointing well-qualified SRSGs and other senior mission staff, the United Nations has embarked upon the identification and training of well-qualified candidates for senior management positions for peacekeeping and peacebuilding operations, such as SRSG, DSRSG, Chief of Staff, Force Commander and Police Commissioner.

15. This was very much in line with what Hedi Annai, the Assistant Secretary-General of DPKO, indicated during his first briefing to me when I took up my assignment in July 2002.

16. Three force commanders were Lieutenant-General Phattiyakul (Thailand) May 2002–August 2002; Major-General Tan (Singapore) August 2002–August 2003; and Lieutenant-General Mat Yusof (Malaysia) August 2003–May 2005.

17. UNMIT press release dated 15 November 2006.

18. United Nations Department of Peacekeeping Operations and Department of Field Support, *United Nations Peacekeeping Operations: Principles and Guidelines* (18 January 2008), paragraph 106.

VIII

Legacy of UN peacebuilding in Timor-Leste

In this book, I have provided an account of how the Timorese leaders interacted and dealt with numerous challenges in peace- and nation-building. I have also documented the state-building efforts made by the Timorese leaders and how I assisted them during the period of my assignment in Timor-Leste from July 2002 to September 2006.[1] I then probed the Timorese leaders' commitment to peace and national interest, as well as their mindset and outlook.

Principal factors contributing to successful peacebuilding

There are four factors that contributed to the successful peacebuilding in Timor-Leste:

The Timorese leaders' ownership of peacebuilding processes, which contributed to the successful peace- and nation-building efforts in Timor-Leste. They developed their own understanding of what was key to these efforts, while accepting many of the security and governance approaches advocated by the international peacebuilding community. As national leaders became confident and insisted on the pursuit of their own peacebuilding approach, the differences in understanding between international policymakers and national leaders emerged in the issues of truth, justice and reconciliation.

Indonesia's acceptance of the independence of Timor-Leste as a nation, which contributed directly to the restoration of security and stability. It

Primordial leadership: Peacebuilding and national ownership in Timor-Leste, Hasegawa, United Nations University Press, 2013, ISBN 978-92-808-1224-4

is noteworthy that unlike other post-conflict countries, Timor-Leste was left alone by the former occupying power, as it established its own political structure for governance, and the very conciliatory approach taken by Gusmão and Ramos-Horta helped build a cordial bilateral relationship between the two countries. Their approach contrasted with the international community's concern about Indonesia's intention towards the new country of Timor-Leste, and the decision to deploy the Australian and New Zealand armed forces as part of the UN peacekeeping forces during the initial period of transitional administration. While the intention of Indonesia was not to intervene in Timor-Leste, it became apparent by the end of the first United Nations Mission of Support in East Timor (UNMISET) mandate period that it remained uncertain whether the militia who had fled to Indonesia would return to Timor-Leste with or without the backing of Indonesia.

The solidarity shown by the Security Council members in supporting the continued engagement of the United Nations. Their expeditious endorsement of the Timorese leaders' call for multilateral stabilization forces in May 2006, and establishment of a new UN mission in August 2006, provided the Timorese people with the overwhelming power needed to stop the violent acts by national security personnel. The Security Council reinstalled the much-needed international peacekeeping forces that were lacking at a critical juncture earlier, when UN peacekeepers were withdrawn prematurely.

Transformation of the indigenous political culture that enabled the people and their leaders to recognize that acquiring power and authority peacefully through free, fair and credible elections was necessary. This transformation is what the international peace doctrine considered to be of cardinal importance in achieving sustainability of peace and nation-building in a post-conflict country. The plebiscite and series of elections that the United Nations introduced had a positive effect on the awareness of the Timorese people of the power they held to determine who should govern their society.

Key lessons learned from the peacebuilding experience in Timor-Leste

Premature withdrawal of UN peacekeepers

The Security Council's decision to withdraw all UN armed security forces from Timor-Leste reduced my role as Head of Mission to that of solely an adviser. When the situation became serious in April and May 2006, Timorese leaders still heeded my advice. When FALINTIL (Forças Armadas de Libertação Nacional de Timor-Leste) – Forças Armadas de Defesa de Timor-Leste) (FDTL) (F-FDTL) soldiers and Polícia Nacional de Timor-Leste (PNTL, National Police of Timor-Leste) police officers started shooting at each other on 25 May 2006, I authorized both the UN military liaison chief and the chief police training officer to intervene. However, had I had a small backup security force, as the Secretary-General had recommended to the Security Council, I could have intervened with necessary force and stabilized the situation.[2]

UNMISET was about to complete its mission mandate in May 2005. The Secretary-General and the Department of Peacekeeping Operations (DPKO), along with UNMISET, wanted to keep some residual military forces to cope with any sudden security developments. Assistant Secretary-General Hédi Annabi, who was in charge of peacekeeping operations, expressed his serious concern about the security gap that would be created by the departure of the backup security forces. I also conveyed my concern to the officials of key Security Council members when I visited London, Paris and Washington.

They, however, considered that the situation was quite stable, and that Timor-Leste had matured in exercising democratic governance. This perception led the Security Council to remove all armed personnel and to leave behind just 40 unarmed police advisers to train PNTL officers, and 35 additional advisers (including 15 military advisers) in support of the development of the Border Patrol Unit (BPU).[3] The 2006 crisis illustrated to the Security Council members that the UN mission was rendered incapable of responding to the security situation. They were reminded of the importance of not withdrawing peacekeeping troops and police forces prematurely.[4]

Preventing the unilateral deployment of national armed forces

The series of security incidents that took place in April–June 2006 showed the fragility of the relationship between the key holders of power and authority. It also revealed the commitment of key Timorese leaders to the national interest of the country at the expense of their personal interest. Their determination enabled the country to prevent the power struggle from igniting civil war. Their acceptance of judicial processes, including Rogério Lobato's trials, provided tangible evidence of the restoration of governance based on rule of law. The security incidents also revealed the psychological factors that affected the behaviours of leaders and people.

It is noteworthy that, in order to prevent any misuse of armed forces in 2007, President Ramos-Horta, Prime Minister Gusmão and National Parliament Partido Democrático (PD, Democratic Party) leader Fernado La Sama Araújo agreed that the deployment of F-FDTL could only be carried out with the agreement of the heads of all three state organs. This showed clearly that the Timorese leaders learned from the crisis in April–May 2006 to minimize any risk for recurrence of violence.

Establishing justice and accountability for the security crisis of 2006

The death count of 39 police officers and civilians in April–May 2006 was small in number compared with incidents in Iraq and Afghanistan, but was nonetheless a devastating development for both Timor-Leste and the United Nations. I was convinced that the incidents required a transparent and impartial investigation by an international entity. I also considered it imperative to establish the accountability for specific criminal actions committed. I spoke to Foreign Minister Ramos-Horta and together we persuaded other key Timorese leaders to request the United Nations to invite an independent commission to investigate the armed incidents that took place at the end of the petitioners' demonstration on 28 and 29 April. The series of clashes between police and military personnel from 23 to 25 May 2006 were also investigated.

It is most noteworthy that the three Timorese leaders agreed to the proposal. Secretary-General Kofi Annan responded immediately to the request to conduct an international investigation. An independent UN inquiry commission was then established in record time. It completed its investigation within three months and issued its report on 9 October 2006.[5] A lesson learned from this event is the importance of establishing a relationship of trust and confidence with national leaders to enable the pursuit of justice and accountability in a conflict-prone country.

The Timorese national leaders made conscientious efforts for political accommodation, if not for reconciliation. Their desire to contain their personal ill-feelings towards each was apparent after the change in the Prime Minister. A formal political dialogue was held in November 2006 with the participation of top state officials, political leaders and commanders of the Timorese armed forces and the national police. In December 2006, both President Gusmão and former Prime Minister Alkatiri, along with new Prime Minister Ramos-Horta and President of the Parliament Francisco "Lú-Olo" Guterres, made a public acknowledgement of collective responsibility for the crisis. The commander of the Timorese armed forces (F-FDTL), Tau Matan Ruak (TMR), and the former General Commander of PNTL, Paulo Martins, issued statements of apology on behalf of their respective national security agencies. The decision by President Gusmão to present the Order of Boaventura to Alkatiri in a public ceremony reflected their willingness to forego their animosity for the sake of achieving national unity, peace and stability in Timor-Leste.

Clash between international peace doctrines and national leadership on justice and peace

There were several issues about which the Timorese leaders were not in agreement with UN officials concerning international peace doctrines and policies. The most critical issue was the international insistence on the judicial process to achieve retributive justice against offenders of serious crimes. In contrast to this international doctrine, the Timorese leaders found it desirable to balance the quest for perfect justice with the need to maintain peace and stability domestically and internationally. Forgiveness and friendship in pursuit of truth, in their view, would bring about more benefit to the country.

The Timorese leaders also found it difficult to adhere rigidly to the principle of rule of law when they were confronted by the Indonesian request for release of Martenus Bere. He was the former commander of the pro-Indonesia Laksaur Militia who was indicted for crimes against humanity in a Suai church massacre that took place on 6 September 1999, when more than 30 people, including priests and children, were killed.[6] They felt that it was not in their national interest to uphold the principle of justice to the strictest sense, as advocated by the United Nations. Therefore they released Martenus Bere, without due process of law. The spokesperson of the United Nations, Marie Okabe, stated on behalf of the Secretary-General: "The UN's firm position is that there can be no amnesty or impunity for serious crimes such as war crimes, crimes against humanity and genocide." The UN position was then elaborated by the UN High Commissioner for Human Rights, Navanethem Pillay, who warned that the release of Martenus Bere would have serious consequences for the prospect of sustaining justice and accountability in Timor-Leste. President Ramos-Horta and Prime Minister Gusmão vigorously defended the action they had taken and asserted that fostering a culture of tolerance and friendship would secure peace, stability and prosperity for all people in the long run.[7]

I was no longer in Timor-Leste, but was still the special adviser to President Ramos-Horta. I felt that I had an obligation to advise him of the need to approach the Bere case more carefully and to show his respect for the judicial process. It was the first time that he felt offended by my advice. Knowing the importance the major global powers put on the maintenance of peace in Southeast Asia, Ramos-Horta must have thought that peace was more important than justice, and felt that the Bere case would not become a serious issue and lead to a heated debate in the Security Council. Ramos-Horta's assessment of the Bere case proved accurate, as the Security Council members hardly discussed the case when they met later in the year.

The outcome of the Martenus Bere case in 2009 put the national leaders at odds with the advocates of justice for peace at the United Nations. Yet, the incident also revealed the convergence of concerns held by the national leaders of Timor-Leste and key members of the Security Council, that peace and stability must prevail even at the expense of justice.

Non-linear transitions to democratic governance

Contrary to a common understanding of the sequential transitions from peacekeeping to peace-and nation-building phases, a critical review of the path taken by the Timorese leadership and the people shows non-linear evolutionary changes. The country moved back and forth between peace and stability, as well as between authoritarianism and liberal democracy (Fig. 8.1).

These four elements or types of peace governance are:
illiberal authoritarianism;
liberal democracy;
peace and stability; and
armed conflict.

These are slightly modified versions of four kinds of "hybrid peace governance" identified by Jarstad and Belloni,[8] with its temporal evolution added to the matrix.

As Fig. 8.1 shows, during the period of Indonesian occupation between 1975 and 1999, the locus of governance in Timor-Leste was marked by a high degree of illiberal authoritarianism and armed conflict. From October 1999 to May 2002, UNTAET governed the territory of Timor-Leste. This period was characterized by a high level of legitimacy, as UNTAET held the trust and confidence of both the local population and the international community. It was also a period of enlightened monarchism, as the Transitional Administrator exercised all powers of governance; he essentially acted as head of government, legislature and judiciary. The third period from 2002 to 2006 was governed by the first constitutional government, which initiated acts of governance with the assistance of UNMISET.

After a few years, the government began to consolidate its power and increased its authoritarian rule, resulting in the security crisis of 2006. The following two years were a transitional period, as the security situation remained precarious, although the new government began to uphold the norms and standards of liberal democracy. The assassination attempts on the President and the Prime Minister in 2008 were another turning point for Timor-Leste, leading to consolidation of power by the government, which achieved a high degree of stability and norms of liberal democracy.

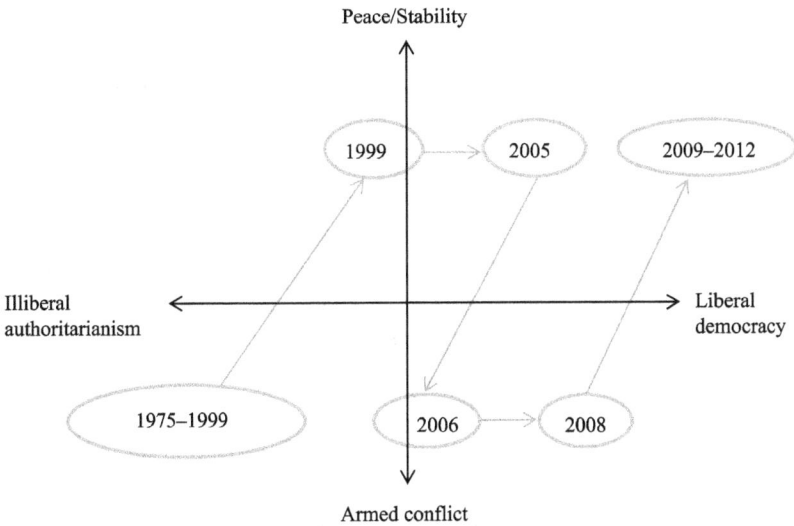

Figure 8.1 Evolutionary development of hybrid peace governance in Timor-Leste
Note: These indicators and the figure are adaptations of the indicators and Figure 3 presented by Anna K. Jarstad and Roberto Belloni, "Introducing Hybrid Peace Governance: Impact and Prospects of Liberal Peacebuilding", in *Global Governance: A Review of Multilateralism* (Boulder, CO: Lynne Rienner Publishers, 2012), vol. 18, no. 1, Jan.–Mar. p. 3.

The outcome of the presidential and parliamentary elections indicated that democracy was gradually taking root in Timor-Leste. As the people were educated about the principles and processes of democratic governance, there was growing awareness among them and their leaders that it was essential to respect the outcome of elections, which are the choices made by a sovereign people.

Primordial national leadership: Key attributes

The Timor-Leste experience showed the decisive role national leadership played in preventing personal rivalry and animosity from erupting into a civil war. The national leaders exercised what I call "primordial leadership", which has five inherent characteristics:
It is authentic and legitimate as it is committed to community interest, identity and unity.
It is fundamental as it is practised locally, incorporating universal ideals and principles of governance by harmonizing them into local community values and customs of governance.

It is primal and emotional, as passion and courage are exercised by leaders who are able to communicate and persuade their followers and the people at large of the efficacy of pursuing holistic visions and universal ideals with appropriate adjustments.[9]

Primordial national leaders are capable of balancing the merits of pursuing the future rather than the past, as seen in their preference for restorative over retributive justice. They are able to balance the need to act on injustices and crimes committed in the past through the retributive justice process, and the need to provide restorative justice to people in need of reconciliation and recognition.

Most importantly, primordial leadership is capable of transforming the mindset and mentality of the people in order, ultimately, to achieve sustainable peace and development.

To bring about the necessary change, the primordial leaders must have a vision of the future of the country as well as its past. Combining all these attributes, the primordial leaders sustain their commitment to national interest and social benefits above their personal interest and gains. In Timor-Leste's case, the key national leaders demonstrated these attributes during and after the security crisis of 2006. They acted jointly to end armed conflicts by placing national interest above their own personal gain. They did not hesitate to seek the support of international stabilization forces in order to prevent the country from relapsing into conflict and civil war.

In any conflict-prone and post-conflict country, I found that the existence of primordial leadership was essential for the country to remain in peace, while acquiring democratic norms and standards of governance. The leaders must uphold their commitment to moral principles and societal interest as a whole. Interestingly, this principle prevails in both the East and the West.

In *The Analects*, Confucius emphasized the importance of morality in personal and governmental conduct. His teachings stressed the superiority of personal exemplification over explicit rules of behaviour, and the attainment of skilled judgment rather than knowledge of rules. The concept of *yi* may be understood as being righteous or doing a right thing, though it may simply mean what it is ethically best to do in a certain context. The term contrasts with action taken out of self-interest. While pursuing one's own self-interest is not necessarily bad, one would be a better – a more righteous– person if one's life was based upon a path designed to enhance the greater good of a community one belongs to or leads.[10]

Thus an outcome of *yi* is doing the right thing for the right reason as understood by the inhabitants of a society as a whole. In the West, as explained by Plato in *The Republic*, a virtuous leader is essential for the proper functioning of state. The ideal state is possible only if it is ruled by a government led by virtuous leaders and trained functionaries. Plato eventually sided with the option of representative democracy and "rule of law" based on sovereign power residing in people as the most practically desirable form of government, given the difficulty in finding a true philosopher–king to lead.

In conflict-prone and post-conflict countries, where the rule of law and other institutional frameworks for democratic governance have not been fully developed, what is needed most is an active engagement of national and local primordial leaders; leaders who can restore or establish the dignity of local people by adhering to locally internalized universal norms and standards of governance behaviour.[11]

The international community needs to find and support such primordial leaders in post-conflict countries, until the rule of law and other institutional mechanisms for democratic governance can be established and internalized fully by the people and society as a whole. This approach supplements the inordinate concentration of effort that has been made on building institutional structures, with no or little attention paid to the local values, traditions and customs that had maintained the totality of social norms. It would also enhance the ethical and professional attributes of the leaders and managers of local governance institutions, increasing their transparency and accountability.

In a conflict-prone society, political leaders tend to come from a small group of elitist families and from those returning from abroad following diasporas. These may be able to outmanoeuvre indigenous people who had been left behind, but many of them are not able to exercise their power judiciously in pursuit of national interest and democratic governance. Under these circumstances, to exercise proper control and political power, the mindset and mentality of leaders and people need to be changed. As demonstrated in Timor-Leste, primordial leadership can play an effective role in bringing about these necessary changes, from a world of traditional norms, values and customs, to one based on the legitimacy accorded by popular consent and universal ideals.

Furthermore, the transformation process to a new group of leaders representing national interest and unity requires the transferral of political power from an old elitist group representing oligarchic power. Primordial leadership must have the qualities of disciplined strong leadership with high moral and ethical standards to restrain their desire to perpetuate their rule. The final and ultimate task of primordial leaders is to prepare for a smooth transition of their functions to successors.

In Timor-Leste, the ethical norms and values of the community have played a more influential role in maintaining domestic peace and stability than have democratic forms of governance. The legitimacy of Timorese national leaders depended on the extent of their commitment to community interest, identity and unity. The ultimate proof of their commitment was the manner in which they had fought against the Indonesian occupation. The fundamental soundness of their leadership was also viewed in terms of how the leaders could incorporate universal ideals and principles of governance into local norms and practices without hindering the stability of society.[12] The leaders discovered that it was essential to communicate and persuade their followers and people to change their mentality.

Timorese leadership proved capable of pursuing the future, rather than the past, as shown in their preferences for restorative over retributive justice. They were able to balance the need to act on injustice and crimes committed in the past through the retributive justice process, and the need to provide restorative justice to people in need of reconciliation and recognition.

Finally, the Timorese leaders were successful in transforming the mindset of people in order, ultimately, to achieve sustainable peace and development. To bring about the necessary change, the leaders demonstrated their commitment to the principle of democratic governance, particularly the right of people to choose their leaders through electoral processes.

In concluding this review of the events of 2006, it is worth repeating that the Timorese leaders acted jointly to end the armed conflict, placing national interest above personal gain. They did not hesitate to seek the support of international security forces in order to prevent the country from relapsing into conflict and a civil war.

Notes

1. My assignment in Timor-Leste started in July 2002 when I began my work as Deputy Special Representative of the Secretary-General (DSRSG) and Resident Co-ordinator of the UN system's operational activities for development. On 20 May 2004, Secretary-General Kofi Annan appointed me as his Special Representative of the Secretary-General (SRSG) for Timor-Leste and Head of United Nations Mission of Support in Timor-Leste (UNMISET). I continued my duty as SRSG until 30 September 2006 and concurrently as Head of the United Nations Office in Timor-Leste (UNOTIL) from 20 May 2005 to 20 August 2006 and the United Nations Integrated Mission in Timor-Leste (UNMIT) from 21 August 2006 to 30 September 2006.
2. Security Council Resolution 1599 (2005) of 28 April 2005 did not authorize the deployment of any backup security force recommended by the Secretary-General in his report (S/2005/99) on 18 February 2005.
3. Security Council Resolution 1599, adopted at its 5171st meeting on 28 April 2005. This compared with 3,500 armed troops and more than 1,000 police officers held by UNMISET when I joined the mission in July 2002.
4. With the adoption of its Resolution 1704 on 25 August 2006, the Security Council reversed its earlier decision and decided to reinstall 1,608 police personnel along with multilateral security forces led by Australia.

5. The United Nations, *Report of the Independent United Nations Commission of Inquiry*, 9 October 2006.
6. This is commonly known as the Suai Church Massacre, which happened on 6 September 1999, two days after the announcement of the results of the independence referendum in Suai, a city in the district of Cova Lima in south-western Timor-Leste. Several hundred persons had reportedly sought refuge from attacks of the Laksaur pro-Indonesia militia in the city's Ave Maria church. Please see the Secretary-General's report dated 31 January 2000 to the General Assembly and the Security Council of the United Nations: A/54/726, S/2000/59, paragraphs 72–82.
7. *The Sydney Morning Herald*, September 7, 2009, and *Australian Associated Press*, 8 September 2009. Bere, a former commander of Laksuar (one of the most violent of the militia groups behind a pro-Indonesian reign of terror in 1999), was arrested after he crossed into East Timor in August 2009 to attend a funeral ceremony for his father and pray at the same church where the killings took place. Locals reportedly beat him severely before police arrested him.
8. Anna K. Jarstad and Roberto Belloni, "Introducing Hybrid Peace Governance: Impact and Prospects of Liberal Peacebuilding", in *Global Governance: A Review of Multilateralism* (Boulder, CO: Lynne Rienner Publishers, Jan.–Mar. 2012), vol. 18, no. 1.
9. Primal leadership in peacebuilding shares the quality of emotional intelligence and resonant leadership identified by Daniel Goleman in *Primal Leadership: Learning to Lead with Emotional Intelligence* (Cambridge, MA: Harvard Business School Press, 2004).
10. *The Analects* is a collection of ideas and teachings of Confucius. It was reportedly written by his disciples around 500 BC, 30–50 years after his death. It is similar in origin to *The Republic* written by Plato, which reflected the teachings of Socrates.
11. Prime Minister Gusmão recognized this point. See RDTL Government Press Release dated 8 August 2012 on his address on the swearing-in of the new 5th Government: "*With regard to the Failed States Index, a very important point that calls for reflection is the ability of the leadership of a country to assume the responsibility to influence and guide the society to the practice of social ethics and politics that is so necessary to instil an environment of tolerance, mutual respect and solidarity and promote harmony and stability.*"
12. For example, the Prime Minister discovered in 2005 the limitations of secularization of the school in a country where the overwhelming majority of the people were Catholic.

Appendix I
Chronology

7 July 2012	Parliamentary elections were held. CNRT, led by incumbent Prime Minister Gusmão won 36.66 per cent of the votes; FRETILIN, led by former Prime Minister Alkatiri won 29.87 per cent; the Partido Democrático (PD, Democratic Party), led by National Parliament President Fernando de Araújo won 11.30 per cent; and Frenti-Mudança, led by Vice-Prime Minister José Luís Guterres won 3.11 per cent. According to the proportional representation formula, CNRT obtained 30 seats, FRETILIN 25 seats, PD 8 seats and Frenti-Mudança 2 seats.
11 May 2012	In the second round of presidential elections, Taur Matan Ruak (TMR) obtained 61.23 per cent of the votes and defeated Francisco "Lú-Olo" Guterres, who received 38.77 per cent of the votes.
17 March 2012	In the first round of presidential elections, FRETILIN candidate Francisco Lú-Olo Guterres obtained 28.76 per cent of the votes; TMR, former commander of F-FDTL and independent candidate supported by the CNRT obtained 25.71 per cent of the votes; and incumbent President José Ramos-Horta followed with 17.48 per cent of the votes.
22–23 February 2012	The Security Council held a debate on UNMIT and adopted Resolution 2037 extending UNMIT's mandate until 31 December 2012.

Primordial leadership: Peacebuilding and national ownership in Timor-Leste, Hasegawa, United Nations University Press, 2013, ISBN 978-92-808-1224-4

18 January 2012	The Secretary-General released a report (S/2012/43) on UNMIT.
12 January 2012	President Ramos-Horta convened a ceremony in Dili marking the closure of the office of the UNHCR in the Timorese capital.
22 December 2011	Timor-Leste's Council of Ministers suspended the activities of martial arts groups in the country for one year.
22 November 2011	The Security Council held a debate on Timor-Leste.
15 October 2011	The Secretary-General's report highlighted the continued progress towards the consolidation of peace, stability and development in Timor-Leste.
14 August 2011	Isolated incidents of violent unrest were reported, including a stabbing that led to the burning of scores of houses.
30 June 2011	The General Assembly appropriated $196.1 million for the maintenance of UNMIT from 1 July 2011 until 30 June 2012.
28 March 2011	The PNTL resumed primary responsibilities for policing in all of Timor-Leste. The United Nations had run policing in Timor-Leste since August 2006.
24 February 2011	The Security Council extended the mandate of UNMIT for a further 12 months.
22 February 2011	The head of UNMIT, Ameerah Haq, briefed the Security Council. This was followed by an open debate where Prime Minister Gusmão of Timor-Leste addressed the Security Council. Representatives of Australia, Japan, New Zealand, the Philippines and the EU also participated in the debate.
2 February 2011	At a meeting of the High-Level Committee on Transition hosted by the President of Timor-Leste, the United Nations and the government agreed to develop a joint transition plan.
19 October 2010	The head of UNMIT, Ameerah Haq, briefed the Security Council. This was followed by an open debate.
12 October 2010	UN police adviser, Ann-Marie Orler, visited Timor-Leste to assess the handover of primary responsibility for police operations from UNPOL to the PNTL.
28 September 2010	The PNTL resumed primary responsibilities for administration and management of the Immigration Department, Border Patrol Unit (BPU) and Interpol Office.
24 September 2010	The PNTL resumed primary responsibilities for the conduct of police operations in Manufahi District.

21 September 2010	The PNTL resumed primary responsibilities for the conduct of police operations in Ailieu District.
10 September 2010	The PNTL resumed primary responsibilities for the conduct of police operations in Ermera District.
7 September 2010	The PNTL resumed primary responsibilities for the conduct of police operations in Liquiça District. Liquiça District had Timor-Leste's first female district commander.
6 September 2010	Deputy Prime Minister Carrascalão resigned following a public disagreement with Prime Minister Gusmão, whom he had accused of embezzling public funds. Carrascalão's political party (the Social Democratic party) remained in the ruling parliamentary coalition.
20 August 2010	Timor-Leste President Ramos-Horta pardoned and commuted the sentences of 26 convicted persons who had been found guilty of the 2006 violence, as well as the attack on the Timor-Leste President and Prime Minister in February 2008.
4 June 2010	Security Council members held a private meeting with countries that contributed police and military liaison staff to UNMIT.
16 April 2010	The PNTL resumed primary responsibilities for the conduct of police operations in Baucau District.
12 April 2010	The PNTL resumed primary responsibilities for the conduct of police operations in Ainaro District.
26 February 2010	The Security Council adopted Resolution 1912 extending UNMIT's mandate until 26 February 2011.
23 February 2010	The Security Council held an open debate on Timor-Leste, during which it was briefed by Ameerah Haq and Deputy Prime Minister of Timor-Leste Guterres.
10–18 January 2010	UN Technical Assistance Mission led by Ian Martin in Timor-Leste.
28 December 2009	Ameerah Haq, the new SRSG, began her appointment.
28 December 2009	A PNTL officer was involved in a shooting in Dili. He was suspended from duty on 4 January 2010.
18 December 2009	The PNTL resumed primary responsibility for the Police Intelligence Service.
14 December 2009	The PNTL resumed primary responsibility for the maritime police operations.
5 December 2009	The PNTL resumed primary responsibilities for the conduct of police operations in Viqueque District.
23 October 2009	Atul Khare and José Luís Guterres, Deputy Prime Minister of Timor-Leste, briefed the Council.

11 September 2009	The PNTL resumed primary responsibilities for the administration and management of the Police Training Centre.
30 August 2009	Martenus Bere, who had been indicted in 2003 by the Serious Crimes Unit (SCU) on charges of crimes against humanity, was released to the Indonesian Government.
30 August 2009	Timor-Leste marked the 10th Anniversary of the UN-organized referendum that led to its independence. In remarks to the press the President of the Security Council commended the people and Government of Timor-Leste on their efforts towards peace, stability and development.
27 August 2009	Amnesty International warned the Security Council that there was a need for a long-term comprehensive plan to end impunity for crimes in Timor-Leste. It also proposed that an international tribunal be set up with jurisdiction over all crimes committed in Timor-Leste between 1975 and 1999.
25 July 2009	The PNTL resumed primary responsibilities for the conduct of police operations in Manatuto District.
30 June 2009	The PNTL resumed primary responsibilities for the conduct of police operations in Oecussi District.
27 May 2009	The Security Council met with troop-contributing countries to discuss the updating of the concept of operations and rules of engagement for UNMIT.
14 May 2009	The gradual resumption of policing responsibilities. Lautem District became the first of Timor-Leste's 13 districts in which the PNTL resumed primary responsibilities for the conduct of police operations.
26 February 2009	The Security Council renewed UNMIT's mandate until 26 February 2010.
19 February 2009	The Security Council held an open debate on Timor-Leste.
15 July 2008	CTF formally completed its final report. It found that the Indonesian police, army and civilian government officials had funded, armed and coordinated anti-independence militias, which carried out activities resulting in grave human rights violations, including crimes against humanity. The Indonesian President Susilo Bambang Yudhoyono and Timorese President Ramos-Horta issued a statement accepting the findings, conclusions and recommendations of the CTF and committed to implementing the recommendations.

13 June 2008   An agreement was signed between the Government and the UNDP on technical assistance and advice for a review of Timor-Leste's security sector. The review was to be finalized by early to mid-2009.

May 2008   The Associação Social Democráta Timorense (ASDT, Social Democratic Association of Timor-Leste), a party in the governing coalition, signed an accord with opposition FRETILIN to form a ruling coalition in a move to force early elections.

17–27 March 2008   A mission of experts, led by UN policy advisor Andrew Hughes, conducted an assessment of the requirements of the national police and possible adjustments to UNMIT police skills sets.

11 February 2008   President Ramos-Horta and Prime Minister Gusmão were both attacked by a group led by former military officer Alfredo Reinado, who was killed in the attack.

24–30 November 2007   A Security Council mission went to Timor-Leste. It comprised South Africa (the lead member), China, Indonesia, Russia, Slovakia and the United States. The mission held meetings with Timorese and UNMIT officials.

Mid-November 2007   Prime Minister Gusmão held talks with a group comprising several of the military "petitioners" whose dismissal from the army was one of the causes of the 2006 violence. The group requested reinstatement of those dismissed in 2006.

September 2007   The Government of Timor-Leste asked that Australian-led international forces cease operations to arrest Alfredo-Reinado, a "petitioner" dismissed from the army in 2006, who had opposed dialogue with the government.

6 August 2007   After many tense days of discussion over who could command a majority in the parliament, President José Ramos-Horta announced that he had appointed Xanana Gusmão as Prime Minister.

Late July 2007   Australian Prime Minister John Howard visited Timor-Leste and was asked by the country's President to keep forces there through 2008. The new parliament was sworn in amid renewed politically motivated violence.

26 July 2007   The spokesperson for the Secretary-General announced that because of the long-standing position of the United Nations against amnesties for genocide,

	crimes against humanity, war crimes or gross violations of human rights, UN officials would neither testify CTF proceedings nor take any other steps that would support its work.
30 June 2007	Parliamentary elections were held. FRETILIN won with a small margin of 29 per cent of the vote against 23 per cent for CNRT.
11 May 2007	José Ramos-Horta defeated Francisco Lú-Olo Guterres to win the presidency.
9 April 2007	In the first round of presidential elections, Parliament leader Francisco Lú-Olo Guterres and Prime Minister José Ramos-Horta, who obtained 28 per cent and 22 per cent of the votes, respectively, earned the right to face each other in the May runoff.
March 2007	Judicial proceedings into the April–May 2006 violence led to the conviction of Rogério Lobato, the former Interior Minister.
22 February 2007	The Security Council renewed UNMIT's mandate for 12 months and increased its police size by 140 ahead of the presidential elections.
February 2007	The CTF began hearings on the 1999 violence.
January 2007	The UNMIT Serious Crimes Investigation Team (SCIT) was established.
26 January 2007	The United Nations, Timor-Leste and Australia signed a security agreement to establish a Trilateral Coordination Body to allow better coordination on security issues.
30 October 2006	The Secretary-General appointed Atul Khare as his SRSG in Timor-Leste to replace Sukehiro Hasegawa.
17 October 2006	Independent Special Commission of Inquiry issued its report on the April–May violence, presenting the facts that led to the violence and recommending the prosecution of several individuals for their role in the crisis.
14 September 2006	UNMIT officially took over policing activities in Timor-Leste with the "blue-hatting" of Australian, Portuguese and Malaysian police contingents.
25 August 2006	The Security Council created UNMIT through Resolution 1704.
14 July 2006	José Luis Guterres, Timor-Leste's Ambassador to the United Nations, was appointed Foreign Minister.
10 July 2006	José Ramos-Horta was sworn in as the new Prime Minister.

28 June 2006	Protesters set fire to some 20 houses in Dili; Secretary-General Kofi Annan appointed a special inquiry commission to investigate the May and June violence.
26 June 2006	Prime Minister Alkatiri resigned.
6 June 2006	A rally of some 2000 called for the Prime Minister's resignation.
2 June 2006	José Ramos-Horta was named Minister of Defence in addition to his post as Foreign Minister; Mari Alkatiri continued to reject calls for his resignation.
1 June 2006	Defence Minister Rodriguez resigned.
25 May 2006	The Secretary-General sent Ian Martin, his representative in Timor-Leste in 1999, on a fact-finding mission to the country. The Council issued a presidential statement supporting the deployment of the multinational forces.
24 May 2006	The Timorese Government requested security assistance from Australia, Malaysia, New Zealand and Portugal. In a statement to the press, the Council expressed deep concern over the deteriorating situation.
23–25 May 2006	Violence continued, with several people killed and several dozen injured. Timorese politicians called on the Prime Minister to resign.
28–29 April 2006	Violent riots took place in Dili leading to the displacement of thousands of civilians.
Late March 2006	Numerous violent incidents occurred in Dili, leading to 48 arrests. Eight of those arrested were dismissed soldiers.
Mid-March 2006	The commander of the armed forces dismissed nearly 40 per cent of the armed forces (591 soldiers).
8 February 2006	Some 400 members of the armed forces demonstrated in front of the President's office in Dili, demanding a response to their petition. They alleged discrimination in promotion and ill-treatment of members of the military from outside the eastern parts of the country.
20 January 2006	President Gusmão presented the CAVR report to the Secretary-General.
28 October 2005	Timor-Leste's CAVR handed over its final report to President Gusmão.
28 September 2005	The COE report was forwarded to the Council, which then requested recommendations from the Secretary-General.

5 August 2005	CTF met officially for the first time.
May 2005	The COE conducted its fact-finding mission. The SCU concluded its activities and UNOTIL was established.
December 2004	Timor-Leste and Indonesia decided to establish the joint Indonesian–Timorese CTF.
November 2004	SCU ceased all investigations.
May 2002	UNTAET withdrew and Timor achieved independence. UNMISET was established.
January 2002	CAVR was established.
June 2000	UNTAET established the Serious Crimes Process.
October 1999	The Indonesian Parliament recognised the referendum. UNTAET was established.
September 1999	Anti-independence violence increased. The Council authorized the deployment of an international force.
August 1999	The referendum took place, showing 78 per cent support for independence.
May 1999	Indonesia and Portugal agreed on modalities for a referendum under UN auspices. Anti-independence violence erupted.
January 1999	Indonesia decided to carry out a referendum concerning independence for Timor-Leste.
1975–1979	The Indonesian occupation was marked by a bloody repression against civilians and armed resistance.
December 1975	Indonesia occupied Timor-Leste.
November 1975	FRETILIN declared Timor-Leste independent.

Source: UN Security Council Document website on Timor-Lest
http://www.securitycouncilreport.org/un-documents/timor-leste/ (accessed 28 July 2012), with additions made by the author.
Explanatory note: This chronology is based on a Security Council report dated March 2012, with additions of events that took place in subsequent months.

Appendix II

Government ministers and senior officials of the Democratic Republic of Timor-Leste

First constitutional government sworn into office
20 May 2002

Prime Minister and Minister of Development and Environment
Mari Bin Amude Alkatiri
Minister of State and Minister of Foreign Affairs and Cooperation
José Ramos-Horta
Minister of Justice   **Ana Maria Pessoa**
Minister of Planning and Finance   **Maria Madalena Brites Boavida**
Minister of Transport, Communications and Public Works
Ovídio Amaral
Minister of Internal Administration   **Rogério Tiago Lobato**
Minister of Agriculture, Forestry and Fisheries   **Estanislau Aleixo da Silva**
Minister of Education, Culture, Youth and Sports   **Armindo Maia**
Minister of Health   **Rui Araújo**
Secretary of State for Defence   **Roque Félix Rodrigues**
Secretary of State for Labour and Solidarity   **Arsénio Bano**
Secretary of State for Trade and Industry   **Arlindo Rangel**
Secretary of State for the Council of Ministers   **Gregório Sousa**
Secretary of State for Parliamentary Issues for the PM
Antoninho Bianco
Vice-Minister of Foreign Affairs and Cooperation   **José Luís Guterres**
Vice-Minister of Foreign Affairs and Cooperation   **Jorge Teme**

Primordial leadership: Peacebuilding and national ownership in Timor-Leste, Hasegawa, United Nations University Press, 2013, ISBN 978-92-808-1224-4

Vice-Minister of Transport, Communications and Public Works
  César Vital Moreira
Vice-Minister of Justice   **Manuel Abrantes**
Vice-Minister of Justice   **Domingos Sarmento**
Vice-Minister of Planning and Finance   **Aicha Bassarewan**
Vice-Minister of International Administration   **Ilda Conceição**
Vice-Minister of Health   **Luís Lobato**
Secretary of State for Electricity and Water at the Ministry of Transport,
  Communications and Public Works   **Egídio de Jesus**
Secretary of State for Tourism, Environment and Investment at the
  Ministry of Development and Environment   **José Teixeira**
Secretary of State for Education, Culture, Youth and Sports
  Virgílio Simith

Constitutional government

On 4 March 2003, the following members of the government were temporarily dismissed:

Minister of Justice   **Ana Maria Pessoa**
Minister of Internal Administration   **Rogério Lobato**
Vice-Minister of Justice   **Domingos Sarmento**
Vice-Minister of Internal Administration   **Alcino Araújo Baris**
Vice-Minister of International Administration   **Ilda Conceição**

On 6 March 2003 sworn into office:

Minister of State in the Presidency of the Council of Ministers
  Ana Maria Pessoa
Minister of Interior   **Rogério Lobato**
Minister of Justice   **Domingos Sarmento**
Vice-Minister of Interior   **Alcino Baris**
Vice-Minister of State Administration   **Ilda Conceição**
Vice-Minister of Development and Environment   **Abel Ximenes**
Secretary of State for Public Works   **João Baptista Alves**

First constitutional government restructured 26 July 2005

Prime Minister and Minister of Natural and Mineral Resources, and
  Energy Policy   **Mari Alkatiri**

Minister of State and Minister of Foreign Affairs and Cooperation
José Ramos-Horta
Minister of Planning and Finance **Madalena Brites Boavida**
Minister of State Administration **Ana Maria Pessoa**
Minister of Transport and Communications **Ovídio Amaral**
Minister of Interior **Rogério Tiago Lobato**
Minister of Defence **Roque Rodrigues**
Minister in the Presidency of the Council of Ministers
Antoninho Bianco
Minister of Agriculture, Forestry and Fisheries **Estanislau Aleixo da Silva**
Minister of Education and Culture **Armindo Maia**
Minister of Health **Rui Araújo**
Minister of Justice **Domingos Sarmento**
Minister of Development **Abel Ximenes**
Minister of Public Works **Odete Vítor**
Minister of Labour and Community Reinsertion **Arsénio Bano**
Secretary of State for the Council of Ministers **Gregório Sousa**
Secretary of State for Youth and Sports **José Manuel Fernandes**
Secretary of State for Environmental Coordination, Territorial Ordering
and Physical Development **João Alves**
Secretary of State for the Coordination of Region I (Lautem, Viqueque
and Baucau) **José Maria dos Reis**
Secretary of State for the Coordination of Region II (Manatuto,
Manufahi e Ainaro) **Virgílio Simith**
Secretary of State for the Coordination of Region III (Dili, Aileu and
Ermera) **Egídio de Jesus**
Secretary of State for the Coordination of Region IV (Liquiça,
Bobonaro and Cova-Lima) **César da Cruz**
Secretary of State resident in Oecussi **Albano Salem**
Vice-Minister of Foreign Affairs and Cooperation **Olímpico Branco**
Vice-Minister of Planning and Finance **Aicha Bassarewan**
Vice-Minister of State Administration **Valentim Ximenes**
Vice-Minister of Natural and Mineral Resources, and Energy Policy
José Teixeira
Vice-Minister of Interior **Alcino Baris**
Vice-Minister for Coffee and Forestry **Francisco Sá Benevides**
Vice-Minister for Primary and Secondary Education **Rosária Corte-Real**
Vice-Minister of Health **Luís Maria Lobato**
Vice-Minister of Justice **Manuel Abrantes**
Vice-Minister of Development **Arcanjo da Silva**
Vice-Minister of Public Works **Raúl da Cunha Mousaco**
Secretary of State for Veterans and Former Combatants **David Ximenes**

Second constitutional government officials

Sworn into office 10 July 2006

Prime Minister and Minister of Defence   **José Ramos-Horta**
Vice-Prime Minister and Minister of Agriculture, Forestry and Fisheries
   Estanislau Aleixo da Silva
Vice-Prime Minister and Minister of Health   **Rui Araújo**
Minister of State Administration   **Ana Maria Pessoa Pinto**
Minister of Planning and Finance   **Maria Madalena Brites Boavida**
Minister of Foreign Affairs and Cooperation   **José Luís Guterres**
Minister of Interior   **Alcino Baris**
Minister in the Presidency of the Council of Ministers
   Antoninho Bianco
Minister of Justice   **Domingos Sarmento**
Minister of Education and Culture   **Rosária Corte-Real**
Minister of Labour and Community Reinsertion   **Arsénio Paixão Bano**
Minister of Development   **Arcanjo da Silva**
Minister of Public Works   **Odete Vítor**
Minister of Natural and Mineral Resources, and Energy Policy
   José Teixeira
Minister of Transport and Communications   **Inácio Moreira**
Secretary of State for the Council of Ministers   **Gregório de Sousa**
Secretary of State for Youth and Sports   **José Manuel Fernandes**
Secretary of State for Environmental Coordination, Territorial Ordering
   and Physical Development   **João Batista Alves**
Vice-Minister of State Administration   **Valentim Ximenes**
Vice-Minister of State Administration   **Filomeno Aleixo**
Vice-Minister of Foreign Affairs and Cooperation   **Adalgiza Magno**
Vice-Minister of Planning and Finance   **Aicha Bassarewa**
Vice-Minister of Agriculture, Forestry and Fisheries   **Francisco Tilman**
   de Sá Benevides
Vice-Minister of Health   **Luís Lobato**
Vice-Minister of Interior   **José Agostinho Sequeira**
Vice-Minister for Technical and Higher Education   **Víctor da Conceição**
   Soares
Vice-Minister for Primary and Secondary Education   **Ilda da Conceição**
Vice-Minister of Justice   **Isabel da Costa Ferreira**
Vice-Minister of Development   **António Cepeda**
Vice-Minister of Public Works   **Raúl Mousaco**
Secretary of State for Veterans and Former Combatants   **David Ximenes**
Secretary of State for the Coordination of Region I   **José Reis**

Secretary of State for the Coordination of Region II   **Adriano Corte Real**

Secretary of State for the Coordination of Region III   **Carlos da Conceição de Deus**

Secretary of State for the Coordination of Region IV   **Lino de Jesus Torrezão**

Secretary of State resident in Oecussi   **Albano Salem**

Source: Historical Archive, Democratic Republic of Timor-Leste http://timor-leste.gov.tl/?cat=25&lang=en, http://timor-leste.gov.tl/?p= 130&lang=en (accessed 14 February 2013), with some editorial modifications.

For Product Safety Concerns and Information please contact our EU
representative GPSR@taylorandfrancis.com
Taylor & Francis Verlag GmbH, Kaufingerstraße 24, 80331 München, Germany

9 781138 481565